- XXII

3̶0̶

$ 15⁰⁰

*On the Plain of Snakes*

## BOOKS BY PAUL THEROUX

FICTION

*Waldo*
*Fong and the Indians*
*Girls at Play*
*Murder in Mount Holly*
*Jungle Lovers*
*Sinning with Annie*
*Saint Jack*
*The Black House*
*The Family Arsenal*
*The Consul's File*
*A Christmas Card*
*Picture Palace*
*London Snow*
*World's End*
*The Mosquito Coast*
*The London Embassy*
*Half Moon Street*
*O-Zone*
*My Secret History*
*Chicago Loop*
*Millroy the Magician*
*My Other Life*
*Kowloon Tong*
*Hotel Honolulu*
*The Stranger at the Palazzo d'Oro*
*Blinding Light*
*The Elephanta Suite*
*A Dead Hand*
*The Lower River*
*Mr. Bones*
*Mother Land*

CRITICISM

*V. S. Naipaul*

NONFICTION

*The Great Railway Bazaar*
*The Old Patagonian Express*
*The Kingdom by the Sea*
*Sailing through China*
*Sunrise with Seamonsters*
*The Imperial Way*
*Riding the Iron Rooster*
*To the Ends of the Earth*
*The Happy Isles of Oceania*
*The Pillars of Hercules*
*Sir Vidia's Shadow*
*Fresh Air Fiend*
*Dark Star Safari*
*Ghost Train to the Eastern Star*
*The Tao of Travel*
*The Last Train to Zona Verde*
*Deep South*
*Figures in a Landscape*
*On the Plain of Snakes*

# PAUL THEROUX

# On the
# Plain of Snakes

## A MEXICAN JOURNEY

*Houghton Mifflin Harcourt*

BOSTON   NEW YORK

2019

*Library of Congress Cataloging-in-Publication Data*
Names: Theroux, Paul, author.
Title: On the plain of snakes : a Mexican journey / Paul Theroux.
Description: Boston : Houghton Mifflin Harcourt, [2019] |
Identifiers: LCCN 2019004920 (print) | LCCN 2019005663 (ebook) |
ISBN 9780544866485 (ebook) | ISBN 9780544866478 (hardcover)
Subjects: LCSH: Mexico—Description and travel. |
Mexican-American Border Region—Description and travel.
Classification: LCC F1216.5 (ebook) | LCC F1216.5 .T54 2019 (print) |
DDC 917.204—DC23
LC record available at https://lccn.loc.gov/2019004920

Book design by Chloe Foster

Excerpt from *To Die in Mexico: Dispatches from Inside the Drug War* by John Gibler.
Copyright © 2011 by John Gibler. Reprinted by permission of The Permissions
Company, Inc., on behalf of City Lights Books, www.citylights.com.
The chapter titled "Along the Border" originally appeared, in different form, in
"Myth and Reason on the Mexican Border," written by the author and published
in 2016 by *Smithsonian* magazine. Text reprinted by permission of the author.
All rights reserved.
Lines from "A Steppe in the Nazas Country" by Manuel José Othon and
"Tarahumara Herbs" by Afonso Reyes, from *Anthology of Mexican Poetry*, compiled
by Octavio Paz and translated by Samuel Beckett. First published in 1958 by
Indiana University Press. Reprinted with permission of Indiana University Press.
Excerpt of six lines from "Late Ripeness," from *Second Space: New Poems* by
Czesław Miłosz. Translated by the author and Robert Hass. Copyright © 2004
by Czełsaw Miłosz. Translation copyright © 2004 by Robert Hass. Reprinted by
permission of HarperCollins Publishers.

*A mis queridos amigos*
*que me acompañaron por los caminos de México*
*No los olvidaré*

An elderly campesino in a battered hat and scuffed boots was stumbling in the bleak high desert, in the sighing emptiness of the Mixteca Alta in Oaxaca state. He was alone on the track that leads from the remote village of Santa María Ixcatlán to the crossroads, miles away. Obviously poor and struggling along, he seemed to me an iconic Mexican figure, emblematic of the life of the land. He could have been a hungry farmer headed to the market, a hopeful worker looking for a factory job, a migrant setting off for the border, or someone seeking help. Whatever his destination, he was on a rough road.

We stopped the pickup truck and told him to hop in. After an hour of bumping along we arrived at the crossroads. The man offered his hand and said, "Many thanks."

"What is the name of this pueblo, señor?"

"It is San Juan Bautista Coixtlahuaca," he said. "See, the old convent."

The broken church was vast and hollowed out and unvisited.

"What is the meaning of 'Coixtlahuaca'?"

*"El llano de las serpientes."*

The plain of snakes.

# CONTENTS

PART ONE   *Borderlands*   1

PART TWO   *Mexico Mundo*   95

PART THREE   *Oaxaca, the* Inframundo   201

PART FOUR   *The Road to Nueva Maravilla*   351

PART FIVE   *The Way Back*   427

# PART ONE

## *Borderlands*

## To the Border: A Perfect Example of Thatness

THE MEXICAN BORDER is the edge of the known world, only shadows and danger beyond it, and lurking figures — hungry, criminal, predatory, fanged, fanatical enemies — a malevolent and ungovernable rabble eager to pounce on the unwary traveler. And the Policía Federal officers are diabolical, heavily armed, stubborn and sullen one minute, screaming out of their furious congested faces the next, then extorting you, as they did me.

Send lawyers, guns, and money! Don't go there! You'll die!

But wait — deeper in Mexico (floppy, high-domed sombreros, mariachi music, blatting trumpets, toothy grins) are the safer, salubrious hot spots you can fly to for a week, get hog-whimpering drunk on tequila, fall ill with paralyzing squitters, and come home with a woven poncho or a painted ceramic skull. Also, here and there, sunny dumping grounds for American retirees — a tutti-frutti of grizzled gringos in permanent settlements on the coast and in gated communities and art colonies inland.

Oh, and the fat cats and petrocrats in Mexico City, thirty listed billionaires — including the seventh-richest man in the world, Señor Carlos Slim — who together have more money than every other Mexican combined. But the campesinos in certain states in southern Mexico, such as Oaxaca and Chiapas, in terms of personal income, are poorer than their counterparts in Bangladesh or Kenya, languishing in an air of stagnant melancholy on hillsides without topsoil, but with seasonal outbursts of fantastical masquerade to lighten the severities and stupefactions of village life. Famine victims, desperadoes, and voluptuaries, all more or less occupying the same space, and that vast space — that Mexican landscape — squalid and lush and primal and majestic.

And huge seasonal settlements of torpid, sunburned Canadians, as well as the remnants of fifteen colonies of polygamous Mormons who fled to Mexico from Utah to maintain large harems of docile, bonnet-wearing wives, all of them glowing with sweat in the Chihuahuan Desert, clad in the required layered underwear they call "temple garments." And isolated bands of Old Colony Mennonites speaking Low German in rural Cuauhtémoc and Zacatecas, herding cows and squeezing homegrown milk into semisoft cheese — Chihuahua cheese, or *queso menonita*, meltable and buttery, very tasty in a Mennonite verenika casserole or bubble bread.

Baja is both swanky and poor, the *frontera* is owned by the cartels and border rats on both sides, Guerrero state is run by narco gangs, Chiapas is dominated by masked idealistic Zapatistas, and — at the Mexico margins — the spring-breakers, the surfers, the backpackers, the crusty retired people, honeymooners, dropouts, fugitives, gun runners, CIA scumbags and snoops, money launderers, currency smurfers, and — look over there — an old gringo in a car squinting down the road, thinking: *Mexico is not a country. Mexico is a world, too much of a* mundo *to be wholly graspable, but so different from state to state in extreme independence of culture and temperament and cuisine, and in every other aspect of peculiar Mexicanismo, it is a perfect example of thatness.*

I was that old gringo. I was driving south in my own car in Mexican sunshine along the straight sloping road through the thinly populated valleys of the Sierra Madre Oriental — the whole craggy spine of Mexico is mountainous. Valleys, spacious and austere, were forested with thousands of single yucca trees, the so-called dragon yucca (*Yucca filifera*) that Mexicans call *palma china*. I pulled off the road to look closely at them and wrote in my notebook: *I cannot explain why, on the empty miles of these roads, I feel young.*

And that was when I saw a slender branch twitch on the ground; it lay beneath the yucca in soil like sediment. It moved. It was a snake, a hank of shimmering scales. It began to contract and wrap itself — its smooth and narrow body pulsing in the serpentine peristalsis of threat, brownish, like the gravel and the dust. I stepped back, but it continued slowly to resolve itself into a coil. Not poisonous, I learned later. Not a plumed serpent, not the rearing rattler being gnawed by the wild-eyed eagle in the vivid emblazonment on the Mexican national flag. It was a coachwhip snake, as numerous on this plain as rattlesnakes, of which Mexico has twenty-six species—not to mention, elsewhere, milk snakes, blind snakes, rat snakes, pit vipers, worm-sized garden snakes, and ten-foot-long boa constrictors.

The joy of the open road—joy verging on euphoria. "Behind us lay the whole of America and everything Dean and I had known about life, and life on the road," Kerouac writes of entering Mexico in *On the Road*. "We had finally found the magic land at the end of the road and we never dreamed the extent of the magic."

But then, driving onward, reflecting on the old twisted trunks of the yuccas and their globular crowns of spiky sword-like leaves ("The leaves are erect when they are young but they become arched when they get older," a botanist writes, seeming to suggest a fogeyish image), each a solitary stick in the asparagus family—and it does seem like a succulent spear that's swelled to become a desert palm rooted in sand, tenacious but bending as it ages. I also think, *It's been a hard summer.* Unregarded, shunned, snubbed, overlooked, taken for granted, belittled, mocked, faintly laughable, stereotypical, no longer interesting, parasitical, invisible to the young—the old person in the United States, and the man and writer I am, is much like the yucca, much like the Mexican. We have all that in common, the accusation of senescence and superfluity.

So, I can identify. But leaving home for Mexico at a time when I feel peculiarly ignored and weakened in status is not sad or lamentable. It is the way of the world. This is a triumphant mood for a long trip, just slipping out and not telling anyone, and fairly sure that no one will notice I've gone.

Again like the despised Mexican, the person always reminded he or she is not welcome, whom no one ever misses: I could not be more sympathetic. I am this yucca with crazy hair and a bent back; I am also (though traveling in the other direction) a shifty migrant. *Yo soy tú*, I think: I am you.

# A Gringo in His Dégringolade

IN THE CASUAL opinion of most Americans, I am an old man, and therefore of little account, past my best, fading in a pathetic diminuendo while flashing his AARP card; like the old in America generally, either invisible or someone to ignore rather than respect, who will be gone soon, and forgotten, a gringo in his dégringolade.

Naturally, I am insulted by this, but out of pride I don't let my indignation show. My work is my reply, my travel is my defiance. And I think of myself in the Mexican way, not as an old man but as most Mexicans regard a senior, an *hombre de juicio*, a man of judgment; not *ruco*, worn out, beneath notice, someone to be patronized, but owed the respect traditionally accorded to an elder, someone (in the Mexican euphemism) of *La Tercera Edad*, the Third Age, who might be called Don Pablo or *tío* (uncle) in deference. Mexican youths are required by custom to surrender their seat to anyone older. They know the saying: *Más sabe el diablo por viejo, que por diablo*—The devil is wise because he's old, not because he's the devil. But "Stand aside, old man, and make way for the young" is the American way.

As an Ancient Mariner of a sort, I want to hold the doubters with my skinny hand, fix them with a glittering eye, and say, "I have been to a place where none of you have ever been, where none of you can ever go. It is the past. I spent decades there and I can say, you don't have the slightest idea."

On my first long trip—to central Africa, fifty-five years ago—I was exhilarated by the notion that I was a stranger in a strange land: far from home, with a new language to learn, committed to two years out of touch, teaching barefoot students in the bush. I was to remain in Africa for six years, learning how to be an outsider. My next teaching job was in Singapore, and when that ended after three years, I abandoned all salaried employment and became a resident in Britain for seventeen years, carrying the compulsory Alien Identity Card.

Partly from passionate curiosity and partly to make a living, I kept traveling. The risky trips I took in my thirties and forties, launching myself into the unknown, astonish me now. One winter I was in Siberia. I went overland to Patagonia. I took every clanking train in China and drove a car to Tibet. I turned fifty paddling alone in my kayak in the Pacific, threatened by islanders, tossed by waves, blown off course in a high wind off Easter Island. Even traveling from Cairo to Cape Town in 2001, and stopping in Johannesburg for my sixtieth birthday, seems an unrepeatable journey—at least by me, when I remember how I was fired upon by a shifta bandit in the Kaisut Desert near Marsabit, and being robbed in Johannesburg of my bag and everything I owned. A decade later, on an African trip for a sequel to that book, resuming in Cape Town and heading for the Congo border, I turned seventy in the Kalahari Desert and defended myself against oafs in the stink and misery of northern Angola. All these trips, ten of them, became books.

"Write the story of a contemporary cured of his heartbreaks solely by long contemplation of a landscape," Camus wrote in his *Notebooks*. Heeding that advice (which has always been a mantra to me) at a time when I believed I might be done with long journeys, I took to my car and went on a two-year trip through the back roads of the Deep South, with a book in mind. I was rejuvenated in the precise sense of the word, tooling along in my car, made to feel young again.

In those years, traveling in the South, I made a detour and crossed the Mexican border for the first time, at Nogales. It was a travel epiphany that woke me to a new world. I marveled how, pushing through an Arizona turnstile in a doorway blowtorched into a thirty-foot iron fence, in seconds I had stepped into a foreign country—the aroma and sizzle of street food, the strumming of guitars, the joshing of hawkers.

"Just across the street Mexico began," Kerouac writes. "We looked with wonder. To our amazement, it looked exactly like Mexico."

I met some migrants then, Mexicans intent on slipping across the border, others who had been deported, and on that visit I saw a middle-aged woman praying before her meal in a migrant shelter, the Comedor of the Kino Border Initiative. She was Zapotec, from a mountain village in Oaxaca state, who had left her three young children with her mother, intending to enter the United States and (so she said) become a menial in a hotel somewhere and send money back to her poor family. But she had become lost in the desert and, spotted by the US Border Patrol, seized, roughed up, and dumped in Nogales. The image of her praying did not leave my mind, and it strengthened my resolve: on my trip whenever I felt obstructed or low, I thought of this valiant woman, and moved on.

Knowing the risks that migrants took emboldened me, and hearing nothing but ignorant opinion about Mexicans, from the highest office in America to the common ruck of barflies and xenophobes (maybe disinhibited by their bigoted leader), I decided to take a trip to Mexico. I studied the map. I had no status except my age, but in a country where the old are respected, that was enough—more than enough.

And a further crucial consideration related to my age: how long would I be able to drive alone in my car over great distances, through the deserts and towns and mountains of Mexico? After you're seventy-six, you need to renew your license every two years. If I failed the eye test next time, my driving days would be over. Knowing that I had limited time—my license with a use-by date—urged me on. My car had served me well in the South. So I contemplated an improvisational road trip along the border and the length of Mexico, from the frontier to Chiapas, with the kind of excitement I felt as a young man.

A Mexico book was on my mind, but there are hundreds of good books about Mexico by foreigners, one of the earliest by an Englishman, Job Hortop, who was a crewman on a slave ship as well as a galley slave himself for twelve years on Spanish ships. He wrote of Mexico and his ordeals in *The rare travales of an Englishman who was not heard of in three-and-twenty years' space,* in 1591, which was included in Hakluyt's *Voyages.* The first comprehensive account of Mexico in English appeared around fifty years later, written by another Englishman, Thomas Gage, who arrived as a Dominican friar in Veracruz in 1625.* Gage's book of travels and the wonders of New Spain appeared in 1648. An important book of the mid-nine-

---

* In that same year, near Plymouth Colony, Myles Standish and his men carried out a massacre on behalf of the Pilgrim fathers, killing so many Indians that they "irreparably damaged the human ecology of the region" (Nathaniel Philbrick, *Mayflower: A Story of Courage, Community, and War,* 2007).

teenth century was the richly detailed, epistolary *Life in Mexico* (1843) by Fanny Erskine Inglis, writing under her married name, Marquise Frances Calderón de la Barca (as the Scottish wife of the Spanish ambassador, she had access everywhere and was habitually indiscreet). Another enduring and insightful work of Mexican travel (which praises Fanny's book) is *Viva Mexico!* by Charles Macomb Flandrau, published over a hundred years ago.

And Stephen Crane, D. H. Lawrence, Evelyn Waugh, Malcolm Lowry, John Dos Passos, Aldous Huxley, B. Traven, Jack Kerouac, Katherine Anne Porter, John Steinbeck, Leonora Carrington, Sybille Bedford, William Burroughs, Saul Bellow, Harriet Doerr, and more—the list is long. Mexico has been lucky in the eminence of its visiting writers, and though they all see something different, Mexico invariably represents for them the exotic, the colorful, the primitive, the unknowable. One of the common deficits of the visiting writers is that they had a very slender grasp of Spanish.

On his short (five weeks) trip to Mexico in 1938, Graham Greene did not speak Spanish at all. His *Lawless Roads* is lauded by some critics, but it is exasperated and bad-tempered, a joyless, overdramatized, and blaming book, contemptuous of Mexico. He traveled in Tabasco and Chiapas at a time when the Catholic Church there was under siege by the government (and elsewhere in the country the government battled with heavily armed Catholic "Cristeros").

Greene, a convert to Catholicism, took the suppression of religion personally. "I loathed Mexico," he writes at one point. And later, "How one begins to hate these people." Again, "I have never been in a country where you are more aware all the time of hate." He describes praying peasants (indigenous Tzotzils probably) in Chiapas with "cave dweller faces" and his having to suffer "unspeakable meals." And toward the end of the book, "the almost pathological hatred I began to feel for Mexico." Yet the novel that was inspired by his Mexican travel, *The Power and the Glory,* is one of his best.

Somerset Maugham visited Mexico for a magazine assignment in 1924, at the same time as D. H. Lawrence, with whom he quarreled. He later wrote a few downbeat, Mexico-inspired short stories, but no book. When

Frieda Lawrence asked him what he thought of the country, Maugham said, "Do you want me to admire men in big hats?"

Hatred or contempt for Mexico is a theme in Evelyn Waugh's obscure and rancorous travel book, *Robbery Under Law: The Mexican Object Lesson,* and in Aldous Huxley's better-known *Beyond the Mexique Bay.* Waugh: "Every year [Mexico] is becoming hungrier, wickeder, and more hopeless." Huxley: "Sunrise, when it came, was a vulgar affair," and "Under close-drawn shawls one catches the reptilian glitter of Indian eyes."

Mexico books continue to appear, many excellent ones: books about the cartels, the stupendous ruins, the border, the savage drug trade, Mexican art and culture, the food, the politics, the economy, get-acquainted books, picture books, guides to hotels and beach resorts, books of tips and hints for potential retirees, surfing guides, books for hikers and campers, books that prettify the country, others that are prosecutorial and full of warnings, such as the helpful 2012 guide *Don't Go There. It's Not Safe. You'll Die, and Other More Rational Advice for Overlanding Mexico and Central America.*

However bitter the foreign writers, no one is more antagonistic toward Mexico than the Mexicans themselves. Carlos Fuentes (the best-known Mexican writer to non-Mexicans) was so conflicted and abused by his fellow writers, he moved to Paris. Other Mexican writers routinely seek jobs in American universities, or expatriate themselves to other countries. You can't blame them: money is a factor. There is a long, sour shelf of lamenting works, epitomized by the hefty, informative compendium *The Sorrows of Mexico: An Indictment of Their Country's Failings by Seven Exceptional Writers. The Labyrinth of Solitude,* Octavio Paz's reflections on death and loneliness, masks and history, is pitiless but also one of the most insightful books I have read on Mexican attitudes and beliefs. ("No," says a Mexican friend whose views I respect, "it's a tissue of stereotypes.")

But I have not found a traveler or commentator, foreign or Mexican, who has been able to sum up Mexico, and maybe such an ambition is a futile and dated enterprise. The country eludes the generalizer and summarizer; it is too big, too complex, too diverse in its geography and culture, too messy and multilingual — the Mexican government recognizes

68 different languages and 350 dialects. Some writers have attempted to be exhaustive. Late in her life (she was seventy, but still game to travel) Rebecca West began to accumulate notes for a book that she hoped would be as encyclopedic about Mexico as her vivid, 400,000-word chronicle of Yugoslavia, *Black Lamb and Grey Falcon*. Though she abandoned her Mexico book, the parts of it, pieced together and published posthumously as *Survivors in Mexico,* are illuminating and at times spirited and insightful.

An implication in all books about the country is that, though Europeans successfully emigrate to Mexico and become Mexican, no American can follow suit: the gringo remains incorrigibly a gringo. In practice, this is not a hardship but amounts to a liberation. Consider the ritualized banter of the sort that social anthropologists describe as "the joking relationship." This foolery is practiced in Mexico to a high degree of refinement. Mexicans allow gringos the singularity to be themselves by trading jolly insults in order to emphasize differences, using the humor of privileged disrespect to avoid conflict. Or, as the anthropologist A. R. Radcliffe-Brown (the definer of this social interaction) put it, "a relation by two persons in which one is by custom permitted, and in some cases required, to tease and make fun of the other, who in turn is required to take no offense."

Owing to Mexican generosity and good humor in a culture that values manners, especially the manners that govern jocular teasing, an American who accepts the role of a gringo is licensed in his gringoismo. A gringo who doesn't abuse that status is given the latitude to be different. Most of the time Mexicans use the word "gringo" without much malice. (*Gabacho* is the insulting word in Mexico for gringo; in Spain, it is a way of rubbishing a French person.) And so the tradition of gringos finding refuge in Mexico is old, and especially now there are permanent communities of gringos all over Mexico, retirees and escapists who have no plans ever to go home, who find it very simple to show up and stay for years. This Mexican hospitality to gringos is in ironic contrast to the present ubiquity of Mexicans who are demonized and fenced in, stamped as undesirable, considered suspect, and unwelcome in America.

Glaring paradoxes like that, and the repetition of stereotypes, also provoked me to take this trip, hoping for more insights in the foreign country through the doorway in the high fence at the end of the road. And there was my anxiety that my driving days are numbered, that my writing life had stalled, that I kept being reminded I was old, and I knew that a road trip would lift my spirits and release me from the useless obsession of self-scrutiny and induce in me (as the English writer Henry Green put it in *Pack My Bag*) "that blessed state when you forever cease to give a damn."

What I intended was a jaunt from one end of Mexico to the other, the opposite of a downfall, which is a dégringolade; rather, a leap in the dark, driving away from home, to cross the border and keep going until I ran out of road. Even the most lighthearted journey to Mexico becomes something serious—or dangerous, tragic, risky, illuminating, or at times bowel-shattering, and in my case it was all of those things.

But no sooner had I gotten behind the wheel than a feeling came over me that was like being caressed by a cosmic wind, reminding me of what travel at its best can do: I was set free.

## "Don't Go Thar! You'll Dah!"

IT TOOK ME four and a half days to drive from Cape Cod to the border. I had left home in a hurry, midafternoon, on a sudden impulse the day before I'd planned to go, impatiently emptying my refrigerator into a big box of food to shove into my car, to eat on the way. I made it to Nyack, New York, by nightfall. Six hundred miles the next day through the mild Dixie autumn, the sadness of southern scenes, melancholy for being overlooked, but familiar to me, like the face of an old friend for the two years I had spent driving on the back roads for my book *Deep South*. Five hundred miles on my third day had me outside Montgomery, Alabama, microwaving noodles in my motel room late at night and watching a football game.

From the supine, somnolent South, I headed to the Gulf, past Biloxi and Pascagoula and New Orleans, puddled with bayous, to Beaumont, Texas, where every motel, big and small, was filled with people who'd lost their homes in the recent hurricane. These were the displaced: shirtless youths and families sprawling in the lobbies, smokers conferring in the parking lot, not desperate but lost, pathetic, fatalistic, like doomsday refugees, a glimpse of what the end of the world will look like: poor, hungry people hunkered down in overcrowded motels with nowhere to go.

Nearer Houston—the wide spot of Winnie (pop. 3,254)—well off the main road, I got a room and a drunken lecture from a motorcyclist who'd ridden there from Billings, Montana.

"Billings, *nice*? Haw, no, it ain't. But you say you're going to the border? I was in Laredo once. Took the wrong damn road. Seen a sign up ahead 'To Mexico' and just swung my bike around—a U-turn on a one-way, the hell with the cops. I ain't goin' near that fucken place. Mexicans would steal my bike and fuck me up. No way am I going to cross that border."

All but toothless, tattooed, greasy hair, round-shouldered from hugging the handlebars of his Harley, leaning on his hog and swigging a beer in the motel parking lot, he was the toughest-looking man I had seen all week—streetwise, knowledgeable about flying saucers and chain saws and back roads, and familiar with life's reverses. He had just picked up his son in a Montana prison ("He done a year and a half—it'll follow him the rest of his life"), and he left me with the thought, "Driving into Mexico? You gotta be out of your mind, man. Don't go thar! You'll dah!"

Another lesson: it's a mistake to disclose that you're passionate about going anywhere, because everyone will give you ten reasons for not going—they want you to stay home and eat meatloaf and play with a computer, which is what they're doing. I heard that refrain again in Corpus Christi the following day, bleary-eyed from the scrubby desert past Victoria and Refugio, having taken a wrong turn and asked for directions to McAllen at a filling station.

A stout squinting man, another tough guy, but sober, gassing up his monster truck, whooped in discouragement, saying, "Do not cross at Brownsville. Do not cross at all, anywhere. The cartels will eyeball you, they'll follow you. If you're lucky, they'll strand you by the side of the road and take your vehicle. If you're unlucky, they'll take your life. Stay away from Mex."

But curious to see the fence, I drove to the Rio Grande Valley, south to Harlingen, over to McAllen, and down Twenty-Third Street to International Boulevard and the frontier at Hidalgo, where the thing was obvious, ugly, and unambiguous. Marking the edge of our great land, it loomed behind a Whataburger stand, a flea market, and a HomeGoods store, an ugly steel fence you might associate with a prison perimeter, twenty-five feet high, like nothing I had seen in any other country. A Texas congressman had called it "an inefficient fourteenth-century solution to a twenty-first-century problem," which was accurate because, like a medieval wall, it was merely a symbol of exclusion rather than anything practical, and easily climbed over or tunneled under. In an age of aerial surveillance and high-security technology, it was a blacksmith's barrier of antiquated ironmongery: old rusty ramparts running for miles, a visible example of national paranoia.

"They're only killing ten people a day," Jorge ("Call me George"), the waiter at the hotel breakfast in McAllen said, turning his cadaverous face on me.

"That was in Juárez," I said. "But I heard it's calmer there now."

Tales of bloodthirsty Mexicans are as old as its earliest chroniclers, such as Francisco López de Gómara in his *Hispania Victrix* (1553), quoted by Montaigne in his essay "On Moderation," mentioning how "all their idols are slaked with human blood." But like many excitable commentators today, Gómara never traveled to Mexico, and all his information was secondhand and questionable. The same is true for Daniel Defoe, who in *Robinson Crusoe* (1719) wrote of Spanish "barbarities" as well as the "idolators and barbarians" they massacred in America for being "idolators . . . sacrificing human bodies to their idols." Crusoe says, "The very name of Spaniards is reckoned to be frightful and terrible."

"And that lady who crashed," Jorge added, wagging his finger, "because the corpse hanging from a bridge fell on her car."

"Tijuana," I complacently observed. "And not recently."

"Those forty-three students who were kidnapped and killed in Guerrero."

"I get the point, George."

"Take a plane. Don't drive."

"I'm crossing. That's my plan."

"But why, in a car?"

"Lots of reasons."

"*Mucha suerte, señor.*"


## "There Is No Business Without Terror"

I PUT JORGE'S warning down to the conventional "Be careful," a plati-tudinous formula all travelers hear when they set out — words that often sound to me empty, resentful, and envious, the sort of precaution that licenses the sullen stay-at-home slug to gloat at some point much later, "See, I told you so!"

"*Me vale madre*," I said to him, claiming I didn't care, in a coarse Mexican way that made him laugh, then groan, then shake his head. He guessed I was foolhardy.

And he was right, because really, I knew nothing, or very little, of the mayhem. Many people had been killed by cartel violence, everyone knew that, but the brutal facts and particularities had eluded me. Or maybe I had ignored them so that I would not allow myself to be deterred in my trip. What I am writing here is all hindsight. The simple statistic, for example, is that more than 200,000 people have been killed or have disappeared since December 2006, when Mexico's government declared war on organized crime. I did not know, when I set out early in 2017, that in the first ten months of that year there had been 17,063 murders in Mexico, and Ciudad Juárez had recorded an average of one a day — more than 300 when I set out, because the Sinaloa and Juárez cartels were vying for dominance in the city, in a turf war to control the drug trade. By the end of 2017, Mexico would record 29,168 murders, the majority of them cartel related.

And in Reynosa, just over the border from McAllen, Texas, where I was standing, oblivious of all this, the violence was chronic, the streets dangerous with crossfire from sudden bloody skirmishes — kidnappings and murders — and a tactic that had become common, the *narcobloqueo*, a roadblock made of hijacked vehicles, sometimes set on fire, to serve as a barricade to protect narcos under siege by the police or army. "Reynosa

Dawns with Narcobloqueos, Persecutions and Shootings" ("*Reynosa aman-
ece con narcobloqueos, persecuciones y balaceras*") was a headline on the *Proceso*
website at the time of another of my crossings, in May 2018, but I missed
the article and all I saw in Reynosa were checkpoints manned by heavily
armed police and black-masked soldiers in dark, boxy armored trucks.

Reynosa was now one of the most violent cities in Mexico because of
a cartel power vacuum, the result of the Mexican army's success in lo-
cating and killing two Gulf cartel bosses: Julián Loiza Salinas ("Comandante Toro"), in April 2017; and the following year, the murder by government troops of Humberto Loza Méndez ("Betito") with three others, in
Reynosa, created greater chaos and more infighting.

Beginning in Reynosa, Los Zetas, who served as enforcers in the armed
wing of the Gulf cartel, had been inspired to form their own cartel, and the
Zetas gloried in being merciless. Most were deserters from the Mexican
army's special forces, who had turned on their officers and decided to use
their killing skills to make real money as *sicarios,* hit men. This fighting in
the streets of Reynosa resulted in as many as four hundred deaths from
May 2017 to January 2018, when I was passing back and forth, bumping
along Reynosa's side streets and potholed roads in a car with conspicuous
license plates lettered *Massachusetts — The Spirit of America.*

I had been beguiled by Reynosa's facade — its picturesque plaza, its
handsome church and friendly shop owners, its good restaurants and taco
stands and flourishing market, the sight of schoolchildren in uniforms, carrying book bags. It took several visits to see what lay behind this convincing display of jaunty Mexicanismo: the back streets, the lurking small-time
drug sellers known as *narcomenudistas* near the slums and shantytowns at
the city's edge, the starved barking dogs, the roadblocks — armored vehicles side by side — manned by scowling soldiers with assault rifles and
jumpy-looking but heavily armed police, most of them masked so that
they could not be identified, ambushed, and murdered later by vindictive
hit men.

Mexican gangs reflect Mexican politics, Mexican states, Mexican geography, and the texture of Mexican life in general, *el mundo* Mexico.
They have too many aspects and moods for anyone to nail it down. The

gang violence is not just the government against the cartels, but the cartels against each other, complicated by ideological splits within the same cartel—ideological in a broad and brutal sense, meaning the side devoted to beheadings being opposed to the side that practiced disemboweling or amputating hands and feet, or hanging bodies from lampposts, or migrant intimidation and enslavement, or the newer tactic of scattering bodies on city streets, as happened when Joaquín Guzmán's goons pushed thirty-five bloody corpses (twelve of them women) off two trucks on Manuel Ávila Camacho Boulevard, near a shopping mall in the prettier part of the port city of Veracruz one day in September 2011, to terrorize their adversaries and show them who was boss. The lack of control by a single cartel meant many contending mobsters and more violence than ever.

Mutilations send a message. A severed tongue indicates someone who blabbed too much, and because *dedo* (finger) is a euphemism for traitor ("He fingered that guy"), the corpse of a betrayer will have a missing finger. And more, as a forensic pathologist elaborates in Ed Vulliamy's *Amexica,* the definitive book on the borderland cartels: "Severed arms could mean that you stole from your consignment, severed legs that you tried to walk away from the cartel." Beheadings are an unambiguous "statement of power, a warning to all, like the public executions of old."

And why such bloody competition among the cartels? Because a successful Mexican drug gang can generate an annual profit calculated in the billions of dollars. The more enterprising cartels reinvest the money in infrastructure. Before he was captured the second time, Guzmán, known as El Chapo (Shorty) for his small stature, ran the largest airborne operation in Mexico; he owned more aircraft than Aeromexico, the national airline. Between 2006 and 2015, Mexican authorities seized 599 aircraft—586 planes and 13 helicopters—from the Sinaloa cartel; by comparison, Aeromexico had a piddling fleet of 127 planes. El Chapo's flights (and he claimed to own submarines, too) mostly serviced the drug habits of Americans, who are the world's largest consumers of illicit drugs, spending more than $100 billion a year on cocaine (including crack), heroin, marijuana, and methamphetamines smuggled across the border, according to a 2014 RAND Corporation report.

Two former allies in the Zetas were themselves rivals now, the Vieja Escuela Zeta (Old School Z) fighting with the Cartel del Noreste (Northeast) faction for control of the main human trafficking and drug routes. What made the Zetas dangerous and unreadable was not only their vicious methods of killing, but also that they were untethered to any one region—unusual for gangsters in Mexico, where villains tended to make trouble in their own territory or on specific routes or *plazas*. *Plaza*, in narco-speak, means turf that is valuable for trafficking. Nuevo Laredo and Tijuana are regarded as coveted *plazas*, thus the mayhem there. The Zetas were everywhere, people said, even in Sinaloa, where they were at war with the Sinaloa cartel, fragmented and in disarray after the arrest of El Chapo. In *Amexica*, Vulliamy quotes a knowledgeable businessman in McAllen saying, "As things are, Los Zetas and the cartels are infiltrating the US side—they're in Houston, they're in New York City, they're all over the Indian reservations."

One Zeta atrocity I knew nothing about took place in 2010, in the small town of San Fernando, south of Reynosa. A roaming band of Zetas stopped two buses of migrants—men, women, and children from Central and South America, who were fleeing the violence in their countries. The Zetas demanded money. The migrants had no money. The Zetas demanded that the migrants work for them, as assassins or operatives or drug mules. The migrants refused. So they were taken to a building in the village of El Huizachal, blindfolded, their hands and legs bound, and each one was shot in the head. Seventy-two of them died. One man (from Ecuador) played dead, escaped, and raised the alarm.

The gory details of this massacre became known when one of the perpetrators was arrested, Édgar Huerta Montiel, an army deserter known as El Wache, or Fat Ass. He admitted killing eleven of the migrants personally, in the belief (so he said) that they were working for a gang hostile to his own. A year later, near the same town, police found 47 mass graves containing 193 corpses—mostly migrants or passengers in buses hijacked and robbed while passing through this area of Tamaulipas state, about eighty miles south of the US border.

Looking for money, menials, or women to traffic across the border, the

Zetas and other gangs routinely hijacked buses and vans and kidnapped travelers—migrants, laborers, commuters, and wanderers like me, the sort of cartel abduction known as *levantón*, a lifting. Attracted by the low wages in Reynosa (most employees start at $10 a day), hundreds of American and European factories operate there, and as many as 100,000 workers live in colonias (communities) around the town.

"There was a gringo here, a plant manager," a man told me in McAllen, which is fifteen minutes from Reynosa. "He used to cross the border every morning, wearing a suit and tie, in a big SUV. Then one day he was caught in a *levantón*, and the company had to pay a big ransom. So they changed their vehicles. Now the plant managers go over in old clothes, in beat-up pickup trucks."

This man, a Mexican immigrant, originally from Monterrey, living at the edge of the Mexican border, told me he had not crossed it for more than twenty years.

"I'm happy here in Texas. And I don't want trouble," he said. "We are just a mile from the middle of Reynosa, and you know what? We never hear news from there. It is never in the papers. All I know is what people whisper about—just the local talk. Rumors, gossip. Nothing official."

But that was much later in my trip.

Another schism happened in El Chapo's Sinaloa cartel when its band of gunmen formed a new gang, the Cartel de Jalisco Nueva Generación—the Jalisco New Generation—notorious for their violent massacres and killings of police, including the first instance of the use of rocket-propelled grenades in shooting down military helicopters. This cartel was one of the most feared criminal gangs, headed by a psychopath, Nemesio Oseguera Cervantes, known as El Mencho, a former avocado seller and policeman. El Mencho's ambition to dominate the drug trade and sideline the Sinaloa cartel had resulted in a vastly increased murder rate. In Tijuana, for example, the number of homicides reported in 2017—1,781—was greater than in any other year. Most of them were cartel killings by the Tijuana cartel, a niche gang of drug and human traffickers allied with the Sinaloa cartel, which was protecting its turf against the Jalisco New Generation. A clearly written note, an ominous message known as a *narcomensaje* (narco message), was pinned to the bullet-riddled bodies of a man and woman found in a Tijuana neighborhood in January 2018. It read, *Welcome to 2018—the plaza is not Sinaloa's, it belongs to Nueva Generación.* A year later, cartel violence in Tijuana exceeded all other years, nearing 2,000 murders.

Another horror: in March 2018, three film school students from Guadalajara took a trip to Tonalá, in Jalisco, where they were planning to make a movie. Picturesque Tonalá is noted for its ceramics, its colorful shops, and its colonial churches. Having little money, the students stayed with one of their grandmothers, but in walking around the town scouting locations, they were mistaken for members of a rival bunch called the Nueva Plaza Gang. They were abducted, tortured, and murdered, their bodies handed over to a fairly well-known Mexican rapper, Christian Omar Palma Gutiérrez ("QBA," his rap moniker), who, with some others in the pay of the Jalisco New Generation, admitted dissolving their bodies in vats of acid. The same year, three Italian men who were selling Chinese merchandise to hawkers in provincial markets disappeared in the town of Tecalitlán, Jalisco. They were abducted at a gas station by a band of local policemen on motorcycles and sold for $53 to a gang who eventually killed them and burned their bodies.

Decapitation and mutilation became something new in Mexican gang warfare. "The machete is the most convincing form of argument," Charles Macomb Flandrau wrote in his *Viva Mexico!* (1908). The cartels had favored bullets, significantly placed, the *tiro de gracia*—a shot in the back of the head meaning the victim was a traitor, a shot through the temple indicating a rival gang member. But in the early 2000s headless bodies began to appear, tossed by the roadside, while human heads were displayed in public, at intersections, and randomly on the roofs of cars. This butchery was believed to be inspired by a tactic of the Guatemalan military's elite commandos, known as Kaibiles.

A man I was to meet in Matamoros, on my traverse of the border, explained how the Kaibiles were toughened by their officers. The officers encouraged recruits to raise a dog from a puppy, then, at a certain point in their training, the recruit was ordered to kill the dog and eat it. From what I heard of them, the Kaibiles deserved that rare classification of "apex predator," the fearsome creature in the animal world at the top of the food chain (tiger, grizzly bear, lion) that has no natural predators, dominating all others. When the Kaibiles became mercenaries in the Mexican cartels, the first beheadings occurred, the earliest known taking place in 2006: a gang in Michoacán kicked open the doors of a bar and tossed five human heads on the dance floor. Decapitations are now, according to one authority on the business, "a staple in the lexicon of violence" for Mexican cartels.

Instead of hiding bodies in mass graves, corpses were triumphantly displayed, as when the Jalisco New Generation (while still part of El Chapo's Sinaloa cartel) dumped the thirty-five bodies on an avenue in Veracruz in September 2011. In reply, the Zetas scattered twenty-six corpses in Jalisco and a dozen in Sinaloa. On closer inspection, the bodies were those of ordinary citizens, not criminals: they were workers and students who had been abducted and murdered and displayed in order to strike fear in the heart of anyone who doubted the murderous resolve of the Zetas.

There are killings contrived with such diabolical cunning they seem un-imaginable. In *To Die in Mexico: Dispatches from Inside the Drug War*, John Gibler writes about a related series of bizarre and violent episodes that took place in Torreón, in Coahuila state, bordering Texas: "Who would believe, for example, that the warden of a state prison would let convicted killers out at night and loan them official vehicles, automatic assault rifles, and bulletproof vests, so that they could gun down scores of innocent people in a neighboring state and then quickly hop back over the state line and into prison, behind bars, a perfect alibi? Who would believe that a paramilitary drug-trafficking organization formed by ex–Special Forces of the Mexican Army would kidnap a local cop and torture him into confessing all of the above details about the prisoners' death squad, videotape the confession, execute the cop on camera with a shot to the heart, and then post the video on YouTube? Who could fathom that the federal attorney general would, within hours of the video-taped confession and execution being posted online, arrest the warden, and then a few days later hold a press conference fully acknowledging that the prisoners' death squad had operated for months, killing ten people in a bar in January 2010, eight peo-

ple in a bar in May 2010, and seventeen people at a birthday party in July?"
Yet all of this actually happened.

I was often encouraged to cross the border at Laredo, into Nuevo Laredo.
During April 2012, when El Chapo was at war with the Zetas, fourteen
torsos—armless and legless bodies—were found in a car by the side of the
road in Nuevo Laredo. Dead Zetas. Some of the torsos were in the trunk,
for which there is a specific narco term: *encajuelado* ("trunked"; therefore,
trunks trunked). A month later, nine bodies were found hanging from a
bridge across Federal Highway 85 in the middle of Nuevo Laredo, a *narcomensaje* banner near them, identifying them as members of the Gulf cartel,
killed by Zetas. The next day, some ice coolers were found in front of
Nuevo Laredo's elegant town hall (Palacio Municipal), and in the coolers
were fourteen headless bodies—more Zetas, but this time with a note
from El Chapo, claiming it was the work of his cartel, as a way of insisting
that the *plaza* of Nuevo Laredo belonged to him.

The Zetas were not intimidated. On May 9, 2012, they left the hacked-
apart bodies of eighteen men inside two vehicles (some of them *encajuelado*) in Chapala, Jalisco, all of them headless, though the severed heads
had also been stacked in the cars. Soon after, in Michoacán state, the Zetas
met their match in the person of Nazario Moreno (called El Más Loco,
the Craziest One), leader of the ruthless Templarios, the Knights Tem-
plar cartel, whose recruits were required to eat human flesh—their victims'—as part of their initiation rites. When Moreno was gunned down
by the Mexican army in 2014, the Zetas flourished, and remain dominant.
But there was a posthumous bonus for the Craziest One: he was promoted
to sainthood. In and around his birthplace in Apatzingán, shrines and altars were erected to Saint Nazario, the dead capo represented as a holy
figure in robes, venerated by credulous Michoacanos.

The massacre that was on many people's minds—and which I knew
a little about, because as a gratuitous outrage it had received extensive
publicity—occurred in 2014, in Guerrero state, when forty-three students
from a school in Ayotzinapa were abducted from buses and murdered.

Only one of the bodies had been found. A vigorous campaign had been mounted on behalf of the bereaved parents, but the crime remained unsolved. The state prosecutor in that case said that the students had been handed over by corrupt local police to a criminal gang, which killed them and burned their bodies. This assertion was disproved in a comprehensive oral history of the massacre by John Gibler, *I Couldn't Even Imagine That They Would Kill Us,* in which he quotes a woman reflecting on the corrupt relationship between drug gangs and police in her murder-plagued state of Veracruz. She said, *"Es que ya sin terror no hay negocio."* (There is no business anymore without terror.) This harsh summary expresses one of the dominant themes in the mayhem of Mexican life.

In the course of my Mexican travels I spent some pleasant weeks in Baja, one of the areas of Mexico that had remained peaceful, frequented for its beaches and sportfishing, its salubrious resorts and hotels. But a few months after I left (and still praising the hospitality and the great food), in December 2017, six bodies were found hanging from bridges in Los Cabos: two near the international airport at Las Veredas, two on the bridge over the highway that connects Cabo San Lucas with San José del Cabo, and two on a third bridge near the airport, the work of drug gangs claiming Los Cabos — on its way to becoming a profitable tourist destination and a market for drugs — as their turf.

Mayhem and uncertainty in Mexico caused the US State Department to devise, in 2018, a new, four-tier advisory system for travelers to the country, to replace the previous system of unspecific travel warnings and travel alerts: Level 1, Exercise Normal Precautions (much of Mexico); Level 2, Exercise Increased Caution (Cancún, Cozumel, Mexico City); Level 3, Reconsider Travel (Guadalajara, Puerto Vallarta, Jalisco); and Level 4, Do Not Travel (Acapulco, Zihuatanejo, Taxco). I knew nothing about this until after I returned from my trip, though I was warned repeatedly to avoid driving in Guerrero state and not to visit Acapulco — warnings I heeded.

Barrancas del Cobre, Copper Canyon, in Chihuahua state, lies in the Exercise Normal Precautions zone and is visited by tourists and hikers. After I finished my Mexican journey, I read of a young American teacher, Patrick Braxton-Andrew, backpacking in Mexico, who left his hotel on

October 28, 2018, wearing sandals for a short, predinner stroll just outside the Copper Canyon town of Urique. He was killed that same day by a member of the Sinaloa cartel, a man identified as El Chueco (the Crooked One), who remained on the loose.

In many killings and abductions the Mexican police or the Mexican army had been involved as abettors or perpetrators. A 2018 Human Rights Watch document on Mexico reported that in August 2017, the Mexican government admitted that the whereabouts of more than 32,000 people who had gone missing since 2006 remained unknown. And in August 2016, the National Human Rights Commission (CNDH) concluded that federal police arbitrarily executed 22 of the 42 civilians who died in a confrontation in 2015 in Tanhuato, Michoacán. Tanhuato, famous for its fiestas, is also an important depot on the northbound drug trafficking route.

"Police fatally shot at least 13 people in the back," the CNDH report stated, "tortured two detainees, and burned a man alive, then altered the crime scene by moving bodies and planting guns to justify the illegal killings. Nobody had been charged with the crimes, and a federal investigation into the Tanhuato killings remained open."

The Mexican army and police also routinely tortured suspects. The CNDH had received almost 10,000 complaints of abuse by the army since 2000. Mexico's own national statistics office, the Instituto Nacional de Estadística y Geografía, reported that in a 2016 survey of more than 64,000 people incarcerated in 370 Mexican prisons, more than half of the prison population had suffered some type of physical violence at the time of their arrest: "19 percent reported receiving electrical shocks; 36 percent being choked, held underwater, or smothered; and 59 percent being hit or kicked. In addition, 28 percent reported that they were threatened that their family would be harmed."

Journalists were targeted by both the cartels and the police on whom they reported. From 2000 through October 2017, 104 journalists were killed and 25 disappeared, according to the Mexican attorney general's office, and between January and July 2017, 8 journalists were murdered and 1 abducted. All of them had published stories about cartel crime and police corruption, and the more vindictive Mexicans claimed the journalists had gotten what they deserved, quoting President Donald Trump's assertion, "The press is the enemy of the people." The International Press Institute, in its report in December 2017, stated that Mexico is "the deadliest country for journalists, edging out Iraq and Syria."

This, then, was the recent history of mayhem and the general situation in Mexico when I drove toward the border, unaware of it and smiling into the sunshine, squinting at the open road and blessing my luck, thinking, The coachwhip snake is not poisonous! And I was to find that no one in Mexico ever used the word "cartel" or spoke the name of a gang—"Zeta" or "Golfo" or any other. You could be killed for uttering these forbidden words. What I heard, when I asked, was always a hot whisper, no louder than a shallow breath, and the whisper was "mafia," with a widening of the eyes as a warning. I also found that the common fear of the so-called mafia—the drug gangs and traffickers—had unified good people and created watchful communities.

The nearer the border, the shriller the warning, until, on the border itself, the US immigration officer answered one of my questions by saying, "I have no idea. I don't have a clue. I have never been there"—and raised his blue arm and the yellow nail of his hairy finger to point across fifty feet of sunny road to Mexico.


## To TJ: "Aquí Empieza la Patria" (The Fatherland Begins Here)

WISHING TO HAVE a notion of the whole border—because the border was on everyone's mind—instead of crossing from McAllen to Reynosa, I decided to drive straight to Tijuana to make a slow, uninterrupted traverse of the entire *frontera*, a road trip from west to east, San Ysidro, California, to Brownsville, Texas, which was also Tijuana to Matamoros, zigzagging from the United States to Mexico and back, from one border town to the other. And then on the eastern end of the line I would head seriously south from Reynosa.

The Texas town of McAllen and its surrounding towns, Hidalgo, Mission, Progreso, Pharr, and some others, are where many Mexicans who live near the border do their shopping. And many Mexican laborers with visas crowd the bridges each morning from the states of Nuevo León and Tamaulipas, returning in the evening when the workday is done. Like most other large US border towns, these places are bilingual and buoyant, their prosperity based on the spending of Mexican visitors and the tenacity of Mexican farm workers, without whom little would be plucked from the fields at harvest time. Texans don't go to McAllen for a good time, but many Mexicans do.

I should add that McAllen and the nearby towns are also beset by incursions of migrants from deeper in Mexico, the poorer states of Oaxaca and Michoacán, who have been spirited across the Rio Grande from Reynosa by traffickers, known variously as coyotes or *polleros* (a word for chicken farmers). On occasion, migrants run through suburban yards pursued by the Border Patrol, or huddle, thirty at a time, in "drop houses" in middle-class neighborhoods until the cartels and traffickers can move them farther north, eluding US checkpoints. Often the traffickers hold them hostage in the drop houses, forcing them to call their relatives in Mexico to send ransom money.

I spent the night in McAllen and set off in the morning, heading west along Route 83, which follows the border—the Rio Grande here—past Roma (where I could wave to picnickers on the other side, at Ciudad Miguel Alemán) and, at Zapata's watery edge, Falcon Lake, two miles wide, swelled by Falcon Dam at its southeast end. At Laredo, the road took me inland to the farming towns of south Texas and then eastward through the pale clay cliffs and deep ravines of Box Canyon and the twenty-mile-long Amistad Reservoir, which straddles the border and is surrounded not by forest but by a greeny-blue sea of head-high junipers and stunted oaks. Farther on, real wilderness, not the Texas of desert stereotype but a low forest of mesquite and cedar that seems dense and impassable, and uninhabited except for the migrant-spotters in vehicles on the service roads and the occasional checkpoint, with sniffer dogs and Border Patrol officers and their blunt greeting at the stop sign: "Are you an American citizen?"

As darkness fell, I was climbing to the high plains, farther from the border—the border from Langtry west to Big Bend here is too rugged for roads, a wasteland of arroyos and clawed ridges, and a much greater challenge to border jumpers. Finally, after driving 560 miles from McAllen, I came to Fort Stockton, the motels filled with workers, glassy-eyed and weary from their arduous day in the oil fields northwest of town.

The next morning, I took I-10 west to the prosperous sprawl of El Paso, with a panorama of the dusty horizontal colonias of Ciudad Juárez, and onward on the straight roads and high desert of New Mexico to the simple hills and placid, wooded valleys of southern Arizona. I gloried in the emptiness, the dry roadsides patterned with leafy shadows, and then past Tucson and the solid single mountains and flat gray plains, where I chose a town at random, Gila Bend, and a motel for the night.

The road the next day slipped closer to the border, and at Yuma and Calexico, Mexico was again on the horizon: beyond the green fields of Date City, the glare of Mexicali. I passed El Centro—a beaten-up grid of hot streets and faded bungalows—and then Imperial Valley, chronicled by William T. Vollmann in *Imperial*, an exhaustive work of social observation, scholarship, and vagabondage. Into the stony hills toward Ocotillo and the Jacumba Wilderness Area, mountain slopes composed entirely of smooth boulders, and finally I took a detour to the desert road that led to Potrero and Dulzura and the small, poor, silent town of San Ysidro—Tijuana bustling and rackety on the other side of the fence.

## *A Traverse of the Border*
## *(Una Travesía de la Frontera)*

SINGING BIRDS — warbling, cheeping, sounding piteous—were hidden in the tangled thickets of lanky shrubs, the flowering mule fat, or water-wally, and spindly willows. I had begun my traverse of the border, walking on a sandy path at the margin of Border Field State Park in San Ysidro, a township south of San Diego. It was obvious to me this early in my trip that the border is not a discrete knife cut, a slash mark in the landscape, except in the minds of politicians and cartographers; it is like most other national boundaries, a muddled blur, and it is obvious in many places that Mexico does not butt up to the border but spills over it and puddles willy-nilly—*troche y moche*, as Mexicans say—giving many border towns a jumbled cultural ambiguity.

San Ysidro looked as Mexican and as poor as any town in Mexico, and the last census, in 2010, showed it to be 93 percent Hispanic. Yet compared to the humble houses in distressed San Ysidro, the villas on the Mexican side in Tijuana, on the heights of Calle Cascada, looked proud on their natural palisade. Up there, on the far side of the fence, a Tijuana resident was unknotting a garden hose, two big dogs lolloping around him. He caught my eye, saw me staring, and waved in a neighborly way, from his own country.

This was the far western end of the frontier, which is marked by a tall, rust-colored, iron-slatted fence—paralleling an older, lower fence—blistered with corrosion, which extends below the tidemark, its end sunk in the Pacific Ocean. It happened to be low tide that midmorning, and I was to discover that this detail mattered: a low tide allows migrants to splash more easily around the fence and sprint up the oily beach into the American thickets.

So, along with the twittering birds in the park, there are often some desperate human fugitives, too. Three birds, once endangered, have been brought back from the brink of extinction, and are diligently nesting in this area, through the efforts of conservationists—the least tern, calling *kip-kip-kip-kiddeek;* the western snowy plover, chirping *o-wee-ah;* and the clapper rail, this last one seldom visible, but its clanking *ik-ik-ik* call echoes in the bushes here. The migrants make no sound.

Cars are forbidden from entering the park, which is not bosky or park-like at all but a sandy waste of gritty paths in low dunes and muddy swamp, the brittle scrub just high enough to hide anyone in its density, diminishing to salt marsh nearer the Tijuana River estuary. Only hikers and bird watchers are allowed inside the park gate. I was on my own that hot day.

The only sound was birdsong, soon overwhelmed by the headlong buzz of two Border Patrol officers on all-terrain vehicles, zipping past me much too fast on the flat paths, their big wheels tossing up damp sand.

"They're looking for someone who just came over, because of the tide," a passing park ranger told me. I had hailed him in his truck to ask directions. "He's over there somewhere."

The migrant had gone to ground in the brush on the northern side of the wetland, near the Tijuana River, hiding in the tall grass that was within sight of Imperial Beach. The men on the ATVs were scouring the area, and a helicopter had now arrived and was hovering near the raptors, kestrels, and harriers.

"If he manages to elude them until dark," the ranger said, "he'll make a run for it in the middle of the night." Then he smiled in reminiscence. "Years ago it was so different. I'd see thirty or forty guys bum-rush the fence, on the assumption that two or three would make it. You don't see that anymore."

Hiking onward, nearer the fence I saw the Tijuanero on the Mexican side with his frolicking dogs, his arms around the green garden hose, the two dogs barking at him as though trying to provoke him to play. With the hose in his hand he looked toward the fence and faced me.

I waved. He waved back again. Then he dropped the twisted hose and began to play with his dogs. I walked as far as I could go—the Plaza Monumental bullring looming above me on the Mexican side, and a mural of the joined US and Mexican flags lettered LOVE TRUMPS HATE and EL AMOR VENCE AL ODIO—to where the iron-slatted fence extends, and ends, about a hundred yards from shore, half submerged in the ocean. The Border Patrol ATVs were still buzzing, the helicopter still yakking, and a Border Patrol officer was standing by his distinctive black-and-white car, scanning the bush with binoculars. Somewhere in the swamp grass, between the river and the Sunset Spur trail, a man was hiding like a rabbit in a thicket, dead still, his head down, his heart beating madly.

What he had done was not remarkable. Having taken note of the low tide, he had made his way through central Tijuana, to the west end of town through the Jardines Playas de Tijuana residential district, crossed the coastal highway, Avenida del Pacífico, descended to the *malecón* and the promenade by the beach, Paseo Costero, and then vaulted from the low wall onto the sand itself, walking north along the beach until he came to the fence, bisecting the beach. Had he been a strong swimmer, he could have swum a bit out to sea, paddled around the end of the fence, and body-surfed sideways through the riptide into the United States, landing on the beach at International Friendship Park.

But he had set off at low tide, probably clinging to the fence, and having splashed onshore had made a dash for it into the bushes, where he was spotted at about the time I had started to hike, ten in the morning. Now he was crouched, blinking and sniffing, counting on the dark camouflage of his wet clothes, instinctively rigid until the danger passed. He was waiting for night to fall, so that he could insert himself farther into San Diego County. If he made it across the river and into the streets of Imperial Beach, he could be in Chula Vista by morning.

The hunted man was alone and living by his wits. Other migrants, with money, often had help, from cartels or from the facilitators known as coyotes. In a seven-month period, at the time I was walking by the fence, 663 Chinese nationals had been arrested trying to cross from Tijuana, a number of them snared at the end of a long tunnel under the fence. It was estimated that they had paid anywhere from $50,000 to $70,000 apiece to be shepherded into the US. China is now one of the world's leading sources of illegal migrants, along with opportunists and economic migrants from the Middle East and south Asia.

Not long after I was in that sector of the border, a California congressman visited the US federal prison in Victorville, expecting to find persecuted Central Americans seeking asylum. He was startled to find that of the 680 detainees under lock and key, 380 were Indian nationals who had flown from India to Mexico City, where they paid thousands of dollars to coyotes to be smuggled into the US. Twenty percent of the detainees at the Immigration and Customs Enforcement (ICE) facility in the Adelanto Detention Center, near Victorville, were Indian nationals. In the first half of 2018, the *Los Angeles Times* reported (August 13, 2018), more than 4,000 Indian nationals had been caught crossing the US border illegally. After being caught, they claimed they were seeking political asylum (from the country known as "the world's biggest democracy"). Around the same time, 671 Bangladeshis were arrested crossing the border near Laredo, Texas—helped across the river (so they claimed) by members of the Zetas cartel, to whom they paid upward of $27,000 apiece.

These non-Mexicans are the SIAs—Special Interest Aliens, who, along with Chinese, included Iraqis, Afghans, Pakistanis, Syrians, and Africans (predominantly Nigerians). Most were aided by coyotes, who worked for cartels. But some arrived by more ingenious strategies—on Jet Skis glissading through the surf, and a dozen at a time in panga boats (a simple, seaworthy design, with an upswept bow, powered by an outboard motor, and favored by third-world fishermen, Somali pirates, and human traffickers). Such boats were routinely seized by the California Border Patrol as they deposited migrants sprinting across Imperial Beach.

The helicopter was still circling over Border Field Park as I walked to the entrance, and drove—not far—to a parking lot near the entry to Tijuana. I walked across the border, filled out an immigration form, and had my passport stamped. Then I took a taxi to Avenida Revolución, the heart of Tijuana, and walked to a restaurant, Cenaduría la Once Antojitos, which had been recommended to me for its posole. Sitting there, bringing my notes up to date, I was happy—well fed, amazed at the ease of my border crossing, and enlightened by a conversation with a man at the Cenaduría.

"We go to California all the time," he said. "We buy jeans, shirts, TV sets. A lot of it is made in Mexico. Even with the Mexican duty we have to pay on the way back, it's cheaper for us."

This explained the many Mexicans I saw struggling with bundles at border posts all the way to Brownsville. And like most of the Mexican border towns I was to visit, Tijuana was thick with pharmacies, dentists, doctors, and cut-price optometrists.

"Properties, customs offices, real estate deals," Carlos Fuentes writes in his sequence of border stories in *The Crystal Frontier*, "wealth and power provided by control over an illusory, crystal border, a porous frontier through which each year pass millions of people, ideas, products—in short, everything (sotto voce: contraband, drugs, counterfeit money, et cetera)."

In a routine that served me for the next few weeks, I wandered around the busy, seemingly safe part of the city. As in other border towns, I was welcomed as a harmless older gringo who might buy a sombrero, a leather jacket, or a belt buckle bulging with a dead scorpion encased in epoxy.

"What do you think of Donald Trump?" was a frequent question. Predictably, he was not a favorite with Mexicans, whom he characterized as rapists and murderers. But many members of the US Customs and Border Protection agency I engaged on this subject acknowledged they'd voted for him, and their union, the National Border Patrol Council (more than eighteen thousand members), for the first time ever involving itself in a presidential election, had endorsed his candidacy.

Retail business was slow in Tijuana, and though the dentists were busy and the pharmacies crowded (Viagra at $5 a pill), the bars and strip clubs and brothels at the north end of town—Zona Norte, around Calle Coahuila—were so thinly visited that when I entered a bar I caused a buzz of attention, being one of only a few gringos in the place. The bars are grim: beer-soaked, smoky, and noisy; the girls, old and young, sitting in clusters at banquettes, hoping to ensnare a client to buy an expensive drink and then negotiate a price for an hour in one of the rooms upstairs, in what is advertised outside as a hotel.

"*Solo mirando*," I said at each place. Just looking, the theme of my traveling life.

The Zona de Tolerancia—Zona Norte in Tijuana, "Boys' Town" elsewhere on the border, and the Zona Rosas deeper in Mexico—is the Mexican answer to regulating sex workers: a designated neighborhood, usually at the edge of cities and larger towns, where prostitution is legal. On these streets, in these seedy bars, sex workers are licensed and given routine medical checks. Though this seemed a rational solution to an age-old issue, it was obvious in Tijuana that this Zone of Tolerance attracted pimps and parasites, the drug trade, pests, and hangers-on.

In midafternoon the bars and hangouts smelled of mildew and spilled beer and were mainly empty; I was assured that they would liven up after dark. But people I met said that if I insisted on seeing the border, I should do so in daylight. As night fell, I was in a queue of perhaps four hundred people, none of them gringos, crowding to leave Mexico, while a gruff American immigration officer at a turnstile shouted at us.

"Back up! Hey, lady. Yes, you—did I tell you to move?!"

I approached him, holding my passport, but he waved me away.

"Back in line!"

The border is not the simple line it seems, and it's hard to believe that in time—so we are promised—it will be the site of the battlements of the Murus Hadrianus Trumpus. It has altered greatly over the past 170-odd years, been disputed and redrawn. The United States has expanded; Mexico has shrunk. Much of what is now our West and Southwest—Texas and New Mexico, all of Arizona, and most of California—was once Mexican territory. But that northern one-third of old Mexico was ceded to the United States after the Mexican-American War (1846–1848), which was provoked in 1845 by the US annexation of Texas. California at that time was still sparsely settled, just a chain of missions on the Camino Real, from San Diego to San Francisco, as Richard Henry Dana described in *Two Years Before the Mast*, when he sailed as a deckhand up this Mexican coast of Alta California in 1834. (On a second visit, twenty-four years later, Dana noted how the Gold Rush had turned the tiny mission of San Francisco into a big city.)

After Texas became part of the Union, its southern border followed the Rio Grande. Arizona did not become a state until 1912, but earlier, when it was still part of the territory of New Mexico, its southern portion was defined by a patch of the Gadsden Purchase (1854)—straight lines, as the border is designated today, inconvenient and hard to police, across stony hill and dusty dale, in the desert.

Throughout the border disputes among the colonials and newcomers, the Native Americans, who had occupied this region for hundreds of years, were regarded as a nuisance. They were fought for objecting to the interlopers and for asserting their ancestral claims to their home. The

Apaches (to use the popular term for a collection of nations) were particularly tenacious; for their veneration of the land, they were seen as warlike, and slaughtered. The descendants of the depleted populations of all these native peoples remain, and following the border today, one encounters the reservations and tribal lands of indigenous folk—from the Cahuilla people near Coachella, California, to the Ewiiaapaayp Band of Kumeyaay Indians (also known as the Cuyapaipe) near San Diego, from the Cocopah at the Arizona state line to the Tohono O'odham farther east, from the Mescalero Apache in southern New Mexico to, in Texas, the Ysleta del Sur near El Paso and the Kickapoo people in Eagle Pass. Among other things, the borderland is a living repository of native peoples.

The Mexican border we know today was established as an international frontier in about the middle of the nineteenth century. For more than a hundred years, from before 1900, Mexicans were encouraged by American farmers to cross the border to work in the fields—much to the Mexican government's disapproval, because their labor was needed at home. These men and women were the primary source of agricultural labor in the Southwest and California. To regulate the flow of fieldworkers, the Bracero Program (Mexicans working on short-term contracts) was established in 1942 under an agreement between the US and Mexico.

The American need for cheap labor has defined the border culture. Once, the border had been porous, and in many places informal and notional, people strolling across in both directions to work, to shop, to find entertainment, and to settle. Mormons fled south across the border to escape US persecution for polygamy, sanctioned in their church's Doctrine and Covenants (132:61–62: "If any man espouse a virgin, and desire to espouse another . . ."). Mexicans headed north for work. The border itself was relatively harmonious. "We used to go across all the time," people told me, on both sides. The Bracero Program allowed hundreds of thousands of Mexicans to cross the border to work as manual laborers in the US. After twenty-two years and five million braceros, the program ended in 1964; the remaining braceros were sent home. It has been proven that the braceros—the term means "men who work with their arms"—were generally exploited and manipulated as low-wage workers.

Still, the border remained lightly policed and simple to cross until the Clinton administration activated Operation Gatekeeper in 1994. The border was beefed up with more officers, and characterized by high fences, patrol cars, security technology, and massive deportations of illegal border crossers. Crime, the drug trade, illegal immigration, cartel violence, and the fears raised by the first bombing of the World Trade Center, in 1993, created the need to tighten the borders further. And that is where we are today, the border a front line in what sometimes seems a war, at other times an endless game of cat and mouse.

America's tattered southern fringe is 1,952 miles long, from the rusty fence in the slosh of the Pacific at Tijuana to Matamoros, near the mouth of the Rio Grande, where the soupy green river pours into the Gulf of Mexico at the estuary, just south of Boca Chica, and its brown, burgeoning surf.

People begged me not to cross. My idea had been to drive along the border and nip over whenever convenient to the Mexican side. These dozen or so crossings were a revelation to me, putting the whole border debate into perspective, giving it a human face—or rather, many faces. It is at once more heartening and more hopeless than I had imagined. Nothing fully prepares you for the strangeness of the border experience.

The first thing to know is that, though gringos seldom cross to any of the border cities and towns, tens of thousands of Mexican Americans and Mexican nationals cross every day, in both directions. They have visas and passports, or an ID that allows them access. Renting or buying a house on the US side is prohibitive for many, so a whole cross-border culture has developed in which American citizens of Mexican descent live in a house or an apartment—or a simple shack—in a Mexican border city, such as Juárez or Nuevo Laredo, and commute to work in El Paso or Laredo.

It is a fairly simple matter to walk to Mexico at any point, but there is always a crush of people—all of them with documents—waiting to enter the US to work, go to school, or shop. As the man told me in Tijuana, clothes and electronics are much cheaper in the US. A busy, bilingual Walmart can be found on the American side of most border crossings. There are always discount shops on the US side, always discount phar-

macies on the Mexican side, though the Boys' Towns — Zones of Tolerance — see little roistering.

"We used to go across all the time" was a common refrain I heard on the
US side, usually by a laughing older man. And then I would sit through a
sordid reminiscence of his less rational youth in a Boys' Town bar.

But the old American habit of crossing the border to carouse is over.
The souvenir shops are empty, and so are the bars. Sombreros, ceramic
skulls, and beads sit unsold and unremarked upon. During the day the
Mexican towns are tranquil enough; after dark, not so much. In most there
is a curfew that is strictly enforced by the police or the army ("who take
no prisoners," a man told me in Nuevo Laredo). And for all the downtown
serenity — the lollygagging, the churchgoing, the taco stands, the mariachi
bands, the shoe shiners in the plaza — one is urged by locals to avoid ven-
turing out of town, even to the nearer country areas ten miles away, which
they refer to as *los ranchitos,* where the cartel gangsters are holed up, and
well armed, and predatory.

Most people on either side of the border are reasonably content, going
to work and to school, living their lives, saluting their respective flag, vot-
ing in local elections, raising children. They are settled, they stay home,
they merely fantasize about the country over the fence or across the river.

At the same time, like a rumble on a lower frequency, there is a constant skirmishing, the equivalent of a border war, as migrants — which include Pakistanis, Syrians, and Africans; desperate, criminal, opportunistic,
or tragic — attempt to get to the other side, often with the help of human traffickers, nearly always cartel members, who demand large sums of
money from the migrants. And there are more than twenty-one thousand
Border Patrol agents who work day and night to thwart them.

Not only men and women trying to secure the border, but twenty- or
thirty-foot steel fences that run for miles. Also shorter fences, vehicle barriers, drones, helicopters, bottlenecks at bridges, checkpoints on back roads
and on the interstates, sniffer dogs, and over the Texas towns of Zapata and
McAllen huge white balloons, the sort deployed for antiterrorism in Iraq
and Afghanistan — enormous dirigibles used for surveillance, tethered to
the border, listening and watching.

And the river, and the desert, and coils of razor wire. The notion of building a wall strikes most people on either side as laughable. The belief is: show me a thirty-foot wall, and I will show you a thirty-five-foot ladder.

Leaving San Ysidro the next day, driving through the desert and the rubbly hills, many of them composed of smooth tumbled boulders, I thought, How on earth can anyone manage to cross this desert? It was magnificent and parched and inhospitable, much of it Native American land, sand dunes — the Imperial Dunes, like the Sahara — and the snake lairs of stony ravines, and vast stretches of twisted mesquite and disjointed cholla cactus, with drifting falcons overhead and tumbleweed down below.

But the evidence that migrants did attempt to cross were the many flagpoles, set a few hundred yards apart, flying striped flags, indicating white wooden boxes lettered AGUA, containing plastic gallon jugs of water, placed there by Samaritans, some from humanitarian groups such as No More Deaths and the Border Angels, for migrants dying of thirst. The founder of Border Angels, Enrique Morones, has said, "This wall of Operation Gatekeeper, from 1994, has led to the death of more than 11,000 people," on both sides of the fence.

"Killed by the light," in the words of Luis Alberto Urrea, author of *The Devil's Highway*, to my mind one of the best accounts of border crossing, of migrant tribulations and frontier culture and criminality. Most migrant deaths are caused by exposure to the elements — the desert daytime heat, the desert nighttime cold. Urrea describes in clinical detail the stages by which a person in the desert succumbs to death in the absence of water: heat stress, heat fatigue, heat syncope ("contraction"), heat cramps, and finally heat exhaustion — tunnel vision, hallucinations, paranoia, the vomiting of blood. "You dream of pools, seas, you dream of a lake . . . You'd pay all your money for cold water. You'd trade sex, anything, for water. Walkers who find abandoned vehicles break open the radiators and die from gulping the antifreeze."

The US community of Tecate hardly exists, but Mexican Tecate, hugging the fence, is a large agricultural town of nearly eighty thousand people.

It is also the setting for one of my favorite short stories, "Pastor Dowe at Tecate," by Paul Bowles. The morose American pastor in this darkly comic tale has great difficulty in his attempts to convert the locals to Christianity, and he finds their attention constantly flagging when he preaches. He discovers that they brighten when he winds up his old phonograph and plays the 1928 show tune "Crazy Rhythm." And so he plays it over and over as he delivers his sermons. Hoping to please Pastor Dowe, some men in his congregation try to tempt him with a thirteen-year-old girl, who shows up with a live baby alligator she hugs as a doll. Tecate itself is ambiguous, more lush than the border town—it might be a town deeper in Mexico—but it is the place I associate with this masterly story.

Tecate is also the setting of "Big Caca's Revenge," a short story by the American-born Hispanic writer Daniel Reveles. This is a tale of power on the border, of local toughs, and of the stereotypical bully and local *cabrón*, Big Caca, getting his comeuppance. A cop, Big Nalgas Machado—*nalgas* means "buttocks"—faces him down and makes him grovel (mocking his maxim, "We cannot make a piñata of the law"): "In less than an hour Tecate's fattest cop became a national hero."

Calexico, California, about an hour farther along the border, is little more than a crossroads, surrounded by desert, with the smallness and lushness of an oasis. Mexicali, a mile away, is equally humble in appearance, but boosted by factories: Honeywell, Mitsubishi, BFGoodrich, Gulfstream, and other companies that relocated over the border to find men and women—and children in some places—who would work cheaply, some for as little as $6 a day.

Driving south along Imperial Avenue to the border crossing, I found it hard to believe I was still in the United States—most signs were in Spanish, and many of the others bilingual, the American citizens of Calexico living in an overlap of Mexicali that was exuberantly reflected in the innovation of their spliced-together names.

I parked on a back street and walked through a small park and up the steps of the stern gray building of US Customs and Border Protection. I strolled down the ramp and pushed through a turnstile, no one looking at my passport. Glancing through the chain-link fence on the Mexican side of the building, I saw a line of people—a long line, stretching down the stairs and through a foyer and along a passageway, hundreds, perhaps a thousand people waiting to enter the United States.

My idea was that I would have lunch in Mexicali and hurry back to Calexico, but this line of people was daunting, moving so slowly that I decided to skip lunch and just look. I was greeted ("Señor!") by a row of beggars and panhandlers of medieval mutilation—amputees, the blind, women carrying whimpering babies, and more assertive young men ("Geeve!")—and found a taxi. With a friendly but laconic driver named Héctor I made a tour of Mexicali, yet "*Prohibido,*" he said when I asked him if he could take me into any of the factories. It was soon clear as we ground through traffic that though Calexico, California, was a small town, Mexicali, on the other side of the thirty-foot fence, was a city of a million people, with an international airport, a large cathedral, a bullring, two museums, hospitals, four universities, a dental school, several public libraries, and industrial areas, sprawling in the desert of Baja, and subdivisions and colonias of one-story, three-room houses, most of them lived in by local factory workers.

"Pimsa," Héctor said, passing the industrial park.

"What's that?"

"Jet engines."

Fifty years ago, the Beat poet and publisher Lawrence Ferlinghetti (still alive at one hundred years old as I write this) took a bus here, as he writes in his travel diary *Mexican Night:* "Arrived at Mexicali, another dusty town, only worse, in midst of flat brown plain I saw from above at nightfall—bus station crammed with campesinos looking grim, tough & hungry, under enormous hats and ponchos, waiting for country buses and revolutions ... I walk out into mud boulevard & vision of utter Desolation, Dung & Death in the image of crowded streets and dark people. Everywhere I walk & look, the same!"

Ferlinghetti's book is terrible, his observations banal, but he records a particular historical moment of moribund Mexicali. And now: GKN Aerospace, Martech Industrial (medical technology), Furukawa México, Wabash Technologies, Robert Bosch Tool, and many others, along with the necessary ancillary services—banks, trucking companies, supermarkets, fuel depots, and schools.

And here is the great paradox of the North American Free Trade Agreement, the visible result of American companies looking for cheap labor: a few hundred yards from the industrial park, the high-tech and aerospace maquiladoras (factories) of Mexicali, past Cristóbal Colón Road, the fence, and beyond the fence, the spinach fields of Calexico—most of the field-workers are Mexicans on work visas. Fruit pickers here, lab technicians over there.

In that area, and farther east, in the lettuce and broccoli fields, nearly all the workers are Mexicans who have been granted H-2A visas—temporary agricultural visas—harvesting for farmers who have proven they cannot find American field hands. Such visas are issued every year, allowing Mexicans to work for anywhere from four months to a year. How does this visa system work? First an agricultural company applies to the US Department of Labor, declaring that it does not have enough American workers to fill the available jobs in the fields. The company needs to prove that it has made an effort to find American workers. Then US Citizenship and Immigration Services reviews the application, and if it seems in order, and truthful, a certain number of H-2A visas are approved, the great majority of which are for agricultural workers. In the year I passed those broccoli fields, ninety thousand of the visas had been issued. And why? Because the agricultural cooperatives here and in the Yuma area supply 90 percent of the lettuce to America for most of the year, a $2.4-billion-a-year industry.

I was not wrong to be warned by the long line at the border. I had slipped into Mexico in a matter of minutes; returning, it took more than two hours in a line of uncomplaining Mexicans, all of them with valid visas, to pass through the narrow border entrance, each person's papers examined, each person photographed and briskly interrogated. Back in my car, I drove past the lettuce fields and through the desert—magnificent, inhospitable—and the rubbly hills, the thorny scrub, and flowering bushes, fifty-odd miles to Yuma.

Just a few days after leaving Calexico, I read a news item that claimed a Border Patrol agent had discovered a 142-foot tunnel less than a mile outside the town, "the third such tunnel discovered in Calexico in the past year."

The tidy, good-sized town of Yuma is not on the border. I stayed the night there and set off in the morning (MEXICO NEXT EXIT) to drive the ten miles south through the lettuce fields to the border. It was clear: towns don't get much poorer than these blighted communities at the edge of the fence—Gadsden and Somerton, Arizona—shacks, rotted trailers, shuttered shops, abandoned houses, hemmed in by the tall, rusty-ribbed border fence that is the margin of the towns here, the dead end of every street to the west, where the winding Colorado River flows south past the border.

I stopped for a while in Gadsden, named for the American ambassador to Mexico who in 1853 negotiated the purchase (for $10 million) of the lower third of Arizona and part of New Mexico. The small town of Gadsden, at the southwest corner of the purchase, is a semiderelict community of 1,314 people, almost half of them (46 percent) living below the poverty line amid the dusty fields and the cholla cactus. The town of San Luis, just down the road, is larger and slightly better off because it is an important border crossing. Mexicans from the other side at San Luis Río Colorado shop at the Walmart Super Center and the stores on Main Street. Yet even compared to the towns over the border, it is like Gadsden and Somerton and the Cocopah Indian Reservation nearer Yuma: barely there, third-world poor, baking in the desert heat.

Over coffee in San Luis I talked to Javier, a middle-aged man, raised in town. I asked him how the fence affected him.

"The fence is funny," he said. "I used to be a firefighter. One day we went to a brush fire, way over in the boonies, and started to fight it. But it was going pretty good, so we chased it. We came to a little chicken-wire fence and dragged our hoses through, still spraying but not making too much progress. Then one of the guys says, 'Hey, this is Mexico!'"

"What did you do?"

"We hauled ass out of there!"

"You're sure you were in Mexico?"

"Yeah. It was that chicken wire. You think this big fence at the edge of town goes all the way along the border, but it's only a few miles here and a few miles there, and the rest is chicken wire."

"Easy to jump?"

"Used to be a lot of fence jumpers. These days, not so many."

Nearer the border crossing itself—turn right on Urtuzuastegui Street, then proceed over the bridge—the shops on Main Street were patronized by day-trippers from Mexico, buying clothes and hats made in China, boom boxes made in Korea, bicycles made in Taiwan.

Just a walkway, no formalities, no one on either side looking at my passport or asking my name. It was the simplest crossing I'd ever made in a long career of crossing borders, and it happened to be a lovely day, so the idea of strolling so easily into another country lifted my spirits. Now I was in San Luis Río Colorado, on the far side of the fence, a sprawling one-story town, sun-faded but solidly built, with a park, a cathedral, a Plaza Benito Juárez, and a state university. It had many shops—the usual border-town shops, hats, boots, leather goods, eyeglasses, and drugstores; and the usual businesses, dentists and doctors.

At the east end of town was the industrial park, near enough to the fence to hear the radios crackling in Border Patrol vehicles and see the metal barbecues in the backyards of bungalows in Arizona's Las Villas subdivision. It always amazed me to see American factories in Mexico, so near the border that a factory owner could puff a big cigar on his property in Mexico and blow smoke into the United States, flicking the ash through the fence.

Here were Daewoo, TSE Brakes, and the Bose Flextronics factory, which employs two thousand people. The next time you clap on your expensive Bose headphones or fire up your car stereo, you had to consider that they were put together a hundred yards from Arizona by someone living in a hut in the Sonoran Desert, and longing (because the US was easily visible) for something better.

I wandered toward the center of town and Benito Juárez Park, a large city block of palms, where some children were kicking a ball and old men were conferring. I fell into conversation with the men.

"I guess some people swim across the river," I said to one of them, a gap-toothed man who cocked his head at me, as if preparing to deliver a witticism.

The Colorado River, more a wadi than a trickle here, forms the border at the west side of town.

"No swimming," he said, and giggled and showed his gap-toothed smile. "There's no water in the river."

"Then they go over the fence?"

"*Abajo,*" he said with a wink. Under it. "*Tuneles.* They travel in tunnels. There are two or three over there." He faced east, toward the desert. "They are two kilometers in length. They pay a coyote three thousand dollars and they go."

"Or the cartels?"

He winced at the word. "Mafia, maybe."

Tunnels—long ones, short ones, high-tech ones, rabbit holes, rat runs—have been dug wherever the border is fenced. The longest one ever unearthed was recently discovered, running 2,600 feet—half a mile—under the border, from the bottom of an elevator shaft in a house in Tijuana to a fenced-in warehouse on the US side. These resemble the mile-long tunnel that led to El Chapo's cell in his high-security prison, and they are designed and built by serious and experienced technicians. A year after the gap-toothed man winked and said "*Tuneles,*" a 600-foot tunnel was found leading from the basement of a defunct KFC restaurant in San Luis, Arizona, to a trapdoor under a bed in a house just across the border in Mexico. This one was not specifically for migrants, but rather a drug tunnel, the drugs hauled by a rope from Mexico to the US.

"This used to be a mining area," a man said to me farther along the border. "No more mining. But where do you think the mining engineers are digging now?"

And it's true: four tunnels have been discovered near Mexican Nogales, leading to the basements of houses in Nogales, Arizona.

"I don't want to go to the United States," Mario, another of the old men, said, and he pointed—four blocks north was the fence. "My family is here. I was born here. This is my home."

It was almost impossible for him to contemplate crossing, but for me,

San Luis was the simplest border crossing of all — a mere stroll, there and back, no lines, no hassle, then off I went in my car, up the highway, past lush green fields and straw-hatted harvesters bent double over rows of lettuce. And onward, out of the restored and tranquil historic center of Yuma (century-old theater, museum, restaurants), east on Interstate 8, to the checkpoint ten miles away at Wellton (smiling troopers and panting sniffer dogs looking for a whiff of drugs or humans in my trunk), through the glare and heat in the harsh desert at Stoval and Aztec and Theba, to the small town of Gila Bend, and three tacos, and someone to talk to, Lorraine, a member of the Tohono O'odham Nation.

"I speak my language fluently, but my children aren't interested," she said, and pointed south. "Over the border the tribe is more traditional, and more people speak the language."

The Tohono O'odham Nation, half in the US, half in Mexico, divided by the border, resists with its slogan, "There is no O'odham word for wall."

After Gila Bend the road veers away from the border, two hundred miles through the desert of saguaro cactus and distant gray-blue mountains, looping through Tucson, then bending southerly again to the border town of Nogales — or rather towns, since there are two Nogaleses, divided by the big rusty fence.

Back when I was driving through the Deep South, I made a detour to the border here, on a whim, and stayed for four days. I saw a simple painted sign on a wooden board, TO MEXICO, propped near the door in the fence, but it was the fence itself that fascinated me. Some masterpieces are unintentional, the result of a freakish accident or an explosive act of sheer weirdness, and the fence that divided Nogales, Arizona, from Nogales, Mexico, was one of them. This pitiless wall was monumental, a multimillion-dollar symbol in steel that depicts our national obsession with threat and contagion.

In a lifetime of crossing borders, I found this fence the oddest frontier I have ever seen — more formal than the Berlin Wall, more brutal than the Great Wall of China, yet in its way as much an example of the same *folie de grandeur*. Built six months before to replace a wall made of steel plates, this towering, seemingly endless row of vertical steel beams was so amazing in its defiant conceit, you either want to see more of it or run in the opposite direction—just the sort of conflicting emotions many people feel when confronted by a peculiar piece of art.

You could, of course, also go through it, which is what I wanted to do. And there was the entryway, where Morley Avenue in the United States ended. Past the JCPenney and Kory's Clothing, just ten steps from one country to the other, a door in the wall, the foreign country at the end of a hot, sunlit street.

After leaving my car at a secure parking lot ($4 a day), I showed my passport to the US border guard, who asked me my plans for the other side. Business?

"Just curiosity," I said. When he made a disapproving squint, I added, "Don't you go over now and then?"

"Never been there," he said.

"It's ten feet away!"

"I'm staying here," he said, his squint now suggesting that I should be doing the same.

I pushed the turnstile and stepped through the narrow door—no line, no other formalities, into the state of Sonora, Mexico. I was instantly, unmistakably in a foreign land, on bumpier roads, among vaguely distressed buildings and some boarded-up shop fronts, and breathing in the mingled aromas of bakeries, taco stands, and risen dust.

Glancing back a moment later, I could not see Arizona anymore, only the foreground of Mexico—small children chasing each other, men in sombreros conferring under a striped awning, steaming food carts.

I treasure border crossings, and the best of them are the ones where I've had to walk from one country to another, savoring the equality of being a pedestrian, stepping over the theoretical line that is shown on maps, from Cambodia into Vietnam, from Pakistan into India, from Turkey into the Republic of Georgia. Usually a frontier is a river—the Mekong, the Ussuri, the Zambezi; or a mountain range—the Pyrenees, the Ruwenzoris; or a sudden alteration in topography, a bewildering landscape transformation—hilly wooded Vermont flattening into the plowed fields of Quebec. Just as often a border is a political expedient—irrational yet unremarkable—creating a seamless no-man's-land, just a width of earth, bounded by fences.

But this border fence was a visual marvel, something like a stockade, and, as the guard demonstrated, it calls for a decision. Do you go through or stay home? Of course, there was always a fence here. Nogalans on both sides remembered when it was a modest enclosure known casually as La Linea, the line, when the main street was more or less contiguous.

"We had a parade every spring," Nicolas Demetrio Kyriakis had told me on that first visit. Nicolas, from an entrepreneurial family of Greek immigrants to Mexico, was a *regidor,* a Nogales town councilor, and one of the advisers to Nogales's mayor. "Floats went down the street and into Nogales, Arizona. A coronation was held on a platform on La Linea, and the Fiesta de Mayo Queen was crowned. It was beautiful—both towns celebrated."

That was thirty years ago. Back then Nogales, Mexico, was still a destination for servicemen from Fort Huachuca, a US Army post about twenty miles as the crow flies to the northeast. Visitors from Tucson and beyond would pop over for a break from the routine—an opportunity to buy clay pots or sombreros, drink a world-class margarita, and visit a taqueria or sample local street food. And the red-light district on Canal Street was another attraction. In the 1940s, cowboy films were made in the area. Hollywood actors crossed the border to eat and raise mild hell in La Caverna, a well-known club run by Nicolas's cousins.

Such was the close bond of the two border towns that when the old, elegant Hotel Olivia on the Mexican side caught fire in the 1960s, and the fire spread to other buildings, the situation becoming desperate, hoses were hoisted over the fence by the fire brigade in Arizona to help the local *bomberos* put it out, an act of neighborliness that was still fondly remembered by the Mexicans.

But after 9/11, soldiers from Fort Huachuca stopped visiting, and when an American passport was required by Mexican immigration, the influx of visitors slowed to a trickle. And there was another theme: since the emphasis across America was on scrutinizing aliens, why would anyone wish to become an alien oneself? The repeated news stories of the cartels taking over were a dire warning: cross the Mexican border and risk dying like a dog.

"Business stagnated after the bombing of the World Trade Center. Things went down," Juan Cordero, the director of the Department of Economic Development in this part of Sonora, told me. "But it was massage parlors and bars on Canal Street, and curio shops downtown, an old-fashioned business model. Sure, we still had lots of American factories in our industrial area — thousands of people are employed there — but we have just a few tourists."

And yet, here I was, a tourist, savoring the satisfaction of having eased myself into another country to enjoy the difference, with the tourist's presumption that I deserved a good time. And I had the gringo's instant assurance that my country, and my car, was just behind the humongous wall.

So what did I do in those four days in Nogales? I had my teeth whitened, the full *limpieza y blanqueamiento*, for less than what it would have cost across the fence ($54 for cleaning, $250 for whitening). I bought a set of wooden dominos. And I ate.

Dinner at La Roca, which was just minutes from the fence, was pleasurable for my being in the hands of the sort of knowledgeable, dark-suited old waiters that have disappeared from most of the world's restaurants. Many have worked at La Roca since it opened — its fortieth anniversary was celebrated that year. Such men were the stalwarts at the restaurant at my hotel, too, the Hotel Fray Marcos. At La Roca I had tortilla soup and a Mexican mélange of fresh shrimp from Guaymas, on the Sonoran coast. Elsewhere in town, even the smaller places, such as Leo's or Zapata's, offered plates of dried shredded beef, known as *mochomos* (fire ants), and fish tacos. I found the Nogalans courtly and easy to meet, and so grateful to have a visitor that as a demonstration of neighborliness I was offered a swig of bacanora, a drink made of agave, Sonora's gift to the world of drinkable rocket fuel — much stronger than tequila.

At Laser Tech over on Avenida Obregón, Dr. Francisco Vazquez had enlarged his dental practice recently to include a dermatology unit, and his wife (and mother of three), Martha Gonzalez-Vazquez, opened a spa with treatments that included not only massage and steam baths but "ancient rituals" inspired by the Aztecs, and for good measure hired Dr. Angel Minjares, whose specialties are theology and psychology, for "assessments."

Their businesses were among the approximately sixty dental practices here, mainly concentrated in a three-block area, all within easy walking distance of the border gate. Most of the patients were American retirees nipping over for the day from Tucson or nearby Green Valley.

Gerd Roehrig, an older Tucsonian originally from Germany, was seeing Dr. Ernesto Quiroga about an implant. What would have cost him $4,500 in his hometown of Tucson was about a third of that in Nogales. Dr. Quiroga recently invested $150,000 in a 3-D scanning machine for CAT scans.

"I guess Canal Street could now be called Root Canal Street," I said to Juan Cordero after my treatment.

He sighed. "People are worried. They think Nogales is dangerous. You know the expression *poner salsa a los tacos*?"

Slather sauce on the tacos—exaggerate.

Wondering about crime, I asked to meet the secretary for public safety in Sonora and was introduced to Ernesto Munro Palacio, a six-foot-three former pitcher for the Monterrey Sultans and a businessman who, since 2009, had been responsible for security in the state.

"Prior to 2009 there was very little investment in security," he said. "But within the past two years Sonora had invested $100 million—in helicopters, armored cars, and surveillance planes—to find the landing strips of organized crime and the marijuana farms."

Murders are a problem all over Mexico. But Secretary Munro said that in Nogales the murder rate had declined from 226 in 2010 to 83 in 2011. This number has continued to drop in each succeeding year, now averaging about 50 a year.

"Ask your people if they know the name of one American who's been killed in Sonora," he said. "No tourist has ever been killed in Nogales."

I did not know it at the time, but in 2016, a gringo resident in Nogales was shot to death in the course of an armed robbery.

The Bianchis, a retired couple from Tucson whom I met in a waiting room, were content. "We come here all the time," Mr. Bianchi said. "I got bridgework. And, hey, people are nice."

On that first visit, Nogales seemed to me a border town trying to save itself, and I thought succeeding. Walking in the city, I was struck by the distinct air of foreignness mingled with a pleasing ordinariness—children at play on school playgrounds, shoppers, churchgoers—the pleasures and routines of Mexico. The visible absence of gringos gives the city a greater feel of difference, as do the brightly painted houses, the result of a plan by Nogales's mayor, José Ángel Hernández, who created an Urban Image Department, which provided free paint for those who wish to spruce up their home. He has also created schools and sports programs to inspire idle youths, as well as teams of street cleaners and urban renewal projects.

The streets of Nogales were as tidy as any on the American side, and full of surprises. On my way to see the boomtown that lies beyond downtown and the dental clinics, I passed a two-story sculpture of a muscular naked youth spearing a winged reptilian figure sprawling at his feet. It was an unexpected apparition beside an overpass. Officially known as *The Defeat of Ignorance* (*La Derrota de la Ignorancia*), the statue, designed by the Spanish sculptor Alfredo Just in the late 1960s, is fondly referred to by Nogalans as *mono bichi*—the naked guy—in a local phrase that is partly Yaqui. (Nogalans scatter their speech with Yaqui words that are incomprehensible elsewhere: *buki* for child, *yori blanco* for white man.)

I was to discover that the neighborhoods that lie just across the fence are not representative of the town at large, which is a lesson in how to know another country—stay longer, travel deeper. Tourists usually stick close to the fence, which accounts for the density of curio shops, and now the density of dental practices. But that downtown of Nogales is misleading.

Driving a few miles south with Juan Cordero, I saw how Nogales sprawled, with newly built and modern subdivisions near more modest ones, all comprising Nuevo Nogales. "This is the main economic engine driving Nogales," Juan said. The majority of the thirty-two thousand people employed in the city worked in the industrial area, in factories making cell-phone components, semiconductors, air ducts for jumbo jets. Most of the names are familiar: Otis Elevator, Black and Decker, Chamberlain garage door openers, Rain Bird sprinklers, General Electric, B/E Aerospace, which makes chairs and tray tables for high-end luxury jets, and much else. Some companies, like Kimberly-Clark and Motorola, have been here since the late 1960s.

These are skilled workers. Those without education or manufacturing skills, the so-called campesinos, look elsewhere for work, and often cross the border to find it. Many of them in the US without papers are caught, jailed for a period, and bused to the border. This, too, is a revelation from the other side of the high fence.

Nogales is where they are dumped. Peg Bowden, a retired nurse, brought me to the Comedor, a shelter run by American Jesuits near the Mariposa gate, about a mile west of downtown Nogales. Peg told me she was so shocked by the savage attack on Gabrielle Giffords in Tucson, in January 2011, that she decided to do something humane. "I needed to connect with something positive." She joined a group of Samaritans, "a bunch of renegade senior citizens whose mission is to prevent deaths in the desert," and she volunteered at the Comedor, working a few days a week, crossing the border from Arizona.

As a trained nurse she was useful, treating bullet wounds, severe hypothermia, and the effects of starvation and exposure—common among border crossers. "Last week we had a girl who'd been lost in the desert for three days. She was fourteen."

It was another day in Nogales, another revelation for me, and by far the most melancholy. A hundred and sixty lost souls, most of them adults, and four small children, were seated on benches at communal tables, eating breakfast in an open-sided shelter at the side of the road.

Some had been longtime residents in the US. Alejandro was a restaurant worker in North Carolina for thirteen years, Arnulfo a carpenter for eleven.

"I spent twenty years in Napa picking strawberries," Claudia, an older woman in a long black dress, told me. "My husband and children are there. I came to Mexico for my father's funeral"—it was her funeral dress. She couldn't return to the US, nor did she have a home in Mexico anymore.

The people staying at the shelter were soft-spoken, humbled, half starved, and hopeless. A woman in her twenties, Rosalba, had spent four days in the desert. She had blistered feet, a deep wound from a cactus thorn, and a severe infection. Some had been caught making their first crossing. Others had been sent home after years in the United States.

The saddest sight to me was María, a woman in her late forties from Oaxaca. Abandoned, with no money, no prospects, and no hope of making a living in her village, she left her three children in the care of her mother and crossed the border with four other women in the hope of finding work. She had become separated from the others, wandered in the desert for four days, was spotted by a helicopter, arrested, roughed up, jailed for a while, then dumped at the border.

"It's like *Sophie's Choice*," Peg Bowden said.

María accepted her fate, and in my last glimpse of her, she sat alone at a table, a plate of food before her, eyes tightly shut, hands together, uplifted in prayer.

It might have been "The Migrant's Prayer," "La Oración del Migrante," which had been found on a scrap of paper in the pocket of a migrant who had died in the desert, mentioned in Marc Silver's documentary, *Who Is Dayani Cristal?*, about the death of an unidentified migrant.

The prayer begins:

> *Viajar, hacia Ti Señor, eso es vivir*
> *Partir es un poco morir . . .*

The journey toward you, Lord, is life.
To set off is to die a little.
To arrive is never to arrive, until one is at rest with you.
You, Lord, experienced migration.

And ends:

You yourself became a migrant from heaven to earth.

I was just a tourist. The fence had hidden all of this—the downtown, the factories, the restaurants, the residential subdivisions, the mall, the migrants, sad stories, happy stories.

It was here for anyone to discover, and so simple. It was as illuminating to me as any foreign travel I had taken anywhere in the world. In some ways, being so near home and taking less effort, it seemed odder, freighted with greater significance, this wider world at the end of Morley Avenue, just behind the fence.

Those four days I'd spent on the other side of the fence in Nogales were unforgettable. I vowed to return, to travel along the whole border and then to go deeper into Mexico. It was the experience of talking to the migrants that did it—their telling me where they had come from and where they were going. Now I was back.

BIENVENIDOS MIGRANTES DEPORTADOS Y EN TRANSITO was the sign on a small building at the western edge of Nogales, a short walk from the border: Welcome Migrants, Deportees, and Those in Transit. This building was the one Peg Bowden had brought me to, known locally as El Comedor—the Eating Place—run by the Kino Border Initiative, Jesuits and volunteers, offering humanitarian aid to migrants as well as a shelter for women and children. It was more full of desperate and perplexed people than I had seen on my earlier visit.

"Our mission is a humanizing presence," Father Sean Carroll said to me as breakfast was served to the migrants. A native of California who had a parish in East Los Angeles, Father Carroll has overseen the Comedor for seven years. In the midst of this confusion and distress, he is young, energetic, humble, and hopeful.

The majority of the migrants (87 percent) have been deported and dumped over the border; the ones in transit (13 percent) are waiting for a chance to jump the fence. Father Carroll makes no judgments. His organization offers food and clothes (it sometimes snows in the winter in Nogales) and a degree of protection from the cartels and the coyotes.

Talking to some of the migrants, I realized that all of them came from southern Mexico — none from the border.

"NAFTA has had an impact," Father Carroll said. "The new agribusinesses produce and export food crops so cheaply, the small farmers have been driven into poverty. Take a traditional farmer in Chiapas or Oaxaca who grows blue corn. How can he or she compete with a GMO crop?"

The first effect of NAFTA, I learned later, was the emigration of the poor from southern Mexico who had lost their livelihoods as farmers and small manufacturers: the trade agreement had put them out of business. Some of them ended up in maquiladoras, in low-wage border factory jobs, others as border jumpers.

To get some idea of who was passing through the Comedor, I introduced myself and talked to them.


## Deportees and Those in Transit

### LETITIA: A PUNITIVE SENTENCE

Tiny, the size of a small girl, Letitia was twenty-two, from a village in the mountains of Oaxaca, an indigenous Mexican whose first language was Zapotec. Her Spanish was not much better than mine. She'd married two years before, given birth to a daughter, and her husband, from an impoverished farming family, migrated — slipped over the border, without papers — to Florida. He got a job in a fertilizer and chemical plant (there are many in Florida) and because of his status did not dare to return to Mexico. He urged Letitia to cross. She had made two attempts.

"My agreement with the mafia was that I'd pay $7,000 altogether, first a down payment and then $4,500 when they got me to Phoenix."

After three days spent walking in the desert beyond Sasabe, a popular smuggling point in the desert west of Nogales, on the Arizona-Mexico border, Letitia was arrested and given two and a half months' detention — a punitive sentence. She was dazed from her confinement in the jail cell, and her sudden deportation, and she was conflicted—her husband in Florida, her daughter in Oaxaca. After a period of recovery at the Comedor, she said she would be headed back to Oaxaca.

## NORMA: "I'M GOING TO TRY AGAIN"

Norma was a well-built Zapotec woman in her early fifties from Tehuantepec, with the strong Tehuana features you see in Diego Rivera peasant portraits. Her husband, Juan, had been working undocumented for fifteen years in the fields in Fresno, picking peaches, oranges, and grapes. Norma had worked in the fields, too, but then got a job in a chicken processing plant and had worked there for nine years. She was called back to Mexico by her family in the Isthmus, in southern Oaxaca, four thousand miles from Fresno. A family funeral was planned, and Norma wanted to pay her respects. And she had another reason to return.

"I have three children in Mexico, from a different husband. I missed them. I wanted to see them. So I took a bus from Fresno to Tijuana. I was so eager to see my children, I didn't think about not having papers. When I decided to go back to the States, I went to Coloso and walked to the border through the mountains."

She had paid $500 to the cartel for the privilege, as a sort of entrance fee, with $4,000 promised to the coyote. The coyote escorted her to the border with some other migrants, three men, and directed them by cell phone.

"The Border Patrol found us on the edge of the highway, the three men and me.

"That was six weeks ago," she went on. "I decided to try again fifteen days ago, from Altar"—near Sasabe—"in the same way. One coyote brought me to the border, another one was waiting on the other side. I would pay $3,500 to the coyote when I was back in Fresno with my husband.

"But this time I was arrested and put in detention. They sent me here on a bus. My husband said, 'Don't go back to Oaxaca.' You see, when I went back to Tehuantepec, they rejected me, for leaving them. I don't want the same thing to happen with my daughter."

Her small daughter was in Fresno.

Norma was lame from walking in the desert.

"I'm going to try again," she said, and put her hands to her face and began to cry.

## TERESA: "I'M AFRAID TO BE HERE BECAUSE OF THE MAFIA"

"Four days ago I was released from detention in Douglas,"Teresa told me. She was forty-eight but looked much older, sad and awkward. Her wish was to work somewhere in the US, "making beds and cleaning — another life. I worked as a cook in a restaurant in Morton, Minnesota."

She'd had four children in Morton, but they were grown, and her husband had run off with another woman. She had gone to Mexico on an ID that someone had sold to her, but on her way back it was spotted as a forgery. She was arrested, imprisoned, and deported.

"I'm afraid to be here because of the mafia," she told me. "And I am not sure what I can do in Mexico. The problem in Mexico is that jobs don't pay enough, even the factories here."

## ARTURO: "MY FEET ARE BAD"

For ten years, Arturo, thirty-seven, worked in a restaurant kitchen in Ventura, California. He was deported after being stopped by a policeman, who saw that he was driving erratically.

"Five beers," Arturo said, shaking his head. He'd been dropped across the border. Attempting to return, he had walked for four days in the desert near Puerto Penasco. "My feet are bad. I had to go to the hospital for medicine. I can't walk."

## DANERIS: RIDER ON THE BEAST

Daneris, from Honduras, was sixteen but looked much younger, like a schoolboy. And he was very skinny from his recent ordeal. Persecuted by the thugs in Tegucigalpa ("*Muchas maras,*" he said; many gangs there), he resolved to leave, and traveled through Guatemala. He hopped the train from southern Mexico known as La Bestia — the Beast — and spent eighteen days riding on the roof of a freight car. He was hoping to be granted political asylum and had an appointment to meet someone here at the Comedor who would advise him on the process.

## JACQUELINA: "I KNOW ABOUT MEAT"

She was thirty-one, wore a green headscarf, and was slender, smiling, and seemed composed, but it was fatalism; she had seen the worst. A single mother with three children—fourteen, ten, and five—she was worried for their future most of all.

"I'm from Mexico City—a poor and dangerous place, Ixtapaluca." The community at the southern edge of the city was a notorious mega-slum and the haunt of cartels and drug traffickers. "It is not safe anymore, because of kidnappings, robberies, and crime. I had a business, organizing social events, such as children's parties and fiestas.

"My idea was to go to Denver and work in a meatpacking plant. I know someone there. It's hard work but I like it—I had worked in meat plants before. I know about meat.

"I tried to cross the border three days ago. I had paid the coyote and entered from Sasabe, and got pretty far, walking in the desert with four others, but we were arrested near Tucson and deported here.

"I don't have any money, so I'm going back to Mexico City. My children are there, and now I need to work, because I had to borrow money to come here—about 20,000 pesos [$1,000] to get to the border."

## ROSELIA AND LEONARDO: "THERE IS NO MONEY IN CHIAPAS"

A brother and sister from San Cristóbal de las Casas, Roselia was eighteen—young, heavy, sad, serious, in a thick black dress, bewildered and lost; Leonardo was twenty-three, tough, worldly, determined, in an old wool coat, protective of his sister.

"I was working in construction in Chiapas, fixing houses," Leonardo said. "I wanted to go to Atlanta, where my cousin works in a restaurant. There is no money in Chiapas.

"We crossed the border to the pickup place. But the men who were supposed to help us on the border did not show up. We were to be taken to Tucson to meet another car and be driven to Atlanta. The coyote was supposed to arrange the car.

"Nothing happened. So we walked two days from the border. On the third day we saw a helicopter and tried to hide, but a motorcycle found us. We were brought to Tucson on Monday and deported on Wednesday.

"We'll go back to Chiapas now. I had to pay $1,500 to the coyote, my sister the same amount. It would have been $6,000 more when we got to Atlanta."

Roselia said, "I'm not married. I worked in the kitchen of a restaurant in San Cristóbal. I don't have much education—I went to elementary school but didn't finish. I was planning to work in a restaurant in Atlanta.

"I'll go back to Chiapas with Leonardo. Our parents are there. We'll try to find some work."

## JUAN: A STORY FULL OF HOLES

His name was not Juan. He said, "I don't want to tell you my name." He was about forty, handsome when he smiled, which was often, ironical rather than bitter. He was one of the few who spoke to me mostly in English. I felt there was a lot of experience and perhaps some deception behind the summary of his story.

"I'm from Chiapas—Villaflores, a small pueblo. I had been working in the fields in Chiapas, planting and harvesting melons.

"I've been in the States for quite a while. I just got out of prison—I had been in for two years, for reentry. I tried four times. The longest period I had been in the States was four years, working in construction in Russellville, Arkansas. The police picked me up on a DUI. I had a problem with probation, and was arrested a second time for speeding.

"So I was deported. I tried to cross the border again and was picked up. I made three more attempts, and then they put me in jail. Now I'm out and going home, but I'll try again to go back to the States sometime, to see my son—my ex-wife and son are in Tennessee. She's a gringa," he said, and smiled, but after I looked at my notes of his story, it was full of holes.

## ERNESTO: A TEARDROP TATTOO

A man of seventy, the oldest of the migrants I'd met at the Comedor, another English speaker, another ex-convict, Ernesto had thick white hair swept back and a white beard and various tattoos, including a teardrop tattoo just under his left eye — this ink sometimes indicates a murderer, but can also mean he'd done hard time. He was unlike any of the other migrants in his bearing and his tone, which was haughty and aggrieved.

"I first went to the States when I was seven, to El Paso, then Los Angeles," he said. "I was in LA for thirty-five years. Then Nebraska. I went to school — everything American. I was a house painter.

"I was busted for illegal entry — arrested in Lincoln, Nebraska, where I was working. I got ten years. When I got out they dropped me here. What can I do at my age? My parents are dead. I've got four children, but they're old now and not in touch, because I was in the joint."

Ten years in prison for illegal entry was not believable, but when I pressed him, he walked away, holding his coat over his shoulders like a cape, and with the same strange hauteur.

## MARCOS: "I GOT SAD AND DRANK A LOT"

His teeth bulging in his smile, Marcos was forty-three and philosophical, tugging at the bill of his baseball cap. He came from distant Apatzingán, originally, in Michoacán, and had traveled with his parents as a child when it was easy to cross the border. He had no memory of the crossing, but remembered the work and his home in Greeley Hill, California.

"I didn't go to school. No one ever helped us or told us about it. I worked in the fields in Greeley and Tulare and Fresno from the time I was ten or eleven. We picked oranges, grapes, nectarines. I made about seven or eight dollars a day — the whole family was picking.

"When I turned eighteen I went to LA and worked in roofing — houses, buildings, all sorts of roofs. I'm not married but I have three children in Colorado, two boys, one girl. They live with their mother. They're students.

"I got picked up in this way. My mother died six years ago. My brother didn't call me about it. When they finally told me the news, I got sad and drank a lot. I was in Colorado then. My girlfriend tried to help me. I was drunk, I hit her, she went down, and a policeman saw us. I was arrested for domestic violence. Because I had a DUI, I got three years in Cañon City, Colorado.

"But they sent me to ICE in Aurora. They gave me a paper and said, 'Sign this paper.' I said, 'No sign.' They said, 'You're illegal.' I signed. They flew me in a plane to San Diego and then in a bus here. I guess I'll try to work here."

### MANUEL QUINTA: "I WANT TO BE A ROOFER"

Manuel was small, wiry, dark, and looked defeated, his face pinched, as he talked about his failure to cross the border. He was well spoken; he said that he had gone to school in his hometown of Los Mochis, near the coast.

"It was my first time trying to cross. I was arrested last Monday in the desert. I had been walking alone for four days. I was going to Phoenix to get a roofing job. I want to be a roofer. I know they need workers. My brother works in construction there—he told me.

"My agreement with the coyote was that I would pay him $1,500 when I got to Phoenix." Manuel shrugged. "Now I'll go back to Los Mochis, and the fields and my wife and three children. My wife works in the fields there."

### JAVIER: "I COME FROM A VERY DANGEROUS PLACE"

"I arrived here yesterday," he said, "from Honduras." He was much younger than most of the migrants—in his late teens, and standing apart from them. He had distinct Mayan features, the profile you see carved on some temple walls. He had just arrived by road and rail—the Beast again—from Tegucigalpa.

"I come from a very dangerous place. I am going to the US. I am the oldest of four children. My mother died. I was working as a bricklayer. I want to go to Maryland. I have some cousins there, but I am not sure where.

"La Bestia took fourteen days from the border. There were about two hundred people on it, from all over—Chiapas, Salvador, Guatemala.

"I have no work in Honduras. But I have to support my brothers. My father is in Honduras, with another family.

"I'm crossing with another guy, but we have no support. This guy knows the area."

## UBALDO: "I'M GOING TO TALK TO A LAWYER"

"I lived in California for twenty years—twenty-eight altogether in the US," Ubaldo said. In Oregon, Idaho, and Washington state. He was forty, his English excellent, and he was forthright, with a level gaze. "My brother and sister are there.

"I worked in construction, in landscaping and tiles. My ex-wife is in Wyoming—we have no kids.

"They put me in jail for drinking in public—a couple of nights. Then ICE took me to a detention center, for five months in Eloy, Arizona, where I was fighting my case.

"They brought me here yesterday. Right now I'm going to talk to a lawyer, then get some money for a bus to Ensenada. I have a friend there. I'll work, make some money, and then try to get back to the States."

## GUILLERMO: "I BROKE MY ARM IN THAT DESERT"

His arm in a sling, in a bright new plaster cast, Guillermo was small and cautious, his knitted hat pulled over his ears, in ill-fitting clothes the Comedor might have found for him. He was hardly twenty.

"I came from Oaxaca alone," he said. "I crossed at Sasabe alone. I walked for ten days and got near to a town. But I entered a ravine full of rocks, and I fell against a rock. I broke my arm in that desert.

"Soon after that I was picked up by the police and brought to a hospital. They fixed my arm and put me in detention, then sent me here.

"I will go now to Hermosillo and try to find some work. After that, I don't know."

## RAMÓN: "IT'S BEEN TWENTY-FIVE YEARS"

Ramón was forty and thin, but apparently in good health. At the age of fifteen he left his home in Zacatecas and crossed the border near Tijuana. "There was no fence then. It was easy." He went to the Bay Area, and then to Seattle, where he got a job on a horse farm. Having learned how to handle horses, he was hired to look after racehorses, as a farrier. He had been married, and his two children were now living with his ex-wife.

"My parents are old and sick, and I missed them, so I took a chance and went to Zacatecas to see them. I thought I had a good ID, but I was stopped at US immigration when I tried to reenter. I might go back to Zacatecas, but it's been twenty-five years."

In making these snapshots of migrants at the Comedor, I intended to follow the example of Chekhov, who, on his trip through Sakhalin Island in 1890, did the same, composing small portraits, before describing the place as a whole.

And so they huddled in El Comedor, under the benign gaze of Father Sean Carroll and his helpers. They prayed, they healed, and then they dispersed, some southward to their old homes, others to make another attempt on the border. Judge not, lest ye be judged, Father Sean might have said.

Hearing so much about the police and Border Patrol, I drove a few miles farther along the border, looking for a patrol vehicle. Very soon I found Mike Coruna in his black-and-white cruiser, on his two p.m.–to–midnight shift at the edge of Nogales, Arizona. He was a beefy man in his early thirties, his hand on his holstered Glock, glancing around as we spoke, always monitoring the fence.

"We get fence jumpers here," he said, which was surprising, because this was a residential part of town, the iron-slatted fence about twenty-five feet high. "The way they jump the fence here is they wedge their feet between the bars and shimmy up like monkeys."

"Any jumpers lately?"

"A few days ago, on my shift, forty guys were caught—more than usual," he said. "I personally have caught about twenty. I estimate about a hundred a week jump in this sector"—he meant this stretch that abuts the town of Nogales, Arizona—"but it used to be thousands."

"How do you catch them?"

"It's tough—catching them is really tough," he said. "They run. They're young, some are carrying bundles of drugs. They watch the fence carefully before they jump." He gestured to the hill of multicolored huts and bungalows that looms over the Mexican town. "We're being watched right now from over there."

The Border Patrol had a demanding job, driving day and night along the bumpy service road that paralleled the frontier, doing sentry duty at checkpoints, engaging in foot chases with desperate migrants. But perhaps the pressure of the job had taken a toll, because for years the officers also had a reputation for vindictiveness: shooting at unarmed fence jumpers, sometimes killing them; roughing up suspects; separating children from their weeping mothers; and harassing the humanitarian organizations that offered medical treatment to wounded migrants. I'd heard that they also vandalized the efforts of the Samaritans of No Más Muertes, the ones who set water stations in the desert for desperately thirsty migrants.

From Nogales I drove east, past Tombstone and the horse country of Bisbee, through the dry rocky hills and pretty pastels of low woodland, to the border town of Douglas—hot, flat, horizontal, on a grid of streets—which faced another rusty fence and the Mexican town of Agua Prieta.

In Nogales, Peg Bowden had given me the name of an activist nun based in Douglas, Sister Judy Bourg, whom I had hoped to meet. A member of the order of the Sisters of Notre Dame, Sister Judy and her companions—both nuns and lay people—placed water bottles and food in the desert for migrants. They also participated in the Healing Our Borders vigil, a weekly ritual that has been observed for the past seventeen years. By carrying crosses that bear the names of the dead, the participants in the ritual honor the thousands of migrants who have died crossing the border. Many of the crosses have no names, but are marked DESCONOCIDO — Unknown. In a public statement, Sister Judy had said, "It's prayer, not protest."

Though Sister Judy was not in Douglas that day, I met a border activist who was — Mark Adams, a friend of hers, who also took part in the vigils. "Let's take a walk," he said soon after we met, and we strolled across the frontier, past the border guards, to the little town of Agua Prieta, with friendly nods and greetings from the immigration officers on both sides.

Douglas had prospered as a town with one local industry, the smelting firm and foundry of Phelps Dodge. But that was gone. The industries were just over the border in Agua Prieta now, twenty-five factories in the small dusty town, making everything from Velcro to seat belts and window blinds.

"The fence doesn't define us," Mark Adams said. After eighteen years on the border heading Frontera de Cristo and its outreach programs (health, education, cultural), he said he'd seen more similarities on the border than differences. Neither the US nor the Mexican government provided services here, so the work of welfare was left to missionaries, as in the third world. Mark said, "It's simple, really. Do justice, love mercy, walk humbly with God."

It was Mark's contention that Mexican immigration is "net zero," neither a surplus nor a deficit — a wash. The growth now was from Central America, thousands of people fleeing violence. And what the US authorities call Special Interest Aliens — Africans, Indians, Pakistanis — who crowd the detention cells up and down the border.

A concert would be held the following day, Mark told me, half the choir on the Mexican side of the fence, the other half in the US, singing together, an event, he said, to promote unity, growth, and peace. Perhaps it was working; side by side, Douglas (a town that had lost its industries) and Agua Prieta (a town that had gained many factories) stood out as the safest and most serene towns I saw in the whole of my traverse of the border.

On the back road from Douglas to Las Cruces I passed through the small ranching town of Animas (pop. 237), a suggestive name and a place conspicuously mentioned in Valeria Luiselli's short but passionate nonfiction book, *Tell Me How It Ends: An Essay in Forty Questions.* "As we approach Animas, we also begin to see fleeting herds of Border Patrol cars like ominous white stallions racing toward the horizon."

Luiselli and her family feel intimidated by this presence of authority, though in the book the Luisellis don't appear to get very close to the border, nor do they see that such vehicles are a feature of the whole frontier. (I had seen Border Patrol vehicles searching for migrants as far as eighty miles north of the border, such as at a checkpoint in Falfurrias, Texas.) Animas is forty miles from the nearest border town, Antelope Wells. Along much of the border is an unpaved service road, specifically for the use of these vehicles and closed to the public. Luiselli seems surprised that the border is patrolled by officialdom, usually armed, often in vehicles. But most national boundaries are guarded this way, including the border between Luiselli's native Mexico and Guatemala, notorious for the ferocity of policing on both sides.

She writes that in the summer of 2014 the Luisellis — Valeria, her husband, and two children, Mexican nationals — took a road trip from New York City to the Southwest. For the three previous years, the family had lived in the city, awaiting green cards as "nonresident aliens" (a designation Valeria objected to, but standard in many countries: I carried an Alien Identity Card for years in Britain). That road trip, and Luiselli's work as a volunteer interpreter at an immigration court in New York City, helping migrants navigate the bureaucratic twists and turns — the anfractuosities in the system — resulted in *Tell Me How It Ends.*

The family trip is briefly sketched. They pass through New Mexico and Arizona but don't cross the border, which seems odd, since as Mexican citizens, with valid passports and US visas, it would have been a simple back-and-forth, and they would have seen (as I did) the good relations, the outreach, and the spirited, twinned communities (south of where they were in Animas) of Douglas and Agua Prieta. Now and then, the Luisellis, stopped by Border Patrol officials, smile, show their papers, and move on. Within a few pages, the trip is over and they are back home in New York. Soon, all but Valeria have green cards. Awaiting her green card, preoccupied with her status as a migrant, Valeria is motivated to become a volunteer translator at the immigration court. Her experience working with undocumented migrants—most of them children—is what informs her short but powerful (and occasionally contradictory) book.

The forty questions of the title are from the "intake questionnaire" used in the court, questions that Luiselli was employed to ask, noting the answers. Most of the questions are simple and direct, such as "Why did you come to the United States?" and "When did you enter the United States?" and "Did you go to school in your country?"

But there are questions that evoke painful memories, like "Did anything happen on your trip to the US that scared you or hurt you?"

These elicit horror stories. Luiselli writes that so many of the women and girls who get to the border are raped on the way (she says 80 percent of them are sexually assaulted), they begin taking contraceptive pills before they set out. She mentions that in this inquisition, the majority of her cases have arrived from Honduras, Guatemala, and El Salvador—fleeing violence, with stories of privation, of gang brutality, of becoming lost in the desert, of abandonment and victimization. The migrants come in search of parents and relatives, for refuge, to be safe, to find a life—and some discover the streets of New York City are just as dangerous as those of Tegucigalpa.

On their trip through Mexico, in vans or riding the Beast, migrants are brutalized, abducted, or forced to work on Mexican farms, as virtual slaves. In the past decade, 120,000 migrants have disappeared en route, murdered or dead and lost, succumbing to thirst or starvation.

Luiselli emphasizes an anomaly I discovered in Nogales, that Mexican child migrants are an exception from the child asylum seekers from Central American countries. Young Mexicans are treated differently, with less sympathy or patience, than all others. If they cannot prove they are victims of trafficking or persecution, they can be seized and immediately, forcibly deported ("voluntary return," in the official euphemism) without any formal immigration proceedings.

The book achieves greater power, and some of its muddle, because Luiselli herself is living a migration story of her own, desiring—like the children—to live in the United States. "Why did you come?" is a pretty simple question for an underprivileged child fleeing endangerment or hunger or a broken family. But what about an articulate, intelligent, well-off, widely traveled university-educated, prizewinning writer from a good family in Mexico—someone like the privileged Valeria Luiselli? She is clearly pained by this knowledge, and says she doesn't have the answer. Here she describes the process of a foreigner's contemplating residence in the US:

"Before coming to the United States, I knew what others know: that the cruelty of its borders was only a thin crust, and that on the other side a possible life was waiting. I understood, some time after, that once you stay here long enough, you begin to remember the place where you originally came from the way a backyard might look from a high window in the deep of winter: a skeleton of the world, a tract of abandonment, objects dead and obsolete."

In a word, home, the place you left behind—from the heights of the imperial city now looking like wreckage, a place you never want to see again.

"And once you're here," she writes, "you're ready to give everything, or almost everything, to stay and play a part in the great theater of belonging. In the United States, to stay is an end in itself and not a means: to stay is the founding myth of this society."

This is eloquent but tentative, self-deceiving, and hedging the bet. She speaks about "staying" and not taking the next step, what should be the triumph of a migrant, becoming an American citizen. Her sidestepping the word "citizenship" is telling, and I think shows how nebulous some migrants regard this desire for transformation. Even for this bright woman the commitment is vaguely expressed. And her saying "to stay is an end in itself and not a means" is not entirely true, since migrants I met—many Mexicans—wished only to get a job, save some money, and return home. And you could probably say the same about the large number of British writers, Irish musicians, Nigerian novelists, Indian techies, French intellectuals, Russian hockey players, and Brazilian surfers who come to the

States—like the despised Mexican—for the space and spontaneity of a convenient and roomy country, and an opportunity to enrich themselves.

On my way to El Paso, I stopped in Las Cruces and talked to Molly Molloy, a librarian at the University of New Mexico. Born in swampy southwestern Louisiana, she said she was happier here in the high desert, and she made it her mission to keep a chronicle, detailing crimes and murders on the border.

"It was always gritty and dangerous, but not like it is now," she told me over a meal in the township of Mesilla—as Mexican-looking a town as any in Mexico, with an old plaza and a nineteenth-century church, and of course Mesilla had been an important Mexican pueblo that was swallowed by the Gadsden Purchase. "The standard story is that in Juárez it was one cartel fighting another. But that's not the truth."

In her scrupulously maintained database of statistics and eyewitness accounts of violence in Juárez, Molly had concluded that the murder rate rose when, in 2008, eight thousand Mexican federal troops were sent to the city. Within days, the murders, abductions, and lynchings increased, reaching their peak in 2010. "It was a kind of terror," Molly said. "The troops were responsible for most of the killings. The murders declined when the troops left."

She remembered, like most people, when a border crossing had been a fairly casual affair, but that ended with Operation Hold the Line in 1993 in the El Paso sector.

"The idea was to put a huge number of Border Patrol agents in urban areas," Molly said. "They closed the border crossings to pedestrians without papers"—the shoppers, the cross-border workers, the part-timers—"and this stimulated illegal immigration."

And President Clinton's success in concluding the NAFTA accord meant that American manufacturing slid into Mexico, crossing the border but not descending very far. In fact, it seemed to be a rule that these companies were determined to stay within hailing distance of the United States, a few minutes' drive for their products to be shipped over the border. Most American factories in Mexico were visible from the US. And, of course, NAFTA went into effect in January 1994 with Clintonian fanfare about creating jobs. But the majority of jobs were created in Mexico.

"The first effect of NAFTA was the emigration of people from southern Mexico who had lost their livelihoods, both farmers and small manufacturers," Molly said, echoing what I had heard in Nogales. "Some of those people ended up in the maquiladoras, and others tried to cross any way they could."

During our dinner in Mesilla, Molly became more and more dispirited as she described the mayhem on the border, the bad government in Mexico, and the desperation of migrants.

"I don't go there now, I don't cross," she said. "It's—what's the word?—it's so cruel."

On my way to El Paso the next day, I passed through a checkpoint and stopped to allow a Border Patrol officer to ask me questions, and for his dog, straining on its leash, to sniff the perimeter of my car.

"How's business?" I asked the man.

"We've got eight on the bench inside," he said, tugging at the leash.

"Did you find them in vehicles?"

"Some from trucks and cars. Some from the fields. We get ten or twelve a day."

"What do you do with them?"

"We process them according to various protocols. You're good to go," he said with a hint of impatience.

"One more question?"

"You can head on out now, sir," he said, his dog seeming to pick up his agitation and slavering at me.

From the window of my motel just off the interstate on the western outskirts of El Paso, I saw a garage advertising oil changes, no appointment necessary. While waiting for my car to be serviced, I wandered over to a used car lot to kill time.

"This car is perfect for you," I heard, a salesman's tone of encouragement. "You need this car."

This was José, a man of about fifty, who was soon accompanied by a colleague, Luis. When I convinced them that I did not need another car, and that the oil in mine was being changed next door, we talked about the border.

"Juárez was always richer than El Paso," José said. "And much bigger. Juárez made El Paso rich. But it's all different now."

"There were ten murders the other day in Juárez," Luis said casually.

With a shrug and a yawn, José said, "It's getting worse."

"Cartel killings?" I said.

"Government killings. The PRI. They're behind it all." He meant the Institutional Revolutionary Party, the entrenched ruling party of Mexico, which was defeated a year later by Andrés Obrador's National Regeneration Movement, MORENA.

And after listing the horrors of Ciudad Juárez, each man told me that he lived across the border, in various colonias of the city. Juárez might be dangerous, but housing was much cheaper than in El Paso, food was a bargain, and commuting from one city to the other every day was very simple. Thousands of Mexicans, all with visas or US passports, crossed the border daily to work or shop in El Paso.

Luis, with American nationality and a valid passport, had lived and worked in various border states. He had the confrontational manner of a tease, the familiarity of a salesman, and a certainty he put down to his intransigence. "I can't help it. I'm stubborn. God made me that way. Ha!"

"Give me an example," I said.

"Sure. The other day in Juárez I'm in traffic. I look at my cell phone and — *beep!* — a policeman pull me over. 'You're talking on your cell phone.' I say, 'Not talking. Looking!' He say to me, 'Give me ten dollars.' I say, 'What for?' 'Talking on phone! Ten dollars! Or I take your license.' I say, 'I not give you ten dollars. Not even five dollars.' He say, 'Give me your license!' I give him my license — Arizona license. I say, 'Now I go online and get another one.'"

This was indeed an illustration of stubbornness, because to get a duplicate license he would have to pay $25.

"I refuse to give the police a *mordida*." A bribe.

"Mexican police," José said. "Always problems."

"You're lucky," Luis said. "You're a gringo. You can tell them anything."
"Like what?" I said.

Luis became animated, shortening his neck, gesticulating. "You have to be an actor with the Mexican police. He say, 'Give me money.' You say, 'I'm a German. I don't speak English.' Play dumb! Be a great actor! Tell them bullshit stories. Get a Golden Globe! Then the police can't touch you."

"You're the only gringo who's come over the bridge today," said Julián Cardona, a lean and sardonic journalist in Ciudad Juárez, who'd been quoted (in *More or Less Dead* by Alice Driver) as saying, "The level of sadism [in Mexico] is overwhelming, and it is largely a reflection of the impunity in the country."

Julián, in his mid-fifties, proved to be an astute observer of life in Juárez, where he has spent his whole working life reporting on its excesses. The excesses have included many beheadings, bodies strung up on telephone poles, and corpses dumped in the streets.

I may have been the only gringo who crossed the bridge to Juárez that day, but there were thousands of Mexicans hurrying to the US side, who then returned to Mexico when their work was done. Many children in Nogales, Mexico, go to school in Nogales, Arizona. "Yes, I speak English," I often heard along the border. "I was educated over the border."

Juárez is infamous for achieving the 2010 world record for violent homicides: 3,622 shootings, stabbings, lynchings, and deaths by torture. "Don't go there," people said in El Paso. Yet it's next door, and the murder rate had dropped to less than Chicago's 468 homicides in 2016. When the wind is southerly, the risen dust of Juárez can make you sneeze in El Paso. Juárez's cityscape twinkles at night; by day it is tawny brown and low-lying, scattered along the south bank of the Rio Grande, visible from its sister city across the river as a set of low, treeless hills and dense colonias. You can hear its honking horns on the Texas side, and in its year of mass murder the rat-tat of gunshots was easily audible. Some bullets fired in Juárez poked holes in the bricks and stucco of El Paso's buildings.

In an uncommon move, a young US Border Patrol officer in El Paso, Francisco Cantú, disenchanted with his job, quit to become an activist on border abuses. In *The Line Becomes a River: Dispatches from the Border,* his 2018 account of his conversion, he describes working in El Paso at the periphery of anarchy in the most violent years: "The insecurity in Juárez drifted through the air like the memory of a shattering dream. In news, in academic texts, in literature and art, the city was perpetually presented as a landscape of maquiladoras, narcos, *sicarios,* delinquents, military, police, poverty, femicide, rape, kidnapping, disappearance, homicide, massacres, shootings, turf wars, mass graves, corruption, decay, and erosion—a laboratory of social and economic horror."

The river is theoretical here, just a cement culvert tagged with indignant graffiti, a trickle of sour shallow water rippling through, like a dry riverbed you might see in drought-stricken Syria, the surrounding hills just as sunbaked, sandy, and Syrian. The contour of the culvert marks the *frontera,* which, with the crime rate, had been much in the news.

On a day of dazzling sunlight, I crossed the international bridge to the city of the wicked superlatives.

In contrast to peaceful and salubrious El Paso, Juárez is nearly all one-story dwellings, small cement bungalows, flat-roofed and ruinous huts, and *jacales* (rough shanties) on an immense grid of broken stony roads—1.5 million people, roughly a quarter of them employed in the maquiladoras, most of them US-owned. The Mexican employees generally work ten-hour factory shifts, for an average daily pay of $6 (the grim details of their employment were elaborated by Alana Semuels in "Upheavals in the Factories of Juárez," in the *Atlantic,* January 21, 2016). In spite of the hoopla about NAFTA, this does not translate to a living wage. Juárez is hard-up, crumbling, and bleak, with an air of pervasive sadness that seemed to me a border mood—the anxious melancholy of poverty and danger.

In the bewildering short story "Paso del Norte," by the Mexican writer Juan Rulfo (author of one of Mexico's best-known novels, *Pedro Páramo*), a man asks his son, who is headed for Ciudad Juárez, "And what the hell will you do in El Norte?"

"Well, make money," the son replies. "You saw, Carmelo came back rich, even brought a gramophone and charges five cents a song . . . and he makes good money and people even line up to listen. So you see; you just need to go and come back. So I'm goin'."

In the tradition of border ballads and border short stories, this one ends badly. The son pays a coyote to help him and some others across the border. They are fired upon, and all are killed except the son, who, when he arrives back in his Mexican village, finds his wife has left him.

I had arranged to meet Julián Cardona at the café El Coyote Inválido, next to the Kentucky Club, a once boisterous and thriving bar, these days thinly visited and subdued.

"Maybe you're the only gringo all week," Julián said over coffee, and he laughed. "Maybe all month!"

Gringos don't go to Juárez anymore, he said. They don't go to Nuevo Laredo, or Ciudad Acuña, or Reynosa, or Matamoros, or many other border towns.

"They used to come over for women, for drugs, for dinner, or to get their cars fixed at the body shops," he said. "And up to about 1993, Mexicans used to pay two dollars to float across in an inflatable raft below the Avenida Juárez to go to work—women to clean houses, men to work in construction."

In the 1990s the casual, porous border became much more formal and heavily policed, first as a series of security measures and then as a consequence of NAFTA, which had the effect of turning the Mexican side of the border into a plantation, a stable supply of cheap labor, and the workers' confinement behind the border fence was considered essential.

"And gringos gradually stopped coming across," Julián said. "The city had changed from its emphasis on tourism to manufacturing."

This was the border city with the largest number of maquiladoras, he said—auto parts, computers, electrical appliances, and many other manufacturers. "We were making TVs before China." These factories employed over 275,000 workers. Their workers live in gritty neighborhoods.

"Half a million people live in this colonia," he said.

We were driving in his pickup truck in a community of dirt roads and flat-roofed houses of cement blocks. They were obviously do-it-yourself homes, poorly put together, the masonry asymmetrical, the wood framing uneven, clumps of electrical wires hanging from the eaves, and the sight of women carrying buckets spoke of no running water.

"There is one high school."

In the period of massacres, he said, there had been twenty-five killings in one day; ten homicides a day had been the average.

"You'd be driving and there'd be a body on the ground, sometimes several." He had slowed his truck to allow a skinny three-legged dog to hop-limp across the stony road. He said, "The soldiers were doing most of the killing and the torture. They and the police were behind the violence. This happens even now. Everywhere they send the soldiers, there are house burnings, torture, killings — this violence promotes the narrative that it's a cartel war."

"But surely the cartels are also doing a lot of the killing, as they fight for control over a territory," I said.

"Yes, no question," Julián said, "but if you send ten thousand soldiers to Juárez, you get massacres. Juárez's bad reputation is well deserved, but you have to understand the reason why."

He showed me a video on his cell phone that happened to be circulating in Mexico that week, of a woman in Guerrero state being tortured by soldiers, a plastic bag tightened over her head as she was being interrogated. "Do you remember now?" a torturer in an army uniform kept repeating.

The woman choked as she was suffocated, and the man removed the bag only long enough to demand answers.

*Tell me*, the man says, *or do you want the bag again?*

The woman, who is tied up, continues to cry and say she knows nothing as the soldier pulls the bag down so hard, the woman sucks it into her mouth and silently gags and struggles.

"See his uniform? He is in the federal police," Julián said. "This also happened in Juárez. This happens every day in Mexico."

Soon after this video went viral, the Mexican government apologized for the criminal aggression of the police.

Over lunch at El Coyote Inválido, Julián talked about border culture.

Border music, he said, was not just the *narcocorridos,* the drug ballads celebrating the frontier exploits of the Mexican cartels, but *norteño* music, northern border ballads. This music was given its peculiar flavor through the use of a border vocabulary that has grown up on both sides. And the cultural mix occurs on the American side, too, much of which is saturated with the jolly *vida mexicana,* as well as the odious *narco cultura.*

The proof that criminals the world over are in love with euphemism shows in the use of *piedra* (stone) or *foco* (headlight) as words for crystal meth, *perico* (parrot) for cocaine, *choncha, mota, mostaza* (mustard), or *café* for marijuana, and *agua de chango* (monkey water) for a strong but cheap liquid high. *Montada* is the Spanish word for being mounted, as on a horse, but it is the border word for torture, usually by the Mexican military. *Albergue,* the word for a traditional inn, is used on the border for a rough shelter made by a migrant.

It was Juan Cordero who told me the border word *gabacho,* which most Spanish speakers would recognize as "frog," the slur in Spain for a French person. But on the border—and it has traveled deeper into Mexico—*gabacho* is an insulting word for a gringo. Border gringos return the compliment, with the much more offensive "beaner" or "frijolero." *El Gabacho* can also refer to the United States as a whole, as in *Mi hermano se fue al Gabacho.* (My brother went to the States.)

A *punto* is a place for buying drugs—*punto* meaning "point," as in "point of sale." *Picadero* (*picar* means to jab or prod) is the word for a heroin house. Another common word, *puchador,* is derived from the English word "pusher." And if you were robbed, there was an odd locution not used elsewhere in Mexico: *Me hicieron*—They did me. One way they might do you was to engage in a housejacking: the English term was used by border Mexicans to mean being burgled in a specific way, the villains breaking into your house to steal your documents, your passport, your visa—the papers you needed to cross the border.

"I'm sure you saw *halcones* along the border," Julián said. This word for falcons is the border term for lookout or spy, and many have an Artful Dodger jauntiness. Yes, I told him, I saw them on the hills near the Comedor at Nogales, standing on the hillsides, scoping out migrants likely to need the services of a coyote or a cartel *pollero,* who were always in search of clients willing to pay to be led across the border.

"Border cities are immigrant cities," Julián said. "They're populated by people from all over. You can talk to anyone." From San Ysidro in the west (across from Tijuana) to Brownsville in the east (across from Matamoros), the spillover means a non-Spanish-speaking American is at a distinct disadvantage when shopping, buying gas, eating in many US border restaurants, and fraternizing with workers. "It's not like Mexico City or Chihuahua, where there are hierarchies. There's no rigid class system here."

That was the reason he was staying in Juárez, he said. He had a house, and as a photographer and journalist—one of a diminishing number here—he could be an eyewitness to whatever happened next in this desperate city.

He seemed to me an example of great resolve, because he had a visa to cross the border, and at any time of day or night he could look across the culvert that holds the greenish residue of the Rio Grande and see the booming city of El Paso. The irony was that much of El Paso's prosperity was based on immigrant labor and the profits from sweatshops in Juárez.

The day I left El Paso, I fell into conversation with a Texan in a restaurant—a man with a book in his hand I took to be someone I might have something in common with, and so it turned out. He was a reader, the book was a collection of poems, the man himself wrote poems, and he was glad to talk over coffee at the Good Luck Café, which served home-style Mexican food. We could see Juárez from where we sat, and so my natural question was, if he was so enthusiastic about *comida mexicana,* wouldn't the best meals be found over there?

"Maybe," he said, and pointed with his face, the half mile to the border. "God, I haven't been over there in years."

The valley of the Rio Grande on the Texas side was irrigated farmland—stony Chihuahuan Desert on the far side.* And then I was back amid

---

* About forty miles south of Van Horn, at place called Porvenir, a melancholy sign. On January 28, 1918, a group of Texans, Anglo ranchers, and soldiers snatched fifteen Mexican men and boys and massacred them on a bluff overlooking the river, the burned Porvenir to the ground.

the beauties of Big Bend and the high desert, descending to Box Canyon and Amistad and Del Rio, Texas, where a quarter of the working population lived over the border, filing across the bridge every day to mop floors, trim gardens, or go shopping. I had lunch in Del Rio, served by Myrta, who told me she crossed to the US every day to cook Mexican food in this restaurant.

"They make car parts and safety belts there now," Myrta said. "But workers earn seventy-five pesos a day [about $4.00]. I'd rather commute to Del Rio and make tacos."

Many of those Del Rio workers were American citizens who lived over the river in the once raunchy and roistering but now hollow-eyed Mexican town of Ciudad Acuña. A garage mechanic I met in Del Rio said he commuted every day from Ciudad Acuña, where his rented house cost him $100 a month. "A similar house would cost between five and eight hundred here." Food was cheaper across the border, and it took only ten minutes to cross.

"I bought a house in Ciudad Acuña for less than twenty grand," Roy, another car mechanic, told me in Del Rio. I heard this same tale many times. "I cross every day."

Del Rio's prosperity was based on its nearness to Laughlin Air Force Base, eight miles away, and the base's need for civilian workers. Ciudad Acuña had survived by having attracted sixty-three factories in five industrial parks, making auto parts, air bags, and Oster appliances (blenders, toasters, coffee machines, microwaves), and was about to conclude a deal for a car assembly plant. The Mexican factory workers I spoke with were reluctant to give details, but they confirmed that the starting salary was the equivalent of about $4.00 a day, rising to $7.50 a day. And most maquiladoras ran two shifts, 7 a.m. to 4 p.m. and 4 p.m. to 2 a.m. There are about fifty thousand workers in Ciudad Acuña, which is greater than the entire population of Del Rio. Because Acuña boasted of its aversion to labor unions, American companies were still relocating there, attracted by the promise of being able to pay factory workers less than $8 a day.

"They're glad to have those jobs," an American consular official had said to me in Nogales, rebutting my skepticism.

Maybe so, but desperation is often a rationale for exploitation, and it was clear to me on my short walk across the border to Acuña that it was a city of poor housing and low spirits, of people living in the hovels Mexicans call *jacales*—workers' quarters, like plantation housing—and that none of the workers in the Oster factory had in their shack one of the coffee machines they toiled to make.

When tourism had dominated Ciudad Acuña, there had been concerts and dances and weekend bullfights.

"Bullfighters came from Spain and Mexico City," Jesús Rubén told me in his souvenir shop. "Lots of gringos came to see them. A local man, Señor Ramón, supplied the bulls. This town was lively!" He pointed to the empty main street, Calle Hidalgo, and the unvisited curio shops, boot sellers, hat shops, and faded postcards. "People everywhere!"

Gringos drove down from Houston for the restaurants, and the air force men from Laughlin had come across to get drunk and chase women at the Boys' Town at the edge of the city. But this was no longer the case. There were saloons signposted LADIES BAR—"where you could find a lady to take home," Jesús said—but these bars were boarded up. And the Plaza de Toros had become a market square.

Route 277 out of Del Rio to Eagle Pass followed the contour of the border, which was the meander of the Rio Grande, sparkling in morning sunlight, slow-moving, and easily swimmable. With meadows and low green hills, pecan farms and fruit orchards, this part of Texas owes its lushness to its proximity to the river and to irrigation. Its harvesting it owes to migrants.

Eagle Pass seemed a town in decline. Its decorous colonnaded mansions spoke of a prosperous past, its faded bungalows of a moribund present. But it had a good-sized golf course. I walked across the low bridge to Piedras Negras and strolled to the large and newish Plaza de las Culturas, and I was struck—as I had been in some other Mexican border towns—by the number of families with children on outings—playing in parks, eating ice cream, kicking soccer balls. The sight of these families gave color and vitality to the towns south of the border, and while there was a large museum in Piedras Negras and a substantial public library, there was nothing comparable on the US side.

The Museo de la Frontera Norte in Piedras Negras stated as its purpose, "impressing, preserving and fortifying the identity of the people of Coahuila."To that end, the history of the town and the state was explained in maps, documents, tools, weapons, and paintings. (No mention, though, that nachos were invented in Piedras Negras by Ignacio "Nacho" Anaya, who in the 1940s combined a dish of tortilla chips, jalapeños, and melted cheese at the Victory Club in town, for gringos from Eagle Pass.) The library on the ground floor was busy with browsers and borrowers and readers, and the motto of Sala Gabriel García Márquez—note the name of one of the greatest writers of the twentieth century—was *Leer para vivir mejor*—Read to live better.

And perhaps the reason was simple. Piedras Negras was another town where factory workers were stuck in low-wage jobs. A population with a small income, without television or video games, unable to afford a car, spends its leisure hours in parks and museums, and borrows books from libraries.

"In the States, the kids are playing with their Xboxes," Mike Smith said to me in Laredo, half a day's drive through farmland from Eagle Pass. Mike was with the Holding Institute, promoting adult literacy and welfare for the underserved in Laredo. "Over the border, they go on outings and picnics. The families tend to create their own activities."

But the bright streets, the newness and efficiency of Laredo, and my days in the pleasant Hotel Posada, on the old plaza, made Nuevo Laredo on the Mexican side look positively horrific—an effect, as in Juárez, of the cartels battling each other and the Mexican military battling the cartels. Laredo, Texas, was a city of museums and colleges—Texas A&M International among them—of sports stadiums and schools. Its stores were thronged with shoppers from over the border, who were so numerous on the bridge that, while crossing from the US to Mexico was a ten-minute walk, a crossing from south to north might take an hour or two, as the line narrowed and was slowed at US immigration. These border crossers were in general holders of visas or work permits.

I knew from experience that it had once been very different. Forty years before, as a restless young man, energized by long overland trips through exotic cultures, I had decided to travel by train from Boston to Patagonia, roughly thirteen thousand miles, a journey of many months. I arrived in Laredo on a train from Fort Worth, to travel south, a trip I described in *The Old Patagonian Express.* I had stayed the night in Laredo, which I found quiet but well lit. "All that light, instead of giving an impression of warmth and activity, merely exposed its emptiness in a deadening blaze." The city had a population of about eighty thousand (it is now three times that size); it was a place of churches and shops, sedate and small, and after dark not much moved. No traffic, no pedestrians.

Laredo then had been a modest-sized border town of small industries, known mainly for its college; and Nuevo Laredo—meretricious and vulgar, noted for whores and silliness—had been thick with tourists, thrill seekers, and drunks.

Back then, the sky glowed over Nuevo Laredo, the lights of saloons and restaurants, and standing near the riverbank I could hear cars honking and music playing from across the river, a beckoning fiesta. "Laredo had the airport and the churches," I wrote, "Nuevo Laredo the brothels and basket factories. Each nationality had seemed to gravitate to its own area of competence." I walked across into a city that seemed lawless, smoky, scented with chiles and cheap perfume, overcrowded, and noisy—"the urchins, the old ladies, the cripples, the sellers of lottery tickets, the frantic dirty youths, the men selling trays of switchblades, the tequila bars and incessant racketing music, the hotels reeking of bedbugs . . ."

Emphasizing the honky-tonk and the wickedness, I sounded disapproving, but I was happy. This was life to me, and I was joyous on those seedy streets, pretty women in doorways snatching at me. I was a thrill-seeking traveler, looking for something sensational to write about, but I did not look very deeply.

Under the influence of Graham Greene, I had found the contrasting sides of the border dramatic, as in the Greene story "Across the Bridge," which takes place in those two frontier towns, American policemen pursuing an English criminal on the run, finding their quarry in Nuevo Laredo:

He said, "This is rather a dreadful place, don't you think?"

"It is," the policeman said.

"I can't think what brings anybody across the bridge."

"Duty," the policeman said gloomily. "I suppose you are passing through."

"Yes," Mr. Calloway said.

"I'd have expected over here there'd have been—you know what I mean—life. You read things about Mexico."

"Oh, life," Mr. Calloway said. He spoke firmly and precisely, as if to a committee of shareholders. "That begins on the other side."

Back then, I had made a little tour of Nuevo Laredo and finally boarded the train, named the Aztec Eagle, for San Luis Potosí and Mexico City.

The years had not been kind to Nuevo Laredo. Decades of petty crime and vandalism and cartel violence had left scars—actual marks of terror, bulldozed houses and broken windows and threats scribbled as graffiti on most walls. The usual factories in the usual places—guarded industrial areas—but the dominant note was anxiety. The town was as ruinous and unvisited as Juárez, and for the same reason: the cartels had left their stink of violence in the streets and battered neighborhoods.

The small border towns up to now had been pleasant enough because they were on back roads, many of the roads unsuitable for the big trucks that lumbered up from the depots of central Mexico or the nearer maquilas. Along with Juárez and Tijuana, Laredo was an important entry point, a trafficking corridor—thousands of trucks, allowing the smugglers of cocaine to find ways to sneak it across.

For the past decade, the Gulf cartel, the Sinaloa cartel (El Chapo in charge), and the Zetas had been in a three-way struggle for domination—the Mexican army and police fighting all three, and sometimes joining them. The cartels were known to recruit their toughest members from the ranks of the poorly paid but highly trained and better-armed killers in the Mexican army's special forces. The bloody and prolonged cartel turf war had been chronicled in half a dozen books, among them Ed Vulliamy's *Amexica: War Along the Borderline; Bloodlines* by Melissa del Bosque; Joe Tone's *Bones: Brothers, Horses, Cartels, and the Borderland Dream;* and Guadalupe Correa-Cabrera's *Los Zetas Inc.: Criminal Corporations, Energy, and Civil War in Mexico.* One of the important things to know about Mexico is that—based on its literature and journalism—the country exists in a frenzy of self-analysis and often self-flagellation, in books and articles that are little known north of the border, but easy enough to find.

The mayhem that continued to disrupt Nuevo Laredo for the past ten years has been well documented—the stories of bodies strung from bridges or left on streets, the bombings, the massacres—enough to discourage anyone from crossing. And it continues to be written about, though the journalists who have done so have paid a heavy price, being targeted by the cartels. Eighteen journalists were killed in 2017, several of them in Nuevo Laredo.

An absence of gringos visiting the city meant that it was easy to find a taxi; they surrounded and implored me. But the driver I chose, who gave his name as Diego, found my inquisitiveness alarming. "Don't write," he said, seeing me scribbling into my notebook, taking me for a journalist.

"*Periodista?*" Diego asked.

"*Pensionado,*" I said. Retiree.

He said he would take me on a tour of the Zona de Tolerancia—he used the expression "Boys' Town"—if I promised to put my notebook on the floor and my pen in my pocket. And he suggested that I sit back and not gape out the window. He grew increasingly nervous as he drove, becoming erratic in his turns, saying that he did not come here often, and that—whispering the word "mafia"—he was agreeing to my request because it happened to be three in the afternoon. Boys' Town was not safe at night.

"It's far," Diego said, as though the distance might make me change my mind. When I said I didn't mind, he added, "And dangerous."

"In what way?"

"Drugs, crime," he said, dropping his voice, and then the words no traveler likes to hear, "*Gente mala*"—Bad people.

"How bad? Very bad?"

"Mafia," he whispered.

"I'm thinking," I said. *Estoy pensando.*

"Okay. But don't talk to anyone. No writing. No pictures. These people don't want their faces shown."

He drove, muttering "Dangerous," from poor street to poor street, for about a mile and a half, around the marshaling yards of the railway where I had embarked all those years ago, when this city had been raucous and sleazy, a frat boy's dream. I had only the dimmest memory of looking around then, and when I read what I wrote in my book, I see a young man breezing through the town, eager to take his trip, laughing when a man tells him that in Boys' Town "there are one thousand whores!"

"What is this street?"

"Calle Monterrey."

A red-light district, the Zona Rosa in the Zona de Tolerancia of Mexican social life, evokes an image of neon promises and dazzling lights, winking drabs and knaves, strip shows and skin flicks, of harlotry and whoredom, the Hispanic Mistress Overdone queening it over "sanctified and pious bawds, the better to beguile." For the mindless, blameless fun of male fantasy and reckless roistering, Boys' Town, in its wicked cuteness, is the perfect name.

Now Diego and I were passing an eight- or nine-foot wall that ran parallel to the street, the sort of solemn unmarked wall that might enclose a school. Diego (sighing, blowing out his cheeks in anxiety) was slowing the taxi at a gateway in the wall, which was more like the entrance to a degenerate cloister than a school, because it suggested discreet exclusion. An entry and an exit, each one so narrow only a single car could squeeze through at a time, with just inches to spare on either side. A sentry box of cement blocks and barred windows stood in the middle, two boys in ragged shirts and matted hair in the sentry box window, and one boy swung himself out, his dirty hands clinging to the rusty bars.

"Gringo," he said, as a mocking greeting.

And as we slid through this slot in the wall, I thought how easy it would be to become trapped inside, because as we passed I saw an iron pipe uplifted in a twist of wire, the sort of iron pipe, a simple immovable obstacle, you see at roadblocks.

*"Dónde?"*

"Anywhere. Just keep driving," I said, and looked back at the toughs manning the gate.

Now in the walled compound, it was as though we had entered a fortress — a small one, that had suffered a defeat, that was mostly empty: one or two parked cars, no lights, no signs except street markers. The enclosed compound was the size of a city block; the inner road around its walls was a beltway, a *circunvalación,* named Casanova; and the roads crossing inside were signposted "Cleopatra" and "Lucrecia Borgia," suggesting that someone in Nuevo Laredo's department of urban planning had a sense of humor.

Low, one-story gray cement huts, ulcerated and stained, lined these roads, some of the huts with old painted signs, most of them stenciled with numbers, all of them dark and grim, windows broken. As we drove along the stony, potholed road called Cleopatra I looked for other cars, or other customers. But only young men, like the mockers at the sentry box at the gate (I took them to be *halcones,* lookouts), were prowling or lounging, and because ours was the single moving car, the youths took an exaggerated interest, yelling as we passed.

Amazingly, some of the huts were open for business. At two or three of them, women sat at the doorway, singly or in companionable groups. They were older women, and the ones I saw were heavy, not coquettes but like hawkers in a Mexican market, and with the same screech, beckoning to our slowly moving car from where they sat in folding chairs, the way an impatient mother might scold a child or hector him at dinnertime.

The clubs — Martha's, and at the top end of the zone, La Zona de Antros (Zone of Caves, or Grottoes) — were shuttered. I was summing up its emptiness and squalor as dreary and woeful when I remembered that, bumping past the huts, we were the only moving thing in this walled compound, and that the way out was the narrowest of exits — so narrow, in fact, that it would be easy for the ragged youths to lock the iron pipe and trap us and rob us.

Diego must have had the same notion, because without my saying anything he headed toward the exit, the car rocking in the ruts, while the women still screeched at us, and two more women in black yelled from the doorway of a hovel called Disco Amazona.

The ragged youths at the gate hooted as Diego sped through, gasping. When he was safely back on Calle Monterrey he said, "Ten years ago it was okay. But this city changed with all the violence."

As we came to a stoplight, a car drew alongside. Diego rolled up his window and looked alarmed again, and when I asked him if anything was wrong, and was he okay, and what was the name of this neighborhood, he would not answer.

Dropping me back at San Dario Avenue, which was the road to the international bridge, he said, "You should leave."

"Thanks."

But it was not easy. The entire walkway on the bridge was filled with people, all of them Mexican, obviously with visas or papers, headed toward the door with the sign US IMMIGRATION — not shuffling toward the door, not moving, but just waiting, and I was waiting with them. After an hour I was greeted, I showed my passport, and was waved through.

In Laredo, over lunch, I talked with two board members of the Holding Institute, the nonprofit offering help to the border towns of Laredo and Nuevo Laredo—GED classes, health care, humanitarian relief, tutoring, English classes, and much else. The institute had started in 1880 as the Holding Seminary of Laredo and had evolved into a community welfare service infused with a spiritual element, though the men I talked with, anything but pious, seemed secular and forthright.

I mentioned that I had just come from a tour in Boys' Town.

"That's very risky," Jaime Arispe said. "You have no rights there, because it's a Zona de Tolerancia. They have their own police."

His colleague Mike Smith said, "If you get arrested, be prepared to buy your way out."

Jaime had been born in Ciudad Acuña in 1953. His father, a civilian worker at Laughlin Air Force Base in Del Rio, started his shift early, and at noon crossed to Acuña for lunch and a siesta, then crossed back to the base until it was time to clock out. Mike's mother was Mexican, but he'd been born in Laredo and was roughly Jaime's age.

"No one goes to Nuevo Laredo for pleasure," Mike said. "It's a factory town now. Sony has a plant there—they have one here, too. They make the same things—electronics, small appliances, components for products. It's a huge plant over there—ten-hour shifts. They provide transport and food. The difference is that the Sony plant here pays fourteen dollars an hour and the one in Mexico pays a dollar."

When I remarked on the prosperity of Laredo, Jaime said, "Laredo is the largest inland port in the US. There are three bridges—World Trade Bridge is just for trucks."

"Good business here translates to good feeling," Mike said. "All along the border, people are very prideful of their town. They hate being lumped with the others."

"We're not McAllen," Jaime said. "Statistically, Reynosa is the most dangerous border town these days."

I asked whether they'd seen Mexicans crossing the border illegally.

Jaime said, "Riverview Park—it's right in town, facing the border. I've been there with my kids, and people have come up to me and asked, 'Can you help me?'"

"They swim across," Mike said. "If they make it, they can blend in. Most people I know in Nuevo Laredo—and I know a lot—want to live here, for economic reasons. They know that they're underpaid at the factories."

I mentioned that the amounts paid to coyotes and cartels seemed very high.

"It's like this," Jaime said, "a sliding scale. To just cross they pay the smallest fee. The next highest gets you across and to a safe house. Pay more money and you're given new clothes and a haircut and the safe house. The most money—maybe five thousand dollars—gets you clothes, a haircut, the house, and English lessons. And what's the risk for the cartel? Very small compared to drug trafficking."

"You've probably heard this before, but it's true," Mike said. "The cartels own the border. Here it's the Zetas—they ran the Gulf cartel out of town."

Jaime suggested that on my drive east I detour at a town called Rio

Bravo, take a side road at El Cenizo, and look at the river, where I would see a popular crossing for migrants. He drew me a map, naming the streets.

Driving out of Laredo, I followed his directions, turned south at Rio Bravo, parked at the tiny village of El Cenizo, and walked downhill to the river. There I found an idyllic spot—a grassy bank, thick drooping stands of riverside willows and bamboo canes, no houses or fences in sight, and what looked to be an easy swim from one side to the other, probably fifty yards of slow-moving water.

The loveliest sight that day on the near bank were yellow sulphur butter-flies, fluttering over the mud like confetti, some poised with folded wings, others scattered, dipping and circling. But in contrast to the butterflies in the scoop of shore was the rubbish and litter of migrant swimmers who'd made it across: knotted clothes, cast-off shoes, water bottles, old socks, and a piteous touch, the discarded toothbrushes of the fleeing Mexicans.

Blue plastic sheeting, cracked and taped, and tied in the bamboo grove, completed what a border Mexican, seeing an improvised shelter, would euphemistically call an *albergue*—an inn—and in that small hiding place the mashed-down canes and culms identified it as a spot where people had recently sought refuge or had slept.

This was about two miles off the border road, Route 83, which is scenic, straight, and bucolic, with farms on either side. But here's a correction: on such a rural road near the border there is always a reminder of the thwart-ing or hunting down of migrants. Driving along that road, I soon came to a checkpoint, as formidable as any international frontier, with armed Border Patrol agents and sniffer dogs and a fleet of vehicles. And overhead, at the town of Zapata, hundreds of feet in the air, a great white blimp tethered to a cornfield—a surveillance balloon.

Later that day, beyond the border bulge of Falcon Lake, I came to Roma, decaying but singular in its decay. Roma was a fossilized nine-teenth-century trading town, still with some attractive but abandoned brick and stucco buildings. Like many once elegant US border towns (Del Rio, Eagle Pass, Douglas, and others), Roma—neglected, underfunded, and overlooked—barely existed.

But it was well built and venerable, originally Mexican, founded as an adobe town in 1765 and made into a brick and mortar marvel 120 years later by a German trader, Heinrich Portscheller. A brief version of his story was given on a slab of bronze in the plaza—the deserted plaza. But the text on the slab left out the more colorful details: that as a twenty-something immigrant to Mexico from Germany, Portscheller had ended up fighting in the army of the soon-to-be-executed Emperor Maximilian; that he deserted and hid in Texas, then changed sides and fought for the Mexicans in several battles. Settling in Texas, he became a US citizen, a brickmaker, and an architect. He oversaw the construction, using hand-cast bricks in the 1880s, of the elegant buildings with ornate pilasters and cornices that surround the symmetrical plaza in Roma—and the church, the ornamental iron balconies, even the iron bridge that spans the river to Ciudad Miguel Alemán. This main plaza in Roma had a moment of renewed glory when in 1952 it was chosen by director Elia Kazan as the setting for a number of scenes in his film *Viva Zapata!*, with Marlon Brando as Zapata. Today, picnicking families, fishermen, and small children idled on the south bank, and waved to the gringo on the Roma bluff.

There was not a soul in the plaza or the church or in any of the shops in old Roma, though present-day Roma had a Dollar Tree store, a Dairy Queen, a gas station, and a school. I walked across Portscheller's iron bridge—no more complicated than crossing a street (a smile, a greeting, no questions on either side)—and walked into Ciudad Alemán.

On the other bank, I fell into step with a man headed to Monterrey—three hours by bus, $13—and remarked that it seemed an easy swim across to the US.

"Not easy," he said. "The current is fast here."

He said that Ciudad Alemán was a peaceful town. "Not like the others."

But Omar, a man of about twenty, a shopkeeper selling piñatas just off the Plaza Principal, said, "Yes, a nice place, but"—and emphatically—"don't go outside town. Twenty miles away are the *ranchitos*, and the mafia." His voice dropped and he began to whisper. "Here we have Los Golfos—they fight the Zetas for control. Drugs, people smuggling, extortion—they are into everything . . ."

Speaking in this way, he became short of breath and choked a little, the gasping of a border Mexican when answering a question about the cartels. It was a physical change, a lapse into euphemisms. He slowly began to hyperventilate in an excess of anxiety, struggling to speak, becoming reluctant and evasive, panting a bit, then abandoning the effort altogether and turning away. It was fear.

The subject was hideous; any mention of the cartels was dangerous. The gangs were brutal, merciless, unforgiving, and well armed, advertising their brutality everywhere. Where could you go for help or protection? The Mexican police and army inspired the same fear.

And what made this fear peculiarly surreal was that Omar sold piñatas, large ones, and they hung around us from the veranda of his shop, comic painted images, doll-like, of Mickey Mouse and El Chapo, of Bernie Sanders, of big-breasted women, of beer bottles, and a fat, orange-haired piñata of Donald Trump.

Omar had gone to school across the river in Roma but had no hope of ever returning. His was a family business here — party favors, costumes — and he would continue to run it, because Mexicans were willing to spend lavishly on parties and fiestas. And Ciudad Alemán, in spite of the cartels, was a well-regulated town. The factories ran twenty-four hours a day, the streets were clean, the buildings painted and presentable, even if business was slow.

One of the common denominators I noticed of the Mexican towns was this civic pride. The street sweeper with his handcart was a feature of every border town I visited, and the local boast was that life was quite a bit better in your own town than in others on the border — in spite of the fact that, wherever you were, a violent drug cartel dominated the place. This *Our Town* feeling of belonging, the assertion that "I was born in Ciudad Alemán, I grew up in Ciudad Alemán, this is my home," gave me hope, because the speaker was a ten-minute walk from Roma, Texas.

I had lunch at a taqueria, ate an ice cream, and sat in the plaza and talked to a local man about the maquilas (auto parts) — and he laughed and called me a *gabacho*. Returning to the US side, I mentioned the piñatas to the immigration officer.

"I'd like to take a swing at the Bernie Sanders piñata," he said.

"What about Trump?"

"He's doing a good job. We need him."

"To build a wall?"

"For everything—everything that's wrong in this country. So much needs to be fixed."

"Have you been across?" and I jerked my thumb toward the bridge.

"Not for years. I hear it's like the Wild West."

I was nearing the towns I had left weeks before—Rio Grande City, Mission, and McAllen. But instead of stopping, I continued forty or so miles to Brownsville, the last bridge into Mexico—Matamoros in this case. Brownsville was another example of the blurred border, of Mexico brimming against the US and lapping over it, leaving a margin of Mexico on the north bank of the green river. The streets and shops of Brownsville were indistinguishable from the streets and shops of Matamoros, except that owing to its reputation for danger, gringos were absent from Matamoros.

Still, it was a short walk to the other side, and although much of Matamoros was stinking and sun-scorched and crumbling, a taxi driver named Germán promised he'd show me the high-priced neighborhood of Matamoros. This was a bluff on the east side near the river, a community called Villa Jardín—where the US consulate general sat behind bomb-proof exterior walls (with armed guards and barriers)—an enclave of shaded streets of big trees and leafy boughs, and mansions, some of them decaying and haunted-looking, others with mansard roofs and landscaped gardens and perimeter walls higher than the consulate's.

"Narcos," Germán said as we passed.

"In those big houses?"

"Yes. They control Matamoros. The narcos live in big houses."

"Trafficking people?"

"People and drugs—*choncha*," he said, using the slang for weed. "And coke. But mainly it's *piedra* [meth], because that's the cheapest and most popular. The users in your country don't have much money."

The Zetas were the traffickers here; they controlled Matamoros and Reynosa. Ciudad Alemán was dominated by the Gulf cartel, Juárez by the Juárez cartel, Nogales by the Sonora cartel, and all of them, plus the Sinaloa cartel, fought for Nuevo Laredo.

I had hired Germán for my day in Matamoros. I liked his temperament — easygoing, fatalistic in a comical way, anxious to please, grateful for the work of being a guide, and candid about his exploits. He'd been born in San Luis Potosí, he said. It wasn't at all like Matamoros; it was quiet, traditional, but without many job opportunities. The action was on the border, he said. He had bounced around.

"I've been to the States," he said. "I lived there for three years. My girlfriend here has a US passport. We have three children." He glanced at me. "I might marry her!"

"How did you get to the States?"

"I went with twenty guys to Miguel Alemán," he said.

"The bridge or the river?"

"We swam across. It was easy, and most of us got jobs nearby in Rio Grande City. If we'd gone up the road, the Border Patrol would have arrested us at the checkpoints. But we stayed on the border. I worked as an electrician and earned good money. After three years I swam back."

A crossing similar to this occurs in Yuri Herrera's novel of the border, *Signs Preceding the End of the World*. This highly praised book ("masterpiece," "epic," "legend-rich") is an oblique and euphemistic narrative of a confident young woman, Makina, in search of her migrant brother in the United States. She goes from her village to a town to "the Big Chilango" (Mexico City), then takes a bus to the border and a short but turbulent inner-tube journey across the Rio Grande. She suddenly capsizes, is rescued, and then has adventures on the opposite bank. Makina is a Mexican of the present moment: constantly on the move, in space, in time, in cultures. That aspect of its being cosmopolitan seems to me the book's value.

Though the novel is portentous and incoherent in the way it chronicles the stoical Makina's travels, this blurring also accurately represents the incomprehension of a Mexican migrant in the US. Herrera is deft in rendering the insights of an alien. The brother, reluctant to return home, admits his migrant confusion: "We forget what we came for." Authority figures and officialdom are a menace throughout the book, with the paradox of Makina needing help in the strange land: "And what was the point of calling the cops when your measure of good fortune consisted of having them not know you exist."

This paradox was Germán's, too, as he led me through Matamoros. We had left Villa Jardín. He would show me the arts center, which was the pride of Matamoros. He was still talking.

"The second time I crossed, I swam again, but nearer Brownsville, and I avoided the checkpoints."

"How did you manage that?"

"By going around them, through the woods," he said, and he had ended up safely near Harlingen, Texas, thirty-odd miles away. "I walked for nine hours."

He showed me the parks near the river, the Olympic Plaza with its arts center, a museum, and—in a border city with the worst reputation today, worse now than Ciudad Juárez or Tijuana—an auditorium for dance and music recitals, a reminder that life goes on. At the river, I took a path down the bank and saw that it was overgrown on both sides, the bushy banks identical. You'd never guess here that this was a border, the narrow green river an international frontier.

"What about the Zona de Tolerancia?"

"We go."

He drove west through the hot streets, descending into the back end of the city, the numbered streets in the city grid—one-story houses here, small shops, garages, fenced-in bungalows, barking dogs, and no trees.

"Calle Ocho," Germán said.

"*Putas.*"

"*Sí. Muchas.*"

Flat-fronted, low cement huts lined Eighth Street, the entrances at sidewalk level, no stairs, and most of the doors were open. As Germán slowed the car, a young woman stepped out and waved. Germán stopped and asked me if I wanted to go in.

"Yes, but wait for me."

She was perhaps twenty but could have been younger, fresh-faced, in a

T-shirt and shorts, and had she been walking near any of the twenty colleges or universities in Matamoros—say, the Instituto de Ciencias Superiores, which we'd passed an hour earlier—you would have taken her to be a student. Squinting in the sun, she grimaced in the glare, and I saw that she was wearing braces—unexpected in a prostitute, but lending to her smile an aspect of awkward girlishness.

"Come with me," she said, and walked through the open door. Next to the door a sign, ROOMS FOR RENT, and just inside an odor of ambiguous sweetness that was both sticky perfume and disinfectant. This was the lobby; the rooms, a bed in each, were to the left and right, and on the wall, as tall as me, a poster of Santa Muerte, Holy Death, a skeleton in a hooded cloak, with a grinning skull, her bony hand wrapped around the shaft of a scythe. The saint of desperate people, and of criminals and drug traffickers and whores; the saint who offers hope and does not blame or ask for repentance. All that Santa Muerte asks is veneration.

Two women sat cross-legged in upholstered chairs on either side of the lobby, where a fan moved its face back and forth. They were dressed in black, heavy and middle-aged, with fleshy arms. They were holding mirrors and applying makeup, painting smoothness onto their faces, pinkish cheeks and red lips, giving themselves unconvincing masks of youth.

"What do you want, señor?"

Now the odor of sweetness had faded and lost its ambiguity, and a stronger note was mildew and dampness and dirty sheets—I could see the rumpled coverlets through the bedroom doors. And Santa Muerte was grinning at me in defiance.

"How much for an hour?"

The young girl began to say a number when the heavier of the seated women lisped in Spanish, "Fifty dollars."

The other woman nodded at the young girl and said, "Go with her," and now a wink. "Tell her the things that make you happy." *Las cosas que te ponen feliz.*

Instant bliss for fifty bucks. Apart from all other considerations, something that bothered me was the glazed look on all the faces, a hint that they might be *tóxicas*—addled, users.

"I'm sorry, my friend is waiting," I said, and slipped outside into the sunshine.

Germán laughed at me when I got back into the car and told him what the woman had said. "Gringo, she could have made you happy!"

"I would have made my wife very unhappy."

Looking at his watch, Germán said, "I'm going to drop you at the bridge. You don't want to be in Matamoros after dark."

I stayed in Brownsville, small and tame compared to Matamoros, but just as Mexican, only tidier, with a zoo, the well-stocked Gladys Porter Zoo, but with far fewer colleges. This was a year before migrants arrived at the bridge from gang-haunted towns in Honduras and El Salvador, and those of them who were mothers with children—babies in some cases—were ordered to one side and their children snatched from them, the children screaming, the mothers weeping. The children were brought to chain-link cages in Brownsville (not unlike the western lowland gorilla cage at the Gladys Porter Zoo), the mothers locked in detention, in holding pens. Two and a half thousand children incarcerated, the mothers (and some fathers) bereft.

The justification for the United States government's barbaric and inhumane violence to the families was a biblical injunction to submit, preached by the attorney general, Jeff Sessions, smiling over his notes: "Persons who violate the law of our nation are subject to prosecution. I would cite you to [sic] the Apostle Paul and his clear and wise command in Romans 13, to obey the laws of the government because God has ordained them for the purpose of order."

After a public outcry against the children being taken from their parents and locked up, the US government relented and changed the policy. But the authorities did not reunite all the parents and children, nor was any solution found for the other eleven thousand child migrants held in detention centers in twenty states, in tent cities in Texas, and some in holding pens as distant as Oregon and New York.

To complete my frontier journey, I drove east from Brownsville, about twenty miles on sandy, narrow Route 4, through low, marshy wetland—no houses on the way, though in the distance a factory for making oil rigs, upright girders, sculptural and strange. Nearer, in the marsh grass, were shorebirds, snowy egrets and cattle egrets and cranes, and the fluttering of migratory birds, hugging the coast, heading south from Padre Island, mocking the human border guards on the ground.

At the end of the road, which grew sandier until it was covered with a thickness of ribbed sand, the beach was awash with breaking waves — and sandpipers, plovers, turnstones, and a flock of eight brown pelicans flying in formation overhead, across a sign in the dunes that warned TURTLE NESTING SEASON. I left the car on the road and walked along the beach, through Boca Chica State Park, to where the green river poured into the Gulf of Mexico.

No fence, no buildings, nothing but sawgrass and low dunes and birds and nesting turtles.

I was stopped at a checkpoint on the narrow road back to Brownsville, and although the Border Patrol officer waved me past the barrier, I stopped and asked what he was looking for.

"We're looking for people."

"Do you find them?"

"Now and then. We find them in cars. They cross the river and come down this road. Smugglers have them in vans sometimes."

I had more questions, but the officer interrupted me with an order.

"You can go, sir."

I ended my traverse from Tijuana with the vision of the border as the front line of a battleground — our tall fences, their long tunnels. We want drugs, we depend on cheap labor, and, knowing our weaknesses, the cartels fight to own the border. The migrants were restless young men, tough guys and desperadoes, ambitious would-be students and field hands, and women who wanted nothing more than a low-paying job in a meatpacking plant or a chicken farm. And weeping mothers, separated from their children, struggling over the fence and walking in the desert to save their families.

One encounter in particular stayed in my memory, like an apparition I had been privileged to experience: María, in the Comedor in Nogales, who had related to me how she had left her three small children in Oaxaca. Abandoned by her husband, destitute, with no chance of supporting her family, she had left her children in the care of her mother and crossed the border with four other desperate women.

"I wanted to find work as a cleaner in a hotel," she said softly.

Separated from the other women in the Arizona desert, she'd become lost, was arrested, roughed up, jailed, and then deported. Her eyes filled with tears when she talked about her children. Later I saw her alone, praying before she ate, an iconic image of piety and hope. Far from her children, she seemed like the tragic mother of a Mexican legend, the ghost La Llorona, the weeping woman, lamenting her loss.

Sometimes a whispered word, or a single image or glimpse of humanity, can be a powerful motivation for looking deeper into the world.

## PART TWO

# Mexico Mundo

## Over the Border

I LEFT MY car on the US side and walked across the border from McAllen to Reynosa to solicit information about obtaining a Vehicle Importation Permit. Bring your car and your papers tomorrow, they said, and we'll help you.

"Business is bad, but at least it's quiet here," Ignacio, a shoeshine man, said to me in the plaza at Reynosa, brushing goop on my shoes. "How old do you think I am? I'm fifty-eight, a grandfather. Black hair, because I'm an Indian. And see, Indian eyes — they're green. Look. Pure Indian."

I mentioned that I was planning to drive to Monterrey.

"The roads are dangerous," he said. "Maybe you'll be lucky. Do you have a pickup truck?"

"No. Just a normal car."

"Good. Because if you had a *camioneta*, someone would steal it," he said. "Notice there are no gringos here? They don't come anymore. No more *gabachos*!"

Reynosa has a terrible reputation for cartel violence. But Reynosa's two large hotels on the plaza were inexpensive and pleasant, and I had a good meal at the restaurant La Estrella.

"And on Calle Dama there used to be many *chamacas*," a man named Ponciano told me, using the local term for young girls. "Many gringos used to come here looking for them. Not many these days. Now we make seat belts."

Schoolchildren hurrying through the streets in school uniforms, hugging books; old men selecting red peppers and women buying tortilla flour; a youthful population, some youths in identical T-shirts canvassing for votes for their candidate in a coming election; parishioners going in and out of the cathedral on the plaza; and on the back streets and the pedestrian mall people shopping or chatting at taco stands. Nothing could have looked more peaceful.

Curio shops and boot shops and hat shops, but there were no American buyers: the gringos of McAllen stayed at home, knowing that the Zeta cartel controlled Reynosa. But the criminal activity was nocturnal and cross-border: mainly drugs — crystal meth and "monkey water" and weed; and the trafficking of desperate migrants; and the rounding up of girls and women for brothels in Texas and farther north.

The next morning, I drove across the border at nine, over the Rio Grande — green and narrow at this point, worming its way to the Gulf. I was apprehensive for my being conspicuous: Ignacio was right — no gringos visible, either in cars or walking. I paid a deposit of $450 and some smaller fees for my Vehicle Importation Permit, about an hour of paperwork, the back-and-forth generally friendly. There was no line, no one waiting; I was the only person being processed in this building full of clerks and policemen.

"You will drive out of here and on to Monterrey — lovely Monterrey," the parking lot security guard crowed as he affixed my permit to the proper place on the windshield, making a business of it, in expectation of the tip he saw me chafing in my fingers. "A beautiful day for a journey, sir!"

And within ten minutes I saw the reality of Reynosa, no longer the sedate Plaza Principal, but the broken roads and back streets and shacks of the scary town, scattered on both sides of a stagnant canal, shabbier and bleaker than what I had left behind.

I took a wrong turn. I found myself on a bad narrowing road, among splintered fences, surrounded by sinister shacks. But a man lying on his back under an old dented car rolled over and crawled out to give me precise directions to the bridge over the canal, to the main road to Monterrey.

And passing through Reynosa proper I saw how the pretty plaza near the border was misleading for being unthreatening and decorous, with its church and narrow streets of shops and taquerias. The full horror and hodgepodge of Reynosa was hidden from the pedestrians who wandered across to buy discount Viagra; it was deeper into the town, the disorder, the ruinous buildings, the litter, the donkeys cropping grass by the roadside. Reynosa was not its plaza, but rather another hot, dense border town of hard-up Mexicans who spent their lives peering across the frontier, easily able to see — through the slats in the fence, beyond the river — better houses, brighter stores, newer cars, cleaner streets, and no donkeys.

At the first stoplight at the intersection of a potholed road of Reynosa, a fat, middle-aged man in shorts and wearing clown makeup — whitened face, red bulb nose, lipsticked mouth — began to juggle three blue balls as the light turned red, and a small girl in a tattered dress, obviously his daughter, passed him a teapot which he balanced on his chin. The small girl hurried to the waiting cars, soliciting pesos.

At the next light, a man in sandals and rags juggled three bananas and flexed his muscles while making lunatic faces. A woman hurried from car to car with a basket, offering tamales. Farther on was a fire-eater, a skinny man in pink pajamas gulping smoky flames from a torch. And I thought: the odd, medieval strategies of the very poor, clowning, performing, selling homemade food; but not begging.

Masked policemen and masked soldiers manned checkpoints on the main road, Boulevard Miguel Hidalgo, and peered at me before waving me on. Within minutes I was out of Reynosa and headed into open country, over the state line from Tamaulipas into Nuevo León. It was the same sort of Texas landscape of mesquite and cactus and browsing cattle, the other side of a river that, owing to an 1836 treaty and a war ten years later, turned this river valley into two countries, which had lately reverted to its earlier condition as a war zone, of fence-jumping, of Mexicans splashing madly across the river, of human trafficking and the drug trade and random killings, the cartels contending for dominance. I was now deeper into Mexico than I had driven so far.

My head was buzzing with anxiety — it was all those warnings — but relief came in the form of butterflies of the sort I'd seen on the riverbank at El Cenizo. But there was just a small clutch of them there. I was not prepared for the masses of them here, the weird intrusion of them, first the small, crippled clusters of fluttering bits of yellow, toppling forward across the road, looking uncertain and slow, and then gouts of them, a straggling mass of buttery beating wings, and after a while clouds of butterflies so thick they blinded me briefly and smeared my windows and left powdery streaks of scales on the hood of my car when I smacked into them. And for miles the rabble of butterflies batted along the road to Monterrey, funneled through the passes in the valley in a mass migration, borne by the soft air and the sunlight. This wilderness of preposterous winged confetti continued to tumble, keeping low to the ground, but never falling far or flying straight, an interrupted progress that made their onward flight seem like a struggle.

Long ago I had read of this butterfly migration, the seasonal movement of monarch butterflies, but it had slipped my mind, and only when I saw them sprinkled everywhere, emerging in their yellow labors from between the mesquite trees, did I remember how they came annually from the northern US states, converged in Texas, and flew through this part of Mexico. It was my luck to be crossing their path at just the right time, and the sight of them cheered me. "Many cultures associate the butterfly with our souls," I later read. How some religions regard the butterfly as a symbol of resurrection, and how some people "view the butterfly as representing endurance, change, hope, and life." And in Mexican life these days the butterflies are identified with migrants, making their way to the border and beyond.

The undulant butterflies did not cease; they fluttered and bobbed all the way to Monterrey—and Monterrey was another surprise. Yet before I reached it, I was uplifted by the thought that almost a whole morning into my journey across the border, nothing bad had happened to me, neither at the hamlets of La Vaquita and General Bravo nor the turnoff to the cattle town of China on its lake and dam, Presa el Cuchillo, a place well known for the goat meat in its cuisine—no roadblocks, no bandits, only sunlight and mesquite and mariposas, the blue-gray silhouette of the Sierra Madre in the distance and the enormous, mostly new city of Monterrey up ahead, looking like a city jackhammered into a quarry, set off by the glittering Cerro de la Silla, Saddle Hill. Mexicans tend to refer to some mountains as hills, though Cerro de la Silla's highest peak, Pico Norte, is more than a mile high.

Butterflies prettified the oil cracking plant and sprinkled themselves among the Monterrey steel mills and the campus of the Tecnológico de Monterrey. Tec de Monterrey, Mexico's most important technical university, is the reason for the city to have transformed itself from an industrial hub to a leader in software development, with four hundred IT companies in business and still expanding. The school has been so successful, producing graduates who staff the software companies, that it now has campuses in twenty-five Mexican cities.

And this is another reason Mexicans feel belittled and misunderstood. Monterrey, Mexico's third-largest city, is a mere hour or so from the nearest town in the US, which would be sad little Roma, Texas, or its bigger neighbor, Rio Grande City, where the schools are struggling and there are no technical colleges and nothing to compare with Monterrey, hidden and growing behind its saddleback mountain.

A simple detour in this surprising city—surprising for its obvious wealth, its boomtown bustle, and its intensive building—brought me near the campus of Tec de Monterrey. It was lunchtime, and by then, having been on the road for a few hours, I was less nervy about driving, calmer, having made it to here from the border and feeling less conspicuous, still among butterflies, and in the rattle of traffic.

Another surprise was that the taqueria I chose for lunch was also near the Felix U. Gómez station of the city's metro—the Metrorrey—twenty miles long, thirty-one stations, and more lines under construction. Who knew Monterrey had a rapid transit system? But it made sense, because this city of manufacturing, IT companies, schools, and a sprawl of colonias would be unsustainable without cheap transport.

Outside the taqueria, I fell into conversation with a motorcyclist, Manuel Rojas, who was also a software engineer at a company nearby ("And it's based in Massachusetts"). Manuel and his biker friends were trying to take a group picture of themselves. I volunteered to be the photographer, and I introduced myself.

"Tec de Monterrey is the best school of its kind in the country, and it's the reason this city is so busy. I went there, and so did most of these guys." Manuel gestured to the other bikers. "There's a medical school, too. Pretty soon we'll have more software development here than manufacturing or heavy industry."

"What's the pay like for someone in your company?" I asked.

"Salaries depend on experience," he said. "You might start at 15,000 pesos a month"—$833—"but if you're good and experienced you can make 100,000." That pay of $5,555 a month worked out to $67,000 a year, and represented a top salary, modest by US standards, but enough in Mexican terms for Manuel Rojas to afford (like his friends) a newish Harley-Davidson and a reasonable apartment near the city, or a house in one of the many colonias.

The demand for workers in Monterrey had created a housing crisis and meant that this mountain valley was crammed from one end to the other with cubicular two-story houses of whitewashed stucco, looking from a distance like a mass of dusty sugar cubes and, up close, mute and unadorned like orderly mausoleums in a graveyard of subdivisions. They were thick on the lower slopes of Cerro de la Silla on one side, and on the pair of mountains on the north, Sierra El Fraile y San Miguel—neither of which looked like a friar (*fraile*) or a saint, but more like a stupendous pair of slag heaps—treeless, stony, sharp-featured. But even with the five-star hotels and the tall buildings, Monterrey had the stung and wounded look of a Mexican city that had blasted its way into existence in a rocky landscape.

Rents varied, Manuel said. A house on the outskirts could be had for $300 a month, but nearer the city center was ten times that.

Manuel was in his early thirties, well spoken, handsome in his motorcycle leathers, patient with my questions, and polite in declining a drink or a meal. He had to go, he said. He was headed with his fellow bikers to a rally in León and wanted to hit the road (*salir a la carretera*), as it was 350 miles away.

"How far is Saltillo?"

"You can be there in an hour and a half."

So I drove to Saltillo on a good road in afternoon glare, through the steep brown hills of the Chihuahuan Desert—no traffic going south, but a succession of convoys of eighteen-wheelers passing me, heading north, many of them car haulers, stacked with Chevys and Mercedes on their way to the border, reminding me that I was on Route 57, known as the NAFTA Highway.

Saltillo is called the Detroit of Mexico for its automobile production (of the twenty-five car plants in Mexico, five are in or around Saltillo), but it had Detroit's disorder, too, the sprawl of working poor and bad housing and agglomerations of shops. Yet the center of the city, also like Detroit, had two good museums and a sculpted, busily baroque eighteenth-century cathedral and plazas of venerable municipal buildings befitting Saltillo as the capital of its state, Coahuila. I drove through its center, looking for a hotel, but got honked forward and quickly found myself headed out of town.

In the interest of greater freedom on the road, I had made few plans in advance and no onward reservations. My method from the start of my trip and along the border was to look for a place to stay for the night at around four or five in the afternoon, spotting one by the roadside ("That'll do"), swinging into the forecourt, and asking whether they had a room and a safe place to park my car. They always did.

That was how I found myself at the Hotel la Fuente, set in a walled compound at the edge of Saltillo. To a casual onlooker it was seedy, with greater scrutiny it was adequate, and as a desperate traveler I found it just right. As with the cheapest Mexican motels, its main asset was its secure parking lot and its unsmiling guard, recommended in a country noted for car theft. My room hummed with the sting of mildew, the lighting was too dim to read by, the bed was lumpy and the bathroom was dusty, but after an anxious day on the road, driving from the border, it seemed perfect. The restaurant looked spartan, but the food was excellent in the simple way of provincial Mexico.

From my inquiries on the border, I had the name of a man in Saltillo, Lopez, a friend of a friend, who had been living in the US until he was stopped for a minor traffic violation and, unable to explain his status, was arrested as an illegal and sent back to Mexico. After ten years working in a factory in Texas, he had gained the experience to be able to get a job in Saltillo and apply his expertise to a factory here. He met me at the Hotel la Fuente, his arms hanging loose, a polite, somewhat sad, and serious man. It was hard to tell how old he was. In a country where people matured early and worked hard, they often looked old in middle age. I took him to be fifty or more, but he could have been much younger. He was jowly, heavy-set, in shirtsleeves—Saltillo was warm—with a soft handshake.

"I have never been here," Lopez said in the restaurant, looking around. Glancing at the menu he remarked that many of the items were local specialties, such as pulque bread, roasted baby goat (*cabrito*), and *machaca con huevos* (shredded beef and eggs). Lopez had the *cabrito*. I had tortilla soup and enchiladas and marveled that in a single day I had made it this far.

"Not far from the border here," Lopez said. "But over the border—that's really far!"

"What sort of work were you doing in the States?"

"Plastic injection molding," he said, poking his fork at the goat meat. "That's what I'm doing here."

The term was new to me, and seemed like a conversation killer, but he said it was important for automotive parts. He was in quality control, and I liked his description of defects: "delamination," "blisters," "burn marks."

"Do you miss the States?"

"I miss my children. My girlfriend and I split up, and she's raising them there. There's no way I can visit them, but my ex sometimes brings them to Nuevo Laredo. They come over the border and we have a meal." He looked a little tearful. "Two boys, eight and twelve. They're getting big."

"Tell me more about the factory where you work," I said.

"Thermoplastics. It's not interesting. The pay is about a quarter of what I was making in Texas—and we have educated people here. There's sixteen universities in Saltillo and lots of colleges." He chewed a little. "I'll manage. It's just that everything's so different now. Twenty years ago I had no problem crossing the border—all of us shopped there, when we had money. But it got worse and worse." He sighed. "Politics!"

"Ours or yours?"

"Both! Our government is bad, yours—well, you know the talk. 'Mexicans are criminals and rapists.' And really, I was working hard, and all the Mexicans I knew were good workers."

He spoke about uncertainties: how NAFTA might be renegotiated to the detriment of Mexico, how stringent immigration policies meant his going to the States again was out of the question, how the current president, Enrique Peña Nieto, was as poor a speaker and as much a liar as our president. But he laughed. "It's not in my hands!" And so we talked about happier things — his new girlfriend, her job at GM, their trips to visit her family in Monterrey, and outings to San Luis Potosí, where he had friends. A lovely city, he said, and urged me to stop there.

Reflecting on Lopez's mood, it struck me that the experience of living under a corrupt government and trying to stay honest yourself made people cynical and distrustful of authority, but at the same time self-sufficient and dependent on friends and family, because no one else would help you.

"Any advice for me? I'm driving south."

"Don't drive at night. You'll be fine. You'll learn a lot. And Mexico City is a lot safer than it used to be."

He had to go, he said — he didn't like driving at night either.

Writing my notes after he'd gone, I was unaware that a couple had begun to eat at the next table, but then I heard them murmuring in English, so I said hello to the first gringos I had seen since Texas.

They announced themselves as Canadians, who had taken a wrong turn at Ojinaga and had fought their way here in an old car from Chihuahua, well over four hundred miles.

They were Beth and Warner — not married, they quickly added. But Warner's wife, Judy, was Beth's best friend, and when Beth said she was driving to Mexico to spend the winter, Judy said, "Warner needs a vacation. He can help with the driving, and fly back when you get there." So off they went, "sharing a room," as Warner explained to me, "but separate beds." They were pleasant, and I admired them for not making a hoo-ha about their journey through the desert.

I wanted to talk about Mexico and the roads. They were preoccupied with their children and their challenges.

"My daughter's bipolar," Beth said.

"My stepson's autistic and borderline troubled," Warner said.

I asked them to amplify a bit.

"She refuses to take her meds and then it's awful," Beth said.

"It's criminal tendencies with my stepson," Warner said. "But in some ways he's an idiot savant."

"In what way criminal?"

"It's the girlfriend—not really girlfriend, because she's gay, but he dotes on her, which is a problem for her gay lover, who's crazy, by the way. Anyway, they go to gay bars and he chats up a fellow and dances with him, and while they're dancing, his girlfriend picks the fellow's back pocket. The gay lover sometimes freaks out, and in fact she called the cops on him, but before it went to trial, she dropped the charges."

"That was considerate."

"Turned out she was wanted in connection with a homicide in which she was named as an accomplice, for driving the getaway car."

"So your stepson was off the hook?"

"Not really. He still went to jail, but that's a whole different story."

Fascinated to know more, I joined them at breakfast (*huevos motuleños,* Yucatán-style eggs layered on tortillas with ham and beans) and learned about the scams and petty crimes and the time the gay girlfriend broke into Warner's house and began smashing things, while the stepson (flourishing a pellet gun) was charged with assault with a deadly weapon ("because it looked like a gun, see") and ended up in jail.

For as long as I talked to Beth and Warner, I ceased to think about Mexico and even forgot I was there, because their stories about madness and mayhem—told plainly, in a Manitoba monotone—held my attention. And I kept having to apologize for my questions. But they forgave me my curiosity.

I was reminded of the observation by the ghost story writer M. R. James, in his creepy tale "Count Magnus": "His besetting fault was pretty clearly that of over-inquisitiveness, possibly a good fault in a traveller, certainly a fault which this traveller paid dearly enough in the end."

All this time, while I was drinking the tea I had brought from home and asking questions, Beth was trying in English to get the waiter's attention. But English was not much use in the Hotel la Fuente.

"What do you want?" I asked.

"A cup of hot water."

I beckoned to the waiter and translated the request; the cup of hot water was delivered.

"The Chinese do that—drink hot water," I said. "They call it white tea."

"I'm going to have real tea," she said.

I smiled in confusion.

"With your tea bag," Beth said, and reached across the table to the saucer where my discarded tea bag lay like a dead mouse. Being a resourceful traveler, she popped the thing into her cup.

South from Saltillo, I was on the straight sloping road through the brownish, gravelly valleys of the Sierra Madre, which bristled with thousands of dark single yucca trees, the so-called *palma china,* which had put me in mind of an army of bent-backed old men with wild hair. No traffic on my side of the highway, but a fourteen-mile backup of trailer trucks (I counted the miles on my odometer) stalled on the other side, waiting to pass a wrecked car.

The highway for most of the way to San Luis Potosí was a *cuota,* a toll road, as opposed to a *libre* road, no tolls. The *libre* roads were less well maintained and tended to cut through the small towns that the *cuotas* bypassed. The *libre* roads were crossed with speed bumps, called *topes,* which bounced even the slowest car and scraped the undercarriage. The *topes* could be maddening but they did the trick, taking their revenge on speeders. The towns on these side roads had the restaurants, little inns (posadas), and motels, which the *cuotas* lacked; but *cuotas* were generally faster and safer, except when there was a wreck and the eighteen-wheelers might be stalled for miles.

CAPILLA DE SANTA MUERTE was daubed in blood red on a sign in a roadside settlement about twenty miles south of the small town of Matehuala. On my map this whole area was termed El Llano del Lobo—the

Plain of the Wolf. Tempted by the names, and remembering what I'd seen of Holy Death in the brothel of Matamoros, I pulled off the road to pay a visit.

"Good day, sir." It was a woman, fanning herself in a plastic chair just outside the entrance. There was nothing ecclesiastical about her faded dress or white apron, but she said the chapel was hers and she was the priestess—and, waving her fan, said, "Come in—you are welcome."

The chapel, a one-story cement building that perhaps had once been a shop, stood in a row of old unvisited shops coated in grayish dust—selling cold drinks, farm equipment, tamales—and one of the roadside tire-repair businesses seen frequently in rural Mexico, "vulcanizing."

Incense wafted from the chapel, the inside walls draped in white bunting and bouquets of plastic flowers. Next to the altar on the back wall was a life-size statue of Holy Death, with all her attributes. I had seen portraits and posters of this skeletal image, but this was the first time I beheld the whole frightening figure of La Santísima Muerte, in a white satin robe and virginal bridal gown, staring from hollow eye sockets and fixing me with a lipless grin. She held a sickle, as the image of Death the Leveler, and a globe and scapular, aspects (like the bridal gown) of the Virgin Mary, a familiar figure—and a helpful one, a protector, a shield, offering hope to everyone, fortune to the poor, protection to criminals and narcos.

"I have pictures, I have beads." The woman with the fan was whispering behind me. Seated outside, she'd had an air of authority; standing in the shadows of the chapel, among the skulls and bones, she was small and slightly humpbacked, one hand clutching her apron.

"I want to buy a picture," I said.

The woman went to a table at the side and selected a ghoulish picture the size of a playing card.

"How much?"

"What you wish."

I gave her some pesos, saying, "I'll come back."

"This"—she tapped the picture—"will keep you safe."

Back on the road, I thought how, even in the grip of NAFTA newfangledness, the eternal Mexico persists. No matter how modern the Mexican motorway, with toll booths, service plazas for gas and food, and mechanics in blue uniforms saluting customers at the word *Lleno*—Fill it up—old Mexico is always at the periphery, in the form of iconic figures at the margin of the highway, the weedy roadside, in the grass, the nearby meadow, under the trees, the creek bank, the little shed, the just visible casita under the spanking-new bridge.

The panorama of emblematic Mexicans begins to appear next to the slick *autopista,* a great relief to the eye and the mind. The vaquero on his horse, wielding his switch as he gathers in his grazing cows; the goatherd in a straw hat chasing a stumbling, bowlegged kid; the boy in sandals and rags, leaning on a guardrail, watching his flock of sheep; the caballero rocking on his bony horse and adjusting his reins; the old woman with a bundle on her back struggling through the tall grass; the mule cart heaped with melons or sacks of beans, a slouching man tapping the mule's flanks with a whip; a woman in a white apron seated under a sign, TAMALES and CARNE SECA; a skinny child chasing a skinny dog chasing a skinny chicken—and in the distance an old town, its cheese-colored church spires visible. I was reminded of Ray Midge in Charles Portis's *The Dog of the South:* "I waved at children carrying buckets of water and at old women with shawls on their heads. It was a chilly morning. *I'm a gringo of good will in a small Buick. I'll try to observe your customs!* That was what I put into my waves."

So, driving across the plateau of these bittersweet reminders of the antique past persisting into the present, and what the *Potosino* poet Manuel José Othón (1858–1906) described as "immensity above, immensity below . . . in the deep profile of the haughty sierra, and the horrendous gash of its mine-works," I came to San Luis Potosí. After days of overnighters in motels in my long drive from home and along the border, I thought: I'll stay here a while.

San Luis Potosí is a victim of the usual Mexican pattern of the old harmonious colonial city brutally martyred in the cause of modernization—officialdom destroying it in order to make it live. It has an ancient city center of noble churches, temples, and cathedrals; a bullring, Plaza de Toros Fermín Rivera; paved plazas surrounded by arcades of shops and restaurants, ringed by buildings that grow uglier as they sprawl into suburbs; and finally, flat-faced factories in the industrial part of the city that produce jobs and income. In the case of San Luis Potosí, the factories make cars, aircraft parts, robotics, glass doors, medical technology, and much else, its workforce composed of assembly-line workers as well as highly educated graduates of the city's sixteen universities and institutes of technology.

Driving into the old part of town, I saw a sign on the roof of a tall building, HOTEL MARÍA CRISTINA, so I steered toward it. In spite of its snooty name, it was a serviceable hotel, $40 a night, within walking distance of every historical sight, and it provided a garage where my car would not be stolen or vandalized.

In this city of a million people, and all the disruption of manufacturing and traffic, you would think of a place turned upside down and modernized out of recognition. But Potosí was poor, and *Potosinos* were oppressed by the weakening peso and the high cost of living, and in such a situation—I had noticed this all over the American Deep South on my previous road trip—people hold on to their culture. Rich people, arrivistes, and new-money snobs emphasize their enhanced status by chucking the homespun traditions that the poor cling to—they have little else to cling to. The English writer V. S. Pritchett noticed this in his travels in Spain and elsewhere: "The past of a place survives in its poor."

This is what accounts for Mexico's density and variety, for its fiestas that have their origins in Aztec ceremony, for its beliefs that have their roots in death worship, for the masks worn by schoolchildren and revelers in plazas today that have their counterparts among Zapotecs, who flourished and wore those same masks two thousand years ago.

Cuisine is culture, and traditional cooking persists in places that have been ignored by gourmet chefs or high-end restaurants. Mexico's street food (*antojitos*) is local and usually delicious, often preferred by diners who eat it, snacking at picnic tables or on stools, rather than have a three-course meal in a restaurant. Among the best meals I had in Mexico were the ones I ate in Potosí—and the relief of being able to walk around without having to search for a parking place added to the pleasure of strolling to a Potosí restaurant.

"You're my namesake!" the owner of one restaurant said to me when we exchanged names. He was Pablo, and a namesake (*tocayo*) is an ally and a potential friend. He introduced me to *enchiladas potosinos* and his variation of *enchiladas suizas* (the Swiss part is hyperbole, referring to the dish's thick cream sauce). Good manners also persist in societies so poor they are ignored and uncorrupted by hustlers and money people, as politeness is a habit of life, a way of getting on. A further point about Mexican politeness, summarized in a shrewd observation by the English philosopher and traveler R. G. Collingwood in his book *The New Leviathan* (1942): "The most beautiful manners I have met with are in countries where men carry knives, and if anybody gives them a nasty word or a nasty look, stick them into him." As my *tocayo*, Pablo became a helpful informant.

"What's that fuss in the plaza?" I asked the next night (*pozole verde*— hominy, chicken, green tomatillos, sliced avocados, much else).

Passing through the grand Plaza de Armas, with its spectacular cathedral and ornate eighteenth-century governor's palace, I had heard a woman screaming denunciations into a microphone under a flapping banner and being watched by a stern-faced crowd.

"She is with the Caravan," Pablo said.

And he explained: The Caravan was a movement of concerned Mexicans determined to keep the memory alive of the forty-three students who had been abducted and had disappeared—almost certainly murdered—in Guerrero state three years before. The students' deaths had remained unexplained, the parents still grieving and angry.

After dinner, on my way back to the hotel, passing through the Plaza Fundadores (Founders' Plaza, commemorating the city's beginning in 1592), I lingered in the Plaza de Armas to listen. Now the wind had slackened, and I could read the banner: AYOTZINAPA! LOS ASESINOS ESTÁN EN LOS PIÑOS! The Murderers Are in the Pines!

Ayotzinapa was the place where the forty-three students had been abducted in September 2014.

Spread across the cobblestones under the banner were large portraits of young men, each one titled in Spanish WE ARE MISSING, and their names, Marco Antonio Gómez Molina, Jorge Álvarez Nava, José Luis Luna Torres, and others.

This was another example of Mexican simultaneity, like the goatherd by the motorway: in the lovely old plaza, on a fiesta evening, among families enjoying the night air, youths costumed as witches and goblins, bikers in leather jackets labeled *Rebeldes* (Rebels) leaning on their motorcycles, children playing with flashing toys, the balloon sellers, and the idle, mildly curious bystanders like me, a frantic woman was howling about murders and drug gangs.

"When will we know! How long will we have to wait!" Gesturing with her microphone to the Palacio de Gobierno, a vast brown edifice that looked implacable, she shouted, "Listen to me about this injustice. I tell you, those people in the government know more than they say—and because they are silent, they are complicit in these horrible murders."

Though the children went on playing, encouraged in their jollities, and the smiling men hawked their balloons and toys, the older people in the plaza watched with alarm.

"Think of their mothers! Think of the families of these murdered students! How they have not been buried properly—how their spirits cry out for justice!"

When she was done, I talked to her a little—and I was the only one. The families and the revelers were shy, embarrassed perhaps by her accusations, wary lest anyone notice that they might be part of this demonstration. Mexicans generally were outraged by the murders, but the anger of this woman, her boldness in this sedate setting, made the outrage more public, and perhaps the onlookers feared consequences.

But the woman was fearless.

"I'm a stranger here," I said, "just a wandering gringo. But I've been listening, and I'm interested in what you're saying."

She said her name was María. She asked, "Where are you from?"

I told her.

"We brought the Caravan to the United States two years ago, to inform the people, and many listened and shared our concern. They were very sympathetic."

And María told me the facts. It was a mass kidnapping at Ayotzinapa Rural Teachers' College in Iguala, Guerrero state. The students had been in two buses, intending to travel to Mexico City to commemorate the 1968 massacre in the plaza at Tlatelolco when hundreds of protesters—the number of deaths remained secret—were killed by armed snipers and riot-control police. But the Ayotzinapa students on the buses were stopped, arrested, and handed over to a cartel gang. It was thought, María said, that the students were taken to a garbage dump and killed on the orders of Iguala's mayor, who was in cahoots (*en cohorte*) with the drug gang and the police. Only two bodies were found and identified; the rest vanished, "and they are crying out for justice."

"Have you made progress with the investigation?" I asked.

"It's three years since the murders took place, and still we don't know what really happened. All we know is that the boys are gone. Forty-three murders in one place."

"And no one is suspected?"

"The mayor is in jail, but he's not talking. Someone knows—someone in the government, or the army, or the police. This is a government of secrets. If there are secrets, there can be no justice."

I asked her why she was doing this here, and now—denouncing the government and demanding answers.

"Because we have not had any answers. The families are so sad—they lost their children. I am here as a reminder. And I am not the only one. If you go to Mexico City, you will see a big encampment at the Ministry of Justice, demonstrating."

"What about writers—are they protesting?"

"Yes, many," María said.

"Juan Villoro?"

"Villoro has written a great deal, and he is a friend to our movement."

In the late-night shadows of the plaza, María and her little band of truth seekers unfastened the banner and rolled up the portraits of the dead students—the limp cloth tattered from use, the colors of the faces cracked and faded—as the gathering of onlookers dispersed, and the plaza became festive again.

This mention of Juan Villoro was fortuitous. He is one of Mexico's most illustrious writers, a novelist and short story writer and a prolific journalist and social critic. I had been in touch with him for some time. I made a note to ask him what he knew of the murdered students. Like María, Juan was a necessary reminder, in this case, of the dark side of Mexico, the Mexico that everyone whispers about. You don't need to be in Mexico long to understand that it is a country of obstacles, a culture of inconvenience.

The obstacles in Mexican society range from—as María said—mass murder to serious hardships to mundane nuisances. You might ask: Why would a young mother of small children—like many I met on the border—take the risks of hopping the fence and enduring the privations of hiking in the desert just to labor for minimum wage in (as some told me) a meatpacking plant or a hotel? One obvious answer is that the risks and privations in Mexico are much worse that those endured in a border crossing.

These inconveniences, big and small, are suffered by everyone except the fat cats, for whom life is a shuttling back and forth in limousines, guarded by goons, or flying over the chaos in their private helicopters.

Paranoia is the chronic condition of fat cats, who are well aware of the disparities in income. The peculiar resentment for the rich or well-off in Mexico is expressed in the sarcasm of popular speech: *fresas* (strawberries) are wealthy conceited people, and their overdressed, obscenely privileged children are *niños bien* (rich kids). These beautiful people exist in an atmosphere thick with suspicion, often accompanied by intimidating muscled bodyguards.

I discovered this in a small but unusual way in San Luis Potosí. The Hotel María Cristina claimed its laundry facility wasn't working, but a staffer said I would have no trouble finding a laundry about six blocks away. Walking out of the hotel, down the narrow Calle Juan Sarabia to the corner of Calle de Los Bravos, I saw a large SUV pull up and obstruct traffic, illegally parking in front of the unadorned Hotel Nápoles. Two men in black, wearing opaque sunglasses, got out and snatched the rear door open for a middle-aged man wearing a fedora, with a fawn-colored jacket like a cape over his shoulders. This cosseted, well-guarded figure, with an aura of power and money—a *cabrón* (big goat) in the admiring sense, a *padrino* (godfather), perhaps—took three strides to the Hotel Nápoles and the entrance to the café just inside, La Colomba, where he was greeted by a sinister smiling mustached man, who hugged him and led him into the shadowy café, which was closed to the public.

This dramatic arrival seized my attention and, eager to know more, I stopped and stared, wondering who this *cabrón* might be. As I gawked, the two heavies who had been in the SUV turned their goggles on me and approached, visibly swelling as they came nearer. It was then I realized that my arms were full of laundry, an absurd tangle of clothes in which, a suspicious bodyguard might suppose, I was hiding a weapon.

"*Hola?*" the larger of the heavies mumbled, and crowded me, poking my armload of clothes.

"Laundry," I said, and slipped away.

But the *lavandería* was closed. This meant that I had to return with my great ball of clothes to the corner of Juan Sarabia and Calle de Los Bravos, and this time both musclemen watched me with mounting suspicion, their mouths tightening, shoulders lifting, as though I was an assassin circling his prey, still with his absurd tangle of clothes, his hands hidden. They looked poised to take me down.

"Laundry!" I said again, my voice rising, and walked quickly past them.

The rich in Mexico are protected, their progress is eased in every phase of life, so they are allowed to have airs. The poor, in their mild way, struggle to maintain their dignity.

And half the country lives in poverty. A recent survey concluded that 55.3 million Mexicans can be described as poor or destitute, this in a population of 127 million. The average Mexican worker earns slightly more than $15,000 a year. For them, suffering under political incompetence and the threat of crime, life is hard and bureaucracy stalls everyone; nothing is simple. Even the plainest aspects of life are a challenge—finding work, finding a place to live, finding a doctor, a school, a parking place.

You'd think the unfairness, the scrimmaging in such competition, would create conflict. But my experience in Mexico, with certain exceptions, showed the opposite, an avoidance of confrontation and a sustaining refuge in the comforts of family life. The realization that everyone is in the same boat, under siege by bad government—the word *malgobierno* is a continuous sigh of frustration—tends to create the like-mindedness of sympathy helpful in making a community coherent. That families are intact, children are valued, and the elderly are respected helps to shore up the social framework and keeps Mexico ticking over, even in the worst of times. What I had learned on the border from the mothers intending to cross was not that they wished to make a new life in the States, but that they hoped, as a solution, to make enough money to keep their family together in Mexico.

But hope and determination and a willingness to take risks are not enough to overcome the curse of bad government or the hostility of the everyday, the warding off of evil. Another feature of Mexican life is the seeking of mediation or protection in rituals. Not prayer alone, though everyone prays; but the ceremonial fiestas, dances, music, the dressing up, the making of offerings and altars of flowers and relics, the veneration of such figures as the suave, cowboy-looking ideal of the superior *cabrón,* or the truly frightening skeleton, Santa Muerte, whose main shrine in Mexico City I hoped to see. All this propitiatory magic, and the ancient remedy of appeal, the masquerade—in most of the world the wearing of masks is a way of making magic by creating a new self.

The African masks at the Trocadero Museum of Ethnology in Paris caught the eye of young Pablo Picasso: "A smell of mold and neglect caught me by the throat. I was so depressed that I would have chosen to leave immediately," he said. "But I forced myself to stay, to examine these masks, all these objects that people had created with a sacred, magical purpose, to serve as intermediaries between them and the unknown, hostile forces surrounding them, attempting in that way to overcome their fears by giving them color and form. And then I understood what painting really meant. It's not an esthetic process; it's a form of magic that interposes itself between us and the hostile universe, a means of seizing power by imposing a form on our terrors as well as on our desires. The day I understood that, I had found my path."

Masks in Mexico are nothing new. The exhibits in the well-stocked Museo Nacional de la Máscara, the Museum of the Mask, in San Luis Potosí, is proof that this land has relied on masquerade for millennia — the superbly crafted jade and turquoise Zapotec masks on view are more than two thousand years old, and similar ones are worn today at festivals.

Skull masks are everywhere in Mexican fiestas, but so are bat masks, and I had wondered why. The museum had the answer. In the persistence of memory, the past informing the present, the bat mask, *murciélago,* is represented with its jaws open, its dark wings flared in a frozen beat, its claws hooked in the air. The bat was a presiding deity in Monte Albán thousands of years ago, and the bat lived in Xibalba, the Kingdom of Night and Darkness. Related to fertility, the bat was known in Zapotec as *bigidiri zinnia* — flesh butterfly (*mariposa de carne*) — and was a benign god. There are sixty-three species of bats in Mexico, ranging from the three-inch-long bug-eating free-tailed bat to the carnivorous spectral bat, with a three-foot wingspan, which feeds on reptiles, small mammals, and other bats.

Needing to walk, and having tramped the narrow streets of the *centro histórico,* I decided to hike up to Cerro Potosí, the hill above the town, beyond Tangamanga Park. The guidebook recommended good shoes, water, and long pants against the *agave lechuguilla* — thorny agave. I started on a cool morning, setting out on the trail at 6,800 feet, and plodded upward about four miles to 8,000 feet. Beyond that I was slow and breathless, and discovered that *lechuguilla* (little lettuce) is a misnomer — it's common name, shin-dagger, is more apt. Lying on a flat, sun-heated rock to get my breath, procrastinating, I soon abandoned my effort to get to the top of Cerro Potosí. But I was thrilled by what I saw below me and beyond, the stone mountains that stretched in all directions, the rough beauty of the rocky crags.

I had been driving through this mountainous landscape for a week and regarded it as simply another tumbled heap of the Sierra Madre Oriental.

But that name was too pretty. Much of the sierra I had seen, southward from the border, could more accurately be termed wasteland—vast, dramatic, hard-edged, inhospitable, and in the words of Manuel José Othón, Potosí's best-known poet, "wild desert," "barren and immensely sad," a place of "savage ravines," "gigantic block upon gigantic block," baked dry by "desolate and burning air." And more—the "bitter and brackish plain," the "dry dead ocean basin."

In the poem "Una Estepa del Nazas," Othón describes the landscape of Nazas, which is a bit to the northwest, near Durango:

> In the gloomy bowl the monotonous river
> rolls, with never a rapid, never a gorge,
> and, low on the horizon, the setting sun
> reverberates, like a furnace mouth.
>
> And here in this grisaille that never is
> lit up by any color, here where the air
> scourges the scorched plant with fiery breath . . .

In fits of romantic masochism, Othón rusticated himself to the arid communities of this region. But he was also a federal judge, and some of these lonely outposts were assigned to him. He made the best of his various places of exile, reporting in agonized poems the physical details of the hard world around him.

I had never heard of this poet until, a day or so after my hike up Cerro Potosí, I visited his house on narrow Madero Street, behind the cathedral. There is not much to see in the dusty house, just some decomposing books, his tiny desk, his inkpot, his iron bed, his portrait photograph—bristling mustache, gentle eyes—and some framed, faded letters.

The little pamphlet (5 pesos) about Othón mentioned how, as a judge, he was summoned from the elegance of San Luis Potosí, the state capital and center of culture, to the hinterland in the late nineteenth century—in small-town Cerritos, in the northeast; in Santa María del Río, stony mountains with steep sides and jagged summits, among dry basins and rocky arroyos. A tortured note of desperate fatalism runs through his poetry, as in remote landscapes he celebrates the savagery, the howling wilderness. It is as though, among all these rocks, by a leafless tree, he is dressed in rags, waiting for Godot.

Look more closely into the shadowy literary history of Othón and you see that his poems were translated into English by Samuel Beckett. It was not his wasteland weariness that appealed to Beckett — though the wasteland predominates — but rather Beckett's need for money. How this translation happened is an unusual story. Although Othón was celebrated in his town for his "Wild Idyll," "Hymn to the Forest," and "In the Desert," this admiration was the national pride of many Mexican writers. But Othón remained obscure to the wider world.

The obscurity was a bit like Beckett's, who in 1950 was forty-four years old, unknown outside his small circle of friends, depressed, frustrated by publishers' rejections, living in near penury in Paris, and writing about loss, misery, and death. Though some of his poems had appeared in small magazines, he had yet to publish any of his novels or plays. He had finished writing *Waiting for Godot*, but it had not been staged. He was open to any reasonable offers of work.

A young Mexican student in Paris — the unknown and yet to be published Octavio Paz — approached Beckett with a proposal to translate one hundred poems by thirty-five Mexican writers. This would be financed, as a worthy cultural project, with funds from UNESCO. Beckett accepted. "The money was a godsend," Beckett's biographer Deirdre Bair writes, "but the chore was almost insurmountable." What made it difficult was that Beckett did not know Spanish very well — awkward, in the circumstances, for a potential translator. But with the help of a dictionary and the assistance of a friend fluent in Spanish, he turned all the poems into English and, in his perseverance, made them his own.

He was glad for the money, but the book was not published then. A year later, *Godot* was staged to great acclaim and Beckett became a literary celebrity. In 1958, at the age of fifty-two, Beckett had at last found the acceptance he had sought, and with his work now in demand, a university press seized the opportunity to use his name, and the *Anthology of Mexican Poetry* appeared.

But there is a singular connection between Samuel Beckett, "the grammarian of solitude," sunk in his comical Irish gloom, hiding in a tiny apartment in Paris, and the condition of Manuel Othón, the late-nineteenth-century Mexican recluse, brooding in the parched wasteland in the middle of Mexico. Seemingly at a loss for words around 1900, Othón, in a despairing poem, wrote the Beckett-like line "the desert, the desert and the desert."

## First Communion in San Diego de la Unión

IN PLACES, THE desert of broken stones and stinging dust in Potosí state, which extends into the state of Guanajuato, is relieved by the dramatic heights of the Sierra Madre, the wasteland flanked by magnificent mountains of sharp, shining granite peaks, some like shattered knives and others like fractured black bones, or marked with odd, inky splashes of obsidian. I had reclaimed my car from the hotel parking lot and set off in the morning from San Luis Potosí, and at Santa María del Río, where the good road ended, I was traveling south in sunshine, euphoric again, on the open road.

It was Saturday, market day, so I turned southwest onto side roads and came to the huddled town of San Diego de la Unión. After the big city of Potosí, I was attracted by its smallness, surrounded by the deep green meadows of Guanajuato state. I stopped simply to look around, in the idle curiosity that is available to any person with a car in Mexico and no particular place to go.

The image that dominated—a dazzling sight—on the main street of the town was that of small girls, nine or ten years old, dressed in shimmering white dresses with veils of white lace, their black hair neatly coiffed, some wearing white gloves, their faces whitened with powder, too, mascara on their dark eyes, their lips reddened—little brides in full makeup tripping down the cobblestone lanes. They were hovered over by adoring attendants, older women — mothers and aunts — and big sisters, serving as chaperones in humble street clothes, made humbler in their proximity to the exquisite princesses.

Fascinated, I followed them, and chatting on the way with admiring onlookers, I learned that the girls were headed to their First Communion at the twin-spired church in the center, the Parroquia de San Diego de Alcalá, named for the patron saint of the town.

It was a poor town — the meagerly stocked market was proof of that. The houses were plain, the side roads in bad repair; I imagined the place was hardly visited by outsiders. Mexican tourists flocked to San Luis Potosí for the lights, the plazas, and the restaurants, but there was not much in San Diego to detain a visitor.

I had been reminded in Potosí of Pritchett's insight, "The past of a place survives in its poor." Here was the strongest evidence of it: the finery of First Communion day, the persistence of the tradition of dressing the young girls in the white of purity and in a Saturday procession, the numbers growing as it passed through town, arriving at the parish church in a joyous parade, the girls, perhaps for the first time in their lives, elegantly dressed, the center of attention.

I waited until they had all filed into the church, the communicants, the families, the gawking townspeople — and these last included farmers, mechanics in blue overalls, and stallholders, some of them from the *carnicería*, their aprons gathered and bunched in their hands, the white cloth reddened with blood spatter from the slabs of cow meat, pigs' heads, and pigs' trotters they had knifed apart that morning.

I took a pew at the back and listened to the wheezing organ and the hymns sung with gusto by the people standing and swaying. When the parishioners were seated, the priest leaned from the carved pulpit and delivered a homily about innocence and purity, and he called upon the girls to come forward, which they did, on skinny legs and in white silken dresses. As they shyly tottered forward, the priest spoke about this special day, "a new day in your life."

"A special day," he added, mentioning the saint whose feast day this was, San Judas — not the betrayer, but Saint Jude Thaddeus, the patron saint of lost causes, last resorts, long shots, and dead ends, and perhaps because of the hope his image offers to desperate people, a popular saint in Mexican hagiology—the Saint Jude chapel in Potosí was plastered with scribbled appeals, and offerings, and flaming racks of votive candles. Saint Jude is the second-most-popular saint in Mexico. The most venerated one is Our Lady of Guadalupe, who appeared in 1531 at Tepeyac (a hill near Mexico City) to the Aztec peasant Juan Diego Cuauhtlatoatzin. The Virgin, speaking in his own language, Nahuatl, commanded him to build the much-visited shrine in her honor, which stands today. (But both of these saints have heavy competition in popularity from Santa Muerte, the robed skeleton whose bony image and lipless grin is everywhere.)

One by one the girls in white tiptoed to the altar rail and knelt to receive the host, their veils trembling as they tilted their heads back like choristers and put out their tongues.

I sat, comforted by the peacefulness of the occasion, buoyed by the smiles of pride on the faces of the relatives and friends, their pleasure in the old ritual, and in this poor town the beauty of the girls, dressed for the occasion.

Then I slipped out and walked the main street of San Diego de la Unión, looking for a place to eat.

A man squinting into the sun laughed when I asked him if there was a restaurant in town. Only *antojitos,* street food, he said, and not much of that; the nearest restaurants were in Dolores Hidalgo, a short distance away.

More back roads and blowing wildflowers and then another small town, but this one of great historical importance and much visited (thus the restaurants), celebrated as the birthplace of Mexican independence. The local priest and committed guerrilla fighter Don Miguel Hidalgo rang the church bells on September 16, 1810. He summoned the townsfolk, whom he energized by repudiating the Spanish conquerors with his *Grito de Dolores,* his Cry of Dolores, raising an army with a powerful denunciation of *malgobierno* and oppression—the beginning of the Mexican independence movement, but far from the end of Mexicans denouncing corrupt government, a cry heard all over the country to this day.

I dined on posole and grilled cactus leaves and returned to the road, heading for the nearby town of San Miguel de Allende.

## San Miguel de Allende: The Dark, the Light, and the Gringos

SMOOTH SAILING, SUNNY days, good roads, especially the country roads of Guanajuato—green pastures of browsing cows, old timber corrals and tile-roofed *ranchitos*, wildflowers, butterflies, and hawks drifting in the cloudless sky.

This is Mexico by day. But it is a delusion for anyone who travels in the country to believe this to be the whole story. From the mutters and guarded warnings, I became aware—as anyone would in the sinister rustling of these whispers—that there is a substratum of criminality even in Mexico's prosperous places, especially in the prosperous places, and it takes unexpected forms.

San Miguel de Allende is fussily picturesque, tastefully restored in parts, well preserved in others, and beautifully maintained in the retention of its traditions, the refuge of artists and weekenders from Mexico City and throngs of tourists both Mexican and foreign. In most respects the town is the apotheosis of highly colored Mexicana—a lovely plaza with trees, El Jardín, a baroque cathedral, many art galleries and souvenir shops, concerts most evenings, excellent restaurants, friendly bars, botanical gardens, and some four- and five-star hotels. All this and a salubrious city center, a town hospitable to eaters and drinkers and strollers and shoppers, as well as to thousands of retirees, most of them gringos.

Built against the steep slopes of the Hill of Moctezuma—its altitude of six thousand feet can moderate the pace of many gasping upslope trudgers—San Miguel has been a destination for expatriates since the late 1930s, when an American artist, Stirling Dickinson, helped found an art school (and attracted other arty expatriates), and later the Peruvian artist Felipe Cossío del Pomar, sent into exile for his left-wing views, received government permission to open an art school in the town's former convent.

The muralist and revolutionary David Alfaro Siqueiros (one of Los Tres Grandes—Orozco and Rivera were the others) taught mural painting here at the Escuela de Bellas Artes in 1948. His mural in the nuns' refectory in the convent is a bright patchwork of abstraction, even if incomplete: the story is that the temperamental artist abandoned it, and San Miguel, in a fit of rage. He and other visiting Mexican artists helped create a receptive mood of artistic congeniality in the town.

"The gringos came in large numbers after the Second World War," Lupita, the manager at my hotel, told me. Stirling Dickinson stimulated these arrivals. "They had the GI Bill and they liked the ambience here and the good weather."

It is still the haunt of potters and painters and pensioners. Thirteen thousand, or roughly 10 percent of the population, are expatriates, committed to living here and—rare for Mexico—the resident gringos, eager to give back, are engaged in any number of charitable projects. The philanthropy is a good idea, and is acknowledged by locals. But the dominant, or at least the most visible, presence is gringo. As foreigners, fairly well-off and living in a bubble, by its very nature privileged and parasitical like expat communities elsewhere in the world, they have a complex relationship with actual Mexicans, peasants generally, who are inevitably their menials. And also, like such places elsewhere, gringos are hyperalert to the servant problem, and the rattle of stories being swapped, the echo chamber that most expat communities become, places driven by gossip.

The colonial classicism is undiminished in the historical center of town, but the sprawl of trophy houses, mansions, condominiums, gated communities, and exclusive townhouses that clutter its margins have given it what seems like an unsustainable urban density and a maddening parking problem that makes being in San Miguel like being trapped in a cyclorama of colonial cuteness.

The building continues unchecked. When I asked about zoning or regulation, Mexicans smiled and made the money sign, not finger-rubbing but the Mexican version, a hand gesture, forming an upright claw with the thumb and forefinger.

San Miguel de Allende by most accounts is one of the most desirable retirement destinations in the world. Houses in its so-called planned communities, such as Rancho los Labradores, are priced in the millions, and so are the luxury townhouses behind secure gates in town, though many apartments and condos cost much less. But as with other towns in Mexico that attract the wealthy and well connected, San Miguel has its share of whispered crime stories and violent incidents.

Without warning, bombs were exploded in bars on three occasions in 2016, and some people were injured. No motive was established; perhaps extortion, intimidation, revenge—no one knew. There were no government investigations, no arrests, no police reports. The absence of verifiable news provokes rumors, and the whispers in San Miguel were that it was gang related. I asked a local man who owned a business not far away what he knew. "Probably a fight among narcos trying to stake their territory," he said. "It has not recurred since."

This was another example of the Mexican mantra, "There is no business without terror." Stories of nighttime muggings abounded, and I saw more policemen walking the beat in San Miguel than in any other place I passed through, as a reassurance to the retirees and an encouragement for more outsiders to take up residence.

Because much of San Miguel's prosperity rested on its real estate boom, many of the dark whispers I heard concerned land scams.

"I bought a building and fixed it up," a Mexican woman told me. "Then I bought an adjacent piece of land and thought I could put in some condos. This investment would see me into my old age, I thought. Years went by, I kept making improvements, renting the condos I'd built. And I was planning to sell everything when I got some bad news."

We were seated in a restaurant. She had been eating slowly as she spoke, and then she put her fork down, sipped some water, and tried to resume, but the memory of this bad news made her stammer and go silent.

I said, "It's all right. You can tell me some other time."

"We say, 'Better not to say too much about such things.'" She shook her head and went on. "At the tax office, when I was applying to pick up a copy of my deed, they said, 'That's not your deed. This land belongs to someone else. We have the deed here.' And they showed me the paperwork proving that my land, my building, the condos—everything—belonged to a man I did not know."

"How is that possible?"

"*Mordidas*," she said. "*Sobornos*." Bribes. She shrugged and went on, "A dishonest lawyer. A dishonest notary. They drew up a whole set of false papers which named this man as the owner of my property."

"That seems incredible," I said. "For one thing, it's about as crooked as anything can be."

"Yes," she said, and favoring her manicure, using her knuckles, she pushed her plate aside and stared toward a fountain that was plopping water into a basin. A hummingbird hovered, poked its beak into a nasturtium, backed away, hovered some more, and darted into a new flower, not flying but levitating itself from blossom to blossom.

"I can't sell if I can't prove I own it. And to prove I own it, I will have to show that this deed is a forgery. This could take years—and I'm not getting any younger."

The scam was diabolical, a stranger falsifying a deed of ownership, having it notarized and backdated, inserting himself into this woman's life by claiming that he owned her considerable property, and not only preventing her from selling it, but maintaining that he had owned it all along.

She swore that she would fight it, but that she had limited resources—her money was tied up in the property, in improvements and repairs. She had a lawyer, but she had no certainty that she would win against someone who was not only a crook but had enough money to bribe the officials who had connived to create the fake deed, pulling the rug—her own expensive rug and much else—out from under her.

She was a besieged woman, but a brave one, and I wished her luck. I heard other tales of land deals gone bad and the pressure for bribes in order to speed up transactions or anything requiring government permission. But these stories were mild by comparison with the saga of Walmart's corruption in Mexico, reported in the *New York Times* (December 17, 2012). Walmart wanted to build an enormous store near the ancient pyramids at San Juan Teotihuacán, outside Mexico City, much visited by tourists. But a zoning regulation specified that commercial development was prohibited near this historical area, elaborated on a zoning map. So Walmart bribed Mexican officials to redraw the map in its favor, the map was published, and the big-box horror store was built, its obscene size swelling over the pyramids. But this was not the end.

"Thanks to eight bribe payments totaling $341,000," the *New York Times* story continued, "Wal-Mart built a Sam's Club in one of Mexico City's most densely populated neighborhoods, near the Basílica de Guadalupe, without a construction license, or an environmental permit, or an urban impact assessment, or even a traffic permit. Thanks to nine bribe payments totaling $765,000, Wal-Mart built a vast refrigerated distribution center in an environmentally fragile flood basin north of Mexico City, in an area where electricity was so scarce that many smaller developers were turned away."

Still, San Miguel de Allende was praised by many for being a great place to live. The retirees who flocked there, and thronged it on weekends, have made it more Mexican, and for both sentimental and practical reasons have helped preserve its character, enlivened it with concerts, festivals, literary occasions, and art exhibitions.

But you could find such events in many retirement communities, I said to a man from California who had decided to make San Miguel de Allende his home during his later years.

He said, "Mexico is a great option for older retired people."

"For the cultural activities? The weather? The low cost of living? What?"

He said, "All of that. And in Mexico you can always find someone to look after you."

And cheaply. For 1,000 pesos, or $50, a week, you could hire a maid to work an eight-hour day (Sundays free), cleaning and making simple meals. Perhaps double that if she lived in. A night nurse would be about $25 a week. Gardeners and menials were paid a pittance.

It was easy to see why people were attracted to San Miguel de Allende. The city was made for strolling, for shopping, for drinking and dining. For almost a century, until 1990, the largest employer in the town had been Fábrica La Aurora, a textile factory, a fifteen-minute walk from the main plaza. When it closed, instead of tearing down the building, solidly made with a four-acre footprint, it was turned into a center for the arts—gallery upon gallery, with coffee shops and restaurants. Here and there iron clumps of machinery have been left on pedestals, looking like vorticist sculptures.

Most nights there's a concert on the bandstand in Benito Juárez Park, or in one of half a dozen theaters or concert halls. The plaza El Jardín hosts mariachi groups and elaborately staged music nights, such as one I came upon by chance, Grupo Mono Blanco—eleven musicians strumming and slapping their instruments, including a harp, ukulele, and mandolin, while a handsome hopping señorita in a gauzy gown swished her skirts, stamped, and flirted in a traditional step dance—the *jarabe tapatío*—whirling around a smug, round-faced young man dressed as a farm boy in a crushed straw hat, or perhaps mimicking the white monkey of the group's name, he too clicking his heels in a percussive, thumping dialogue of happy feet.

In the Parroquia San Miguel Arcángel, the iconic church—pink steeples, ornate facade, courtyard scuffed smooth by centuries of churchgoers, the weathered stone, like a superior cicatrized sand castle, abraded by light rain—I attended one of the many Mexican weddings that weekend, as an uninvited, eavesdropping celebrant. This display of elegance and poverty side by side—the elegance self-conscious, the poverty exuberant—resembled a Hieronymus Bosch painting or a Mexican mural, both alike in their portrayal of the grotesque in the flurry of their multilayered strangeness and their distortions of body types.

The wedding party was in the process of gathering, greeting and kissing in the cobblestone courtyard at the church entrance. The plump, nervous bride, flicking at her veil, posed in a voluminous gown and glittering tiara, attended by a bevy of young men in black suits, slicked-down hair, wide shoulders, and confident smiles; the bridesmaids, all shapes and sizes but dressed in identical purple gowns, stumbled badly in stiletto heels on the cobblestones. Surrounding them were potbellied matrons in tight dresses, portly husbands in yellow suits with stupendous sideburns and droopy mustaches, overdressed children, and heavily made-up crones in bombazine and shawls.

Add to this surrealistic spectacle of wealth the ragged children of San Miguel standing a few feet away, gawking and kicking at the stray, whining dogs, provoking them to bark at the wedding party, tugging balloons and pull toys. Workmen in paint-splashed overalls puffed on cigars and pointed, and shrouded white-robed nuns hovered over pots of soup, ladling it into bowls, while nearby at a smoking stove one woman was deep-frying meat and another slapping tortillas on a skillet.

As a spectacle, it was an opportunity for townspeople to gape, to tease, to eat, to become part of the throng, as a pack of imploring beggars lined up for alms, some with bowls of coins, others slumped, one nursing a child at her breast, another wildly gesturing to her comatose baby and pleading for help—and a few feet away, the taffeta gowns, the silken shawls, the gleaming suits, the misshapen wedding guests, grinding out their cigarettes under their expensive shoes in anticipation of the ceremony.

Then some trumpeted chords from inside the church, organ music. The wedding party stood at attention and, tugging at their clothes, began to shuffle through the archway and down the main aisle. It was easy to see, from the energy and enthusiasm of this eventful town, why people wanted to come here.

"*Reposado, tranquilidad*," Lupita, the hotel manager, said, praising the place.

But I was not looking for repose or tranquility. This weekend was an aberration. It is pleasant in Mexico to sit by the beach, inert and sunlit, sipping a mojito, but who wants to hear about that? What you crave in reading a travel narrative is the unexpected, a taste of fear, the sudden emergence by the roadside of a wicked policeman, threatening harm.

## A Shakedown: "How Can We Resolve This?"

I UPPED AND left San Miguel in a mellow mood early on a Monday morning of blue sky and sunshine, heading to Mexico City. I kept to country roads in order to bypass the big city of Querétaro, but after fifty miles I found myself back on a racetrack toll road, rolling into the outskirts of the city of twenty-three million. Half of this huge number of *chilangos*—as the Mexico City dwellers call themselves—are classified as enduring dire

poverty, many enjoying extreme wealth, and an estimated fifteen thousand children live on the street. Driving from the Periférico into the
sprawl—low hills of houses, dusty air, blur of distant buildings—the city
seemed immense and daunting, visibly ramshackle and overcrowded, an
almost unimaginable farrago of the nastiest version of urban life.

The sign BUENA VISTA stayed in my memory, not only because the
view of tenements and factories was unpleasant, but because it was near
there that a policeman on a motorcycle drew up next to me, indicating
with the fat finger of a leather-gloved hand that I must follow him.

In the heavy traffic—trucks, buses, speeding cars—this was a challenge, and what made it particularly difficult was that he led me to an
off-ramp of stalled vehicles, and then beyond it, to a side road and then,
bumping in front of me, into a series of slummy streets, where he came to
rest, waving for me to park behind him, in a barrio of rundown tenements,
in an alleyway, on a dead-end road.

Some startled pedestrians—poorly dressed, looking seedy—glanced at
me and then at the policeman and hurried away, ducking behind fences
and into doorways, and it was clear to me that they had a better idea of
what was about to happen than I did.

When the policeman dismounted, swaggering to my car, I could see
he was short and bulge-bellied, his face almost level with mine, and I was
seated. His helmet framed and seemed to squeeze his face, concentrating
the fury in his muscly cheeks, the cruel glint in his black eyes. But by
then—even as he approached, pigeon-toed in big boots—he was shouting at me.

I rolled my window down and said, "Good afternoon, sir."

His screams drowned me out, and at first I had no idea what he was
saying. I said, "My Spanish is poor. Please speak slowly."

"The license plates on your car. They are not Mexican plates. And you're
driving on our roads!"

"I have the documents. My Vehicle Importation Permit, my insurance,
my visa. Would you like to see them?"

They were in my briefcase, in the trunk, but I was hesitant to get out
of the car. I was much taller than the policeman, and he might make my

height a cause for provocation, but I also feared his physical proximity and felt safer speaking to him through the car window.

Interrupting me, he shouted, "What I am saying is that your plates are illegal. Do you understand? You are breaking the law by driving on our roads."

"I have a permit," I said.

He had now worked himself into a froth of spitting rage, and as he screamed out of his congested face I saw that he was wrapped in belts, a holstered pistol in one, handcuffs in another, a truncheon, a phone, chrome-plated chains, and his uniform was tight against his hard, fat body, as though in his fury, his body — in the way of some panicky animals — was swelling to add greater menace to his threat posture.

"Do you want to see my papers?"

The hot stink of this decaying part of the city clawed at my nose as he leaned and put his darkening face closer to me, shouting, "Do you know what I can do to you? I can take you over there" — he flapped his hand in the direction of the dark end of the alleyway where the slum dwellers had fled. "I can take your car. I can do what I want."

"*Sabes qué te puedo hacer?*" Do you know what I can do to you? Spoken by an enraged policeman in Mexico, that statement seizes your attention, and so does "*Puedo hacer lo que quiero*" — I can do what I want. After all, this is a country where police have been responsible for arbitrary killing, kidnapping, suffocation, and torture, including electrocution and medieval strappado. And in my anxiety, I remembered, because he had mentioned my license plates, how on some days of the week, certain cars, designated by the numbers on their plates, were prohibited. "*Hoy no circula*" — No driving today — to combat Mexico City's toxic (and visible as a brown cloud) air pollution.

I said, "Is it because I can't drive today with these plates? *Hoy no circula?*"

But he was too worked up to listen. His eyes were very small — tiny, dark pebbles, pierced with a wicked glint — and his nose was an enlarged snout, like a stabbing weapon. His gloved hands were now two leather fists. It seemed that his anger was partly theatrical, that he was amping up his shouts to intimidate me.

It worked. I was afraid. This *I can do what I want* was the most worrying threat. I have written elsewhere about how I have been frightened in travel, nearly always by someone with a gun—a boy in Malawi, a shifta bandit in the north Kenya desert, and three boys with rusty spears had accosted me in a lagoon in the Trobriand Islands, threatening to stab me to death. There was also the apprehension bordering on fear that I had felt, paddling on a river heading into Mozambique, when a fellow paddler—a Malawian, who knew this stretch of the river well—pointed to a reach in the stream ahead, a bank of mud huts partly hidden by tall reeds, and said, "There are bad people in that place"—a place we could not avoid passing.

Fear is a sense of physical weakness, the certain knowledge that you are trapped and helpless and in danger. And what made this sense emphatic was that all this time, as the policeman was screaming, local people—slum dwellers, barefoot children, women with bundles—were passing by, glancing at me, and moving on. They knew what was happening, and so I was also alarmed by their reaction—their fear was added to mine.

"I can take your car to the *corralón*."

I did not know this word, which he kept repeating. I should have figured it out—*corral* is clear enough, implying an enclosure. I later found out that *corralón* is a car pound or tow yard. But you do not simply pay a fine and pick up your car. You must first prove that you own the car, and this requires notarized documents, a lawyer, visits to various offices, and a fine of up to $500 for inconveniencing the police department and the car pound. Being berated by an infuriated cop in a side street of a slum, I did not know how serious that threat of a *corralón* could be.

But I was still alarmed. The accepted way to broach the subject of a bribe in Mexico is to say, "How can we resolve this?" ("*Cómo podemos resolver esto?*"), but I was too numb to remember this delicate proposal, so I said bluntly in Spanish, "What do you want?"

"Give me fifty."

"Fifty pesos?"

"Fifty dollars."

"I don't have fifty dollars." I took out my wallet. I had a twenty, some smaller bills, and a thickness of pesos. "Here," I said, and offered him a twenty-dollar bill.

Flicking it with his leather fingers, he said, "I want three hundred."

"You said fifty."

"It's now three hundred." His teeth were square and stained, his fat face pitted and crusted with badly healed acne scars.

"What's your name, sir?" I had found that sometimes that works to lower the temperature in a confrontation.

He screamed, "Antonio! Three hundred dollars!"

"Thank you, Antonio. I'm Paul." He had not seen any of my papers, nor asked to examine my license. "I am visiting Mexico. I have a visa and a vehicle permit. I am a pensioner. I don't have a job. I'm an old gringo—a gabacho. I'm not rich. I don't have three hundred dollars to give you."

"You have cards in your wallet"—silly me for opening the thing. "Use the ATM machine."

"Not possible."

He was breathing hard. "Go to a bank!"

"I can't do that." And the very idea of finding a bank in this squalid corner of Mexico City seemed laughable.

This provoked him to shouting, untranslatable fury, and I thought: He has the gun, the cuffs, the truncheon. He is the law. He can arrest me on any charge, or invent one. He can plant drugs on me. I can be locked up and lose my car.

"Excuse me." I got out of the car.

He did not back away, he hovered, and now the bystanders who had lingered to gape hurried off a little distance and eavesdropped on the scene from behind piles of rubbish and the tenement fence.

I went to the trunk of my car and, concealing my movements, slipped a fifty-dollar bill out of an envelope in my briefcase. I locked the trunk and handed him the fifty, the twenty, and some smaller bills.

"I said three hundred!"

"I don't have it."

"Get it! Go to a bank!"

It was past four o'clock on a hot afternoon in a Mexico City slum, and though I was being browbeaten by a cop on a side road, the roar of traffic on the overpass beyond the ruined buildings was unnerving—the beeping, the banging. And the number of bystanders had grown, the poor people fascinated to see a gringo offering a cop the equivalent (in Mexico City, at the lowest level, which this neighborhood was) of an average worker's three months' salary—and the cop slapping it away. I was fascinated but anxious, because this crooked cop was someone to fear, the embodiment of what all Mexicans fear: corrupt authority.

Meanwhile, I had gotten back into my car. I repeated that I was a *pensionado* and did not have the cash. He repeated that he wanted three hundred dollars, and his anger had not diminished, as with spittle on his discolored teeth he threatened me again with the *corralón* and the torture of endless litigation and documents.

Why did I not hand over the three hundred? I had, under pressure, handed over bribes many times before. Nothing moves in India without a bribe, and bribes had been demanded of me in China, Africa, Brazil, Pakistan, and Turkey. As I was seated in a cubicle in the immigration office of Ngurah Rai Airport in Denpasar, Bali, a frowning man in a uniform loomed over me and said, "Give me what I want or I put you on the next plane to Kuala Lumpur." (I gave him $120.) I'd had my wits about me in those places. But here I had become disoriented and somewhat irrational. I had forgotten the right answer. I was anxious, my senses assaulted, my heart fluttering, existing in a distorted reality in which time was suspended, as near to a surrealistic dream as I had ever experienced in travel.

And more (as I concluded later): I was too fearful to change my story of not having the money; and, of course, I did not trust him. If I gave him three hundred, he would demand more. Nor was I smart enough to figure out that his shout of taking my car and putting it into a *corralón* was a common threat, often acted upon. *I can do anything* was worrying, but for the moment, in the blur of my fear, my numbness of mind, I was too slow to react, and I suppose it seemed to him like stubbornness.

About fifteen or twenty minutes had passed—not a long time, normally, but a tortuous length of time in an intimidating interrogation endured in a back alley in a Mexico City slum.

Finally, in frustration, he screamed, "*Su billetera!*"

Wallet. I produced it.

"Open it!"

I opened it, and as I did, he put his stubby fingers in and took it all—the ninety or a hundred dollars, the thickness of pesos, perhaps two hundred altogether. He jammed it into his pocket.

"I want a receipt, please," I said.

He obliged, because this was a usual thing, and even the thievish police have rules, preventing a second cop from shaking you down. He took a scrap of paper and wrote: XL-TOTAL. DF-OMEGA, and the date and time. He handed it to me and rode off.

I sat quaking in my car for a while, and I was trembling and a bit breathless as I drove away. Stunned, in my delirium I took the wrong road. I kept driving, to calm myself, and I ended up two hours later on the road to Toluca, beyond the western edge of Mexico City. Because the cop had taken all my pesos, I could not use the toll road (cost: 40 pesos) that would have sped me back into the city.

So I followed the line of dawdling cars in the traffic jams that led to my hotel, La Casona, in the Roma district, arriving six hours late.

"I'm so ashamed," the hotel owner said when I arrived and told him my story, which he listened to, clucking. His name was Rudi Roth, from a Swiss family, but born and educated in Mexico. Rudi was an adventurer who said he liked my books, but he was braver than me—a yachtsman who had sailed alone across the Atlantic, a pilot who had flown solo all over Mexico in his small plane. He had suffered a debilitating stroke just a few months before and was now confined to a wheelchair. Sympathetic, highly intelligent, and courageous, he became a good friend. "But this does not happen very often." He was a *cazador*—a hunter.

Yet it did, again, not far from the hotel. Headed three blocks away to find the apartment house where William Burroughs had lived in 1950, with twenty-eight-year-old Jack Kerouac as his pot-smoking houseguest (at work on an early version of *On the Road*), I turned into their street, Calle Medellín, and did not see the DIRECCIÓN ÚNICA sign. I went perhaps fifteen feet into oncoming traffic and, promptly realizing my mistake, began to make a U-turn. As I was turning, a young policeman approached. He told me to wait. He beckoned another, older policeman, obviously his superior.

The senior officer was armed and well built, and he spoke to me in reasonable tones.

"You have broken the law," he said. "This is a one-way street. I can take your car. I can put it in a *corralón*. You will need to pay a lot of money to retrieve it, and it will require special papers and an attorney. I could also arrest you for breaking the law. A fine would be involved. You must realize how serious this is."

I did not challenge him. This was perhaps an intimation of what many people of color in the United States experienced from arbitrary stops by some police. I did not say that I was a pensioner, an old gringo without a job, wandering in his wonderful country. I said, "*Cómo podemos resolver esto?*"

He said, "Two hundred and fifty."

"Pesos?"

"Dollars."

I went to my hidden stash of money. I counted twenties into his hand. When I got to $240, he said, "Two-forty, okay," and stopped traffic so that I could complete my U-turn. And to my list of the inconveniences of life endured by Mexicans, I added: police.

My experience with the police was a piddling example of corruption, but a good lesson. Mexicans acknowledge that the police force in many towns is staffed by narcos, who extort and murder with impunity. The historian and anthropologist Claudio Lomnitz has written that the Mexican state exists on bribery and coercion. In a brisk, persuasive essay Lomnitz suggested three causes for this crisis of corruption. The state was weakened and bankrupted in the nineteenth century by fighting small, costly wars with Spain, France, the United States, and with its own indigenous peoples. Mexico's financial instability carried over into the twentieth century and beyond the Revolution of 1910.

So how is the country sustained? By informal trade—folks working outside the law—that dominates as much as two-thirds of the Mexican economy, and its improvisational infrastructure. This involves minor infractions, on the whole, millions of them. "But informal economies can only be regulated with petty corruption—by police who are bribed to look the other way." This corruption has become systemic, a way of doing business. Cops make money by shaking down anyone they can.

The narrow tax base is the second cause of corruption. Mexico, like Saudi Arabia, essentially a petrocracy, survives because 30 percent of its tax revenue comes from one reliable source—Pemex, the national oil industry. Most people don't pay tax, either because they are too poor or because they exist outside the system. "Such a narrow tax base fosters low levels of accountability."

"Mexico's quagmire of impunity has also been affected by the American drug and gun control policies." The border is historically lopsided, Lomnitz writes, describing the third reason. The US has criminalized the economy that services its vast appetite for drugs. This means that because Mexican law enforcement is weak and corrupt, "the temptation to outsource illegal activities is natural—even perfectly predictable." Border traffic is stimulated, too, because guns are banned in Mexico but sold freely in the States. The consequence is that Mexico pays "a disproportionate share of the cost of the American gun and drug habits," further weakening the state and creating paradoxes that are clearly apparent on the border.

For example, in the year Ciudad Juárez had a higher murder rate than Baghdad, El Paso, just across the river, was ranked as the second-safest city in the US. "But where did Juárez's drug gangs purchase their guns? El Paso. And where did the drugs that moved through Juárez end up? El Paso."

"You must be careful, Don Pablo," Rudi Roth said at his hotel. "Mexico is surrealistic."

Gabriel García Márquez, who had lived not far from Rudi's hotel, called Mexico City "Luciferian" and "as ugly a city as Bangkok." Leonora Carrington, an English expat, writer, and surrealist painter, whose studio was four streets south in this Roma district, on Calle Chihuahua, once said, "I felt at home in Mexico, but as one does in a familiar swimming pool that has sharks in it."

## *Juan Villoro: The Massacre*

IN THE PLAZA in San Luis Potosí, the defiant woman, loudly denouncing the government for not investigating the murders of the forty-three students in Ayotzinapa, had acknowledged that the writer Juan Villoro had written extensively about the massacre. Villoro was my friend, and soon after arriving in Mexico City we had dinner to discuss the teaching I had promised to do.

Tall, bearded, an athletic sixty-one, Villoro is one of Mexico's most accomplished and respected writers, a novelist, short story writer, playwright, and journalist. He writes about books, sports, politics, and rock music. He has a weekly column in *Reforma*, Mexico's largest newspaper, as well as a monthly column in Madrid's *El País*. He explained his work ethic and his being prolific as the necessity of a freelance writer in Mexico. "To make a living we have to keep writing."

A modest man, he deferred questions about himself and told me about his father. Luis Villoro was born in Barcelona in 1920 and began his study of philosophy there. In the turmoil of the Spanish Civil War, he moved to Belgium, where he continued his studies. Aware of the approaching shadow of World War II and the impending invasion of Belgium by Germany in 1940, he set his mind to emigrate to Mexico. Settled in Mexico City, he finished his degree in philosophy. He had written on Descartes, Wilhelm Dilthey (German philosopher, 1833–1911), Wittgenstein's *Tractatus*, political and medieval philosophy, and the ingredients of ideology. A close observer of the people in Chiapas, he wrote the seminal book on the consciousness of indigenous people, *The Major Moments of Indigenism in Mexico*. One of his books on systems of belief has the untranslatable title *Creer, Saber, Conocer*. These are subtle variations on the Spanish verb "to know," for which we have only one English word, with multiple shades of meaning.

"An amazing man," I said. "A great mind."

"With an eye for the ladies," Juan said. "He had five wives. My mother was his first wife."

Juan was reluctant to talk about himself, but I had read his work and knew he was well read and widely traveled, and having lived and studied for periods in the United States, he spoke English with casual fluency, often using colloquialisms he picked up from his knowledge of rock music. The author of more than thirty books, he has won a number of literary awards, notably the prestigious Herralde Prize, for his novel *El Testigo* (*The Witness*). A collection of short stories, *The Guilty*, and a novel, *The Reef*, have appeared in translation.

"Welcome," he had emailed, when I told him I'd arrived and explained the circumstances. "You can always count on the Mexican police for an illegal surprise!"

We met at La Casona—Rudi Roth was his friend and former schoolmate—and walked to a restaurant nearby called MeroToro. We shared the specialties, the hog jaw (*quijada de cerdo*) and the fettuccini with rabbit, and then—this being Mexico: tasty food, grisly murders—he told me about the fate of the students from Ayotzinapa.

"I have to go back a bit and explain the school," Juan said. "Lázaro Cárdenas, our best president, in the late 1930s, was deeply interested in education and encouraged the growth of rural schools. For many years we had *escuelas normales*, which were meant to prepare teachers to go to the countryside, to teach in these schools. In the beginning there were thirty or more *escuelas normales*, but these days there are only thirteen."

Now he smiled a grim smile and shook his head, so I asked the obvious question: "Why so few?"

"The Mexican government began to close the schools for various reasons—in any case, rural schools are not a priority in this country. Teachers in the schools criticized the situation, because the reasoning behind the closures was so unfair." He leveled his gaze at me and said with conviction, "The government, so corrupt."

Juan had impressed me in years past by speaking publicly of government corruption in Mexico, and had repeated the assertion in his newspaper columns. His straightforwardness, imaginatively set out, is but one reason to value Villoro's work.

"As a result of this government attitude, many rural teachers became social activists—and some even became *guerrilleros,* including some of the teachers and students at Ayotzinapa. This happened early. One teacher was Lucio Cabañas, who was kidnapped and killed. Another was Genaro Vázquez Rojas, who was also killed. Both of these murders were in the 1970s."

"What had they done to be singled out?" I asked.

"They wished to change the rural schools, like the other teachers, and to liberalize education." He smiled again, and a smile from Juan Villoro always seemed to introduce a contradiction. "But consider this. After 1968 there was a lot of rhetoric by the government calling for an open country. At the same time they were repressing social activists in the state of Guerrero."

"Why there exactly?"

"The rural schools," he said—implying new ideas, a kind of enlightenment. "Education in Mexico turns people into activists. They see problems. But in Mexico it's very hard to find direct solutions to problems."

"You mean solutions arising from the government's actions?"

"Yes," he said. "The idea is usually, 'Let them solve it themselves. Give them time. Ignore them.' Look at the Zapatistas. After all this time"—he meant since the uprising by the Zapatista Army of National Liberation in 1994—"they now have health, education, and welfare. They have created a country within a country."

It seemed he had gone off on a tangent, because he had started by saying that the *escuelas normales,* which produced teachers for the rural schools, had become fewer and fewer. How had that happened?

"Okay—there's an unwritten law that if a school has no new students, the school has to be closed. 'We have to close the school,' they say. 'There aren't enough students to justify keeping them open.'"

"But that makes sense. If there are no new students, why should the school be kept open?"

Juan raised his hand in a cautioning way and said, "But why are there no new students? The reduced numbers are caused by various means—lots of obstacles. The government 'forgot' to send applications, or 'forgot' to process them. Or they 'lost' the applications. Or they simply ignored the whole application process."

"Suppressed the entry of students," I said.

"Exactly. The students had to fight for their education, and when this happens a fighting tradition is developed in which social struggle is part of their education. Fighting against poverty, they become social activists simply by being students. Their enemies are the corrupt politicians and drug lords"—he smiled again and paused for emphasis—"who are often the same. The real owners of the state of Guerrero."

I said, "It's as though it's a settled belief by the Mexican government that any defiance is subversive. The poor, objecting to being poor, are subversive."

"Especially in Guerrero."

Guerrero may not be widely known to non-Mexicans, but many of its cities and towns are, notably the coastal resorts on the Pacific: Acapulco, Ixtapa, and Zihuatanejo, the luxury hotels and the beaches. The tiny town of Ayotzinapa, however, was in the poverty-afflicted hinterland, the mountainous dead center of the state.

"I am the grandfather of this generation," Juan said. "I try to guide them. They are fighting for the right to study, and in the process they become activists. For example, as a protest they closed the main highway to Acapulco—the Autopista del Sol, and in that action, two students were killed by police—Federales."

That was in 2002, but closing the main road from Acapulco to Mexico City was a standard form of protest—nonviolent but disruptive. Just five months before my dinner with Juan, teachers in Guerrero occupied two tollbooths on the Autopista del Sol, allowing motorists to drive through only after handing them pamphlets explaining the reasons behind their strike. They also demanded the handover—alive—of the forty-three missing students from the Ayotzinapa teachers' college.

"Students are used to closing highways as part of their protests—or commandeering buses. It's an accepted tactic."

The students have no money, no vehicles, no access to the power structure. I said, "It's class warfare."

"Yes."

As we talked, we continued to eat, and I was writing down Juan's words
in my notebook—ideal, really, because I could ask him to repeat certain
statements, or spell names, or clarify his assertions. And this was a small,
quiet restaurant, where we sat without interruption. We were now served
a chocolate dessert, and somehow this delicacy made me self-conscious
about our peaceful surroundings and the bitter conflict he was describing—typical Mexican incongruity.

I said, "What about the forty-three students?"

"I was coming to that. You need to know the background—the plight
of the rural schools. The attitude of the government—suspicion and oppression." He sat back in his chair and said simply, "The situation was
structurally damaged from the beginning."

He reminded me of another massacre, the killing in 1968 of four hundred or more students by Mexican army sharpshooters in the Plaza de las
Tres Culturas in the Tlatelolco section of Mexico City. And how, after
1968, the government was suspicious and disapproving of any gatherings
of youths. Concerts were banned. Rock music was forbidden to be played
on the national radio station, and these sanctions had lasted about ten
years, at which time Juan himself started a radio program, featuring Led
Zeppelin, Pink Floyd, and David Bowie. But no one forgot the horror of
the 1968 massacre.

"So, in September 2014, the students in Ayotzinapa were preparing an
event to commemorate that massacre. They needed money to go to the
capital of Guerrero state, but having none, they took five buses."

"Commandeered the buses?"

"Yes, as I said, this was a normal tactic. Just using buses at random. It
was not a problem at first. A large group of students went to the town of
Iguala for the buses. They were escorted by the local police, the Federales,
and the army. Then the commander in chief of the armed forces, who was
in charge of the whole action, said the buses had to stop. The mayor was

in touch with all the forces the whole time. Why did the buses stop at that precise moment?"

"*Quién sabe?*"

"The mayor's order. Because of one particular bus, which was equipped to smuggle drugs to the US—very sophisticated concealments and compartments. A similar bus was stopped in Chicago some years ago, a normal-looking bus but full of drugs inside the walls."

"This mayor was part of the plot?"

"José Luis Abarca, a known and proven drug lord—he's in jail now. His wife was also an accomplice. He had killed people. He's a criminal. This is an established fact."

"And the students?"

"Abducted," Juan said. "Disappeared. Obviously killed. International experts came and unearthed most of the story. But when they asked if they could interview members of the army, permission was not granted. So a great deal of the story is untold. But because the bus had drugs on it, they recovered it and killed and cremated the students who were on it, after kidnapping them."

"What was the point of killing them?"

"If they were aware of the drugs in the bus, and the collusion of the police and the drug lords, they were witnesses who had to be dealt with. This is such a violent country, they wouldn't think twice about killing forty-three students."

"After all this time no one has gotten to the bottom of it?"

"It is known that the students were killed. But where are the bodies? Only two have been found. The government has done everything possible to obstruct justice."

"But why?"

"They are counting on people to forget."

But in a poor country, people value what little they have: their dignity, their lives, their children most of all—and their long memories. Their memories are merciless.

· · ·

They remembered everything—the students who survived, the teachers, the grieving parents, the bystanders, the bus drivers. And when the American journalist John Gibler (*Mexico Unconquered, To Die in Mexico*) traveled to Iguala and Ayotzinapa to seek these people out, and over a two-year period listened to their stories, he heard things that surprised even Juan Villoro. His account of these revelations appeared a few months after my dinner with Juan. *I Couldn't Even Imagine That They Would Kill Us*, Gibler's book, contains the testimonies of scores of people who witnessed the massacre or suffered in the aftermath of the mass kidnapping.

As Juan had said, the students from—to give it its full name—the Raúl Isidro Burgos Rural Teachers' College of Ayotzinapa had hoped to find some buses to take them to an event in Mexico City, a demonstration and memorial service to commemorate the massacre in 1968 by the Mexican police and military (and hidden snipers) at Tlatelolco. This action was ordered by the Mexican president, Gustavo Díaz Ordaz, who later denied that a massacre had taken place, calling it a confrontation. The anniversary was October 2. The Ayotzinapa students set out on September 25 to commandeer the buses in Iguala. They were attacked the next day, six murdered in skirmishes on the highway in Iguala, one left in a coma with a bullet to the head, and forty-three Ayotzinapa students, most of them nineteen or twenty, one of them seventeen, abducted, "forcibly disappeared," a monumental *levantón* in which none of the *levantados* were heard of again.

The only trace found of the forty-three students was a single bone fragment, which was later proven to have been planted by the police to back up a concocted story. The detail that Juan had heard, about the one bus possibly containing heroin to be smuggled north, was mentioned to Gibler by various informants. But there were five buses, and all of them were attacked.

What emerges from the eyewitnesses to the armed assault on the buses is the shock of the students, which is reflected in the title of the book. They knew there might be a hassle or an argument, but they had not imagined that the police would shoot to kill. Taking buses to attend a demo was an accepted practice—many bus drivers colluded with the students and used the hijacking of their buses as an excuse to spend a few restful days off.

In testimony after testimony, the students described to Gibler the buses setting off and, within minutes, the horror of being ambushed by the municipal police, the windows shattering, bullets flying, students being hit—many were wounded—the sight of blood and shattered bones. And then the police boarding the buses, screaming insults, demanding names, threatening the students, and dragging them away. The chain of voices in the book is consistent, one account backing up another, and adding detail. But all of it comes from the students' point of view, and the effect is chaotic—fearful, frustrating, a hellish bewilderment, as the assault continues into the night, the students refusing to leave their fallen comrades, seeking help.

But no one helped. Forty students were wounded, many of them seriously with gunshot wounds. Even when their fellow students managed to take the injured to various hospitals—bleeding, some in grave condition—they were met with indifference from nurses and contempt from doctors. One doctor who refused to attend to the wounded students, interviewed by Gibler, dismissed the whole business and denigrated the students as agitators. "That school is worthless," the medical man told Gibler. And the students, the *ayotzinapos,* "they are criminals." Their protests are disruptive—"dirty, ugly"—they deserve what they got. A bullet-riddled corpse of one student found on the street had its face flayed and its eyes gouged out. The limbs of others had been severed.

"So, cutting off their faces, taking out their eyes, cutting off their limbs, and incinerating their bodies," Gibler asks the doctor, "that seems right to you?"

"Yes," the doctor replies. "Truthfully, yes."

Sorting the evidence, examining the accounts, Gibler proved that the government explanation for the killings and abduction was false and self-serving—untrue that a cartel masterminded it, that students were mistaken for a rival drug gang, that after the kidnapping the forty-three students were shot, their bodies incinerated at the local trash dump, and their ashes put in bags and tossed into the Iguala River.

"An overwhelming amount of evidence describes a very different reality," Gibler writes. "On September 26–27, 2014, scores of Iguala, Cocula, and Huitzuco police collaborated with Guerrero state police and federal police to carry out hours of horrific violence against unarmed college students, while the Mexican army watched from the shadows."

About those police: they are not the protectors they seem. Gibler was assured by various people in the know in Iguala—among them a journalist and a city councilwoman—that there is no separation between the police and the narcos. Almost the entire police force is comprised of narcos in police uniforms, using police weapons and squad cars. They are known as *los bélicos* (the belligerents), and it was they who carried out the assault on the students.

"In Mexico, police and military at every level have fully merged with forces of organized crime," Gibler concludes. "It is no longer accurate to speak about corruption—if it ever was."

But why did the attack happen? Why the deaths? Why were the forty-three students kidnapped, and why have they never been found? These questions are not answered in Gibler's book, nor can answers to them be found in any other book, nor in any official report, nor by the students' parents or any informants.

What is clear is that the prevailing tone of the attackers is vindictiveness—against protesting students, their leftist views, their civil disruption, and their actions resulting in social dislocation. The resentful attitude of the doctors and nurses who were so little help to the wounded reflects this bitterness. The students—poor, despised, studying at a small rural college known for its radical views—were hated for their taking buses, hated for their ideas, hated for their sense of grievance and political activism.

One theory finds the mayor and his wife behind it all. As Villoro said, the mayor, José Luis Abarca, was also a drug lord. His wife, María de los Ángeles Pineda Villa, was ambitious politically (as well as related to members of a powerful local cartel), and on the night of the killings and kidnappings, she was hosting a celebrity event in Iguala, speaking to dignitaries, and (perhaps) ordered the police action so her speech would not be disrupted. She disappeared with her husband after the night of mayhem, but the couple was eventually found, arrested, and jailed, though not convicted of any crime. To this day, the Mexican government has not charged anyone with the abduction and disappearance of the forty-three students. The pain of this injustice has been traumatic.

"Something about the events in Iguala—the combination of horror, state culpability, and well-crafted official incompetence—struck at the very core of a people exhausted by violence and government depravity," Gibler writes of the aftermath. "Anger was everywhere palpable."

The anger has not subsided, the protests continue, and the grieving parents ("victims of our own government," one mother says, "because we are campesinos") go on seeking answers and have refused any money as compensation: "Our children are not for sale."

Wishing to know more, I wrote to John Gibler and asked him about the Mexican government's involvement in the massacre.

"There is an overwhelming amount of documented information as to federal involvement in the attacks," Gibler wrote me. "But also, and this is a key point for me and something I try to emphasize in the afterword [of the book]: I consider the federal government's 'cover-up' to be a part of the attacks themselves. Since 43 students were and continue to be disappeared, the violence is not only contained or concentrated in the past (as with the murders and injuries) on the night of the initial physical aggression. The violence, material as well as emotional, against the students and their families is maintained and extended into the present by the act of forced disappearance.

"The administration of that disappearance—the lies and torture and omissions carried out by the federal government in its cover-up—is itself constitutive of the atrocity."

He went on to say that the federal government, having connived in the cover-up, cooked up evidence, destroyed the evidence of eyewitnesses, and tortured people to force them to lie. Though all of this crookedness had been documented by independent investigators, the government continued to falsify its part in the massacre.

"There is no doubt that the federal government participated in the attacks," Gibler went on. "And there is no doubt that the federal government coordinated a massive and grotesque cover-up. What we still do not know is why. You ask: What motivated the attacks? The GIEI [the Group of Interdisciplinary Independent Experts, impartial lawyers and human rights advocates] poses the hypothesis that the students may have unknowingly commandeered a commercial bus loaded with a major heroin shipment.

"That is a logical hypothesis that could explain the chaotic and escalating nature of the attacks. If it were to be proven it would show that, indeed, the police and army control and administer the drug trade. However, I think that independent of the motivation that sparked the attacks, the precise nature of the brutality—the combination of killing, mutilation, and mass forced disappearance—was targeted directly at the students for being radical, organized, poor; rural and indigenous students of a school noted for its anti-government organizing and historic links to insurrectionary armed movements."

Ayotzinapa is tragic but instructive, and every aspect of it explains the mood of Mexico, from the poor, to the middle-class doctor or dentist who sees students as complainers, to a government that feels no obligation to be fair. People in power—police, politicians—believe they can get away with murder. Above all, Ayotzinapa reveals the penetration of the cartels in all Mexican institutions.

This is also why an authority figure who demonizes Mexicans and stereotypes them with insults—such as the American president—or who belittles the poor and subjects them to arbitrary arrest, is a familiar tyrant, inspiring cynicism. Mexicans spend very little time railing against the US government, because in their experience, government by its very nature is corrupt, often criminal, and the poor are its victims.

## El Taller, the Workshop

WITHOUT WARNING, AN invitation was circulated by the Mexican writer Guillermo Osorno to a number of Mexican novelists, editors, journalists, and broadcasters, asking whether they would be interested in taking part in a *taller* ("tuh-*yair*"), a workshop, for ten days at the Centro Horizontal, a cultural center on Colima Street in the Roma Norte district of the capital. Greater Mexico City had been particularly hard hit by the recent Puebla earthquake — there were areas of fallen houses, closed-off streets, yellow warning tape, and avenues piled with the rubble of collapsed walls. And much later someone said to me that because of the trauma of the event, many citizens yearned to be part of a sympathetic group, to talk, to write, to share stories, to ease the pain wrought by the earthquake.

The recipients of the invitation were asked to submit a piece of their writing. If it was deemed suitable — intelligent, original, well written — a place would be reserved for its creator, and tuition was free.

Nor was the teacher to be paid. But it was suggested that the teacher — a gringo writer — might wish to improve his Spanish. And though the classes, mainly conducted in English, would be held from ten to noon each day, any students who were inclined might have lunch together with the teacher — more literary discussion — or go on field trips to sights in the city in the afternoon. A further detail: this gringo writer was self-supporting and had no connection to the American embassy or any foreign organization.

I was the gringo writer. Juan Villoro and Centro Horizontal's director, Guillermo Osorno, examined the entries and chose twenty-four students. They were young and middle-aged, a few oldish, men and women, all of them accomplished, most from Mexico City but others from the nearer cities of Querétaro and Cuernavaca, or more distant places, Oaxaca and Durango. One was American but a longtime Mexico resident, another had dual Mexican-US citizenship. They were bright, funny, insightful, generous, and friendly, glad to be included in the ten days of talk and writing, and most of them spoke English well.

They were candid, too, and all but one — Adán Ramírez Serret, an impish, genial fellow but a tenacious and resourceful journalist — had been to the United States. Valerie Miranda, the dual citizen, worked for an important internet site, dividing her time between its offices in Los Angeles and Mexico City. Valerie was a stylish, dark-haired woman of Mexican and Scandinavian ancestry, taller than the average Mexican, and could have passed for English, French, or American, an ambiguity that was at the heart of the story she told on the first day of the class.

"My husband and I were in Utopia, Texas—please take note of the name—with my husband's friend," Valerie said, standing and commanding the attention of the room. "We decided to get a cup of coffee, and he was talking with his friend on the sidewalk, so I said that I would get the coffee. One thing I should say—my husband and his friend look very Mexican. I know I don't look Mexican in a conventional way. There was a line inside the coffee shop, but I didn't mind waiting. Pretty soon I heard a man behind me say, 'There's a couple of Mexicans outside. Let's go fuck them up.' I slipped out and told them we had to leave at once."

In the shocked silence that followed, Diego Olavarría signaled with his hand. He was a slender, bearded fellow, his head often cocked to one side in a scrutinizing way, who described himself as a *cronista*, a chronicler, an occupation to which I could relate.

"I was in Liège, Belgium," he said, stroking his frizzy beard. He was as fluent in English as Valerie, and as young. "A friend and I nearly got in a fight with three xenophobic teenagers. One of them appeared to be of North African descent, and the other two might have been Eastern European. They came at us on a dark street in a bad neighborhood, late at night, and hurled a lighter at us. They then insulted us and demanded that we speak French. My friend and I had been speaking in Spanish, and this apparently sparked the whole confrontation. They yelled, *Tu es en Belgique! Parle français! Parle français!*"

The class murmured at Diego's sudden lapse into French.

"This xenophobia was quite a surprise," he went on. "I wondered if, many years before, their parents had been yelled at or harassed for not speaking the language. Perhaps these kids felt it was their turn to exact revenge on those who seemed even more like outsiders than themselves. Either way, it was sad. In the end, we walked away unscathed, but disheartened."

Valerie's and Diego's helpful candor and their ability to tell a story set the tone of the workshop. I blessed my luck that I would have a week or more with such wonderful students, and told them how—a traveler's blessing—I felt I now had twenty-four friends.

In the trunk of my car were thirty-odd books that I had brought from home, all of them Spanish translations of my own books: *La Costa de los Mosquitos, En el Gallo de Hierro, Mi Otra Vida, El Tao del Viajero, Elefanta Suite*, and other titles that had been accumulating in boxes in my basement. I took them to class the first day and gave them out to those who could answer my literary quiz.

They looked a bit apprehensive. Students hate being conspicuously quizzed.

My questions were at first all Mexico related: Who wrote *Mexico City Blues*? In what city did *Under the Volcano* take place? Name D. H. Lawrence's Mexico novel. Give the titles of Graham Greene's, Aldous Huxley's, and Evelyn Waugh's Mexico books. B. Traven wrote *The Treasure of the Sierra Madre*—what was his true nationality, and name another book by him set in Mexico. What gringo poet died leaving Mexico by ship? What American writer supposedly died in Chihuahua?

They correctly answered all except the Waugh (*Robbery Under Law*) and the last two: Hart Crane and Ambrose Bierce. Having run out of Mexico questions, I asked them more general ones: What novel begins, "Call me Ishmael"? Who wrote the short story "The Lady with the Little Dog"? What novel begins, "Stately, plump Buck Mulligan came from the stairhead, bearing a bowl of lather"? Which writer began a poem, "Whose woods these are, I think I know"?

They missed the Chekhov short story, but they got the rest. I felt I was in good hands.

Then Héctor Orestes Aguilar piped up, saying he had a question for me. "Sir, can you tell me which novel begins, 'The past is a foreign country; they do things differently there,' and who wrote this novel?"

Putting the new teacher on the spot on the first day of class is an age-old tease, and a challenge, a form of veiled hostility, a student's way of asserting power and entertaining his fellow students. One of the older students, formally dressed, wearing a blue necktie, Héctor had the look of a bureaucrat or an insurance salesman.

I asked him, please, to repeat the question, which he did, with a greater air of pedantry than the first time.

"That's a hard one," I said, and saw him smile with renewed confidence. "I wonder if anyone in the group knows the answer."

Héctor glanced around the room, defying anyone to reply. But in the general shaking of heads it seemed that no one knew, not even Villoro or Osorno.

"Can you give us a hint, Héctor? Or any sort of clue?"

"So you don't know this?" Héctor said.

"*Estoy pensando,*" I said, and put my fist to my head, a thinking gesture.

Now the class began to squirm, because it seemed that Héctor had gone a bit too far, revealed himself as a wise guy, a *sabelotodo,* a *listillo,* or even worse, a *pedante,* amusing enough in an informal setting of guys yakking in a bar, but unwelcome in a classroom in an attempt to show up the new teacher.

To create a more excruciating atmosphere of suspense and give Héctor an air of superiority, I made the most of my hesitation. I put on a ham actor's pained expression. I clawed my hair. But realizing that I was over-doing it, that the students were embarrassed for the gringo, I spoke up.

"They're the first lines of *The Go-Between,* by L. P. Hartley, English writer," I said, and seeing that Héctor was deflated, I went closer to where he was seated and asked, "Now please tell me, if you can, the names of other novels that L. P. Hartley wrote."

After this banter, I told them why I was traveling in Mexico: because the notion of ranging widely in a big country attracted me, and because in the United States, under the current presidential administration, Mexico and Mexicans had been reduced to stereotypes. One great reason to travel, I said, was to destroy the stereotypes.

"By driving from my home, I hoped to show that we are close," I said. "I get in my car and drive south, and in a week or so I'm over the border." I let this sink in, and then said, "Friends, we're on the same road."

Each day we would deal with a different subject, I said. Today would be about travel, about leaving home. And on successive days: memory, wit-ness, reading, and writing. During the ten days they would write a short story. I would suggest some subjects. At the end of the workshop we would read and discuss them.

And so I encouraged them to talk about travel, about the changes they felt in their mood and self-awareness in separating themselves from home. One by one they described this experience, the individuation so important to the creative process.

"I have traveled in Ethiopia," Diego Olavarría said. He had also spent time in Cuba and Honduras, and had reported on them. He was a slender, frizzy-bearded young man in his mid-twenties whose English was precise. He had studied in the United States, worked as a translator, and published a book on Ethiopia, *El Paralelo Etíope*, which I discovered later had been awarded a coveted literary prize in Mexico.

Diego spoke about the discoveries in his African travel, about the poverty he'd seen. But he also said that if Oaxaca and Chiapas were sovereign nations, they would be among the poorest in the world.

Others spoke up: Claudia Muzzi, of Italian ancestry, had traveled in Italy and indeed spoke Italian. But her most memorable experiences had been in the United States, specifically in Georgia. She planned to write about it later in the week.

Héctor was not the bureaucrat I suspected him to be, but rather a former diplomat, linguist, and essayist. He had served for many years in the Mexican diplomatic service, as cultural attaché in embassies in Belgium, Austria, Slovakia, Hungary, Bulgaria, Croatia, and elsewhere. He spoke German and French, and had traveled widely in Europe. He urged us all to read L. P. Hartley.

Luisa was an editor of a travel magazine who had visited many countries. Raúl was a broadcast journalist who had lived for years in El Centro, California, and reported on the border. Ernesto was a businessman and an aspiring poet. Emilio was a scientist who had camped in many countries, studying meteorology, and he was an artist, too, who'd exhibited his work in Europe. Yael Weiss was from a Mexican Jewish family and had had a memorable experience in Las Vegas, Nevada, which she would write about. Rosi Zorrilla was an art dealer and writer. Michael Sledge, the American, was writing a novel based on the life of Edward James, an English aristocrat (and perhaps illegitimate son of King Edward VII), a collector of surrealist paintings, and the creator of a mansion (La Pozas) and fabulous garden near Xilitla, in San Luis Potosí state. Guadalupe Nettel was a mother of two and, as I was to discover, a well-known writer — several of her books had been translated into English.

Others were just as singular and well traveled and full of promise. I felt I was in good hands. We talked that first morning about leaving home in order to fulfill literary ambitions, the obstacles to becoming noticed or published, and — these days — the difficulties of traveling to the United States. It used to be so simple, they said.

Julieta, who had said she had begun to write about the behavior of dogs, and who spoke candidly about how she had been married twice, to the same man, after an interval of separation, said, "What would you like to do, and how can we help?"

"One of my ambitions in Mexico City is to see the chapel of Santa Muerte," I said. "I've heard it's tucked away in a corner of the city and that it's worth seeing. I've been to a Santa Muerte chapel in the north, but this is supposed to be where pilgrims go."

I had spoken with enthusiasm and eagerness, but when I finished, hoping for a response, none came. I filled the awkward silence by saying how I'd also seen images of Holy Death on the border, usually in the poorest huts and colonias.

"Could be dangerous," Diego said at last, and as a traveler in El Salvador and Ethiopia, he knew a thing or two about danger. "They might object to our visiting. They might prevent us. There could be trouble. I think we should talk to someone beforehand. Maybe later in the week."

"Have any of you been there?"

No, in murmurs, around the room, like the rustle of leaves, the susurrus slowly dying away to a vibrant silence.

"Do you know where it is — the church?"

More murmurs, the students conferring, a shaking of heads: no one had a clue.

"So this is something we have to do!" I said, and they laughed.

"Let's eat first," Julieta said, and six of them took me to Coyoacán, to a restaurant called Los Danzantes, at the edge of the plaza of gardens, Jardín Centenario, a fountain splashing nearby, children playing, some strolling musicians plunking guitars.

The first course was *hierba santa*—sacred leaf, a green aromatic leaf with soft, warm cheese.

"Coyoacán was once a small village," Julieta said.

"It was part of the lake," Guadalupe said.

And then we were served *tacos con chapulines*—tacos with toasted grasshoppers.

"Hernán Cortés lived here," Adán said.

With a Mexican sense of historic time, Adán cast his mind back five hundred years and imagined the conquistador in his hacienda at 57 Higuera Street, though there is no sign that he lived here with his mistress, Doña Marina, known as La Malinche.

About twenty years ago a reporter knocked on the door of Cortés's house and asked why a place that represented a defining moment in national history was not a museum. Cortés, after all, wrote his chronicles here. The owner of the house, Rina Lazo, a painter, said, "For Mexico to make this house a museum would be like the people of Hiroshima creating a monument for the man who dropped the atomic bomb." And as for the mistress, La Malinche, the name was a form of abuse—to be a *malinchista* was to be a lover of foreigners, a traitor.

Meanwhile, Adán was tugging my sleeve, saying, "And Frida Kahlo and Trotsky."

"We can walk to their houses later," Rosi said. "Here's your tortilla soup, Don Pablo. Have some wine."

And I thought: I am content. I have achieved that elusive objective in travel—a destination. I have arrived. I am happy, one of the hardest moods to describe.

As I was finishing my soup, the fried plantains were served, then a plate of split-open cow bones, gelatinous gray matter trembling inside.

"We call it *tuétano*," Rosi said.

"Cow marrow," Raúl said.

"None for me, but I can tell you these are femurs," I said, poking the bones with the tines of my fork and realizing I was slightly drunk. "Notice this knob or head, which connects to the pelvic bone." They laughed as another plate was slid onto the table. "Ah, more tacos."

"*Patos,*" Yael said. "Ducks."

Then tostadas with tuna tartare, cactus leaf, corn smut, more grasshoppers, pork belly (*base de nopal, huitlacoche, chapulines, y chicharrón*), and more.

Raising her glass, Julieta, in a tipsy giggle, uttered something to the effect that we had "*cogieron demasiado.*"

To the laughter—had I heard that right?

She corrected herself: "*Comieron demasiado!*"

That's better: not "fucked too much" but "ate too much." *Coger* versus *comer. Coger* is "to take" in Spain, but "to fuck" in Mexico.

We talked about words. Rosi said, "*Gilipollas* is used in Spain, not here. When we want to say 'asshole,' we say *pendejo* or *cabrón,* but *que cabrón* can be praise, too."

"What kind of *cabrón* is Donald Trump?"

At first they wouldn't be drawn out, but it was now late in the afternoon, and we were sitting among the splashings and remnants of a long lunch, platters of tacos, ripped tortillas, some long bones of cow marrow, and lip-smeared wineglasses.

"He does not like us at all," Raúl said.

Trump's crude insults were well known, and they were so hurtful in their stinging bluntness that most Mexicans I'd asked about them just shrugged, regarding it as beneath them to comment. Of Mexican immigrants he had said, "They're bringing drugs. They're bringing crime. They're rapists." And, "The Mexican legal system is corrupt, as is much of Mexico." To the cheers of his supporters, he'd crowed, "Mexico is not our friend."

"Worse than a *cabrón,*" Rosi said. "And different."

"Give me a word," I said.

"*Mamón,*" she said. "Thinks he's better than anyone."

*Mamón* is cocky. The literal meaning is unweaned, still suckling. But in colloquial Mexican Spanish it has a much broader meaning, implying conceited, idiot, scrounger, dickhead, mooch, jackass.

"*Estúpido,*" she added. "*Boolgar*"—her pronunciation of *vulgar.*

"*Cínico*," Guadalupe said. "*Mentiroso*"—liar. "*Engreído*"—vain.

"*Tonto, perverso, payaso*," Julieta said. Stupid, perverse, clownish.

"*Astuto*," Yael said, not astute, but in the Mexican sense, cunning and tricky. "*Decadente*."

"*Loco*," Raúl said. "His talk about building a big wall. He doesn't know that Mexicans travel back and forth every day to work in the United States, or to buy things. When I lived in El Centro, California, I was a radio journalist and I covered the border. In my time, in 1990, a fifteen-year-old boy was climbing the fence, and when he got to the top, a Border Patrol agent shot him. He fell back onto the Mexico side and he died."

"I'd like to check on that," I said. "Do you remember his name?"

"Eduardo Zamora," Raúl said. After twenty-seven years, the name was still fresh in his mind.

When I looked into this case, I found many others: unarmed Mexicans shot to death while attempting to cross the border.

"But half the voters in the States wanted Donald Trump," I said.

"*Por qué?*"

I told them that based on my travels in the Deep South in the Obama years, I understood the Trump voters, and how rural America felt overlooked and disregarded by Washington politicians, who seemed out of touch and pompous and casually corrupt. Many Americans were bewildered by having to accommodate themselves to the resettlement of Syrian, Somali, and Afghan refugees—their care and feeding—when many local communities were hard-up. And why were they unemployed? Because their town's manufacturing had been outsourced to China and India and Mexico. The larger proportion of American soldiers came from such communities, and they, and their parents, resented being instruments of regime change abroad. America seemed insecure, violent, and wayward; and President Obama appeared detached and indecisive. He had belittled the police, and his attorney general had called the police racists.

Add to this the presumptuousness of Hillary Clinton, who was so certain of winning that she campaigned halfheartedly and did not understand voters' anxieties. Trump saw into this anxiety and discontent, and promised to fix Washington and the border and put America first and stop fighting foreign wars and create jobs. There was a subtext of xenophobia, too, in many of his speeches. He played on the distrust of the Clintons and subtly disparaged the Republican Party. To the complex problems America faced he offered simplistic and persuasive answers. His message resonated, and as I had spent the previous two years driving on the back roads of middle America, listening to people, I was not surprised that he won.

At that point, I changed the subject to the Mexican police. Most of this group had been stopped by policemen, and Rosi said, "It's almost as if you're more afraid of the police than anyone else." Part of the reason for police shakedowns was that they earned so little, between $150 and $300 a month.

"This is getting depressing," Julieta said. "Let's go to the Casa Azul."

The Blue House, in Coyoacán, a short walk from the restaurant, was where Frida Kahlo had been born, grew up, and lived with Diego Rivera. She had died there, too, in an upper room. Now a museum, it was filled with Frida's startling paintings and also many of Diego's, family photographs and paraphernalia, such as the corsets and leg braces that the wounded (thirty operations, including an amputated leg) Frida had worn. Out of the small, stifling rooms, the courtyard was a suburban jungle of tamed vines and trimmed trees, the whole house a work of art, a kind of habitable sculpture.

"What do you think?" Rosi asked. She was the art dealer, always inquisitive.

"Lovely—I could live here," I said.

But I thought: Frida's house, her art, and her clothes, especially her *china poblana* peasant costume, were deeply personal expressions of a passionate self. I could not formulate this for Rosi, but I felt that for art, for writing, for anything creative to have value, it must be passionate and personal. Yet Frida was a special case.

She had become one of Mexico's exports, though in Mexico her style was recognized for being self-conscious and somewhat dated. Foreigners adored her, so she was promoted, with her image on T-shirts and refrigerator magnets, as well as a fairly expensive Frida Barbie doll. Her house and wild garden were widely advertised as attractions for the tourist buses.

She is "ghastly but unique," in the summing up of the narrator of Juan Villoro's story "Amigos Mexicanos," in which the nosy American journalist Katzenberg is searching for meaningful Mexicanisms. "Katzenberg didn't understand that [Kahlo's] famous traditional dresses were now only to be found on the second floor of the Museo de Antropología, or worn on godforsaken ranches where they were never as luxurious or finely embroidered."

For the traveler contemplating Mexico, Frida is a detour and a distraction. It was her genius as an artist, and her neurotic narcissism, to turn her whole self into art — her love, her suffering, her accident-prone life — and in the process make herself an icon, for the Mexican tradition is full of icons, especially of madonnas. It did not hurt her career that the forty-three-year-old Diego Rivera dumped his wife and married the teenage Frida (she was nineteen). And Diego was not just any old bridegroom. "This 300 pounds of gesticulating, brush-waving, manifesto-writing flesh," as Rebecca West describes him in her posthumous *Survivors in Mexico,* "who looked like Mao Tse-tung but was an amalgam of Pantagruel and Barnum and Baron Munchhausen." Frida loved him as a wife, as a daughter, as a protégée, as a mother. But Frida as a mutilated, mustached, and unibrowed madonna was perhaps more admired in Europe and the United States than in Mexico itself.

Trotsky's house, not far away, near a busy road, was less a house than a shrine to its former occupant, who's buried there. His skull had been smashed in 1940 by a Stalinist assassin, the weapon a *piolet,* a mountaineer's ice ax. The murderer, Ramón Mercader, was made a Hero of the Soviet Union after his release from twenty years in a Mexican prison. "Depressing," Julieta said. "And the building is modernized so badly." Then we went to the Coyoacán market and walked among taco stalls, crates of mangoes, carcasses of animals, dead-eyed fish gleaming on marble slabs, chiles hung like firecrackers, and trays of toasted grasshoppers.

"What did I tell you—Mexico City is surreal," Rudi said, back at the Hotel La Casona, when I described my day.

"A good day," I said, my first as a teacher in Mexico City.

The succeeding days were as full, and as friendly. The recent earthquake had damaged many buildings in the Roma district, where our class met. More surrealism: houses cracked in half, tenements with slumping floors, gaping windows, the rubble of shattered concrete blocks where a building had once stood—and next door, an apartment house untouched by the temblor. In many elegant plazas displaced families were living in tents.

"Here is a strange story," Guadalupe said in class one day. "There's an ancient site, Atzompa, in Oaxaca where some archeologists found the tomb of an important man, a governor. They identified him because his name had been inscribed there—Ocho Temblor."

"Eight Quake," a name indicating his power.

"In this tomb they found a jar," Guadalupe said, "and in the jar many bones and broken clay shards that seemed to be the pieces of an animal. When they began to assemble the clay pieces, they saw that they were making a crocodile. They put the thing together, finishing on a certain day—September seventh. The moment the croc was whole, the earthquake occurred. The epicenter was at Atzompa."

Héctor was dubious. It seemed too neat, he said. Anyway, what struck him was that there was little news about Oaxaca's earthquake—poor villages flattened, humble houses destroyed, and over a hundred people killed. But twelve days later, when Mexico City was shaken by an earthquake—probably the same tectonic plates shifting under the Sierra Madre's fault line—there had been a great outcry, because it involved wealthy people and expensive houses.

"You mentioned Mexico stereotypes," Héctor said. "I agree. There are many. For this reason, when we had a cultural event in the embassies where I worked, I refused to show a Frida image or a skeleton. I am against them as symbols of national culture. Such images created a stereotype. I wanted to show contemporary culture. What about women essayists? What about modern musicians? We are a strong civilization on the cultural side, greater than the stereotypes."

We debated this. Some agreed. Some said that Frida's portraits were powerful icons. And one day, to prove that some people resisted the *malgobierno*, we walked to the Reforma, where in front of the attorney general's office a permanent protest was installed. Dozens of people were camped out—the relatives of the forty-three students who had been murdered in Ayotzinapa, flapping tents, oversized signs and banners, blaring loudspeakers, and defiance. This had been going on, so far, for 1,100 days.

More restaurants, lunchtime seminars, and more outings—to the Bellas Artes Museum, and at the Antiguo Colegio de San Ildefonso—its interior bright with indignant murals by Orozco, Rivera, and others—the exhibit "Che Guevara in Africa." This was a chronicle in photographs and texts of Che's attempt to create a popular rebellion in the Congo in 1965. His *Congo Diary* is a powerful account of an idealistic man's campaign to bring change to Africa, at a time when I was a schoolteacher in the African bush. He was at the edge of Katanga in the Congo; I was in Malawi about six hundred miles away. I could easily relate to his book, which begins, "This is the story of a failure," and ends, "I won't forget the defeat, nor its precious teachings."

Héctor supervised our visit to the National Museum of Anthropology, a building of startling modernity. The guide explained the tableaux of peasant folk in adobe huts, surrounded by quaint handicrafts and simple utensils, tending clay pots on wood fires. There were a dozen or so exhibits: here Las Pachitas, there the Zapotecs, the Mixtecs, the Nawatlaka, each with their distinctive skirts or blouses or headgear, their weaving, their needlework, the beadwork of the Huicholes, the embroidered fabric of the Otomi, and examples of their sixty-two languages and three hundred dialects.

"How they used to live?" I asked.

"How they live now," the guide said.

The Otomi in Tequisquiapan in Querétaro, the Totonac in Veracruz, the Mixtec people in the hills and valleys of Mixteca Alta—and more: all still existed, though perhaps not in the idealized portraiture of the anthropological museum. They were the poorest of the Mexican peoples.

"They are the people who try to cross the border," Diego said. "Many of them want to migrate to the United States."

The memory of María, the mother of three, saying grace over her meal in Nogales, came to mind, her posture and her solemn Zapotec face like the living image of the weeping mother La Llorona; the woman who had become lost in the Arizona desert, been arrested, roughed up, and deported; who in her bravery and desperation had inspired me to travel farther into Mexico—indeed, my mission from the beginning, after meeting her, was to travel to her region, Mixteca Alta in Oaxaca, and look at the conditions that impelled the local people to make the risky border crossing.

"But you have indigenous people, too," Héctor said, sidling up to me. "And just as poor."

I told him what the Tohono O'odham woman in Gila Bend had said to me, how the O'odham Nation was divided by the border, half the people in Arizona, the rest in the Sonoran Desert in Mexico, where they live a more traditional life; how she was proud, and fluent in her language, and, "There is no O'odham word for wall." It had become something of a rallying cry for her nation.

Meanwhile, *el taller*, two hours in the morning, a discussion over lunch, always an outing and often dinner: full days with two dozen students who had become my friends. I had not taught in a classroom for more than forty years, and rediscovered the pleasure of the back-and-forth with intelligent, engaged students. I was eager to meet them each day, I enjoyed their company, and I was grateful for their companionship.

"Time to write something," I said one morning, and gave them a list of topics—ambiguous, challenging their imagination: "The Real Thing," "The Stranger," "In the Mexican Labyrinth," "The Masks of Mexico," and more.

The stories they submitted were all different, with many common themes: identity, misunderstanding, risk, solitude, confusion, often in the long shadow of the United States. They were fluent, confident, some experimental in style, all of them arresting. All argued against stereotypes, many depicted the private lives of individuals, in some cases extraordinary people, or unusual scenes. Death was featured often, along with awkwardness, loneliness, lost love, violence, insult, and the satisfactions and inconveniences of being Mexican.

Many of the students in the *taller* were writers of considerable skill and accomplishment, widely published in Mexico. But only one of them had a reputation—well deserved—in North America and Europe. This was Guadalupe Nettel. Three of her books had been translated into English: a memoir, *The Body Where I Was Born*, about confronting the possibility of blindness; a novel of inconvenient love affairs, *After the Winter;* and a collection of short stories, *Natural Histories.* In a story in *Natural Histories,* a Mexican scientist, who teaches in the US and Europe, "would often say that people only gain recognition in Mexico when they make a successful career for themselves abroad." This had been the case for her: having won prizes and been translated into English and French, Guadalupe became known in Mexico. It's true of writers in many other countries, who, for self-esteem as well as to make a living, need the authority of foreign approval.

The condition of being a stranger, an experience of solitude and loneliness, figured in the most successful stories. The stranger in Julieta García González's story was a man in a restaurant. The narrator, a lonely woman, walks into the place, sees this handsome young man, and says, "Hello, babe! How are you? I missed you!" The man is stunned and embarrassed, but invites the woman to sit with him. The woman asks for a drink of wine. She is comforted by his presence, his odor. "That meant he could also smell me: the traces of unhappiness . . . that he could somehow perceive the six months I was trying to leave behind."

He asks, "How are you, honey?" and she is befuddled. They clink glasses. She says, "Did you miss me?" Her fantasy of approaching a stranger "as if we were friends."

The man plays the game, they talk, drink some more, then the man says, "Shall we go?" When they leave, the woman cautions him, "Don't tell me your name." The man says the same. He asks for a hug. A passionate embrace, but brief: he departs and does not look back. The woman's arm burns where he had touched her, "like a rash. It lingered—and I liked it."

Another stranger, Claudia Muzzi, wrote of her visit to Newnan, Georgia, where she introduced herself as an editor, hoping to write a piece about the latest breast cancer treatments. In her tour of a "luxurious" cancer treatment center she notices the patients' faces, "too ill to reflect the presence of an intruder, a sort of ailment tourist, a vulture." After becoming lost and delayed in a walk, she returns and is treated offhandedly, as a stranger: "The staff had long surpassed their smiling hours"—the Mexican visitor rebuffed on her return.

In Guadalupe Nettel's "El Cuartito"—"The Small Room"—Mexican immigrants are strangers, interrogated on the US border. "Since childhood, I've spent so many hours in US customs queues that I know that the wait can be long and exhausting . . . Everything seemed deliberately designed to foment despair. It's a lottery . . ." In the misery and delay, the thought: "The northern border is a wound that pains all Mexicans." As for the indignity of the interrogation, "Every human being should experience it at least once, so as to know what others go through."

Not long after I read Guadalupe's story, I read the works she'd written that had been translated into English: her memoir, *The Body Where I Was Born,* and her story collection, *Natural Histories.* The memoir was beautifully wrought, deeply personal, and affecting; the stories I found astonishing and original—of people existing adjacent to animals that weirdly and accurately reflected their lives: fish, cats, a snake, and in the last tale a fungus. What impressed me was the wide experience disclosed in the stories, of love and marriage (generally disastrous) and of travel (beautifully observed). And I was struck by how cosmopolitan Guadalupe and many of the others were, since Mexico City was connected to the world, perhaps more to the big world than to the hard-up hinterland.

The gringo in a small village in Oaxaca in Michael Sledge's story does not realize how alien he is until the July celebration of Lunes de Cerro, Monday on the Hill, when the whole town of five hundred families gathers to eat and drink together. The fiesta is raucous, men dressed as women, wearing wigs and masks. The men in drag pounce on the drunken men, spin them around, then move on. When the fiesta becomes rowdy, the narrator is grabbed by a masked woman and they dance pleasantly, but then the mask comes off. It is Felix, the narrator's gardener, an intimate friend. "But the spell was broken. Now that he had shown himself, neither of us could continue dancing, and in fact were slightly embarrassed by the intimacy we suddenly found ourselves in." They part awkwardly, as strangers.

The foreign woman in Héctor Orestes Aguilar's "The Gringa" was Mariana, a Polish refugee. "Tiny, plump, with big green eyes and very white skin," she has arrived in Mexico to make a career as an artist and photographer. In her grand house she presides over salons. But then another stranger is glimpsed by the narrator, who remembers that as a small boy, during a party, "I saw B. Traven in the living room of Mariana's main house. I mean I saw half of his body, everything I could see as a little boy, just his brown boots and his khaki pants. I will never forget that all the children there, including me, called him by his nickname, Skipper."

This is accurate. Traven's widow spoke of how her reclusive husband fancied himself a ship's captain and liked to be called Skipper.

I could see that being a stranger was a fate many of these students of mine understood well. The stranger in Luisa Reyes Retana's "Juana Lao" was a woman who, when her grandfather died, found some unopened letters addressed to an uncle who died twenty-seven years earlier, leading her to Cuba and a revelation of her uncle's deep secret. In "Gringa," Yael Weiss (writer, translator, and editor) described herself as being Mexican but not looking Mexican—like a gringa, freckled, pale, "a mixture of European, Asian, Native American, with both Jewish and Catholic ancestors." Connecting with some black rappers in Las Vegas, and using "Mexican" as a way of blending in, "my Mexican identity was pigmenting me for the first time in my life. I started feeling ambiguous, treacherous, an intruder wearing a Mexican alibi." And, "The new racism against Mexicans made me look brown."

This story reminded me of the different faces in the class: a few like gringos, some dark, some Indian, some Spanish, Italian, Eastern European—all sorts. There is no Mexican face.

Feeling overlooked and disregarded made these writers hyperalert: Rosi Zorrilla in Cuba untangling a misunderstanding, Miriam in a restaurant observing a gringo diner complaining. Maria Pellicer, at the Las Vegas airport, describes a woman just off a plane from England, who falls down drunk in the immigration line and is treated with kindness by the police. Valerie in her apartment recording a sudden hovering helicopter, "like an enormous spider contemplating its prey," that is targeting some Somali terrorists, holed up with explosives in the next-door flophouse. Mexico City, a world of strangers.

At its best, teaching is also an experience of learning from your students. In Adán Ramírez Serret's disquisition on foreign writers, I learned about Jorge Cuesta, who had hosted Aldous Huxley and argued with Octavio Paz. Curious about Cuesta, I looked him up. He was a scientist as well as writer and editor. He married Diego Rivera's ex-wife, started a magazine, went mad, castrated himself, and, hospitalized, hanged himself, at the age of thirty-eight.

I knew the name of José Donoso, a Chilean writer who had lived in Mexico and the US, but Abril Castillo's "Masks" enlarged my understanding. This was a suspenseful account of reading Pilar Donoso's book about her father, José. On her father's death, Pilar spent seven years reading his many diaries, in which she found that he belittled her, that he was a bullying egotist, that (though married) he was a closeted homosexual who recorded how he physically assaulted his wife. In one of José's notebooks an idea is elaborated: the daughter of a famous writer embarks on his biography and, on finishing it, kills herself. Pilar wrote a memoir of her father, *Correr el Tupido Velo* (*Draw a Thick Veil*), and two years after finishing it, at the age of forty-four, killed herself. I did not know about this (so-far-untranslated) book, in which another José Donoso diary entry is quoted: "Behind the face of the mask there is never a face. There is always another mask. The masks are you, and the mask below the mask is also you ... All different masks serve a purpose, you use them because they help you to live ... You have to defend yourself."

I was stimulated and enlightened by the students, the care they took in their stories—most of them in English—and was grateful for their good will, generosity, and good humor. I had forgotten how, with great students, you learned so much. And how in a short time I had made twenty-four friends.

They were a traveler's fondest dream—hospitable, informative, and eager to please.

## The Shrine of Santa Muerte

"WHAT ABOUT SANTA Muerte?" I asked the group one day. "Our visit to La Capilla?"

That provoked a silence, then someone said there were many such Holy Death chapels, and Diego said, "We should make a phone call," and "I don't think they welcome outsiders." Then began a huddled discussion of the risks of such a visit.

Apparently there were many. Though a Santa Muerte chapel in Orizaba, Veracruz, was celebrating its tenth anniversary, and another chapel was to be built in the south of the city, a Santa Muerte shrine in Pachuca had recently been destroyed by the local authorities, enraging the worshipers. The government had targeted some shrines that were associated with drug cartels. As the cult had grown in popularity, so government disapproval had increased.

Holy Death in her medieval monk's robe, her yellow skull grinning in the shadow of her loose hood, gripping her wicked scythe in skinny finger bones, was, among other roles, a narco saint. Although the worship of the Bony One (La Huesuda) dates back to pre-Hispanic Mexico, in the seventeenth century the skeletal figure of Saint Death, "vice-regal" and crowned, was carried in Holy Week processions in Oaxaca, "to demonstrate the triumph of death over the Son of God" (I was to see ancient enthroned skeletons in churches in rural Oaxaca). The Santa Muerte cult, in its florid, more macabre form, is more recent, and the present day has seen a great resurgence of followers, especially among criminals. An elaborate Santa Muerte shrine (offerings of fruit, mescal, and money) had been found in 2002 in the house of a Gulf cartel boss, Gilberto García Mena (El June), according to Diego Osorno in his account of cartel violence, *The War of the Zetas*. Mena's house was in Guardados de Abajo, a Mexican village that was visible from the riverbank near Roma, Texas, near the border town of Ciudad Alemán. Another connection between the skeletal saint and the drug cartels was the chain of altars stretching for 150 miles along the Ribereña — the south bank of the river — parallel to the border, dozens of shrines dedicated to Holy Death, placed there by the narcos for protection.

Offering hope to the desperate (as well as to drug dealers, prostitutes, smugglers, and gangsters) and a spiritual shield from the authorities, Santa Muerte was now the fastest-growing faith in Mexico, with millions of believers. Enterprising cultists were setting up shrines all over the country, some grand edifices and many no more imposing than the shop front I had visited in El Llano del Lobo, south of Matehuala.

The problem with our discussion was that no one was quite sure where the chapel was located. No one had been there.

"But you've been to Ethiopia," I said to Diego.

"Compared to this, Ethiopia might be safer. I think we should have someone meet us and guide us."

Adán was on the phone. He said, "*Hola! Santa Muerte!*" Then he made a face. The person at the other end hung up.

"Maybe forget it," Julieta said. "Could be trouble."

"Just a look," I said. "To see what it's like."

"Where is it?" Adán asked.

"A taxi driver will know," Diego said.

"I used to live near the Plaza de la Soledad," Valerie said. "I think it's somewhere around there." She added that one of the features of the plaza, which was next to the venerable church of Santa Cruz y Soledad, was that at night along with the teenage prostitutes were many prostitutes of advanced age, ladies in their sixties and seventies. "And they attract some customers, too."

All this speculation fueled their curiosity, and they could see that I was eager to visit the shrine — theirs, in a way: this occult oddity, somewhere in their city — and they did not want to let me down. After all, as a *cronista*, I needed to see it for my chronicles.

"I've got someone," Diego said, his phone at his ear. He spoke, he listened, he scribbled an address. When he hung up, he said, "Morelos."

"Yes, that's what I thought," Valerie said.

"A small street—Nicolás Bravo," Diego said.

"Must be very small."

"Near San Antonio Tomatlán," Diego said.

"The church or the street? It's a long street."

"The taxi driver will know," Diego said.

When we found a taxi—my four friends clawing for balance in the back, me sprawled in the front—the driver pulled out a thick road atlas, which he examined whenever we stopped at a traffic light. As the print was very small and faded, he used a magnifying glass, the bulky book on his lap, jammed against the steering wheel.

"Morelos," he said, wagging the magnifying glass.

"I thought so," Valerie said.

"I think I know," the driver said. "But I have never been there."

Morelos, so my friends said, is acknowledged to be one of the three most dangerous districts in Mexico City, the others being Central de Abasto in Iztapalapa, a drug trafficking center, and Olivar del Conde, because of its labyrinthine layout of alleys, walkways, and dead-end streets, which contributed to confrontation, theft, and no easy escape routes.

Morelos looked to me like Bombay, just as dense and disordered. We drove for half an hour in the usual heavy, jolting, contending Mexico City traffic and entered the busy lanes of Morelos. Markets, shop fronts, and stalls crowded the main street, Circonvalación, which was thick with pushcarts and awnings and goods piled high—dresses, shoes, T-shirts, hats, wind-blown racks of brassieres and panties flying like pennants, next to pots and pans, skillets, and rice cookers. The place teemed with shoppers who darted in and out of traffic, an air of anarchy and improvisation, loud music, and the sizzle of frying food.

"Have any of you been to Bombay?" I asked.

None of them had.

"Don't bother," I said. "This is Bombay."

Stalled in traffic, the driver was rotating his magnifying glass over a page of streets in his atlas.

"Ah," he said, and shoved the atlas aside. He turned sharply into a narrow street, and then a crossroads, where a church stood, the bricks of its twin steeples glowing in the afternoon sun.

"Santa Muerte?" I asked.

Adán squirmed free of the others in the back and hurried into the high arched doorway of the church entrance. He was back within two minutes, saying, "No, but I have directions." He spoke to the driver, who set off again, looking confident. "That was the church of San Antonio Tomatlán."

This was Saint Anthony of Padua, known to all Bostonians in the North End for the procession on his feast day in August, his statue fluttering with pinned-on dollar bills, in thanks for his help, as the saint you pray to when you've lost something—money, your keys, a friend, anything.

"Nicolás Bravo," Diego said, reading a road sign. "It's here."

The Unico National Shrine of the Holy Death was a small, whitewashed, flat-fronted building with a square window facing the street, and in that window a statue, a large robed skeleton, with a smaller spidery skeleton just behind her. A deep doorway—more a gateway than a door—was cut into the thick wall. The street was bleak, empty of people, which made the jangling music from the market three streets away somewhat surrealistic. As for the window, nothing in a skeleton's stark bony demeanor or toothy grin spoke of welcome or offered solace.

We lingered, lurked a little, hesitated, then went through the gateway, through a tunnel-like lobby painted with skulls that gave it a garish, ghost-train, haunted-house carnival atmosphere, into the chapel itself, which was cavernous, lit by flaming candles, and filled with skeletons. The rows of wooden pews were empty except for one woman in a dark shawl, her hands wrapped in its folds, her gray etiolated face turned toward the altar and the smoking candles and blackened lamps.

The altar was set like a stage, scattered with the paraphernalia of death—skulls, bones, coffins, and wilted flowers—and a six-foot skeleton of Santa Muerte in a bright white wedding dress and tangled veil, holding her scythe in one hand and a globe in the other. A black wig was tipped sideways on her skull, and at her back a pair of four-foot wings, the Angel of Death dressed as a ghoulish bride. But there were portraits of Jesus on the altar, too, and crucifixes, along with more skeletons of different sizes.

"There's another Santa Muerte shrine in Tepito, not far away," Diego whispered. He had been making inquiries. "But they call this the national sanctuary—they had a service this morning."

I had been hearing children giggling but could not see them. Then I saw them, two boys rolling on the floor in a passageway to the right of the altar, near a stall hung with beads and trinkets where an old woman was dangling a Santa Muerte skeleton before the reverential face of a potential customer. The children were playing and teasing under a forbidding figure of Santa Muerte, this one in a purple prom gown.

A skeleton dressed in cloudy satin was labeled LA NIÑA BLANCA, votive candles of various colors flickering around her, each one representing a particular wish. And plastic spiders, many of them, purple and black, long-legged, clinging to wispy strands hung behind the altar and at the center of wheel-like webs. Another skeleton at the corner of the altar, and a painted image of an ordinary Mexican man in a blue shirt. "A portrait of the founder, maybe," Valerie said, possibly a man named David Romo Guillén, a former Catholic priest and self-anointed bishop of the cult, who'd recently been arrested for kidnapping and money laundering.

On the shadowy walls of the chapel, plaster images of Saint Peter and wooden crucifixes were set next to other portraits, one of them Jesús Malverde, the narco saint from Culiacán—seated as always—wearing cowboy boots, a white shirt and string tie, and holding wads of money.

"*La Santa Trinca,*" Julieta read as she gazed at a portrait of Mexico's holy trinity, Saint Jude, Jesús Malverde, and Santa Muerte—bearded apostle, bandit, and skeleton.

No one had questioned our being there, nor had anyone stopped Valerie from snapping pictures with her cell phone. We walked around, whispering, looking closely at the relics and images. At the stall, it was possible to buy prayer cards that were formulated to be effective. I chose one for someone who was desperate to be rid of an oppressive person.

"*Protector de la Santísima Muerte*," it began. "Blessed Death Protector, I come before you, broken, beaten, lost on my path of life and love. I ask you, my Mother, to please hear my request [*insert request here:* "A member of my family is driving me crazy," I whispered], to help me at this truly troubling time. I am being punished unfairly at the hands of a noncommunicator. They are aware that their behavior is painful and tormenting and yet proceed to do so anyway . . ."

And when I began to examine the trinkets at the stall, the woman behind the counter — mother of the playful boys rolling on the floor — asked whether I wanted something special.

"Something lucky," I said. "To keep me safe while I drive."

"Try this."

She unhooked a string of beads on which a three-inch silver image of Santa Muerte dangled.

"This will help you. This is good for protection."

I paid the equivalent of $3.

"But wait," she said, and uncorked a small bottle, pouring an aromatic liquid over the beads, saying, "Balm [*bálsamo*], to clean it, from all the other people who've touched it."

"It's the worship of death," Diego said as we left the chapel.

"I wonder."

It seemed to me that death worship was not the point here. Santa Muerte was not the image of someone who was once living, but rather a representation of death, and her most appealing aspect was that she turned no one away, certainly not sinners, whom she welcomed, forgiving everyone, especially the wickedest among us. Just as crucial, Santa Muerte did not demand repentance and reform; on the contrary, she embraced the sinner and the sins. People came here for indulgence, and for miracles. She represented acceptance — "Keep on sinning!" was the subtext of her theology — and she granted miracles to those who lit the right candle, offered a piece of jewelry or some pesos, or begged to be helped.

Mexico's other important saint, Jude, promised assistance to the desperate, but to seize Saint Jude's attention, it helped to be in a state of grace, having made a good confession and embraced holiness.

Santa Muerte did not require any holiness or atonement, only sincere belief, perhaps demonstrated (as some adherents did) by crawling on all fours to the shrine and praying on bloody knees. It was easy to understand La Flaca (the Skinny One), Doña Flaquita (Little Skinny Woman), La Huesuda (the Bony One), but there were sixty others listed by Claudio Lomnitz in his exhaustive book on the subject, *Death and the Idea of Mexico,* including La Parca (End of Life), La Grulla (the Crane), La Pepenadora (the Scavenger), La Llorona (the Ghost), La Jodida (the Busted One), La Apestosa (the Stinking One), La Araña Pachona (the Sanctimonious Spider), the vulgar La Chingada or La Chifosca (the Screwed One), and more. These variations spoke to the Mexican who felt flawed, hunted, lawless, hopeless, doomed. Indeed, as the embodiment of death, Santa Muerte is the Idol of Doom.

Veneration had never been greater than at this moment, the popularity soaring to something like twenty million in the past ten or fifteen years, while at the same time such veneration had been condemned by the Vatican in 2013 as sacrilegious. It was well known that Santa Muerte appealed to those who made their money in illegal, criminal, or shadowy trades—picking pockets, trafficking drugs, killing for hire, and prostitution. But in promising protection, and perhaps a miracle, instead of heaven, death worship was the perfect faith for Mexico, where half the people lived in poverty.

"What do you think?" I asked as we headed to the waiting taxi.

I laughed, hearing the Mexico City reply: "*Vamos a comer.*" Let's eat.


## Detour to the Border

MEXICO CITY HAD once, not long ago, been regarded as the City of Dreadful Night, with a villainous reputation for abductions and muggings, for crime and chaos. ("So this gringo gets into a taxi and thinks he's going to his hotel, but instead he's driven to a slum and robbed.") Yet once I settled into the day-to-day of teaching and eating and visiting the sights, the capital appeared to me prosperous and lively, a great multilayered city with billionaires on the top layer and poor slum dwellers on the bottom, and the only wickedness I saw was from the bad-tempered policemen. Away from the districts that were acknowledged to be risky, it seemed as safe as any other city of twenty-three million people.

As time went on, I fribbled the days away as a flaneur, became lazy and presumptuous in the manner of a city dweller, and developed the big-city vices of procrastination, eating late, sleeping longer, yakking in cafés, and pretending to be busy. My excuse was that I had a teaching job, but even when my workshop ended, I continued socializing with my new friends — wonderful friends — telling myself that it was part of my Mexican journey. Mexicans, so stigmatized and stereotyped, respond with affection — as good people do — when they are perceived as individuals. I loved being in their company. I began to slip into the urban routine, not a traveler anymore but living the life of an idle *chilango* and telling myself it was travel. It was easy to see how so many foreigners visiting Mexico City decided to spend the rest of their lives here, while dishonestly complaining it was a shark tank or Luciferian.

The worst big-city vice is forgetting that the hinterland exists — the unglamorous reality of the country. When I got a message from Peg Bowden in Nogales that, for the first time ever, the US Border Patrol had agreed to meet some groups of activists in Tucson, I decided to drop everything and go. "You might want to be there," Peg said.

Leaving my car in a secure parking lot in the Roma district, I flew to Tucson, arriving on a hot Arizona morning of blinding glare and scorched, unbreathable air. I promised myself that I would return to Mexico by bus.

The event was billed as a "Community Forum" and held at a small Episcopal church on a residential street of the city. The pews were half filled with activists, well over a hundred of them, and five Border Patrol agents in green uniforms sat on a raised platform before the altar. One of those men in green was the newly appointed sector chief for Tucson, Rodolfo Karisch, a man with a cold smile and small hard eyes set deep in his fleshy face. The activists in the pews were all sorts: fierce white-haired grandmothers, skeptical Tohono O'odham elders — lean and long-haired, indignant old men in sandals — a delegation from the border humanitarian group No More

Deaths, a sorority of Catholic nuns from the border town of Douglas, led by a well-known activist, the diminutive but iron-willed Sister Judy Bourg, as well as quite a number of young men and women who could have been college students, all of them aiming a fixed and furious gaze at the bulky Border Patrol officers.

A note at the bottom of the "Forum Outline" leaflet promised, "No press will be present at this forum," so I did not advertise my interest or say my piece; instead I listened, kept my head down, and made notes. Various groups took turns speaking for five or ten minutes, introducing themselves and voicing their concerns, and then Chief Karisch—the theme of his introduction was "We are policing a war zone"—invited comments from the floor.

With passion tempered by precision, the activists stood and expressed their frustrations.

"Do you have a policy—a standard operating procedure—with regard to dealing with humanitarian aid workers?" a young woman asked. "There was recently a Border Patrol raid on a No More Deaths camp. This is illegal under international humanitarian law."

"We follow the law," Chief Karisch began, perhaps oblivious of the implications of the law the woman was referring to, which is a set of specific rules that, in the words of the International Committee of the Red Cross, "seek, for humanitarian reasons, to limit the effects of armed conflict. It protects persons who are not or are no longer participating in the hostilities and restricts the means and methods of warfare. International humanitarian law is also known as the law of war or the law of armed conflict"—but the woman was still speaking.

"The Border Patrol agent threatened us. He said, 'No More Deaths will regret this.'"

"We don't approve of threats," the chief said, and called on another raised hand, this time an older man.

"Are you willing to find out if training exists on the topic of not destroying water bottles?"

Yes, the chief was willing.

"And what disciplinary measures will you take if you find someone responsible?" the man went on. "If you have officer misconduct, how do you deal with it?"

"Reprimand to termination," the chief said tersely, while soliciting another speaker, a tall man in a leather vest, string tie, and wide-brimmed hat.

"There is a humanitarian crisis in Mexico," the man said. "Do you recognize that we need to have a humanitarian response in the Tucson sector?"

In the Tucson sector in 2017, the bodies of 128 people had been found, including 57 in the thickets of the Cabeza Prieta National Wildlife Refuge and the desert near Ajo, where No More Deaths had been leaving water bottles. This put me in mind of the horrors described by Luis Alberto Urrea in *The Devil's Highway*, where he recounted the ordeal of migrants in that very sector.

"There's a difference between giving water to migrants and sheltering them," the chief said. "Harboring and smuggling is against the law."

A young man jumped up, saying, "Is the provision of medical care to a wounded or sick migrant regarded as harboring?"

"That's tricky," the chief said.

There were more questions related to the destruction of water bottles, to which the chief's answer was that he would look into it.

No More Deaths had recently released a report detailing the abuses of the Border Patrol. In the period from 2012 to 2015, the group had placed more than 31,500 gallons of water at 139 aid stations on trails used by migrants in and around Arivaca, a bleak stretch of desert east of the Tohono O'odham reservation. They estimated that about 86 percent of the water was used. That was proof that lives had been saved. At the same time, about 10 percent of the water in the aid stations, some 3,500 gallons, was destroyed. The report included two trail-camera videos that showed one agent puncturing water containers and another agent (on a cold winter day) removing a blanket from an aid station.

The Border Patrol had been filmed systematically slashing water bottles and kicking the boxes to pieces. A report published in January 2018 by No More Deaths and La Coalición de Derechos Humanos gave specific figures for the Sonoran Desert in the Tucson sector: 415 jugs destroyed, on average twice a week, the damage affecting 3,586 gallons of water. And clothes, food, and blankets left in the desert by Samaritans had been seized or trashed. This was an example of pure spite.

The Border Patrol had also arrested humanitarian workers for trespassing and littering—in this case, littering meant leaving caches of life-saving supplies in the desert. In the period reported, almost six hundred migrant corpses had been delivered to the Pima County medical examiner. Pima County is an irregular rectangle, with Tucson in the east, Organ Pipe Cactus National Monument in the west, the Tohono O'odham Nation in the middle, and the border forming the bottom edge.

These abuses were not only the result of recent directives from the Trump administration. A spokeswoman for No More Deaths, Caitlin Deighan, said the policy of militarizing the border and forcing migrants into the most dangerous stretches of desert, where thousands died, dated from President Clinton's era, and the deaths and bottle slashings had continued into the Obama presidency. "It's been ongoing throughout every administration," she said.

A back-and-forth began in the church on the distinctions between harboring migrants and the humanitarian camps in which wounded or sick migrants were treated by doctors or activists. This was not resolved, though I could see that the cause of the impasse was the Border Patrol failing to see any mitigating nuance, regarding a sick or dying migrant as someone to arrest and deport, while the activists promoted the notion that such a person was deserving of help.

This was the ethical question that Henry David Thoreau faced in Concord, harboring a runaway slave—often starving, ill, or thirsty—violating the Fugitive Slave Act and risking jail and a fine, to help save the life of a fellow human being. The Fugitive Slave Act made every American complicit in supporting slavery; the criminalizing of humanitarian acts on the border made every American complicit in persecuting migrants.

A woman stood and raised her arms for attention, saying, "Please may we have a moment of silence for the seven thousand found dead on the US-Mexico border because of US policy?"

After this silence—less a silence than a subdued buzz of ten seconds or so during which I could hear cars passing the church—a man spoke up: "In your opening remarks, sir, you called this a war zone. That's pretty serious. So my question is, what is your hiring policy? It seems to me from what I've seen that you have a lot of very young and untested officers, a lot of wannabes and dubious people with a chip on their shoulder. What are you doing to counter that mentality?"

"We grew very fast as an agency," the chief said, acknowledging a lack of strict oversight and conceding that some of the newer officers had been unsuitable, aggressive, or untrained. But they were still learning, he added. "We screen our applicants better. We reject many applicants."

"But they're still destroying humanitarian camps and slashing water bottles. Some of your guys are no more than teenagers."

"There's a provision for eighteen-year-olds to join," the chief conceded.

That reminded me of the many big, swaggering high school kids I'd seen on Arizona sidewalks, laughing much too loudly and shoving each other, or honking their horns at teenage girls at the Sonic drive-in. Not one of the activists was anywhere near that age. It was easy to imagine a boy or girl in their late teens, armed with a Glock and a stun gun, in a green Border Patrol uniform and a Stetson hat—such an armed teenager representing the federal government—facing a defiant activist or a cowering migrant. The ensuing confrontation would not be a meeting of minds.

The tribal elders voiced the same concern: aggressive policing, Border Patrol vehicles violating tribal law by driving across the reservation. One of the legal and cultural complexities of this sector was that the Tohono O'odham Nation of twenty-five thousand people straddled the border, most of them living in the United States, the rest in the Sonoran Desert.

"The greatest casualty is the trust in the US government and the Border Patrol," one of the elders said. He was a slender man in a red shirt, a braid of his lustrous jet-black hair hanging against his back. "In the Nation there's an overwhelming fear of the Border Patrol. Tribal members see the cars driving on our roads—and these cars have no right to be there."

"I'll have someone look into this," the chief said. "That's why I'm here. I'm here to listen."

"This land is our sacred land," the man said in a protesting voice. "What are you going to do to reestablish trust?"

"I am here to develop that trust," the chief said.

But the man remained standing, leaning forward. He raised his hand and waited for silence before saying, with stern authority, "We are not the enemy!"

"Let me say this," the chief said in a subdued voice. "You need to understand that we don't make the rules and laws. It's our job to enforce them."

This elicited a shriek from a young man in a back pew, who stood and said loudly, "You say you don't make the rules and laws, but successive Border Patrol chiefs have changed the rules and made new rules! These have been arbitrary and abusive, like destroying the water bottles and arresting us for giving medicine to migrants!"

"I will be following established protocols," the chief said. "I will not be making new rules."

An older man in a jacket and tie rose to say that he was a teacher in a Tucson school who often supervised students on field trips in the sector, and the students in the vans and buses always had to endure an extensive interrogation at Border Patrol checkpoints.

"These are my students—they are not lawbreakers, and yet they are singled out and subjected to intimidation," the man said. "I want to know what you are doing to eliminate racial profiling. It is having an enormous negative impact on my students."

As the chief said he would look into this, too, adding that he was bringing the meeting to a close, a petite middle-aged woman got up and said, "Before this session ends, I want to remind you that your union endorsed Donald Trump for president, and the Border Patrol Foundation gave an award to Steve Bannon."

This assertion had a dark and tangled history. Bannon, an adviser to the Trump presidential campaign, had received the Courage in Journalism Award from the Brian Terry Foundation at a dinner in Tucson in 2017. The foundation was named for a Border Patrol officer who had been murdered in 2010 in the Tucson sector. The rifle used to kill him had been identified as one of the weapons in the "Fast and Furious" program.

Fast and Furious was a gun-walking plan that allowed more than two thousand high-caliber weapons—assault rifles and semiautomatic handguns—to flow from the US to Mexico so that in a sting operation the weapons could be traced to criminal figures, who would then be arrested. Under Fast and Furious, the Bureau of Alcohol, Tobacco, Firearms and Explosives allowed—indeed encouraged (no proper IDs were necessary)—Mexican criminals to buy firearms from gun stores near the border (the Lone Wolf Trading Company, in a Glendale, Arizona, strip mall, was one) and smuggle them into Mexico.

The twisted thinking behind this idea was that the weapons, traced by the ATF to cartel leaders and drug lords, would identify and undo the villains in the gangs. The program, initiated during the Obama administration, was a failure: the bureau lost track of hundreds of the illegal weapons, and no drug lords were prosecuted. A Fast and Furious .50-caliber rifle was recovered from El Chapo's drug gang, though thirty-four of these big guns (powerful enough to shoot down a helicopter) went untraced. And it was later proven that a Fast and Furious assault rifle, an AK-47, was used to kill Officer Brian Terry. This came to light when a whistle-blower, an ATF agent named John Dodson, made the connection between Terry's death and that particular rifle, sold by the Lone Wolf Trading Company to a Mexican criminal, with the approval of the ATF.

President Obama stonewalled the investigation, defended his Justice Department, refused to release any documents relating to the affair, and stoutly defended his attorney general, Eric Holder, who denied knowing anything about it. But because of intense pressure, crucial documents were unsealed that showed that many subordinates of Holder in the Department of Justice had known of the scheme, and that Holder (combative under Senate scrutiny) had attempted to thwart the investigation. The result of the gun-walking operation was that thousands of US weapons ended up in Mexico and were used extensively in crimes on the border.

Since Bannon was head of Breitbart News, which exposed the whole business—though Breitbart inaccurately portrayed Holder as having prior knowledge of it—he was given the journalism award.

"I have nothing further to say on this," the Border Patrol chief said, and called the meeting to a close.

But the mention of this scandal showed how complicated border issues could be, and how the desperate measure of concocting a sting operation, allowing guns to be smuggled, ended in mayhem, misery, cover-ups, and death.

Listening, making notes, I rehearsed a little speech, which I would begin by saying, "Criminalizing humanitarian effort in the United States is nothing new ..."

In fact, it amounted almost to a national tradition. The Fugitive Slave Act of 1850 — the Bloodhound Law — penalized abolitionists in, for example, my hometown of Medford, Massachusetts, as well as those who kept the safe houses throughout the North that constituted the Underground Railroad. Taking risks, and often arrested for helping people fleeing slavery and persecution in the South, the idealists — Henry David Thoreau was one of many — defied the government and sheltered runaway slaves, hiding them from the authorities and helping them to freedom. Anyone caught harboring or aiding an escaped slave was fined $1,000 — a punitive sum at the time ($30,000 in today's money). But in their humanism, and squarely in the American tradition of justified dissent, opposing the craven political philosophy of "the government knows best," the abolitionists were precursors of the activists in No More Deaths, and of sanctuary cities and churches that sheltered migrants.

But I said nothing.

## The Psychotropic Bus

INSTEAD OF FLYING back to Mexico City to pick up my car and resume my road trip, I decided to ride the bus there by a roundabout route, via the coastal cities of Culiacán, Mazatlán, and Puerto Vallarta, places I was curious to see. And in taking the bus I thought I might also experience a different sort of border crossing — in the company of hard-up Mexicans who could not afford to fly.

The inexpensive cross-border bus from Phoenix ("*Tufesa Internacional — la experiencia más confortable de viajar*") turned out to be mood-altering, psychotropic in a general way, and in a narrow sense, too. The trip

reminded me that most headlong hallucinatory brain-bending drug episodes (at least in my life) begin with the mildest, most prosaic tinkering
and hoo-ha. First you find a couch or a hammock ("This'll do"), get comfortable on it, swallow the poison, and for thumb-twiddling minutes or
longer, wait for the nerves to jangle and the eyeballs to boil.

At first there is only mild discomfort, a pukesome catch in the throat,
and then, in an eruption of phosphenes, blinding light in the lantern of
your head, as the body surrenders to a narrowing liquefaction, and finally a
transformation, as one is borne along a river of lava, or it might be marma-
lade, with a chorus of warping chirrups, perhaps of demented sparrows or
speeding schools of translucent reef fish — only the synapses know. At the
start is the decapitation, and you melt, you vanish, and in a welcome dawn
you are reborn as plasma, until reincarnated as damp flesh, blinking and
wondering, What just happened?

The bus was like that, but it took a while. Travel can mimic such an episode, which is why they are both called trips. From a hot Phoenician noon,
the bus moved through the Arizona desert to the glare of Tucson and the
sting of sand at Tubac, where some saguaro cacti were giving me the finger,
others were like spiky candelabra, and the more symmetrical were monumental menorahs. After twenty miles, the bus slowed over rumble strips at
the edge of the USA, for its insertion through a gateway in the tall rusted
fence, crossing from small, sedate Nogales, Arizona, to sprawling and rackety Nogales in Sonora, where I had been several times.

So far, a simple bus ride in the afternoon heat and no formalities at the
border, except five squat, helmeted soldiers in black, shouldering past us on
the broken pavement and entering the bus carrying assault rifles, prying
open sections of upholstery and poking flashlights into crevices. Mexican
authority figures are meaner, darker, better fed, and more muscled than the
average Mexican, heavily armed and unsmiling.

"Looking for drugs?" I asked my new friend Bonifacio.

"No. The drugs go the other way. They are looking for guns and money."

A dozen of us on the bus, and I was the conspicuous gringo, all the
others fully documented but poor and anxious returnees, burdened with
the Mexican dilemma, extended family on both sides of the border, com-

pounded in Bonifacio's case: "Wife there, with some kids. She don't like Arizona. Other kids here, grandkids too." And his lungs were bad, from the fumes of his work, spray-painting cars in Phoenix. Old Señora Cruz and her daughter were visiting relatives. Miguel had not been to his home-town of Guadalajara in years (it was twenty-seven hours away on this bus); he, like the others, were intending to come back, yet quietly watch-ful—as Mexicans always seemed to me, a reflex that was both social and cultural—in the presence of a detachment of police, as you would be in the presence of shouting drunks or a clutch of madmen. And even the middle-aged man with the boy-gangster face, who was to get off at Los Mochis, was subdued.

In Nogales, Sonora, street food was being served—you could smell the hot fat and its smart of chiles in Arizona through the vertical interstices in the thirty-foot iron fence: a woman with a bundle of tamales, a man with a tray of drinks, an ice cream seller, children hawking candy. Only fifty yards from the United States and the economy was suddenly improvisational, intensified by the heightened awareness of people hungry and poor. News-paper vendors, too, the headlines all mentioning Trump.

"*Café?*" I asked.

"I'll get you one!"

The well-dressed—tie, jacket, golf cap—street vendor hurried into moving traffic with my money, emerging minutes later, a Styrofoam cup in one hand, deftly sorting my change with the other, keeping a handful and reminding me that *propina* is the word for tip.

The bus sped south to Hermosillo, out of the old heart of Nogales, through the precincts of the industrial area (more than a hundred factories, making computers, clothing, appliances, electronics, and plastic and rubber goods to be trucked through the fence), and finally low, grassy, and wooded hills. If you ignored the ordinary miseries, the tenements and tumbled huts of the almost forty thousand workers, the landscape was indistinguishable from that in Arizona, even to the emblematic sight of a crow pecking at the red hash in the crushed plating of a roadkill armadillo.

But that frontier is misleading for giving the impression of poor people jammed against the fence, their shonky houses in the rabbit warrens of dense colonias. They are the unfortunates, the huddled masses yearning to breathe free, making plastic buckets and automobile wiring for the gringo market, hustling tamales for bus passengers, and as in many other Mexican border towns, offering discount dentistry.

You'd never know, contemplating the chaos and squalor and the hope that is palpable by the fence, what natural beauty lies beyond it, that twenty minutes south of the fence is open country: the grandeur of the Sonoran hinterland, the villages of Bambuto and Santa Ana, the mesquite trees dotting the hills, the green-tufted ravines and iron-dark mountains in the distance, the ridge of the sierra to the east, the dry riverbeds in the twilight, their shadows mimicking water flow.

In the gathering darkness, the approach to Hermosillo, the passengers, sunk in their ancestral desert, became calmer and more confident, softened in a way by being back in Mexico, polite to each other, though garrulous and digressive when contending with my questions.

"Trump is crazy—very crazy," Miguel said. "He hates Mexicans, he hates immigrants, he says bad things about the Chinese—and the Chinese are intelligent! All he cares about is money."

This was at the sandwich stall at Hermosillo bus station on the Plaza Girasol. And that was when I saw Señora Cruz's large medallion, the size of a silver dollar, and the way she moved her thumb over its face in a caress, as though venerating San Cristóbal, patron saint of travelers. But this was the narco saint Malverde I'd seen at the Santa Muerte chapel in Mexico City.

"Jesús Malverde," she said, and lifted the medallion, showing me the image of the bandit seated in a chair surrounded by pistols, rifles, and marijuana leaves on one side, and an occult pentagram on the other.

This was so different from driving myself through the butterflies at Reynosa. But the hallucinatory nature of the bus trip did not take hold until after dark, on the dead-straight desert road, to the moan of the engine and slow gear changes, a sound like grieving. And then the visions descended like a fever, with the bus speeding headlong toward the coast on the empty road—few drivers in Mexico risk the nighttime roads—with the silvery glint of low bushes and natural rubble, full moon on the flat backland. I drowsed and dreamed but was jerked awake by the pounding of the bus for unearthly glimpses of the moonlit hills, and the bounce and swerve of the bus rocked me like a dissolving drug. Ten hours into the trip, on the nighttime road, no other cars risking this desert darkness, it was as if we were on a thoroughfare in space, speeding past blobs of stars. But for interludes of wakefulness, I sensed little but gasoline fumes and dampness and, as in all long-distance buses, stale food and feety odors.

The glare of gas station rest stops, mystical, comet-like as they rushed past, but melancholy and ordinary when we paused for the ten-minute breaks. Ciudad Obregón, for example, one man with a mop, a paper plate of warmed-up tortillas, yawning people dawdling over coffee. And then back to the road and a new synesthetic reality, phantom shapes and bursts of light crowding the windows of the speeding vehicle. And many of these flashes of light had the bleached-bone look of Mexico's enduring and much-venerated emblem, the grinning skull of Santa Muerte.

I could not stay awake, but when I dropped off to sleep, I was woken by the road bang on the wheels or the brilliant light of overhead lamps — blazing in the middle of nowhere and leaving me seeing stars and filling me with the nausea of helplessness and the frustration of sudden insights that just as suddenly deserted me. And in such a bus, at such a speed, tunneling through the desert darkness, you always assume you're going to crash.

At Los Mochis, after a hundred more miles of flashes and empty road, no one was awake, no one boarded, and the hallucinatory landscape began again, the bus buffeted by the combined grip of headwind and slipstream, the squirts of light. I slept and woke and slept again, and remembered Señora Cruz saying at one of the stations, "Sometimes they stop the buses. They put up roadblocks and rob all the passengers."

"Who does this — the cartels?"

"Not cartels," she said, as though offended. "But the others," and she named them: *ratones* (mice, but also robbers), *ladrones* (thieves), *cucarachas* (roaches).

But like the vampirism of psychedelia, the hallucinogenic nature of the bus trip began to fade with the waning moon and the watery glow of daylight, and when the sun like a flashing blade penetrated the interior of the bus, I was wide awake, but sluggish with the hangover from a long night of interrupted dreams.

Now we were crossing the river at Culiacán, the enameled flow greeny black in the dawn, the city famous as a hideout, notorious for its cartel violence. Señora Cruz and her daughter heaved themselves past me, Señora Cruz still fingering her medallion of Jesús Malverde.

On the daylit road the banality of the rational world and its street signs and lampposts asserted itself. Though I could not see the ocean, it was obvious that to the west, beyond the flatness of the land, the sea lay under the high sky and limpid air — morning in Mazatlán.

## *Mornings in Mazatlán*

SUNDAY MORNING IN Mazatlán, no traffic, only a few joggers and dog walkers on the decaying corniche in the *centro histórico,* the old part of town, still too early for anyone to be headed to work. I was welcomed at La Siesta, my seafront hotel (ocean-view room, $53). On its facade, a plaque memorializing Jack Kerouac's visit to the town, to this very spot (*"En memoria a su estancia en estas playas"*), with a long quotation.

*"La única gente que me interesa esta que está loca, la gente que está loca por vivir, loca por hablar, loca por salvarse,"* it began, and anyone who has read *On the Road* will easily recognize it as the mission statement of the man who inspired my generation to hit the road: "The only people for me are the mad ones, the ones who are mad to live, mad to talk, mad to be saved." (The end of the book, seldom quoted, was a soberer reflection: "Nobody knows what's going to happen to anybody, besides the forlorn rags of growing old," a condition that Kerouac was never to know, dying in Florida at the age of forty-seven.)

Kerouac had come to Mazatlán, like me, from Arizona by bus, the same route, though in 1951 it would have been a slower trip. He did not stay in Mazatlán; he left the same day for Mexico City to see William Burroughs. I lingered for three days of pure idleness, liking the seedy charm of the old city and cheered by the families on the promenade — and the children, the lovers, the drinkers, the strollers. This end of town, on Olas Altas (High Waves) beach, was an enclave in which Mexicans themselves were tourists, or else visited from nearby.

"They come from the colonias — some of them from far away — for the breeze here," a woman told me, explaining the campesinos seated on the sea wall.

There are two Mazatláns. One is the *centro histórico,* with its market and churches and the Teatro Ángela Peralta — built in 1874, for opera, boxing, movies, and plays; restored in 1992 as a venue for local musicians and dramatists and dancers — its old plazas and small bistros, hospitable to locals. The other, flashier, golden Mazatlán, the Zona Dorada, six miles up the beach, at the top end of town, with its grand hotels and resorts, is dismissed by locals as the destination of rich gringos, and financed to launder drug money, as a man told me with a dismissive laugh: "*Dinero lavar!*"

It is rare in Mexico to meet someone who has no family connection to the US. Many Mexicans I met — working in hotels, restaurants, and shops, driving taxis — had held jobs in the States and been thrown out. In the tale told most often, they had been summoned to Mexico for a family emergency and had been unable to return.

Liliana had slipped over the border and made beds in a hotel in Colorado for a year, then worked in a restaurant for a second year. She told me she'd been paid well, and she remembered the generous tips in the restaurant.

"I came home because my mother was dying," she said. "Now I can't go back." She thought a moment — and looked aged in her reflection. "If I had five thousand dollars, I could get a visa, or pay the mafia to help me cross. But I will never have that money."

Making beds in a good hotel full time in Mazatlán, Liliana earned 700 pesos a week, about $35. Her husband had left her; her children were grown. She was resigned to a life of poorly paid work, just getting by.

Her mention of the mafia prompted my next question.

"There are four here." And she shrugged. "They don't bother me." *Ellos no me molestan.*

"They fight with each other," Miguel had told me on the bus, "and with the police."

Because Mazatlán is a busy and important seaport, the cartels contend for control of its port, essential (and notorious) for moving drugs north. Just a few months before, thirteen tons of cocaine, hidden in barrels of hot sauce and destined to be off-loaded at Mazatlán, were intercepted down the coast at Manzanillo.

A more aggrieved man repeated a frequent Mexican complaint: "If you didn't want drugs in your country, we wouldn't have cartels in ours."

But that is only partly true. The cartels are now more involved than ever in human trafficking, because though it is not quite as profitable, the penalties for smuggling people are far less than for smuggling drugs.

I was often the target of the Mexican taunt, "Yes, we have El Chapo Guzmán, but you had Al Capone!"

This all sounds contentious. Yet the days I spent in Mazatlán were peaceful, strolling on the *malecón*—thirteen miles of seafront promenade—trying out the restaurants, swimming on the hot afternoons, and at night smiling at the frenzied dancers in the joints in the seaside clubs.

"The deep appeal of the seedy" is Graham Greene's expression for certain places (he described it in West Africa), and it was compelling and comforting in Old Mazatlán, an ageless scruffiness, a sense of vitality in decay, an argument against luxury, boutique hotels, and pestering waiters in tailcoats. The pleasure of relaxing on a worn sofa.

That was the best of Mexico for me—inexpensive meals that were delicious, cheap hotels that were comfortable, and friendly people who, out of politeness, seldom complained to outsiders of their dire circumstances: poor pay, criminal gangs, a country without good health care or pensions, crooked police, cruel soldiers, and a government indifferent to the plight of most citizens. I found that in these circumstances, the people I met overcame the infernalities by either being obstinate and wicked themselves, or in most cases being kind, in a mood of acceptance, understanding that voicing objections can get you hurt, or killed.

The Mazatlán public market, the Mercado Municipal, an art nouveau building, was a ten-minute walk from my hotel, filled with people milling among dead fish, flyblown meat, fruit, clothes, appliances, shoes, religious paraphernalia, and the kitsch and souvenir junk that Mexicans call *cháchara-ras*. Although crowded, sensationally so at times, the market was a scene of politeness, friendly beckoning, good-humored bargaining, and no confrontation.

It was there, in a stall selling *cháchara*, as well as icons and crucifixes and ceramic skulls, that I saw that familiar mustached face on a foot-high plaster statue. The skinny, dignified man in the white shirt, string tie, and cowboy boots was unmistakable as Jesús Malverde — an ascetic saint's face, but this idol was holding a wad of money in his right hand, his left hand resting on a stack of bills. Sitting on a throne-like chair, a big, spiky, seven-fingered marijuana leaf as a backdrop, another leaf at his feet: a secular holy man, shocking in its commanding presence and its oddness. It was the image of the seated man I had seen in Mexico City and on Señora Cruz's medallion.

"Tell me about him, please."

The smiling clerk, her name tag reading MINERVA, verified, as Señora Cruz had said to me, "You know this is Jesús Malverde?"

"Yes."

Minerva said that Malverde was a man who had lived in Sinaloa, and gave me to understand that there was a Malverde shrine in Culiacán (where Señora Cruz had gotten off the bus); that he was venerated, given offerings of gold trinkets and money; and that in most respects Malverde worship amounted to a cult, every bit as powerful as the cult of Santa Muerte.

"Malverde is important, but only in Culiacán and Sinaloa generally," she said. "He doesn't matter anywhere else. His statues are here, but not in other markets."

Most of the statues were six or eight inches high, but some were huge — two-foot-high images of the skinny man in the white shirt, black tie, black trousers, and cowboy boots, the thin ascetic face suggesting saintly self-denial. But what of the marijuana leaves and the stacks of money?

"People worship him — they ask him for protection."

"What people?"

"*Marijuaneros*," Minerva said. "Also poor people — they pray to him."

This little glimpse into the arcane belief system in Mexico fascinated me, so when I had time, I looked deeper. Jesús Malverde, called the Narco Saint, had been studied and written about by, among others, the journalist Sam Quinones, who wrote in *True Tales from Another Mexico* how Malverde was known as the Generous Bandit and the Angel of the Poor; how pilgrims left offerings and plaques at his shrine, a large building by the railway tracks in Culiacán; how this Robin Hood figure had lived in the time of the dictator Porfirio Díaz (1877–1911); how he had been hunted down and finally hanged from a mesquite tree by government soldiers on May 3, 1909, now a day of celebration for Malverdistas. Quinones is also persuasive in asserting that Malverde was likely a mythical figure, that he had probably never lived, that he might be a conflation of two prominent bandits or perhaps an invention arisen out of nothing at all except a sense of grievance and a yearning for protection.

Belief gains strength in the absence of facts. Malverde is the more powerful for being pure legend, from the hagiography of an oral tradition. Here is the proof: some worshipers at Malverde's shrine have witnessed miracles—the return of lost cows, the curing of a gangrenous leg. That Malverde never existed, or is an inflated or hallowed version of a person who might have lived, or is surrounded by a nimbus of hogwash and speculation, producing tears, protestations of faith, and verified miracles, gives him a stark similarity to most other saints.

*Malgobierno* has something to do with it, too. Quinones writes, "Sinaloa is one of those places in Mexico where justice isn't blind and the lawless aren't always the bad guys." As for the official disapproval of Malverde: "Having the government as an enemy can improve a reputation." Especially when the government does so little to deal with corruption, ineffective public institutions, widespread poverty, income inequality, underdevelopment, and the police and army getting away with murder.

When the government is not on your side, you look elsewhere for comfort and develop a belief in Holy Death, in the Narco Saint, in (as Poe put it) the grotesque and the arabesque.

On a beach chair on the sand, among the bathers and the families, I felt like Aschenbach—and I mocked myself with that image for a few days, catching up on notes. But one early evening, dusk like a lowering veil, I sat in a corner of the Plaza de la República, getting a $1 shoe shine by Manuel—a youngish man with a small son—who told me, "I live very far from here. I come every day on the bus." People passed, slowed by the heat and the broken pavement, hand-holding couples, a man dragging a reluctant dog, a woman pushing a stroller, a drunk who staggered near until Manuel waved him off ("*Borracho*"), children neat in school uniforms toting backpacks, a priest hugging himself and lecturing an old woman, the flower seller, the ice cream man, the man selling balloons and wind-up toys, all of them circulating in the plaza while Manuel told me about his small child and his tribulations, his sick wife, his unfair rent, his long commute, the price of food, the unhelpful government—the end of another hot morning in Mazatlán.

And I was overcome with sadness, the melancholy of the voyeuristic traveler, and thought: This is what happens when you stay too long in a place. You begin to understand how trapped people feel, how hopeless and beneath notice, how nothing will change for them, while you the traveler simply skip away.

## Tepic: People Who Hide from Evangelists

TO THE INLAND town of Tepic the next morning, a lovely day, sliding down the coast on a bus, someone else driving, a tour of the tomato fields, the ranks and rows of trees in the avocado orchards, cornfields and vegetable gardens, miles of them, all sizable and symmetrical. Even the cemeteries were orderly, the carved mausoleums like small habitable chalets. Only the human huts and shacks in the passing settlements were squalid and ruinous, where the farm workers live, earning a pittance—this, thirty miles from Mazatlán, near the town of El Rosario.

It was restful to travel into the big bosomy landscape, the green hills, shaggy with low trees, too steep to plow or cultivate except in the hidden slopes where (I was assured) marijuana and *amapola* (opium poppies) were grown, making El Rosario more famous for its drug crops than its vegetables or fruit, and as a consequence, a haunt of the cartels, and somewhat disputed here in Nayarit between the Sinaloa cartel and the Jalisco New Generation.

From the swampy coastal plain haunted by herons, the road climbed into the hills to Tepic. That was my destination. Tepic was founded almost five hundred years ago, but you'd never know it: its antiquity was buried by scrap yards and car repair shops, which are the Mexican response to a bad economy and low wages — making do and mending are the answers to mechanical problems. No one has any money, so cars are kept for decades, and cobblers and tailors are busy, too, and so are blacksmiths, welders, and brickmakers. Mexicans still know how to fix things: the body shops of Tijuana smooth the dented cars from California.

In the glare of early afternoon, the rest of Tepic, a town cupped in the mountains, consisted of a few busy commercial streets, and the nearer neighborhoods of cracked and sunbaked bungalows and small fenced-in houses scattered over a hillside, some of them on narrow cobblestone lanes. A whitewashed, walled-off university was the pride of the town, and so was another dominant feature, a remnant of the past: the seventeenth-century cathedral with Gothic steeples, whose fenestration and tapering top gave them the look of a pair of upright, skeletal rockets. An uninviting place, on the whole, the sort that inspires the thought, Let's keep going.

But I had spent the whole morning on the bus, and I was happy to get off at three thousand feet. The air was markedly fresher than in steamy Mazatlán, and I was here for a reason: to visit the nearest settlement of indigenous Huichol people. I was told in Mazatlán that I would have no trouble finding them: "You will see them. You will know them by their amazing clothes" (*ropas sorprendentes*).

In the sunny early afternoon, I walked down the main avenue, Insurgentes, to a restaurant that had been recommended, El Farallón — excellent seafood, traditionally broiled on a *zaranda* (literally a sieve, but in Mexico a grill). I was to find, as I had on the border, that no matter how dreary-looking a Mexican city or town, it nearly always has a good place to eat, which is worth stopping to find. In the absence of any other comfort, suffering poor housing, violent streets, bad government, and wicked cops,

Mexicans defend their food and take pride in its regional differences—in many cases, define themselves and their towns in the uniqueness of their food.

Paying my bill, I stepped into the street at the same time as another man, who had just finished eating and was voluptuously working a toothpick in his mouth. I said hello, we talked awhile—simple pleasantries—and then I asked how I might find some Huichol people in Tepic.

The man made an expansive gesture. "They're everywhere."

"I'd like to go to a Huichol village."

"That might be a problem."

"The village is far from here?"

"Two or three villages—yes, far. But they don't want you to visit. There used to be tours. But they're suspicious of outsiders." He smiled and took the toothpick from his mouth. "They made a rule banning missionaries from visiting." He laughed. "They don't want to see them!"

"Why is this?"

"Christian missionaries—*evangélicos*—many of them gringos from the US—singing, dancing. They wanted to convert them, but the Huicholes have other ideas and other gods." He gestured with the toothpick, making it a spear. "*Evangélicos!*"

"Is there a center of Huichol culture?"

"In Jalisco. San Andrés Cohamiata," he said. "You'll never find it. It's far, it's in the mountains. I don't think there's a road."

"So how do the Huicholes travel?"

"They don't travel far. But when they do, they use the paths"—*senderos*. "They walk."

He wished me well and strolled off, grinning into his toothpick. But not long after that, walking down a side street, I saw two women coming toward me, unmistakably Huicholes, highly colored, billowy blue gypsy skirts, yellow shawls, embroidered blouses, and red headscarves. They walked with the confidence verging on swagger that people possess when they wear traditional dress, asserting their difference.

"*Hola,*" I said, but they didn't stop, so I hurried after them and tried to engage them in conversation.

There followed an epiphany: I had found two people, natives of Mexico, whose grasp of Spanish was as rudimentary as mine.

"Huichol?"

"Yes."

"You live near here?"

"No."

"Where is your village?"

Flinging her hand, one woman said, "There. Far."

"San Andrés?"

"No. Another place. Small place."

"I want to visit your village."

They laughed. "No!"

"To see you make things." They were famous for their embroidery, their sewing, their decorated wide-brimmed straw hats, and especially for their intricate beadwork—tiny beads worked into the surface of wax sculptures.

In their refusal they spoke in their own language, finding this whole encounter ludicrous, the sudden pestering gringo on the hot street in mid-afternoon. They waved me away, but I was encouraged to look further. I walked for another hour but did not see another Huichol. Maybe, as the man said, they were hiding from gringo evangelists—who could blame them?

And so I left, boarding another bus.

## Puerto Vallarta

THE BUS MOVED past cane fields—the untidiest cash crop on earth, great uncombed, flopped-over stalks—and teams of people harvesting pineapples—bulky in padded shirts and gloves, to protect them from the thorns and spines—and into steep-sided hills, and groves of mangoes, and finally the descent to the town of Compostela. Compostela's church was nearly as impressive as Tepic's, and it is a tribute to indigenous resistance that in spite of all the proselytizing and the ecclesiastical architecture, the Huicholes were still venerating the deer and praying to the eagle and prostrating themselves before the jaguar, indifferent to one gringo's speculation that "in the juvescence of the year / Came Christ the tiger."

The palm and banana groves of the coastal plain lay below, wreathing the pretty resort town of Sayulita, and in the distance the enormous bay—the largest in the Pacific, so Mexicans say, backed by mountains—the great scallop of coastline that contains Puerto Vallarta. I could see it all in panorama, and later I learned that Old Vallarta lay in the middle of the bay, the luxury hotels at the top end, and at the bottom end of the bay the South Zone, then Mismaloya, where *Night of the Iguana* was filmed. Miles of beach, of *malecón* and promenade, and bandstands. There were rows of hotels, elaborate ones and gated resorts that possessed great strips of beach, and little posadas on side streets with balconies and ceiling fans.

The Zona Romántica of Old Vallarta—dense with shops and small hotels, on a grid of narrow streets—catered in the daytime to strollers and families looking for ceramics and souvenirs, and at night became a Zona de Tolerancia for roisterers and gawkers, throngs of whores and drunks, seeking each other.

I found a hotel bargain in the northerly Marina district, the four-day midweek special: a modest charge allowed me a room and unlimited food. Its guests were a revelation. Once, twenty years ago, for my book about the Mediterranean, I had spent two weeks on a Turkish cruise ship, which made a circuit of the ports of the eastern Mediterranean. Finding this ship had been a fluke: I had simply happened upon it at its mooring in Istanbul and bought a ticket on a whim. I discovered that one way to understand a culture was to spend a longish holiday in the company of a single nationality. Turks at breakfast, at every meal, playing cards, going on shore excursions, joining sing-alongs in the evening. I was the only non-Turk. I discovered how polite, even courtly, they were to each other; how circumspect they were in foreign ports; how abused and cheated they were in Alexandria and Haifa and Rhodes, screamed at in English, browbeaten by immigration officers; and how secure they felt on their Turkish ship, the MV *Akdeniz*.

The hotel on the Paseo de la Marina Sur had been built around a stack of open-sided lobbies, dampened and mildewed by the hot sea breeze from the Pacific. It was less than half full in spite of the holiday bargain. All the other guests were Mexican, many honeymooners, many middle-aged couples, but mostly families — not just mother and dad and the children, but the grandparents, *abuela, abuelo,* two of each in some cases. It seemed from these hundreds of middle-class Mexicans that they married young, they made their parents part of the holiday, they had many children, they tended to be heavyset, and they favored loose and baggy clothes — you'd see their counterparts at Disney World. Except for the small children — who chased each other, shrieking, around the hotel, bumping other guests, and were forgiven for being cute — the Mexicans were excessively polite, courteous toward each other, patient in the long lines at the buffet, and long-suffering at the pool — only a few risked the ocean.

I saw that a Mexican heaven, a Mexican holiday, is an all-you-can-eat buffet. They were not drinkers, but they were eaters. And the hotel, catering to these appetites, provided two large buffet restaurants, one in the main building below the lobby, another nearer the pool. The tables were always full, the guests padding back and forth, from the raw bar to the roast beef, from the posole and taco station to the pasta stall, from the salad trays and finally to the shelves of wobbly desserts. These Mexicans were a match for the greediest Americans, chewing their way through a buffet on a hot afternoon, going back for seconds and thirds, then looking for a chaise lounge to sleep off the effort of stuffing themselves before heading back once again, to load their plates with gummy chicken legs, fish smothered in white sauce, pizza slices, spare ribs, and an anthology of black clotted beans. None of it looked to my amateur eye like the sort of food you'd find in your neighborhood Mexican restaurant, or even in *their* neighborhood Mexican restaurant. It seemed the epitome of institutional gringo cuisine, but that hardly mattered, because it was piled high and you could eat as much as you wanted.

That was a revelation, but of course the hotel was perfect in other ways, too. The kids could run around, the pool was large enough for everyone, the oldies had places to sit or sleep. And if hunger was the common denominator, mealtime — all day, most of the evening — was a constant: the ritual of bingeing and gorging, the objective of the lanky, mustached gallant, the short-arsed salesman, the duck-butted matron, and the hyperactive tot. A Mexican middle-class vacation meant unlimited access to the buffet and a place for the kids to play and for the grandparents to snooze. No one used the tennis courts, no one was reading.

Now and then I shared a table, usually with a couple or a family, and we talked in general, about the weather, where they lived (many from Mexico City), what sort of work they did (teachers, electricians, drivers, insurance agents, beauticians). None mentioned the president until I mentioned his name.

"Trump hates us." This from a young woman at breakfast, holding her baby daughter on her lap.

"He says we're rapists and murderers." This from a dentist, a man who had studied in Texas.

"He does not know us," an old man said to me, smiling, spooning soup. "He does not want to know us."

"Why do Mexicans go to the States?" a woman said to me, while her husband listened, I think abashed at her assertiveness toward a stranger. "They go to look for work—and they work. All they ask for is to have a job. They are good workers. And what are they paid? Very little. But they don't complain. And Donald Trump says we are bad people."

Her husband said, "And he hires Mexicans at his hotels. I heard that on the news."

When the men were alone, away from wives and children, at the bar, by the pool, and we had talked awhile, establishing a bit of rapport, they howled, "He is crazy. He's a liar! How can a man so crazy become president?"

On another memorable occasion, a man who described himself as a driver (*conductor*), said, "He is a traitor! He is Judas!"—and the word sounds crueler when spoken in Spanish: *Hoodas!*

To get away from the eaters at the hotel and the hubbub of Vallarta, I took a taxi—one I had used the previous day—to the botanical gardens at the edge of the jungle, Selva El Tuito, driven by Ottavio, an older man, who said, "This is my day off. I told my son to take you. But he said no, and you know why? He doesn't speak English. I told him to learn English, that's the way to get business. But he doesn't do it."

"*Pero, hablo español perfectamente.*"

"*Claro,*" Ottavio said, and laughed, continuing in English. "One reason I am busy is, I speak English."

"Have you been to the States?"

"No. Never. I would like to go. You think Mr. Trump would allow me?"

"What do you think of him?"

He lapsed into Spanish, saying, "*Una rata.*"

Out of Vallarta, southward, along the coast. Cliffside hotels and gated communities and villas and bungalows and chalets and mansions. "All Canadians," Ottavio said, indicating a tall building, and at a clifftop development, "Gringos, gringos, gringos." Germans often visited, he said. Some Germans retired to Mexico. British people, too. "Arabians," he said. And after all this: "But if a Mexican wants to go to their country—hah!"

We were on Highway 200, the road that extends for another thousand miles, to the border town of Tapachula and the edge of Guatemala. We stopped briefly so that I could examine the decaying sign and the fenced-in ruin of the Night of the Iguana Hotel, then continued inland, where at a bend in the road Ottavio became very nervous, slowing and finally stopping the car.

"There are no policemen here," he said. "But there should be policemen. A checkpoint. I need permission to go farther."

But there were no policemen on this dark narrow curve, only overhanging trees and an old stone wall, nothing to indicate a frontier.

"This is not Jalisco. It is a different state. I will have trouble when I come back. They'll say, 'Where is your permission?'"

"I don't see anyone, do you?"

"Maybe they see us."

He fretted for a few minutes, gripping the steering wheel, then got out of the car and looked around, called out briefly, shook his head, and, sighing, restarted the car and drove onward.

"We might have trouble," he said.

It was the perennial anxiety that Mexicans feel, faced with the ambiguous threat of authority, usually from the police or the army. But the winding road and the dangerous curves, buses and trucks coming toward us, distracted him, and after twenty miles we came to the botanical gardens.

The best botanical gardens are the oldest ones, with majestic trees like Kew or the one in Singapore, or in Calcutta with its great stands of bamboo, or the oldest of all, the garden in Kingstown, on the island of St. Vincent. The garden here was young, having been planted fairly recently, fifteen years ago or less. But that was not the point. I was merely looking for an excuse to get away from the crowds of eaters at my hotel in Vallarta, and walking the pathways of the gardens with Ottavio was a revelation.

It started when he rushed toward a plant, exclaiming, "These are tasty. You can eat the flowers of these. You can make tea with them, too — good for the blood!"

Birds and butterflies, the sunny day, and we came to a section of cactus plants, various kinds.

"This is *nopal*," Ottavio said, salivating a little. "Those ends — the little ones, see them? They're good to eat. Slice them up. You can have them for breakfast."

A fork in the road. We descended the path to a small pond, dusted with gilded gnats.

"Look at that lily pad — just like a tortilla!" And he leaned closer, looking hungry. "You can eat the roots, you know!"

His excitement grew when he saw orange trees and lemon trees laden with fruit, and a pink pomegranate on a thorny bough. And spotting a smooth, fist-sized blob hanging from a vine, he said, "Pretty. I wonder if you can eat that?"

Craving to be alone, I paid Ottavio for taking me there and spent the rest of the morning in the gardens on my own, loving the solitude and the surrounding forest as much as the gardens themselves. And then I walked up to the road and took a slow, stopping bus, past the resorts and the gated communities and the people on vacation, back to my hotel, where it was always mealtime. The day at the botanical gardens inspired two thoughts:

that it was time to leave Puerto Vallarta for Mexico City, and that it must be by an express bus.

It was an overnighter. Back to Sayulita and Compostela, and then the bus wound through the mountains to Guadalajara, an overbright bus station and a quesadilla there; then to Ocotlán and Atlacomulco. Turning south at Jilotepec de Molina Enríques, the bus arrived at dawn at the Poniente terminal.

This was near the Observatorio metro station, named for an observatory built by the national university for stargazing. But some time after the telescope was installed, Mexico City's polluted air and glary light rendered it unusable.

I took the metro back to Hotel La Casona. Rudi Roth said, "I'm sorry to see you go. I liked having breakfast with you."

My car was where I had left it, in the secure parking lot near the hotel. There was a bulky package in the back seat. One of my students had left this as a present for me, a framed etching by a celebrated Mexican artist, Sergio Hernández, with a note: *Please come back, Don Pablo.*

Touched, a bit dreamy from this sweet gesture, I drove out of the lot, turned the corner, entered a street—unusually empty of cars—and heard a loud yell and a shrill whistle.

A policeman flapped his hand at me and pulled me over.

"You are in violation of the law," he said.

"I don't understand."

"As this is a Sunday, this road is closed to vehicles—notice the bicycles."

That was true—bike riders everywhere, swishing past us in both directions. There was no sign saying the road was closed to vehicles. Apparently, the bike riding was a Sunday tradition in Mexico City.

"We can impound your car for this violation."

"How much?" I asked. He then named his price. I handed him the money. He softened, became polite, and thanked me with a little salute.

"Which way to Texcoco?" I asked. "But not by the Periférico."

I wanted to avoid the ring road because it was patrolled by the sort of motorcycle police who had shaken me down before. It was not the direct route to Puebla, but judging from my map, it was the quickest way out of Mexico City, with fewer cops.

"Straight ahead. Look for signs to the airport," the policeman said with a friendly smile as he palmed my dollar bills. He then slipped them into his jacket and patted the proud little square of thickness in his pocket. "Keep going east. *Buen viaje.*"

## PART THREE

# Oaxaca, *the* Inframundo

## *To Puebla*

LEAVING THE CITY, thinking of my students and the surprise of the handsome gift left in my car, I was glum with nostalgic melancholy. It was the effect of my detour to the border, my side trip to the coast, the end of the writing workshop. I wasn't busy anymore. The cure for idleness was to hit the road. I was not sad to leave Mexico City—my heart sings whenever I leave a big city and see the thinning suburbs and first green hills beyond them—but I was sad to leave the students, no longer students, but friends.

My destination was Puebla, and there was a direct route, southeast from where I'd been shaken down. But this would have taken me through Nezahualcóyotl—sinister "Ciudad Neza"—the densest district of Mexico City, and not only the most populous but the most violent, a place of cops much crookeder than the one who had just extorted me on a leafy boulevard in Roma Sur. Neza was notorious for its slums, its seedy underworld, gangs, drugs, and murder—in particular femicides, the rape and killing of women—where I would also be impeded by the slow traffic through its barrios. By taking a detour, I would be in the countryside quicker, and far from the police.

I was soon in Texcoco and driving clockwise around the slopes of Monte Tlaloc, "the ghost mountain," with a temple to Tlaloc the storm god, the god of rain and fertility, on its summit at 13,600 feet—one of the highest archeological sites in the world, higher than Machu Picchu. Tlaloc is part of a trio of close-together volcanoes, with the 17,000-footers Iztaccíhuatl (the Woman in White) and Popocatépetl (Smoking Mountain). Popocatépetl was still smoking, still erupting, and the grandeur of this trio of steep, symmetrical flanks and peaks was apparent even cloaked in the brown grainy cloudbanks drifting from Mexico City.

A bit farther south I was traveling on the old Camino Real, which linked the great capital to Puebla—the Royal Road in name, but humble in reality, a thoroughfare of farms and cultivated land and small villages, passing through Calpulalpan (celebrated for its annual fair, during which, so the town's tourist office boasted, "people feast on local specialties—maguey worms, pulque, and owls"). This region of plowed fields provided the food for the big city. Keeping to this straight road, I connected to the *autopista,* paying a toll and sailing to Puebla.

At a service area near the town of San Martín Texmelucan de Labastida I stopped for gas. By now, as a road tripper, I had become accustomed to the routine of a Mexican pit stop, a model of efficiency and in many respects superior to its equivalent in the US. Because Mexico has abandoned its passenger trains, and depends on eighteen-wheelers to move its freight north to the border and beyond, and on its fleets of long-distance buses, its main highways are well maintained. The off-ramp always leads to the dusty antique past—to the man plowing a stony field with a burro, to the woman with a bundle on her head, to the boy herding goats, to the *ranchitos,* the *carne asada* stands, the five-hundred-year-old churches, and a *tienda,* selling beer and snacks, with a skinny cat asleep on the tamales.

On the main road, the gas pumps at the service area are manned by attendants in uniforms. You drive in, say *"Lleno, por favor"* or *"Llenarlo,"* and the fellow fills the tank, washes your windows, earns a tip, and offers his elaborate thanks: "At your service, sir."

There will always be an OXXO convenience store at the service area, many of them the size of a small supermarket: beer, wine, T-shirts, hats, chips, automotive accessories, fireworks, balloons, lucky charms, first aid supplies, fruit, canned food, plastic toys, magazines, and newspapers. There will probably be a taco stand next door, or a chicken franchise like El Pollo Loco, staffed by pretty girls in paper hats. The restrooms will be guarded by a woman wrapped in a rebozo and wearing an apron. She will greet you and remind you that you will need to insert a 5-peso coin in the turnstile, and she might discreetly hand you four squares of stiff abrasive paper, expecting a tip. An enterprising man might be seated at a table near the gas pumps, selling watermelons or clay pots. In some of the larger service areas between the big cities there might be a brown motel of fake adobe, and some of the smaller ones feature a decent restaurant selling local food.

After the gasoline ritual, I parked and bought two tacos, a cup of coffee, and a copy of *El Universal,* and sat in the sunshine, reading the paper and blessing my luck. I'd be in Puebla within an hour, and in three or four days—I was in no hurry—in Oaxaca. But no sunny moment in Mexico is without a cloud. On an inside page of the paper, under a photo that looked like a gruesome car crash, I read a news item about how, just the day before, a car—the vandalized and sticky one in the picture—was found in Veracruz with five human heads tied to the hood, the decapitated corpses stacked inside the car. Graffiti scratched into the car's paint, a *narcomensaje,* indicated that it was the work of a cartel, the Jalisco New Generation.

"Sending a message" was the usual explanation, an unambiguous message in this case, stating that this cartel was not to be trifled with. In 2017 there had been 2,200 criminal homicides in Veracruz state, most of them cartel related.

From here to Puebla, every flat area of the fertile landscape was a cultivated field—hardly a tree in sight—smallholdings of green vegetables, onions or cabbages, lettuce or tomatoes. In the north, I had been used to seeing cactus and bleak stretches of desert, roads of washboard gravel, but here in southerly Puebla state the land was fertile, the fields were green, and people were hoeing, their backs bent, clawing at the soil, the iconic postures of peasants.

Passing Cholula, I thought of stopping for the night, but the traffic began to pile up around me, and pretty soon I was shouldered off the motorway by honking cars and, in a maze of narrow streets, going in the wrong direction. I knew I was lost—or at least far from the center of the city—because the streets were slanted and asymmetrical. The oldest parts of a Mexican city, surveyed and laid out by the Spanish, were always arranged in a tight grid of right angles.

I pulled off the road, consulted the map on my phone, and got my bearings. But I was still in a single crawl of traffic on back streets, nowhere near the center of Puebla, passing a residential area of walled-in bungalows, cringing dogs, and tire repair shops.

Such is the revelation of the road trip. Someone says, "We spent a week in Puebla," and the name seems magical: colonial churches, houses roofed with red tiles, the Zócalo lined with cafés and arcades, *mole poblano* drizzled on chicken, brassy music, perhaps folkloric dancing—twirling skirts, stamping feet, shoeshine stalls and balloon sellers, the locals strolling, some of the women outfitted in the Frida Kahlo style, with the colorful Puebla dress, the *china poblana* outfit of an embroidered blouse and full skirt, perhaps a tiara of pompoms and a shawl and an apron thick with floral stitching. All that is accurate, but there is more.

Here is the reality. Puebla is not the compact colonial city it once was. No Mexican city with a romantic name fits that description. Never mind that it is more than five hundred years old. Puebla is a sprawling metropolis of more than four million people, with a Walmart and shopping malls and factories—one of the biggest textile factories in Mexico. It has a Volkswagen plant, another making Hyundais, and eleven industrial parks. Also the industry for which Puebla is most famous, the making of Talavera ceramics—nine such workshops.

There is not a big city in Mexico—no matter how charming its plaza, how atmospheric its cathedral, how wonderful its food, or how illustrious its schools—that is not in some way fundamentally grim, with a big-box store, a Sam's Club, and an industrial area, a periphery of urban ugliness that makes your heart sink. Because this is in Mundo Mexico, on the plain of snakes, its citizens are overlooked by the government, its workers exploited and underpaid, its teachers belittled, nearly all its city dwellers living in small spaces. But the people are making the best of it, because it was my experience that Mexicans might be mockers and teasers, but they are not idle complainers.

When an oppressed group in Mexico airs a grievance, it doesn't mumble. It takes to the streets with resolve, holds a demonstration in the main plaza, camps out in front of a ministry in a defiant vigil, burns a bus, blocks a motorway, or, in the case of the Zapatistas in Chiapas, arrives on horseback out of the jungle and declares an insurrection, taking over an entire state and eventually running it so well that the government (out of shame or indifference or confusion) turns its back on the rebels, pretends they don't exist, and allows them to create a better way of life.

I made my way through the Puebla suburbs, into the numbered streets and the square blocks, following the signs pointing to *centro histórico*. Passing an older but solid hotel, its brick facade decorated with Talaveras, on a corner next to a church — the Hotel San José — I parked and ran inside. Yes, they had plenty of rooms, $50 a night, walking distance to the Zócalo and the museums. And that became my home for four nights.

After a long drive and a long walk, I strolled around the Zócalo, where a klezmer group was playing. Klezmer? Yes, violins, guitars, a drum, a trumpet, a trombone. Two players were bearded, in black vests and black fedoras. None were Jewish, they told me later; they simply loved the sound. They had seen videos of klezmer music on the internet and decided to learn how to play its strangulated and sobbing tremolos, its flatulent oompahs, its Bulgarian syncopations, and its Polish mazurkas, bewitching the many Mexicans who crowded the arcade to hear it. One child was provoked to a stumbling dance at the feet of the fiddler, who was sawing his heart out with his eyes shut.

Looking for the famous seventeenth-century paintings in the cathedral on the Zócalo the next day, I was distracted by a scene that reached back to the Spanish conquest: a tall, white-robed bishop in a sparkly white miter, carrying a gold shepherd's crook, a white giant walking among a congregation of much smaller, much darker people. The bishop was attended by a priest in purple vestments, bearing a bucket. Wielding a dripping silver aspergillum — the knobbed, hand-held sprinkling instrument — the bishop spattered holy water on the upturned faces of the faithful, bringing pious smiles of gratitude to those ritually moistened.

The paintings were soot-darkened and severe, the Altar of the Kings (of Spain) was overpainted and garish, containing the sculpted images of the kings, patrons of the church residing in niches. But two items stood out. One was a glass coffin with a life-size model of the naked Christ inside, lying supine, his tortured eyes turned toward heaven and covered in blood and deeply scored with spectacular lacerations. This was not old, but it was gory enough to be alarming.

And at a side altar, a painting depicting Father Miguel Pro, his arms extended as though crucified, being shot by a firing squad. This image, too, was fairly sooty, but I remembered the name of Father Pro from Graham Greene. He was fondly recalled by Greene in 1938 as the priest who had returned from studying in Europe to serve the faithful in 1926, when the anticlerical laws were being strictly enforced. Celebrating Mass in secret, in defiance of the government, Father Pro was arrested in 1927 on a trumped-up charge of attempting to assassinate a general (Obregón, who was later killed by a militant Catholic for his anticlericalism). Far from quelling the Cristero Rebellion, the execution of Father Pro—as shown in the painting—gave the Cristeros a martyr. And the atmosphere of persecution provided Graham Greene with a plot: godless politicians, brutish soldiers, God-fearing peasants, churches under siege, and priests ministering the sacraments in covert rituals.

What Greene did not mention was that the churches reopened in 1929, except in the two reluctant states where he was traveling, and that the Cristero rebels were militant, crudely armed, but passionate Catholics, willing to commit murder for their faith—a formidable army howling *"Viva Cristo Rey!"* and gunning for infidels. Though the states of Tabasco and Chiapas were suffering the vandalism of their churches, Mexico was being governed by Lázaro Cárdenas, a man mildly disparaged by Greene, whom most Mexicans believe to have been their most enlightened president. Cárdenas was a pacifier: as he repealed the antichurch laws, he was trying to mollify the Cristeros in some states, and the persecutors of the Catholics in other states, while at the same time fending off foreign petrocrats and nationalizing the oil companies.

Puebla was an interlude in my road trip south, a four-day touristic pit stop. I fueled my walks with Puebla's wonderful food: *mole poblano*—goopy, spiced chocolate sauce over chicken; *memelas*—corn cakes topped with cheese and tomato; *molotes*—stuffed pastry; *chalupas* topped with salsa and shredded meat. Hearty meals, stuffed buns, sticky sauces, and street food.

A museumgoer when I have nothing better to do, I avoid writing much about collections, because a visitor should enter a museum innocent of what's to come, be allowed to make discoveries, and not be nagged into seeing specific works. I had been humbled by the museums in Mexico City, especially by the treasures in the National Museum of Anthropology—the giant Olmec heads, the skull with staring bejeweled eyes and overlaid with a mosaic of turquoise, Moctezuma's feathered headdress, and glittering mortuary masks, items harvested from ruins and tombs all over Mexico.

There were no treasures in Puebla's Museo Amparo to equal those. The Amparo's small collection was housed in two old stone buildings on a side street. But I found something remarkable there, a Mexican artist obsessed with the grotesqueries of modern Mexico. Among the colonial paintings and ancient stone carvings was an artist I'd never heard of and who seemed to me a true original. This was Yoshua Okón, who described himself as a performance artist. Young (born in 1970) and widely traveled, he made videos as well as installations and sculptures. One of the sculptures in the Museo Amparo was a shimmering object of chrome and cast bronze, a thing of singular beauty that looked like a throne. And in a manner of speaking it was one, as its label stated: *El Excusado / The Toilet*. It was a superior hopper, as arresting as an Edward Hopper, of lovely proportions, made in the shape of the Museo Soumaya, "an emblem of Carlos Slim's telecommunication empire" and intended to mock both Slim's museum (the Soumaya, in Mexico City) and Slim's wealth, succeeding at both with devastating Mexican mockery.

Looping around that room was Okón's installation titled *HCl,* a symmetrical series of acrylic pipes, each pipe about six inches in diameter and running up and down the walls of two rooms, attractive as a well-made industrial masterpiece depicting the austere geometry of plumbing. This too, at first glance, was a wonderful thing, for the way the bold pipes surrounded the room. The pipes vividly churned with brownish-gray liquid, and the whole business was operated by a gulping, pumping contraption, as impressively made as Carlos Slim's scale-model art museum that was also a "functioning, luxury" toilet.

"HCl is the formula for hydrochloric acid," the label began, and explained that this acid is an aid to human digestion. Then the unexpected detail: the see-through pipes were filled with human vomit, "donated by anonymous patients from a bulimic clinic." You admire the artistry and form, and then, told what it represented, you gaze with nauseated horror.

"Okón is satirizing the fantasies engendered by the relentless corruption of contemporary culture," the label went on, "and the sacrifice of health and well-being to corporate-denominated images of bodily appearance."

I had seen the angels and saints in the big, dark paintings of Villalpando and Cabrera in the church on the Zócalo, the murals of Rivera or Orozco on the walls of public buildings, the self-portraits of Frida Kahlo in plaster corsets, standing on a wooden leg in her Blue House in Coyoacán. And now Okón's puke-filled pipes. Like Rivera and the others, and the Oaxaca artist Francisco Toledo, Okón's work is widely praised and exhibited in museums around the world.

It seemed that the strangeness of life in Mexico, the inequality as well as the vitality, stimulated those artists and provoked the appropriate reply. Such Mexican traits certainly stimulated Francisco Toledo in Oaxaca. When it became known that McDonald's was opening a burger joint in his city, Toledo threatened an episode of performance art, showing up naked in front of the proposed site, offering free tamales to any Oaxacan who supported him in his outrage.

Okón's videos were as odd and shocking, and as essentially Mexican, as his sculptural installations. Sharing Toledo's resentment of McDonald's intrusion, Okón in 2014 made *Freedom Fries: Still Life*, a video loop of a huge, blobby, obese man lying naked on a McDonald's dining table. Okón's video statement on migration is titled *Oracle, a Border Town in Arizona*. Basing this on the tens of thousands of unaccompanied minors who have crossed the US border, Okón filmed a chorus of nine Guatemalan children in Oracle, singing a song to the tune of "The Marines' Hymn" that narrates a history of American aggression, beginning with the invasion of Mexico in the nineteenth century ("From the halls of Montezuma ..."). "In this version," his gallery description explains, "the kids sing about the invasion of their own land—beginning with a CIA-led coup in 1954—with specific emphasis on the complicity of the CIA and the United Fruit Company."

Another video at the Museo Amparo was *Bocanegra: A Walk in the Park,* a sequence shot in Mexico City showing Nazi sympathizers and historical reenactment buffs, all in actual Nazi uniforms, marching, giving speeches, saluting, and drinking beer. The shouts and *Sieg Heils* in the video were audible in the nearby galleries.

The people experiencing these pieces were all Mexicans—or so they looked to me; Puebla seemed without foreign tourists—and I lingered to note their reactions, smiling at the Carlos Slim toilet, shocked by everything else. I caught the attention of a museum attendant, a middle-aged man, his thumbs hooked into his belt. He nodded at the vomit plumbing and winked at me, as one satirist to another.

Mexican art was also a world, as ancient as the monumental Olmec heads in the first great civilization on the continent, and as modern as the bronze hopper and outrageous videos intended to satirize Mexico today.

Walking out of the Okón exhibit, I fell into step with a sedate older couple.

"What did you think?" I asked.

"That man has a good sense of humor," the man said, and his wife nodded in approval.

Art as rebellion, as protest, was a Mexican passion, and protest was a theme in Puebla that day. Hundreds of health care workers—doctors and nurses—were milling about the city's main plaza, airing their grievances. I talked to a woman in a nurse's uniform who said that thousands of such workers had not been paid, or had been laid off, or denied their bonuses. This too was like performance art, because all the protesters were dressed in their hospital uniforms—white dresses, white coats, the doctors carrying stethoscopes as well as signs.

Shouts and agitation, the medical union members howling through bullhorns: I had seen similar protests elsewhere, in Potosí, Puerto Vallarta, and Mexico City. It seemed an eternal urban ritual, the theater of struggle, enacted in the land of bankruptcy and discontent and failed government, making Mexico appear to be a world of broken promises, a land to flee.

## *Cholula*

ANOTHER DAY, I became a time-killing tourist and took the bus to Cholula, famous for its pyramid. At one time Cholula and Puebla were separate towns, with their own distinctive food, music, saints' days, celebrations, and churches. Now, with the sprawl, Cholula is a Puebla suburb, a four-mile bus ride apart, past car dealerships and restaurants and department stores.

What was originally a pyramid of stepped and cut stone is now little more than a steep grassy hill, but it was once the highest pyramid in Mexico, known as Tlachihualtepetl (Made-by-Hand Mountain). Its ancient remains are located in its interior, the labyrinth of tunnels in its base — low, dark corridors linking chambers and stairways, leading to humid grottoes and empty niches. Although my aversion to caves and tight spaces amounts almost to a suffocating nightmare of — perhaps — uterine fear, I bought a ticket and walked in.

And once in, I had to creep along, ducking through the whole complex of tunnels, subjecting myself to an anxious half hour, eager for it to be over, nothing learned except that the guts of this pyramid were lengthy (five miles of them had been excavated). I was so relieved finally to exit the thing that I happily climbed to the church at the top, gasping so dramatically that a man laughed at my discomfort.

"But it's worth it!" he said. *Pero vale la pena!*

Yes, because standing on the steps of the sixteenth-century church of Our Lady of Remedies (Nuestra Señora de los Remedios), I looked north and saw Popocatépetl in the distance, in Malcolm Lowry's words, "plumed with emerald snow and drenched with brilliance," looking in the fading sunset as simple and severe as Mount Fuji, like a pyramidal mountain drawn by a small child.

As with many of the most ancient and historic churches in Mexico, Our Lady of Remedies was built to displace a temple to a potent deity, to rid the people of their old beliefs and insert new ones. "Upon its top there was found by the Spaniards a temple dedicated to Quetzalcoatl, which, with characteristic promptitude, they threw down, and substituted in its place a Christian temple," wrote Thomas Janvier in 1887 in his *Mexican Guide*. (One of Janvier's other books is a strange but little-known novel of disorientation, *In the Sargasso Sea*.)

Because Cholula is also noted for its highly decorated baroque churches, I made a little tour of them, guidebook in hand, admiring the Talavera tile inlays and the gold-encrusted walls, the tortured saints and the gory crucifixions. But this was merely an interlude, a way of working up an appetite for another meal in Puebla, and stretching my legs for the road trip south.

## More Detours: Roadblock, Back Road, Hitchhikers, Yanhuitlán

THE ROAD FROM Puebla to Oaxaca begins near the Walmart, cuts through the industrial areas and poor neighborhoods—small children in the street and starved dogs—passes small shops and garages, extends through farmland and vegetable fields, then rises, mounting into the distance, leaving all traces of humanity behind, and continues after the town of Tehuacán into the heights of the rocky past, not a person in sight, the summits of these nameless mountains looking scalded and bare and terrifying in their flinty emptiness.

I drove contentedly on the narrow road, hardly any traffic, except for the occasional blue long-distance bus or an eighteen-wheeler chugging under its load of steel girders, big, slow-moving vehicles, maddening to pass on the tight curves. The road wound through one of the most dramatic mountain landscapes I have ever seen—past declivities of precipitous ridges, the mile-high Sierra de Zapotitlán, and climbing to their flanks, the steep cliffs and rocky slopes of the Sierra Mixteca, no towns, few villages, perhaps a lone figure leaning against the slope here and there, many goats, and the rest of it a bleak and beautiful expanse of lifeless isolation. I was following the route of Río Calapa, which partly forms the border between the states of Puebla and Oaxaca, a region of outstanding beauty, the high sides of the valleys baked brown, their deepest parts darkened in the shadow of a river trickling south. To the east, more rivers and tributaries swell into the much wider Río Papaloapan—the River of Butterflies—flowing into the Gulf.

I passed long, narrow valleys, eroded hills and mountainsides, meager soils, so sheet-washed and thin from being sluiced with rain, the water pouring across them and carrying the surface away. In the winding river gorges that Mexicans call *barrancas,* the clinging vegetation—yucca, organ pipe and prickly pear cactus, tenacious, bristling with spikes—looked strangely metallic. To the east was the Tehuacán-Cuicatlán Biosphere Reserve, cloud forests at the higher elevations, and on some lower slopes, tall columnar cactus in mazy green colonnades.

I was in no hurry, blissed out by the light and the sky and the precipices, the configuration of mountain ridges, the vertiginous sides, pathless, looking unclimbable—and if these single peaks had names, they were not on my map, or on any I could find.

Descending through valleys of grayish clay and bone-white cliffs, I came to a gas station and saw that the nearest town was Tepelmeme (pop. 419), in the hard-pressed Mixteca region that produces many migrants, to Mexico City, to US border factories, and beyond. But all I saw were the infertile slopes of the sierra and the puffs of blowing clay dust, like hurrying and decaying ghosts.

I had gone about 150 miles and, seeing a diner, went in to find something to eat. Not a soul in the place eating—and it was noon—but three solid Mixtec women encouraged me to order. I had a *queso fonda,* a bowl of roasted cheese with tortillas, and a coffee, and made notes on my progress through the mountains, which had thrilled me.

"I am from Tepel," one of the women said to me in answer to my question.

"What happens there?"

"We are campesinos. We have goats. We grow our food."

"And the church," another woman said. "It is old and beautiful."

"Do you go to Oaxaca?"

"Yes, sir. For the fiestas. And to buy things."

"Is there a bus?"

"Yes. Expensive, though," the woman said, the peso equivalent of $5.

Living in a state with the lowest per capita income in Mexico ($3,400), $5 was around half a day's wage, and for this woman probably much more than that.

I left enough of a tip so that they could each buy a bus ticket, and when I explained this, they laughed and said that when I came back, I must visit their village.

In a sunny mood, I continued south, and hardly ten miles down the road, at the beginning of a long valley, I saw a line of cars—unmoving—from where I had to stop, and winding along the floor of the valley and rising along its sides, to the highest point at a notch, a mile or more of narrow road made visible by the bulky cars and buses and big trucks—a solid, sinuous snake of traffic lying against the land, defining its curves.

After hours of hardly any vehicles, this astonishing traffic jam. I had seen stopped traffic in Mexico before, but never on a road this narrow, all the drivers and passengers lolling by the side of the road, picnicking, drinking beer, some loudly complaining, others walking agitatedly, stiff-legged, shaking their fists into the distance and calling out in futile barks, as though at some unseen villain.

Two mustached bus drivers, uniformed in peaked caps and buttoned-up bumfreezers, were conferring near me.

"What happened?" I asked. "An accident?"

"It's a blockade."

"Up there?"

"No—it's far. Maybe at the tollbooth."

"Where's the tollbooth?"

"Maybe the one at San Cristóbal."

I looked at my map and found the crossroads of San Cristóbal Suchixt-lahuaca (pop. 200), about ten miles ahead. This meant ten miles of backed-up traffic.

"Who are the people who made the blockade?"

"The teachers," said one bus driver.

"It's always the teachers," the other one said.

I sighed, grumbled, kicked at roadside gravel, and slapped my head.

The border fence, Nogales, Arizona. Close relatives live on both sides.

Border Patrol officer, Nogales, Arizona.

PHOTOS BY STEVE MCCURRY

María saying grace at the Comedor, the Kino Initiative's migrant shelter in Nogales. Desperately poor, she left her three children behind to cross the border, to work as a cleaner. Arrested by the Border Patrol, she was roughed up, jailed, and deported. Her stoicism was a continued inspiration.

PEG BOWDEN

In Brownsville, Texas, a cross memorializes a migrant who died on this spot. There is hardly a stretch of border wall that does not have such a cross.

STEVE McCURRY

The author with weavers and campesinos in San Baltazar Guelavila, Oaxaca. All but two of them had been undocumented workers in the United States. MICHAEL SLEDGE

The author at the Comedor in Nogales, talking to a man who had been deported after working for twelve years in the United States. STEVE MCCURRY

Nogales street scene.

Child street performer, Oaxaca.

PHOTOS BY STEVE McCURRY

The author and an indignant citizen in
Ciudad Alemán's main plaza.

Late afternoon mezcal, Oaxaca.

A man at his family grave in a traditional Day of the Dead vigil at a cemetery in Oaxaca.

Celebrant in a Day of the Dead procession, Oaxaca.

The author walking on the Ciudad Juárez side of the border, along the culvert that contains the Rio Grande, a trickle here in the dry season.

The border west of Nogales, Arizona.

A side street in a poor community in Ciudad Juárez, source of much of the labor for NAFTA factories.

The author and Subcomandante Marcos (masked) at a Zapatista event in Chiapas.
MICHAEL SLEDGE

Santa María Ixcatlán, Mixteca Alta. This woman had woven the straw hat that morning to use as payment for milling the maize in her basket. MICHAEL SLEDGE

A shepherd in late afternoon, a remnant of the eternal Mexico, along the sixteenth-century Padre Tembleque aqueduct northeast of Mexico City. STEVE MCCURRY

Noting my frustration, the first bus driver said, "You don't have to stay here. You can take that road."

He was pointing, but I saw no road, only the rubbly hillside beyond the safety fence and the scabious vegetation of *nopal* and low, twisted leafless trees.

The man led me to the fence and, pointing to what looked like an arroyo, an eroded gully leading up the hill, said, "That's a road. You can take it. Go that way. My bus is too big, but your car can do it." He took my shoulder and twisted my body around, the way a schoolteacher directs a small child. "See those men? Go through there."

Fifty yards down the road, a group of men in thick ragged coats sat on the metal fence, beside a break in it that seemed wide enough to accommodate my car.

"Go!" the bus driver said. He slapped my car. "You're lucky!"

"Then what?"

"Just keep going!" He flapped his hand, and when the men sitting on the fence heard him, they perked up.

I made a U-turn and drove back to the opening in the fence and the group of men. As I entered, one man gestured for me to roll down my window.

"Thirty pesos," he said—a quick thinker. It was $1.50. I handed it over and the other men laughed at this man's enterprise, or his impudence, or perhaps at my gringo acquiescence.

I drove up this rutted hillside next to the highway, and at the top of the hill entered a wilderness of dead trees, following what was no more than a bumpy pathway—and thinking, of course, If my car breaks down here, I am out of luck. No villages were indicated on my map, only the tollbooth at the crossing at San Cristóbal Suchixtlahuaca, ten miles ahead. Ten miles is nothing on a highway; on a dirt track (my axles bumping against the ruts, stones kicking into my undercarriage), it is a great distance.

So I drove very slowly, in a state of mild anxiety, somewhat alleviated by the happy thought that I was circumventing the traffic jam of the blockade. I could see a deep gully to my left, a riverbed inside it, obsidian on this overcast late afternoon of blowing dust. And after twenty minutes of washboard gravel I came to a better road—not paved, its ruts apparently filled with cat litter, but signposted to San Miguel Tequixtepec, a community I could see, a scattering of squat, clay-colored huts, a church, two steeples, a red dome, and low hills in the distance, softened by greenery.

I thought with relief that someone in the village would help me if I had a problem, and drove on feeling more confident, further encouraged by a harder-surfaced road, and another sign, San Juan Bautista Coixtlahuaca to the left, San Cristóbal to the right. I turned right for San Cristóbal, reasoning that if the blocked tollbooth was there, I would be first in line when the blockade was lifted.

A mile farther on, I came upon the blockade. A crowd of men and women were milling about, many of them sitting, barriers set up to prevent cars from passing, and about fifty cars parked by the roadside. It could have passed for a yard sale, with roadside junk and people chatting companionably, some looking at their phones, others playing with children. But from their postures, the way they were sitting on the curbstones and leaning against the fences—from the very air of indolence and fatigue and unhurried conversation, not much movement—I sensed that nothing was about to change. It was a relaxed group, no sign of confrontation. The tollbooth had been dismantled, tree limbs had been dragged into the road, vestiges of meals were strewn about—paper plates, plastic cups, crumpled napkins, crushed soda cans—a reminder that in Mexico, political action such as a roadblock or a protest is also a social occasion.

"What's happening?" I asked a man leaning against his car.

"Blockade." He shrugged.

"Any idea when it will end?"

"Maybe soon. Maybe some hours."

"What are they doing?"

"Talking," he said, which I took to mean they were negotiating—in any case, creating enough of a fuss and a backup on the main road to make their point. Like the medical workers I'd seen in Puebla, the teachers had a list of demands for the government.

I went to my car, got my map of Mexico, and approached the same man again, unfolding it. I circled San Cristóbal with my pen, saying, "We're here, right?"

He put his finger on the circle and chafed the map with his fingertip.

"This road," he said. "It's there." He pointed to where the cars were drawn up on the shoulder. "You can go that way. It's the free road."

A road designated *libre* was usually a side road, a country road, or one crowded with local traffic.

"Will this one get me to Oaxaca?"

"Sure." Then he looked unsure. "After a while." *Después de un tiempo.*

Reasoning that I would rather take a detour for hours on a bad road than sit in my car in a traffic jam, I thanked him and drove away, past the parked cars and the children and the protesting teachers, through the bowl of a green valley and into the hills that looked rockier and drier in the distance.

The road was paved but potholed. In places the ruts were a foot deep and very wide, some of them filled with water where goats were drinking. But I was moving, and that was a great thing, and I was in the heart of the country, passing through the small village of San Cristóbal, with its flat-roofed huts, wooden animal pens, and donkeys tethered to dead trees. Skidding on the loose rocks, I was approaching cliffs of spectacular skeletal erosion.

At the far edge of the village, three young, well-dressed women—long wool coats, wide-brimmed hats—stood under a big, thick-limbed tree, looking tense and expectant, as though waiting for a bus. Their shoulders were wrapped in shawls, because we were in the uplands, where it was cool, and the sky had darkened, clouds in the distance threatening rain. I stopped and said hello. We exchanged the polite and disarming greetings that are customary in Mexico among strangers in a country setting.

I then asked, "Do you want a ride?"

Yes, they did, and smiled, looking relieved. They pressed against my car.

"Where are you going?"

"Tejúpam," one said, but the name meant nothing to me and I could not find it on my map.

"Is it far?"

"A little bit."

I told them I was trying to get to Oaxaca.

"We'll show you the way."

"Let's go," I said, and the three of them got into the back seat, none daring to risk the passenger seat with the gringo, laughing softly, unwrapping their shawls, and wriggling to get comfortable.

"What are your names?"

They said they were Shirley, Lucia, and Vianey—Vianey had to spell it slowly for me to grasp it. Not a common name, she said, but her parents liked it.

Now we were in those rough-hewn hills of bluish shattered rock I'd seen, passing a poor hut and a flock of goats, in the deep countryside of Oaxaca's Mixteca Alta, the poorest part of Mexico. None of the land looked arable, and even the goats seemed to be having a tough time nibbling at the ragged tussocks of grass growing sparsely in the hard ribs of clay soil.

"Do you work or go to school?"

"We are students," Shirley said—she was the most responsive. "We are studying education. We intend to become teachers."

"Were you helping with the blockade?"

"Just looking," Shirley said—*observando*.

"How often do they have a blockade?"

"Almost every day. They block the airport in Oaxaca sometimes."

"Who organizes it?"

"*El sindicato*." The union. And she became specific. "*Sección veintidós del Sindicato Nacional de Trabajadores de la Educación*."

Section 22 of the teachers' union, well known for an action carried out a year before, in Asunción Nochixtlán, a town south of here, where buses and trucks had been burned to block the road, slogans painted on the overpass. In the confrontation with police some protesters had been killed. I had come across news stories of it when reading about Oaxaca beforehand. In a piece published by the Institute of Public Education of Oaxaca, I'd read, "The teachers' crisis in Oaxaca is not a conflict merely destined to disappear. It has been a decades-long struggle that has now transformed into a social revolution."

"What do they want, more money?"

"Not only money. But medical care and other things."

"Will they get what they want?"

"The government wants to shut down the union."

All this talk while the road was winding, but rising too, up and around the stony, battered landscape of high desert, scarred slopes, and withered thorn bushes, the whole of it smothered in low clouds—appropriate here, since the name of the region, Mixteca, came from a Nahuatl word, *mixtla,* meaning cloudy land. I opened my window and the chilly air stung my head.

"It's cold!"

The young women laughed, and Shirley said, "May we ask you some questions?"

"Yes, of course."

Was I married? Where did I live? Did I have children? How many? What was my job? How far had I driven?

And when I said that I had come from the border at Reynosa, they said they had heard that Tamaulipas was dangerous. Shirley and Vianey had not been farther north than Mexico City, and Lucia had not been north of Puebla. They wanted to be teachers here, they hoped in a school near their home in Tejúpam.

Black clouds were mounting ahead, building beyond the ridge, as dark as smoke billowing from an oil fire, thunderheads, tall and dense, closing in as they heaped against the hills, as black as clouds could be, and really not like clouds at all but a black bulging wall about to burst.

Just as I said, "I think some rain is coming," the first hard drops smacked the windshield, and more spattering and splashing, with a flash of lightning and a crack of thunder.

"*Aguacero,*" Shirley said—a new word for me. And she explained: a sudden cloudburst, a downpour, frequent here, she added. And we could expect *un inundación,* a flash flood. She had to shout to be heard above the clatter of the rain.

At once rainwater was streaming from the cliffs next to the road, and the road itself was awash, the whole surface lifting in the torrent.

"Were you actually going to walk all this way to your village?"

"If it was necessary, yes. We walk all the time."

But the road was so bad, and the rain so persistent, the thunderclaps making me wince, it took all my concentration to steady the car. Across the steepness of the hillsides the runoff twisted and scarfed through the roots of dead trees and glistened, pouring onto the road. And where there was soil it coursed as mud and silt, sluicing into smooth piles that narrowed the road.

"*Avalancha de lodo,*" Shirley said. Mudslide.

"*Muy lodoso,*" Lucia said. Very muddy.

The hairpin bends concentrated the flow of water, and I drove through a creek bed of tumbled stones to the battering of the rain on my car.

"*Una tormenta,*" Shirley said: a thunderstorm.

"*Una lección de español,*" I said, and they laughed.

Here, where there were more trees, and a thickness of topsoil, there were mudslides — reddish clay tumbled to the roadside, and in places rockslides so wide there was only a car's width between the rockslide and the edge of the cliff. Some of the fallen boulders had sharp edges, as though they'd been split by a lightning bolt. I wondered whether at some point a rockslide would broadside my car, toppling it and my passengers into the deep ravine to my left, or whether the whole unstable road would give way in a stupendous landslide of mud and stones, dropping my car into the abyss, and burying us.

"*Una tormenta eléctrica,*" Lucia added, when the lightning cracked out of the shifting clouds and lit the hillsides briefly before they blackened again.

Some peasant huts, the small rough ones known as *jacales,* built into the steepness, rocked in the wind, their tin roofs streaming. On some of the more level terraces cattle were browsing in the weeds, their coats soaked and dark, the lightning enlarging them and seeming to electrify them, making them stiff-legged and mechanical, like oversized metallic toys.

"Where is this village of yours?" I asked. "Is it far?"

"A little bit."

By now we had been on the road for over an hour, and the rain still hammered down—not a cloudburst, as Shirley had suggested, but a storm, slowly destroying the road under me and reducing the visibility to twenty feet.

"Would you like to go to the United States?"

"Yes, to Los Angeles," Shirley said. "Not to live, but to visit."

"Maybe New York City?"

Lucia said, "Also."

These mentions of big cities seemed bittersweet when, in the driving rain, the road sloped through another valley—more wooded here—and I saw a church steeple ahead, and a sign, and we entered a paved road.

The sign said VILLA TEJÚPAM DE LA UNIÓN, and I could see when we got closer that the church—lovely from a distance—looked hollowed out and ruinous, but Shirley assured me it was solid and well attended; the high cracked wall was misleading. The houses in the village were one-story structures, sodden and dark, and down the road a restaurant, Bugambilias, was shut. The streets were empty on this rainy day, a cowering dog the only sign of life.

The young women humped and buttock-bumped sideways and slid out of the back seat to press against my window, thanking me, their pretty faces wet with the rain, their hair plastered against their cheeks, the rain still falling on their hats and shawls.

"How far to Oaxaca?"

"Stay on this road."

"Is it far?"

"A little bit. You will pass Yodobada and Yanhuitlán."

"Thank you! Thank you! Thank you!" they called out.

I drove on, ecstatic, having met the challenge of Mexican back roads, the hairpin bends, the rockslides, the high desert, all of it ominously enhanced by the thunderstorm. And why had I been confident? Because of the women in the back seat. If I'd had any problem—a flat tire, a crash, a breakdown—I was sure they would have happily stayed with me and helped. Cooperation and mutual aid were keys to the survival of their Mixteca culture. So I'd skirted my way around the blockade, clogged with traffic, that had obstructed the wide highway, and at last I found a kind of delight in the unexpected and dramatic detour, a little victory that seemed essential to my traveling in the Mexican backlands.

The road was straighter after that, the meadows greener, the rain softer, but I had climbed to 7,400 feet. I passed Yodobada (pop. 226, nearly all indigenous), and twenty miles south I again joined one of the oldest thoroughfares in Mexico, the Camino Real—the Royal Road—which for centuries connected Mexico City to the southern regions. I entered the village of Yanhuitlán. I slowed the car for a better look, and stopped—dazzled by the biggest church I'd seen anywhere in rural Mexico.

On the grassy platform of a hill, the church of Santo Domingo Yanhuitlán was tall, high-sided, and austere, braced by stepped squarish buttresses rising almost to its roof, its flat facade inset with niches where stony-gazed saints looked vigilant. What was most impressive was its unadorned immensity, its fortress-like solidity, its stark and solitary position in a country town of plank-built houses and bony huts, the biggest thing in the landscape, bigger than any hill and perfectly preserved, its tawny stone pinkish, having been rosily dampened by the rainstorm that had now abated.

I needed to stretch my legs. I parked and climbed the thirty or so steps leading to the arched entrance that framed its enormous wooden doors. I walked to the door under the bell tower, where a skinny russet-haired dog was skulking, eyeing me. As I approached, the dog became animated, circled me, crouching, then darted and nipped at my foot, then took a bite of my shoe, leaving a blob of slobber on my toe cap, growling when I kicked at him. As I backed away the dog resumed his skulking at the doorway, and I thought, You win, *perrito*.

But when the dog loped after a mangy cat, I slipped into the church, marveling at its immensity. In its time this building was the tallest church in the Americas, its time being around 1558, when it was finished. It took twenty-five years to complete, six hundred laborers toiling at the masonry, the stone cut from a quarry in Teposcolula, a dozen miles away over the ridge of hills to the west. Fifteen Dominican friars from Spain lived in its convent. And who financed its construction? The townspeople of Yanhuitlán and nearby villages, paying tribute, the laborers themselves forking over twenty cacao beans a week for the privilege of shifting and cutting the stone in the quarries and cutting wood for scaffolds, making its buttresses, chiseling the niches, cementing the cloisters for this monastery complex that was also a fortress. And when the church was finished and Christmas and Easter were celebrated, the thousands of townsfolk were required to bring money or cacao beans—"failure to do so would result in public whipping on the church patio."

I knew nothing of this when I stood under the high ceiling and gazed at the gold altarpiece and the strange baptismal font, set on four thick upright snakes. And then I stepped outside into the mist, dazzled by the sight of this great, broad-shouldered stone monolith with a steeple, now obviously restored to its former grandeur—not a crack or a scar anywhere evident on its smooth, pinkish, skin-like sides. It was my luck later to find a book about it, *Building Yanhuitlan: Art, Politics, and Religion in the Mixteca Alta Since 1500,* by an Italian scholar, Alessia Frassani.

The town had once been populous and flourishing, in Frassani's telling—twelve thousand people clustered in neighborhoods paying tribute and attending services, some reluctantly. In preconquest times, Yanhuitlán was the second-most-important Mixtec cult center in the region (the first was at Achiutla, about twenty miles southwest). A number of Mixtecs held to their old beliefs, of annual sacrifices to Xipe Totec (Our Lord the Flayed One), and the veneration of their gods, resenting the fact that the church had been built over their temple to the local deities, obscuring the site, like a frivolous Spanish tea cozy over a sacred Mixtec pot.

This church-for-temple replacement, like the one I'd seen in Cholula, was a missionary stratagem; it happened everywhere in Mexico, it happened in South America, the Christian church built on the foundations of an idol worshiper's temple. You see it vividly in Rome, one example being the ancient temple dedicated to the Indo-Iranian god Mithras, made into the fifth-century basilica of St. Clement. The instigation was the apostle Paul's: "Whom therefore ye ignorantly worship, him declare I unto you." But like the Athenian mockers of Paul and the Roman cultists of Mithraism (many of them soldiers), when the belief was suppressed, some Mixtec elders — leaders known as caciques, and nobles — vocally resented the desecration of their temple, this towering thing squatting heavily upon it.

The Dominican friars demanded that the townsfolk surrender their idols, the carved images of their own gods, to be destroyed, or ritually executed by burning. Xipe Totec was the god of rebirth, and there were four other main deities: Zagui, who controlled the rain; Tizono, the heart of the town; Toyna, the patron of the town; and Xitondoco, the merchant god. All of them (you might say) better suited and more useful to an important agricultural and commercial center, purveying wheat and silk, than the image of a crucified foreigner, encumbered by his dogma of sin and damnation, with the promise of possible ease in a nebulous afterlife.

Images of the Mixtec gods were kept on household altars and propitiated with plumes and cloth and the resin used for incense, known as copal. But in time, with the persuasion of the Spanish friars, the representation of the bloodied and crucified man became familiar as the sort of human sacrifice that was required in Mixtec rituals (men were flayed alive to propitiate Xipe Totec, their skin worn like a cape by the nobles), and the Christian cross looked somewhat like the cosmic tree of ancient lore.

"Not only does the Mesoamerican cosmic tree resemble the Christian cross in its quincunx shape," Frassani writes, "but the growth of the tree itself is strictly connected to the regenerative function of human sacrifice. Since colonial times, the Christian Holy Cross has taken up the meaning and function of the ancient cosmic tree, conflating cosmological knowledge about world order and ritual significance through the enactment of the periodical sacrifice of Jesus."

This syncretic sandwich combining two ritualistic traditions, the Mixtec beliefs and imagery with the Christian system, satisfied a great number of people in Yanhuitlán. But not all: some clung to the old ways. Because of their defiance, three prominent local leaders were declared heretics and forced to undergo severe trials, which became known as the Yanhuitlán Inquisition, two and a half years of interrogation by a Spanish priest, Grand Inquisitor Francisco Tello de Sandoval, and his assistants. This judicial process was not very different from the terrifying Spanish Inquisition of the mother country, which had started in 1478. And it was contemporaneous with many tribunals in Spain involving torture, auto-da-fé, and strict sentencing—heretics fined, exiled, ordered to be galley slaves, or burned alive.

Inquisitions took place all over Mexico. Pictures of executions of idolatrous Indians appeared in histories detailing conversion in Mexico—one, *The History of Tlaxcala,* by the sixteenth-century historian Diego Muñoz Camargo, includes a woodcut that depicts six Tlaxcalans hanging from a gallows for their idolatry, and in the foreground two being burned to death while the pious, impassive Franciscan priests look on. Nor were such executions reserved for Indians alone. One of the first (in 1574) resulted in the death of "twenty-one pestilent Lutherans," and in the mid-seventeenth century, so Claudio Lomnitz writes in *Death and the Idea of Mexico,* a diarist, Gregorio Martín de Guijo, "records the public execution of sixty-six effigies and thirteen live Jews in Mexico City." As for the inquisition in Yanhuitlán, all the proceedings were documented in more than three hundred handwritten pages, one of the most important examples of "New Spain's inquisitorial persecution."

"If their intention had simply been to spread our faith," Montaigne wrote in his essay "On Coaches," a fierce denunciation of the Spanish conquistadors and their cruelties in Mexico—and published in 1580, at the very time this was happening—"they would have thought that it grows not by taking possession of lands but of men, and they would have had killings enough through the necessities of war without introducing indiscriminate slaughter."

What emerged from the inquisition of the Mixtec leaders who openly resisted the imposition of the Christian faith?

Defiance. The intransigent Mixtec leaders had exhorted their people, "Give them your old images—keep the new ones, the better made and precious ones," and "Don't attend mass in the church . . . honor your ancestors here"—at their own altars.

The Spaniards will soon be gone, the Mixtec traditionalists promised around 1540, and then the local people would be able to go back to worshiping their own gods and observing their own traditions. No more paying tribute or heavy fines, no more forced labor, such as their being impelled, under armed guard, to scour the nearby rivers for the gold the priests demanded.

It emerged in the Yanhuitlán Inquisition that the stubborn Mixtec adherents offered food and incense to the gods at their home altars before going to church, "so as to avoid the wrath of their ancestors." And in another devious stratagem, uncovered by the inquisitor, they chewed a narcotic green tobacco (*Nicotiana rustica*) they knew as *piciete,* to become thoroughly stoned during Mass, so blissed out on the weed that they would not hear the alien preaching.

But resistance failed, multitudes were converted, and as a subtle accommodation more old customs were absorbed into the Christian rituals, such as the tradition of placing a greenstone into the mouth of a corpse before burial. And Mixtec imagery was adopted even in such Christian objects as the baptismal font I'd seen, carved from a single stone, in the baptistry at Yanhuitlán, where four plump plume-sided serpents, the Quetzalcoatl of legend, poured from the mouths of serpents' heads at the corners of the font, one snake emerging from another, their upright bodies supporting the great stone bowl adorned with leaves.

As I stood in front of the church, a helpful elevated spot, I could see that the great commercial center of Yanhuitlán was diminished. On his visit in 1953, captivated by the church and wishing to draw vignettes of it for his book *Week in Yanhuitlán,* Ross Parmenter was told there were 2,200 people living there. It was now reduced to a village of fewer than 900, almost a mile and a half high on the cold plateau, the Royal Road bypassed by the toll road. Yanhuitlán was another town in the highlands of the Mixteca Alta that produced migrants to the US. Its singular attraction was the stupendous church in this desolation; yet the grand edifice made me feel weirdly uncomfortable—but why?

"It's a strange and insufferable uncertainty to know that monumental beauty always supposes servitude," Albert Camus wrote in the last volume of his *Notebooks* (1951–1959), speaking of the forced labor that creates great buildings like this. (He was in Rome when this idea came to him.) "Perhaps it's for this that I put the beauty of a landscape above all else—it's not paid for by any injustice and my heart is free there."

I continued down the rain-washed road, the old Camino Real, through the valley and across the hills to Nochixtlán, where the burned-out buses from the teachers' union action a year before still sat in the main street, rusted and windowless, the slogans on the pedestrian overpass still legible: JUSTICE AND RIGHTS FOR ALL PEOPLE. I zigzagged through the farmland of San Jerónimo Sosola, keeping to side roads, until I came to the denser communities at Villa de Etla and San Pablo Etla, and finally at nightfall the sprawl of Oaxaca in its valley, four miles across, at this time of day a mass of restless lights, like a bowl of fireflies.

## Intact Oaxaca

A DEAD CAT lay on the sidewalk. This was in Oaxaca city, on the corner of Calle Tinoco y Palacios and a narrow lane, with an unreadable name on a broken sign, near my posada. The cat was large, not a mere *gato* but what Mexicans called a *gatazo,* a big cat—a flattened, half-inch-high carcass, like a fluffy scrap of carpet, recognizable as a ginger tom, frowning and toothy in death, a bit flyblown but dried out, stiffened, and beginning to mummify. Because the streets were so similar, I used this cat as a landmark—"Turn left at the dead cat"—and always found my way home, never having to humble myself by asking directions.

It was another lesson in Mexican idiom, too, because *dar el gatazo*—to show the big cat—is slang for making yourself look good.

Poor but complex and handsome, like so many of its people, and dignified in its poverty, indestructible in its simplicity, Oaxaca was a proud place, too. As for its name, to the antihero of *Under the Volcano*—Malcolm Lowry at his most florid and hyperbolic—Oaxaca "was like a breaking heart, a sudden peal of stifled bells in a gale, the last syllables of one dying of thirst in the desert."

To me the name was clunky and familiar, because it was my home for the weeks ahead. The city was orderly and joyous without being recklessly licentious, like other Mexican cities I'd seen. But in the harmonious symmetry of its old-fashioned layout, one antique street looked to me much like another. It took me a while to see that an old, unremarkable, one-story corner house, at 600 Pino Suárez, which I passed every day on my way to Spanish class at the Instituto Cultural Oaxaca, had been occupied by D. H. Lawrence when he lived here with his wife, Frieda. On the inner patio he wrote the final version of *The Plumed Serpent* and some of the pieces in *Mornings in Mexico*.

It is worth remembering the way the latter book begins: "One says Mexico: one means, after all, one little town away South in the Republic: and in this little town, one rather crumbly adobe house built round two sides of a garden *patio:* and of this house, one spot on the deep, shady verandah facing inwards to the trees, where there are an onyx table and three rocking-chairs and one little wooden chair, a pot with carnations, and a person with a pen. We talk so grandly, in capital letters about Morning in Mexico. All it amounts to is one little individual looking at a bit of sky and trees, then looking down at the page of his exercise book."

Thus, Lawrence in Oaxaca, at his best, seeing things as they are. And it was pretty much how I spent many days in my posada in Oaxaca, dibble-dabbling with my pen in my notebook.

There was a good reason for Oaxaca being unaltered, and unalterable. A few days after arriving in this colonial town in a high valley, justly celebrated for its beauty and its traditions, I was reminded again of how "the past of a place survives in its poor"—how the poor tend to keep their cultural identity intact. They depend on its compass and continuity and its pleasures for their self-esteem, while the rising classes and the rich tend to rid themselves of their old traditions, except in a showy or ritualized way, because they became wealthy by resisting them and breaking rules. Oaxaca, with its powerful and visible identity and its living culture, was hard-up as a result of staying true to itself.

As proof of this, I met a man, a Oaxaqueño, who said he was aggrieved.

"We are poor in Oaxaca, and I will tell you why. All our houses are hundreds of years old, all our streets are narrow. It is forbidden to destroy any houses, it is forbidden to widen the streets. We cannot build big hotels or resorts here, like other places in Mexico. We cannot change. It is forbidden. So we remain poor."

The old scarred Oaxaca houses, the whole yellowish place of sun-struck and eroded stucco and stone, looked as though it had been carved out of aged cheese. The stone that gives Oaxacan architecture its distinctive mottled yellow-green-tan color is volcanic tuff, known in Spanish as *toba volcánica,* or *cantera verde,* which is quarried from hills all over the region. In spite of their plain facades, many of the larger buildings had shaded patios and courtyards, and large interior rooms, and some interior courtyards with roofed entryways (*zaguanes*) resembled atriums, with fountains, stone carvings, and brittle palms in dusty pots. Many of the ancient churches, the monasteries and convents, and the great temple of Santo Domingo had been confiscated and desecrated under the reform laws spearheaded in the 1860s by President Benito Juárez, who was born in the small village of San Pablo Guelatao, in the mountains northeast of Oaxaca, and raised in the city. "That chapel? It was a stable for horses," Oaxaqueños said of the most beautiful church interiors. "And this convent was a barracks." But when the wave of anticlericalism had passed, the churches and convents were restored to their former glory, along with the plazas and the Zócalo. Still no luxury resorts have been built.

D. H. Lawrence, Malcolm Lowry, and Aldous Huxley—all visitors, inspired in their writing by their immersion in Oaxaca—would recognize the place today, would grow sentimental, would probably find a table in a rooftop bar, the same wobbly table they'd sat at before, and order some local artisanal mezcal to drink, and marvel about how little had changed. The Oaxaca allusions in *Mornings in Mexico, Under the Volcano,* and *Beyond the Mexique Bay* are not dated in any significant way. Lawrence extols the hike to Huayapam, Lowry praises the powerful mezcal, Huxley anatomizes the architecture: they would not be disappointed by Oaxaca today, or much else in the south.

The Mexican republic comprises thirty-one states. The north of the country lies in America's cruel, teasing, overwhelming shadow—a shadow that contains factory towns, industrial areas, smuggler enclaves, and drug routes. Mexico City, in the middle of the country, is like an entire nation, of twenty-three million people—much larger than any Central American republic. But the south of Mexico, the poorest region, is a place apart, rooted in the distant past, some of its people so innocent of Spanish, they still speak the language of the 2,500-year-old civilization of Monte Albán, a few miles outside Oaxaca, enumerating the beautiful temples by counting all ten of them in Zapotec on their fingers: "*Tuvi, tiop, choon, tap, gaiy, xhoop, gats, xhon, ga, tse.*"

The sanctions against bulldozing the classic architecture of Oaxaca and making room for resorts have kept the town's soul intact. Not many cities in Mexico can say that; not many cities in the world. Oaxaca is remarkable for having resisted modernization—a great impulse for any venerable city—and for valuing its cultural heritage. Because traffic is slowed to a crawl by the narrow streets, most people walk. A city of pedestrians moves at a human pace in most other respects, too, and is inevitably a place where small details are more visible, and noticed and appreciated. Strollers see more, and are more polite, than drivers.

Being poor, many Oaxaqueños have had to uproot themselves and become travelers and emigrants in order to make money—a greater proportion of them here, and in the southern states of Chiapas, Puebla, and Guerrero, than elsewhere in Mexico. In the course of three weeks in the city, I met many—men, mostly—who had worked for a spell in the US, or in a maquiladora on the border.

"I labored for three years in a factory that made televisions," a man told me, and thumped a table with his hands, demonstrating the procedure, "fitting a piece of plastic panel with screws, all day, every day."

There was the young man who mopped floors at a Holiday Inn in Dallas, the waiter who had made pizza in Racine, the attendant at a car wash in Anaheim; all—or most—confided they'd been illegal, and some of their stories were of ordeals.

"It was back in '95," the former car wash worker said. "I walked five days in Sonora, and crossed the border. I got to Tucson after a week, and worked in California for eight years. I was eventually deported—just as well, my family is here. I'm staying in Oaxaca. Nowadays I would have to pay the mafia five thousand dollars to get me over the border, and I probably wouldn't make it."

The constant references to the United States, all the talk of people who have relations there, the descriptions of their long and difficult trips there, their sadness, always, at having to return home—"My mother is old," "My father died," "My family is here," "My grandma is sick"—made it seem as though the US was a satellite of Mexico, like a moon, anchored in space, adjacent to Mexico, always visible and seemingly available but kept just out of reach, a terrible tease, circulating in the sky.

Because Oaxaca had remained its old self, the town's human scale allowed you to cross the heart of the city unobstructed in less than an hour, walking from the far south side, up Bustamante from the Periférico, past the Zócalo at the center, continuing to the perimeter road on the north end, the old Pan-American Highway, designated Niños Héroes de Chapultepec. Oaxaca's colonias and newer residential areas lie at greater distances, but even a traditional rural village, such as the settlement against the mountainside at Huayapam, was a fifteen-minute drive. A car is a burden in town, though, because of the slow-moving traffic and the scarcity of parking spaces.

The texture of Oaxaca was apparent in the course of any stroll: the hawkers, the beggars, the squatters, the improvisational buskers and musicians and singers lining the cobblestone streets; the women with small children selling handicrafts—carpets, weavings, carvings, vivid grinning painted skulls set out on a straw mat; the blind man singing his heart out, playing a guitar, while a small, dirty, barefoot child solicited tips from passersby with a plastic cup. They constitute the foreground—the "color"—of all writing about Oaxaca, from D. H. Lawrence's first visit in 1924 onward. Anywhere else, such street life would seem pathetic, but in Oaxaca the blind singer is forgivable, and valued as another example of folklore.

That most of these street vendors are Indians—Zapotec and Mixtec—deepens the town's cultural authority: five hundred years after the conquest—Oaxaca was founded in 1529—the same indigenous people persist, tenacious and undiluted, still speaking their ancient languages, eas-

ily recognizable as Mexico's native aristocrats, their same hawk-nosed pro-
files chip-carved on the murals disinterred from the ruins at Monte Albán
and Mitla, not far away. As Benito Juárez (raised speaking Zapotec) described his own family, they are *"Indios de la raza primitiva del país"*—that
is, Indians of the original race of the country.

Because of the wide doorways that line the sidewalk, and the open
doors, Oaxaca's streets are filled with the fragrance of its characteristic
cooking: the aroma of warm, buttery string cheese, eight kinds of drizzled
*mole,* the creamy fragrance of fresh cacao beans, and the scorched tortillas
of the folded-over *tlayuda.* All this to the sound of guitars and accordions,
the laughter from bars, the vitality more obvious now, in the weeks leading
up to Halloween and the Day of the Dead. Many strollers were already
in costumes—princesses and monsters and villains and the black-suited
troupes wearing skeleton suits, children, dwarfish and disguised, who look
more terrifying in skull masks because of their small size, like demon ho-
munculi, all of them dancing to blatting brass bands and snare drums along
the nighttime streets.

## Lessons in Mexican

FOR WEEKS, MY daily walk in Oaxaca took me from my posada, along
Pino Suárez and Avenida Benito Juárez, to the perimeter road of the Child
Heroes of Chapultepec—the coffee shops, the areas of broken pavement,
the antagonistic graffiti, violating the facades and soaked into the old
stonework:

HOY BARRICADAS, MAÑANA LUCHA. Today barricades, tomorrow the
struggle.

And: SE ALISTAN LAS BOMBAS, SE AFILA EL PUÑAL. The bombs are
readied, the dagger is sharpened.

And: ZAPATA VIVE!

The newspaper kiosks displayed lurid headlines, always of mayhem, car
crashes, or cartel murders, and photographs of bullet-riddled or dismembered corpses. The lampposts and scrawled-upon walls were pasted with

advertisements for snake oil remedies or quack doctors. Farther along the avenue, the Teatro Juárez, with nightly performances of music and dancing; and across the avenue, the park El Llano—the Plain—families picnicking on the grass, lovers embracing on benches, children climbing on the bandstand. El Llano's weekly market, with its many stalls (*puestos*), sold T-shirts and fried grasshoppers, flying ants and maguey worms, and all the varieties of street food, from the simple tacos and *tlacoyos* you could hold in one hand to *gorditas* that took two hands.

I knew that walk, because at the intersection of those two major roads, the Instituto Cultural Oaxaca lay in shady gardens behind a high wall. The Instituto resembled a monastery, as old Mexican school compounds often do, and its scalloped arches, pitted colonnades, and cool verandas made it seem even more cloistral, with an air of muted contemplation, in a garden of royal palms, and bougainvillea and plumeria in bloom.

I walked that way every day for the next three weeks, schoolbooks in my damp hands.

Having signed up to improve my Spanish, I arrived there early the first day for the nine o'clock class, with my blank notebook and my plump, untasted Spanish-English dictionary. And the old first-day-of-school anxiety came back, the sense of confinement and submission that I had felt as a student long ago, the uncertainty—waiting for instructions, feeling small and vague and futile, all reminders of how much I had hated school. How even now I avoided colleges for the way they are smugly sequestered and out of touch. (I have, for almost fifty years, accepted any writing assignment to make a living, in order to stay away from a campus as a writer in residence.) My heart sank as soon as the iron gate clanged behind me at the archway of the Instituto's entrance, and I was, so to speak, walled in. I felt a sense of incompetence—not from any lack of self-esteem, but from a long-ago experience of hectoring and impatient teachers. I also thought: I have been here before, I am too old for this.

But I had vowed to speak the language with more subtlety, and the welcoming staff, while insisting on speaking nothing but Spanish, were reassuring and friendly, joshing me in the way of a new boy. I took an aptitude test—written and spoken—to gauge my proficiency and was assigned to an intermediate group—five other students. But my first acquaintance was startling.

"Are you doing this for college credit?" I asked a young, pretty, pink-faced woman wearing a hoodie with a college logo on the front.

She laughed in a girlish gasping way, became pinker, tugged her hood down over her ponytail, and smiling in confusion, said, "I'm thirteen years old!"

This was Miley. I frowned, trying to think of the last time I had spoken to a thirteen-year-old fellow student in a classroom, and concluded that it was perhaps in 1954, when I myself was thirteen, at Roberts Junior High—the Eisenhower administration.

Alan, the young man to her left, said, "Yeah. I'm picking up a credit."

A Japanese woman entered the room, greeted us in Spanish, and opened a thick Spanish-Japanese dictionary, turned some tissuey pages, and began annotating them. This was Akiko, very thin, very watchful, seated with her legs twisted together and hugging herself this chilly morning. It was only after a few days that I realized that she knew Spanish fairly well but spoke it with such a heavy Japanese accent she was unintelligible.

Two other students arrived, Marcie, a lawyer from Texas, and Dieter, a German émigré, living in Canada, and averse to answering my questions—staring in response to any inquiry. Six of us, awaiting our teacher.

The sunny somnolence of a classroom, the odor of decaying books, the weird apprehension mingled with boredom and impatience; the sense, most of all, of being unprepared and somehow confined, the awkwardness of this assorted bunch being in the same room—I had not been trapped this way for sixty years.

The teacher entered, a stocky smiling man, carefully shutting the door and greeting us as he shrugged off his leather bomber jacket and draped it on the back of a chair. He greeted the others, then leaned toward me and gave his name as Herman.

"*Uno más?*"

"*Si, soy novio,*" I said, and there was laughter, because I had introduced myself as a fiancé or boyfriend (*novio*) when I had meant to say that I was new (*nuevo*).

Both Dieter and Miley laughed the hardest at my stumble, Dieter with a callow giggle, Miley with a snorting hoot. Marcie, the Texan, winced in sympathy and shook her head. She was in her late forties, perhaps: we two were the adults.

Herman asked me my name.

I said, "*Mi nombre es Pablo, pero yo prefiero Don Pablo, porque . . .*" My name is Paul, but I prefer Don Pablo, because . . .

"*Por qué?*" Herman grinned at my presumption.

"*Porque soy un gringo viejo y . . .*" Because I'm an old gringo and . . .

"*Y qué?*"

"*Y tengo muchas . . . experiences . . .*" And I have many experiences . . .

"*Experiencias de vida,*" he suggested. Life experiences.

"*Sí. Soy viejo, y tengo muchas experiencias de vida.*"

Old and experienced, that's me.

"*Pero no soy un pensionado,*" I said, insisting I was not retired.

Herman then launched in Spanish (which I could follow but not write down) into a long and interesting disquisition on retirement in Mexico, emphasizing the strange notion of being a *pensionado* here, because although men and women did retire in their mid- or late sixties after forty or fifty years of work, they received no pensions from the government. Pensions were provided only for people who had paid into a private plan, which only a tiny minority, mostly city dwellers, were able to do. And as salaries were small and it was hard to accumulate savings, the prospect of retirement filled most people with gloom.

Welfare was unknown, Herman said, and even medical care was very basic. In the absence of any help from the government, the children of retirees took on the burden of supporting their parents. That was why I had seen so many grandparents with the Mexican families at the hotels in Mazatlán and Puerto Vallarta, and so many of their careworn adult children. Herman finished by saying that the government did little to help old people.

And then he thanked me, because I had provoked this explanation by saying that I was not a pensioner. "*Bueno, Don Pablo!*" Herman turned to the class, and as it was Monday, he asked us how we had spent the weekend.

"*Has visitado las iglesias?*" Have you visited the churches?

I clawed at my cuff and sneaked a look at my watch, assuming a half hour or so had passed. But it was only ten past nine. What a long time remained between now and the end of this class at one o'clock. I stifled a yawn and copied Herman's question into my notebook.

Marcie cleared her throat and, in clear grammatical Spanish, declared that she had spent Saturday morning at the cathedral and shopping in the Zócalo, and in using the expression *sin embargo,* reminded me that it meant "nevertheless." Alan had gone to Monte Albán with Dieter, and Akiko and Miley reported on their respective weekends.

And when it was my turn I said, "*Sí, he visitado la iglesia de Santo Domingo,*" not because I had visited it, but because I needed to make a coherent reply, and Santo Domingo was near my posada, and I added, "*Sendereando, también,*" because I wanted to use the elegant word for hiking I had heard in Tepic.

"*Fui sendereando, fui caminando,*" Herman said, offering me a choice, helping me out. I was hiking, I was walking.

"*Fui caminando.*" I was walking.

And so it began, improvisation and fumbling and mendacity, the hallmarks of all my studying as a youth in school. I was a student again, bluffing my way through lessons, as I had done for years.

"*Encontraron algunos problemas?*" Herman asked in general. Faced any problems?

Alan and Dieter had a bus problem, Miley had gotten lost, and I was impressed that she knew the verb form, "*Me perdí.*" Marcie had not encountered any problems, nor had Akiko, who stammered a reply.

"Don Pablo?"

"*Sí,*" and I added, "*Sin embargo, un poquito pequeño,*" and then said, "*Un problema por mi, en los pisos mojados y pisos resbaladizos,*" improvising again, because they were words on a sign I had seen in a hotel stairway in Puerto

Vallarta, warning of wet floors and slippery floors. I had chanted the sign, making myself remember, and Herman affirmed that I could also use it for *politicos resbaladizos,* slippery politicians.

"*Has probado la comida Oaxaqueña?*" Herman asked me, making a scooping gesture to his mouth. Have you eaten any Oaxacan food?

"*No, señor. He estado en Oaxaca dos días solamente.*" I've only been in Oaxaca two days — two days exhausted by travel and the altitude. Faltering, I added, "*La comida Oaxaqueña — es sabrosa?*" Is it tasty?

"*Muy sabroso, muy especial,*" Herman said. Very tasty, very special. "Marcie?"

She said, "*Sí. Me gusta comer las tlayudas.*" Yes, I like to eat *tlayudas.*

*Tlayuda,* Herman explained, was a Nahuatl word for a local specialty, a baked corn tortilla spread with *asiento* (lard), beans, shredded vegetables, maybe avocado, maybe *tasajo* — thin strips of beef — or chorizo, and covered with melted string cheese called *quesillo.* The *tlayuda* was sometimes referred to as Oaxacan pizza, but the comparison was inexact.

"*Chapulines?*" Herman said.

He explained, with gestures, that a *chapulín* was small, and it jumped, and it was deep-fried and very tasty.

"*Yo he probado muchos chapulines,*" Alan said, and then, in a patronizing aside to me, "Grasshoppers."

"*También yo he probado chapulines en Africa,*" I said. I'd eaten grasshoppers in Africa. And I asked, "*Hay chapulines en el mercado?*" Do they have grasshoppers in the market?

"*Muchos en el tianguis*" — and Herman explained that *tianguis,* like *tlayuda,* was a Nahuatl word meaning outdoor market. At El Llano park, a few blocks away, on certain days when the *tianguis* was held, I would find fried grasshoppers and, in certain months — and he smiled — "*chicatanas y hormigas.*"

I knew the word *hormigas* as ants, and more, the "big-assed ants," *hormigas culonas* — a memorable name — that were famously eaten in Colombia. *Chicatanas,* a Oaxacan specialty, Herman explained, were flying ants that appeared from the sodden earth in the rainy month of May.

And, of course, worms (*gusanos*), Herman went on, they too were eaten, the *gusano de maguey* that was found in a bottle of local mezcal, and sometimes a red worm (*gusano rojo*) that was fried, or folded into a taco.

And frogs (*ranas*), and the well-known varieties of *mole*, the sauces with twenty ingredients, including chocolate and green herbs, and the tortillas of maize, the folded-over *tlacoyo* that might be filled with lamb testicles (*criadillas*) or grilled goat intestines (*machitos*). The drinks—cold maize and cacao *tejate*, and the hot maize *atole*, two more Nahuatl words for Aztec drinks. An hour more of this—local dishes and ingredients—and correct verb forms for enjoying (*disfrutando*) them. I liked the idea that I was not so much studying Spanish as learning Mexican.

A brief coffee break—God, was it only ten-thirty?—and back to the classroom to continue our conversation, Herman inquiring, "*A qué te dedicas?*" What is your job?

Language learning is an incessant interrogation. I realized that first morning how, in studying a language, being asked and answering direct questions, you reveal yourself; how so much of such a class is revelatory—sometimes simple, often confessional. This is true of school generally, analyzing texts, reviewing historical events, engaging in dialogues with the teacher. But nowhere are you more naked than in the back-and-forth of classroom conversation in the practice of new words and verb forms. It was apparent from the beginning, from "Have you visited the churches?," and I had stammered to answer. But "What is your job?" was a direct question that suggested something deeper.

"*Yo me dedico a estudiar,*" the younger ones replied. They studied. And Marcie was an *abogado.* Lawyer.

Though I had intended to be anonymous, I could not think of evading the question with a plausible answer, and said, "I am a writer," feeling exposed, and to Herman's next question, I added, "*Yo me dedico a escribir novelas y libros de viajes.*" My job is writing novels and travel books.

This impelled Herman to introduce us to a helpful construction: "What is the book you like most?" *Cuál es el libro que más les gusta?*

Miley liked James Patterson, Dieter liked Dan Brown, Alan liked Harry Potter, Marcie liked *crimen ficción.*

"*Don Pablo?*"

It was that bad dream in which you're asked an impossible question, while being judged in your answer by a row of grinning simpletons. A young person can name a favorite book, out of a dozen; someone new to the language might nominate *The Da Vinci Code;* the lawyer might reasonably choose a whodunit.

"Many books," I said. *Muchos libros.*

And at once I became conscious of being elderly and conspicuous, because my hesitation seemed like the doddering of an old buffer. But it wasn't that at all; I was fully alert, my head surveying shelves of books, authors and titles on their spines. *Choose one* is the diabolical demand.

The younger students stared, triumphant. I could not name a single book!

"I have read thousands of books." *He leído miles de libros.*

"*Treasure Hunters* by James Patterson?" Miley asked.

"I hadn't realized he wrote children's books."

"He's written millions of them!"

Herman said, "*En español, por favor.*"

"*Ha escrito muchos libros para niños,*" Miley said.

Dieter leaned toward me and inquired, "*Has leído a Dan Brown?*"

"*No he leído a este hombre,*" I said. I have not read this man.

As if to spare my embarrassment, Herman moved on to a new construction: "What do you most like—or least like—about your work?"

"*Qué es lo que más—o menos—le gusta de su trabajo?*"

"*Lo que más me gusta de mi trabajo,*" I began, and thought hard, because no one in fifty years had ever asked me this question. And what *was* it that I most liked about my work? That I had no boss, no employees, no rivals, no competitors—the freedom of being a writer? That it was a way of dealing with my life, transforming my experiences, finding ways to understand it—recording life's joys, making its tribulations bearable, and also, in writing, easing the passage of time? Making a living this way, my own way, self-employed—that was something to like. Curious to know more about Mexico, I could get in my car and drive from home to the border, and from the border to Mexico City, and then here, making notes at the end of the day, answerable to no one.

But at the bottom of it all was the spell at my desk, bent over a piece of paper—since I had always written in longhand—and saying something new, often surprising myself by what emerged from my unconscious; then afterward, rewriting, improving, polishing, mulling it and making it whole, and so on, for days or years—a page, a story, a book.

In the silence of the classroom, my fellow students waiting for me to reveal what I liked most about my work, the answer came to me, easy enough to translate from English to Spanish, since the words were so similar.

"*El acto de la creación,*" I said. The act of creation.

"*Lo que más me gusta,*" Herman said, cueing me to make a complete sentence.

"*Lo que más me gusta de mi trabajo,*" I said, "*es el acto de la creación.*" What I like most about my work is the act of creation.

The others stared at this weird, unexpected, incomprehensible answer, and then chipped in with what they liked most, and what they liked least, about their jobs. Then it was our travel, our food, our fiestas, an elaboration of pleasures and prejudices. After an hour and a half, we were fairly fluent in explaining how we felt about various personal activities. We knew each other better, and I was sure that I had revealed myself as a pompous ass, or just another old buffer intruding on their fun.

At noon we went outside and sat on one of the verandas for a session of free-ranging dialogues, conversation as greater self-revelation, but in an aside, discussing the concepts of wanting and liking, Herman said, "*Tengo ganas de una chela.*"

It was a Mexican way of saying, "I have an urge for a beer." Not the tourist's "*Yo quiero una cerveza*" or the thirsty Spaniard saying, "*Me apetece una cerveza.*" And as a bonus, *chela* was Mexican slang for beer—brew or suds. Another indication that I was learning Mexican.

After four hours of listening and repeating and answering questions, my first Instituto day ended. I walked to El Llano park, found a restaurant, and nodded over my lunch—corn chowder with squash blossoms—and then went back to my posada. Exhausted, believing I was taking a siesta, I slept the rest of the afternoon, waking in darkness to strange odors and the thin air at five thousand feet.

On a solitary stroll along Calle Porfirio Díaz that evening, past the plaza in front of Santo Domingo church, I heard a brass band and saw a masked man on a gray horse—a skull mask, wide black sombrero, a drooping cape. There were trumpeters and drummers, a troop of small girls dressed as coquettes but with ghoulish masks, small boys as devil-faced monsters, and older children as space aliens—green heads, squinting eyes. And all this time the blaring of the band, the rat-a-tat and syncopation of the snare drums, the boom of the bass drums, the skirl of flutes, this tooting and tapping fanfare bearing them down the road toward the Zócalo—it was comic and macabre and assertive. Masquerade gave the procession confidence: they were poor people from the nearer colonias, dressed as aristocrats and ghouls.

This was to be the pattern throughout late October in Oaxaca—masks, costumes, band music, enlivening the afternoons and evenings; dancing devils and clown costumes and a proliferation of skulls.

That was my first day of formally learning Mexican.

The next entry in my notebook, I see, is headed *Six days later*. What had I done in those six days? I kept track of verb forms, listed vocabulary items, conjugated verbs, learned to say *El cerdo le gusta revolcarse en los lugares lodosos*—The pig likes to roll in the mud. I noted the Nahuatl cognates, but I made no record of my days. I attended classes every morning, and the lessons consumed most of my days and all my energy. I did a little furtive sightseeing, and I found some of the lovely restaurants for which Oaxaca is also famous. I tried to stay alert at the Instituto, but it was an effort, and it exhausted me—not just the effect of disentangling irregular verbs, but the tedium and humiliation of answering questions.

So you're a traveler, and you write books about your trips.

*Qué es lo que más (o menos) les gusta de sus viajes?*

What do you like most (or least) about your travels?

What I like most? *Conocer personas.* Meeting people.

What I like least? *Las demoras y el peligro.* Delays and danger.

"And by the way, Don Pablo, did you know that there is a Spanish saying that goes, There is danger in delay?" (*Peligro en la demora.*)

One day, during the like and dislike routines, I was asked what word I liked the most.

"The word I like most"—*La palabra que más me gusta*—what can I say? I have written millions of words. No one has ever asked me this. I confessed to *resbaladizo*—slippery—the word I had seen above the hotel stairs and chanted to myself.

Another day, the forbidding question, *Cuándo naciste?*

When were you born?

Around the table, the answers tumbled out, and I was amazed once again that Miley was born thirteen years ago, during George W. Bush's second term, and she was the same age as my car. But the intention here on Herman's part was not to shame anyone but to teach the verb form, *nací*, I was born.

I thought hard, then said, "*Nací a mediados del siglo veinte*"—in the middle of the twentieth century—evading a date. During the coffee break, Marcie confided that she had lied about her birth date.

"I do a lot of lying," she said, shaking her head.

"Me too."

"Those personal questions!"

To the question "*Cómo celebras habitualmente los cumpleaños?*"—How do you celebrate your birthday?—the younger students spoke of cakes (*pasteles*) and candles (*velas*), but when my turn came, I thought, What a question! and said, *Yo no celebro este día*—I don't celebrate that day—and who could blame me?

At the end of most lessons, often in the conversations under the trees or on the veranda, Herman was more affable and playful, and I provoked him to share words or expressions that were specifically Mexican.

"No kidding!" was *No manches!* (Don't stain!)

"What did you say?" was *Mande?* (Give me an order.)

*Qué padre!* was "Cool!"

*Qué desmadre!* was "What a mess!"

*Dos tres* was "Okay," an equivocating reply to "How are you?"

And there was the Mexican expression for being tactless or off-base or blundering: *mear fuera de olla*—to piss outside the jar.

"Did I say it right?"

*"No, Don Pablo, se está meando fuera de olla!"*

I shared the words I had learned on the border—*camacha* for chick, *gabacho* for gringo, *halcones* (falcons) for lookouts, *piedra* (stone) for crystal meth, *choncha* and *mota* for marijuana, and *agua de chango*—monkey water. And Herman countered with *Fierro!*—Iron!—a cartel war cry in a gunfight.

"The northerners say that southerners are lazy and short," Herman said in Spanish. "Southerners say northerners are tall and work too much. Most people say the *chilangos* are urbane and educated, and everyone mocks the people in the Yucatán for being rustic and less intelligent."

Most days, I trudged away from the Instituto, had a snack, and went to bed, sleeping through the hot afternoon, rising at dusk to survey the *calaveras* parading down the main streets in costumes, waving banners, and often carrying large images—of monsters and demons and, now and then, a saint, often Santa Muerte. And the following morning at the Instituto, I reported what I had seen, in answer to the question "What did you do yesterday?" Herman told us the main names for the figure of Death: Santa Muerte, Señora Blanca, Señora Negra, La Flaca (the Skinny One) and its diminutive La Flaquita, La Huesuda (the Bony One), and the others I'd heard in Mexico City—the fifty others.

The word for skull, *calavera*, also meant skeleton, and a literary *calavera* was a four-line satirical poem, which Herman assigned for us to compose one night as homework.

Learning Mexican with Herman helped to clarify for me the two skeletons that were often confused. There was Santa Muerte, Holy Death, in a hood, carrying a scythe, and sometimes a globe, an oil lamp, and justice scales, a folk deity, prayed to because she is nonjudgmental and might grant a criminal request—a convenient death, say, or a blameless robbery. And there was another skeleton, the more recent, a mere century-old bony figure that had been drawn by Mexican artist José Posada (1851–1913) as a satirical cartoon image to mock the political and social elites in Mexico at the turn of the century. Posada's skeleton, often referred to as La Catrina, was elaborately dressed, with a wide frilly bonnet on her skull.

Now I saw that the children were dressed as Posada's La Catrina, because this image allowed the skull-faced child to wear finery and a fancy hat. This was dressing up, the macabre comedy of the fiesta. Santa Muerte was another story altogether—the fastest-growing cult in Mexico, and a dark one, nothing funny about it. And though the Day of the Dead was approaching, neither of the bony creatures had much to do with those dead souls, yet all of these skeletons were conflated for the holidays in a daily danse macabre, some of it played for laughs, some a response to the tenor of Mexican life—violent, dangerous, and histrionic.

One of the classes started harmlessly enough with the concept of childhood boredom—"When I was a child I was bored by . . ." (*Cuando era niño me aburría . . .*), and I found myself confiding that I had been bored in church and in school and listening to speeches (*escuchando discursos*). The word *aburrirse* (to be bored) was batted around, and Herman asked, "What sport do you find boring?" *Qué deporte te aburres?*

And as the normally torpid yawning youngsters in the class became animated and expressed their feelings about various sports, emotions ran high. Miley hated baseball, Alan had no interest in ball games, Dieter denounced American football.

"The pauses, the stopping . . ." *Las pausas, las paradas . . .*

I said, "You don't know the rules."

"*En español,*" Herman said.

"*No sabes las reglas,*" I said. "*Este deporte—fútbol—es muy complicado.*" And I became flummoxed and tetchy because I wanted to explain how people in a community identify with a team, get to know the personalities and skills of particular players, enjoy the rivalries and the spectacle, anatomize the coaching, flaunt the colors and the uniforms, become a more unified community because of the team. I like watching all sports played well (*todos los deportes jugaron bien*). A city with a championship team was always a proud and happy place. I tried to express this, but my Spanish failed me.

Perhaps sensing that I was agitated, Herman asked Dieter his favorite sport.

"*Paracaidismo.*"

We stared. And he explained: skydiving. He had made sixty-two jumps. He intended to make many more. He was a German. He lived in a remote Canadian province. I knew nothing of skydiving—did it qualify as a sport if all that happened was you leaped from a plane, and in free fall clawed the air, and then tore open your parachute and hoped to land safely? And sometimes your parachute did not open, and you died.

I said that. "*A veces, las personas—los paracaidistas—mueren.*" Sometimes the skydivers die.

Dieter seemed pleased that I had challenged him, because it gave him a chance to cock his head and declare to the class, "*No tengo miedo.*" I am not afraid.

We returned to the subject of boredom.

Romantic movies bored Marcie as a child: "*Cuando era niña me aburría las películas románticas.*"

Miley had been bored by playing with dolls (*jugando a las muñecas*).

"*Don Pablo?*"

"*Cuando era niño, no estaba aburrido.*" When I was a child I was not bored. And later, to another question about myself as a child, I told a lie. "*Cuando era niño, lo que más me gustaba de comer era la comida de mi mamá.*" When I was a child, I liked my mother's food. But in fact, I had generally disliked it.

All this confession and evasion, in the relentless interrogation of language learning, sometimes led to awkwardness.

"*Mi abuelo era un huérfano,*" I replied to a question about my family, revealing that my grandfather had been an orphan.

"*Mi abuelo también,*" Marcie said, and became misty-eyed.

Both of us resented this accidental intrusion into our private lives.

After a week, in the casual outdoor hour on the veranda or under the royal palms, Herman introduced us to Mexican card games and trivia quizzes, and cartoons that required us to explain in Spanish what was happening to the little dog in the snowstorm, or the bewitched doll in the toy shop.

And there were toys, too, little trucks and cars and tiny buildings, which we held and made the subject of a story. At first I resisted, feeling like a fool, and allowed the others to relate the story of the burning building that was saved by the fire truck, or the lonely child who was comforted by the pretty doll (*linda muñeca*).

"*Don Pablo?*"

"*Estoy pensando.*"

I was thinking of Philip Roth, who had told me of an experience he'd had in therapy, at a crisis in his life; how he had sat in a circle of strangers, all of them similarly undergoing therapy, and been handed a toy car. The therapist had said, "Philip, please tell us a story about this car. Where has it been? Where is it going?"

Roth had balked at first, feeling foolish and put on the spot. He sighed and then (as he told me) said to himself, "I'm a writer. I can tell a story. This is what I do." And he held the toy car in his palm and began to describe its journey.

So when my turn came, I picked up the little doll and said, "*Una vez en una pueblito extraño . . .*"

One day, in a strange little village . . .

Always, afterward at my posada, I lay in bed at siesta time, groggy from class, thinking, What did I reveal of myself this morning? And I covered my face, remembering what I had said—unable to think of a plausible lie—telling the class that I had a chicken farm (*granja de pollos*) and four geese (*cuatro gansos*), or describing a job I had disliked as a young man (*en el supermercado*), or, based on a set of cartoons Herman showed us, inventing a story about a crocodile: "Once, a crocodile that lived in a jungle . . ." (*Había una vez un cocodrilo que vivía en la selva . . .*) Somehow the subject of tattooing had arisen, and I revealed I had *dos tatuajes*. Why?

And there was the trivia game we'd played, selecting cards from a stack and asking each other questions from them. "What is the tallest . . ." (*Cuál es el más alto . . .*) In the trivia quiz some of the others had made embarrassing revelations, too. Miley had never heard of the United Nations. Akiko was bewildered by a question about the Sphinx.

Herman, sensing that I was restless, urged me to get out more.

I said, *"El fin de semana estoy pensando visitar a Monte Albán."*
At the end of the week I'm thinking of visiting Monte Albán.
*"Buena idea."*

With my car safely stowed in a walled-in parking lot, I bought a bus ticket and got myself to Monte Albán. The city lay high and fortress-like on a flat-topped mountain outside Oaxaca, overlooking three valleys, and its pale stone glittered in the sunlight. Following a Mexican group, I rambled around the beautiful ruins, the temples, the astronomical observatories, the steep platforms, the I-shaped ball court, a wilderness of sharply cut steps.

The tombs of the nobles and kings had contained overmodeled skulls and treasures worked in turquoise and gold. The geometric city had flourished for 2,500 years, its people growing their own food, studying the heavens, celebrating the solstice, extolling cripples and hunchbacks as powerful and unusual, and practicing human sacrifice — favoring the death and decapitation of young children especially, because they were regarded as the purest (*el más puro*). Human sacrifices were made to Pitao Cozobi, the god of corn, his name meaning "bountiful harvest." The ear of corn was venerated in Zapotec and later Aztec culture because it symbolized the triumph of fecundity, the source of all life.

Pausing at a central altar, the guide began to speak of the bat mask of obsidian inlaid with precious stones that had once been displayed there, the sculpted black image of the bat god (*El Dios Murciélago*), who was also the god of corn and fertility — the image I had seen in the anthropology museum in Mexico City.

I formulated a question, rehearsed it a few times in my mind, then risked it, asking the guide why the Zapotecs had worshiped the bat: *"Por qué adoraban un murciélago?"*

"Because they revered maize. They believed that they were created from maize, and they knew that the bats ate the rats and mice and insects that destroyed the maize." And he repeated what I had read on a label under a bat mask in San Luis Potosí, how the bat was a presiding deity, related to fertility, inhabiting Xibalba, the Kingdom of Night and Darkness.

Figures danced across the stone surfaces of the temples, where other gods were carved, many of them with agricultural or hunting associations, the half-human, half-jaguar god of seeds and wind, the rain and lightning god, the god in the form of a macaw who represented the sun and war, the mother goddess Huechaana, who guided the fortunes of hunters and fishermen. Pixee Pecala, the god of love and lechery—and many other gods and avatars—gods of misery and unhappiness, the god of earthquakes, the god of the hereafter or death, the god of flowers, the god of turkey hens, the god of disease with a pockmarked face—all were inscribed in friezes on walls, in tombs, on effigy vessels and pots, in glyphs.

On my own, sightseeing, speaking my improved Spanish, I felt liberated and content. At a bar that evening, I tried out some of the Mexican expressions I'd learned (*Tengo ganas de una chela*), and using the verb patterns Herman had drummed into me, I was able to say what I liked most about Monte Albán, what I liked least about American politics, and games I had liked to play as a child. (*Los juegos que había disfrutado de niño . . .*)

Learning Mexican had turned me into an anonymous flaneur, taking notes, sizing up Oaxaca, preparing for the Day of the Dead, and going on day trips, such as my visit to the ruins of the sixteenth-century monastery at Cuilápam—which had the look of a railway station—where I was able to understand the guide describing some of the damaged frescoes.

"And the Aztecs made posole with the intestines of the prisoners they captured," he said. *Los intestinos humanos!*

In a café one night, a youngish man stared at me, then stepped closer and leaned in, smiling, saying, "Paul Theroux—what are you doing in Oaxaca?"

His name was John Pedro Schwartz, an academic and writer living in Oaxaca, a friendly man, widely traveled—he had recently spent seven years teaching in Lebanon. And I was able to tell him that I had come here to learn Spanish, "*Yo vine a aprender español*," and to add in the subjunctive mood, "*Sin embargo, es posible que si fuera más joven hubiera sido mas fácil.*"

However, it's possible that if I were younger this would have been easier.

## *The Day of the Dead*

EACH EVENING, ON the days from before Halloween through All Saints' Day (also called Día de los Angelitos, Day of the Dead Children) on November first, and the Day of the Dead (Día de los Muertos) on the second, Oaxaca was transformed. The *comparsas*—troupes of masked marchers and musicians—subverted the order of the city, asserted their marching multitudes, pushed forward along the cobbles, and sprawled, taking over the streets, thrusting everyone else aside, turning them into spectators. Then the city belonged to the processions of skull-faced children and ghouls and drummers and trumpeters and the Angel of Death.

The masked adults and children and the musicians assembled in the plaza in front of the Santo Domingo church before starting slowly down Oaxaca's main street, Calle Porfirio Díaz. In the beginning, these were the Halloween celebrants, preparing to overlap with the Day of the Dead festivities. As the processions grew larger, more people, more banners, so did the images they carried—a queen, a clown—much taller, the costumes becoming fancier, the masks more elaborate, the music louder, until (as local parades often do) they took over the whole street, filling it all the way to the Zócalo, creating a spectacle. Where there had been pop music and karaoke issuing from balconies and bars, now there was the blare of a brass band.

Heading down Avenida Juárez to language class on one of those days, passing the newspaper kiosks, I saw a headline: SICARIOS DESCANSAN EN LA FIESTA.

The fact that "Hit Men Rested on the Holiday" was good news, and an explanation for apparently fewer crimes and more confidence and safer neighborhoods and parades uninterrupted by gunfire or mutilated corpses.

John Pedro Schwartz had appeared at an opportune moment. He said, "This must happen to you all over the world," but I told him truthfully that I could not think of another time in my travels—fifty years of wandering—when a stranger had confronted me, recognized me, and offered to help me on my way. John Pedro became a friend and a guide, giving advice and steering me to the significant events that took place in the weeklong fiesta that goes under the name the Days of the Dead.

In the transformation of the cities on these days, small altars and shrines—*ofrendas*—sprang up, all of them improvised, bright with a blanket of marigolds, strewn with ribbons, flanked by flickering candles in jars, lovely until you saw at the center the skull and the bony arms and legs of the fiesta's memento mori. But the fixed grin on the skull made it an ambiguous comedy in a festival that was often satirical.

Halloween means dressing up, a sort of rehearsal, but also a time for visiting graveyards. Outside the Panteón San Miguel, Oaxaca's walled-in cemetery, there was a carnival—food, games, rides, beer—and the niches on the high interior walls, where bodies were filed away and labeled, were lighted by candles. At each tombstone inside, at the crypts, vaults, and tombs that were like villas—with roofs and columns—a family was gathered, drinking and eating. I was welcomed: "Have a drink?" "Are you hungry?"

The parades in daylight were jovial, with prancing monsters and the effigies of ghouls and beauties, but when night fell on All Saints' Day—November 1—the vigils began, and I went to the old cemetery in Santa Cruz Xoxocotlán, a center of Day of the Dead activity, where I saw that a vigil was a drinking party or a family picnic or, for some, a solemn, prayerful veneration. The drinking and shouting in a cluster of hearty masked celebrants is so odd you take it to be transgressive, but it is fitting, because the Day of the Dead embodies elements of insult and protest, in the cause of grieving and satire, which is a form of grieving—as well as binge eating.

On the Day of the Dead itself, November 2, I traveled to the village of Soledad Etla for the music, the food, the death watch parties at grave sites. Soledad Etla was eerily lit and noisy with contending bands of musicians, as well as a DJ playing loud Mexican rock songs. The tables of food were laden with *garnaches: tlayudas,* tacos, crepes, popcorn, and sausages, fizzing and bursting in bubbling puddles of fat. It was a party and a masked ball at Etla—a fat man in a Donald Trump mask; a man dressed as El Chapo, dancing and waving a shovel, to symbolize his tunneling to freedom; and a small girl, a diminutive coquette, made diabolical with mascara and fangs in a velvet costume.

"*Hola, Don Pablo!*"

It was Carlos, the owner of my posada, watching a procession of *comparsas*. He said Soledad Etla was the place to be, though I should visit San José Mogote for its music. He offered me a beer and, in his companionable way, narrated the parade and identified some of the masks and costumes — skeletons, turtles, platinum blondes with painted faces, angels, monsters, monks, children as gauchos, men dressed as women, many ghoulish brides in weird wedding gowns.

"They fight," Carlos said. "They mock life. They mock death."

This protest, the rebellion, was a tonic. In the parades, using the freedom of pandemonium, many of the masked and costumed marchers chanted against the government, against Trump, or carried signs boldly lettered MUERA A MALGOBIERNO!

This exhortation — Death to Bad Government! — part of the Cry of Dolores, has old roots in Mexico, dating from 1810 when Father Hidalgo, a Catholic priest (in Dolores, near Guanajuato, where I'd had lunch one day on my way south), shouted it, and much else, to denounce the Spanish and rouse the Mexicans to revolt. This cry is regarded as the commencement of the Mexican War of Independence, but it has been raised as well to many successive Mexican governments.

The images of death, of Santa Muerte, of bony La Catarina, are not mournful, because the mood is festive with a subtext of anarchy. The celebrants are people who work and live humbly all year, then seize this chance to make noise, to protest, to drink themselves silly.

San José Mogote was not far away. The village market was a mob scene, but a mob scene with music — the costumed villagers dancing to three brass bands, vying for attention, the music deafening, the dancers ecstatic and shrieking.

A day or so later, the formal celebrations ended, less raucously, with ritual all-nighters at grave sites in rural villages outside Oaxaca bidding the dead farewell. I was welcomed, but I crept away at midnight. The mourners were still marching with candles at two in the morning. But I wondered about the noise and roistering: what had this cacophony and masquerade to do with the Day of the Dead?

The answer was, everything, because dressing up and dancing and yelling were forms of protest, the daily routine turned upside down. I met a man who explained it. Diego was a musician—he played the guitar and sang—but there wasn't enough work, so he was a part-time teacher, guide, and explainer. It seemed no one in Oaxaca could make any kind of living doing one job.

"Protest is a tradition here in Oaxaca," Diego told me. "There were big protests in 2006, with thirty or forty deaths. No one in the government paid any attention. It was the death of the gringo activist Brad Will that brought headlines. The others were just dead Mexicans."

"What about lately? I saw a protest encampment in the Zócalo."

"In July 2016 there was a big protest in Nochixtlán."

"I drove through there. What was the protest about?"

"Educational reform and demands for better health benefits," Diego said. "See, in Mexico most of the protests are in the south or in Mexico City. Not in the north very often, because the cities of the north—Monterrey, Guadalajara, and others—have car factories and they make things for export. We don't generate money here. We have three million people in the state of Oaxaca and eighty thousand teachers. There's not enough money to pay them. All we have is tourism. Anyway, there are more social protests in the south."

I mentioned that I had heard there were mineral deposits in the state.

"Yes—more protest! The traditional communities object to what they see as exploitation. A Canadian company here is looking for gold and silver, but they are opposed by the local people because they see it as irresponsible. There is uranium here, but the communities won't let them extract it."

Then he came to the point. Protest was a necessary tradition, because in many towns and villages in Oaxaca there were no political parties.

I asked him, "What do they have if they don't have political parties?"

"They have Uses and Customs," he said. Usos y Costumbres—the term for traditional, customary law. The government did nothing to protect people from mining companies creating blight in the countryside, or factories offering cheap wages, or the violence of the cartels. "They protest in their own way."

## Memento Mori

PROTEST WAS MINGLED with the fiesta, the fiesta with ritual, and many of the ritualized masquerades had their origins in ancient Aztec culture, an empire of blood sacrifice and skulls and glittering masks. But the modern masquerade—precisely because the participants were masked—guaranteed anonymity, offering an opportunity for people to take to the streets and act out their grievances.

The Days of the Dead was just such a fiesta. It was a solemn ritual, it was a vigil in graveyards, it was a masquerade, it was a binge, it was an occasion for dressing up and looking fabulous, it included political protest, and it was a party.

Dominating this fiesta was the grinning image of Death. "One of Mexico's national totems," which emerged in the aftermath of the Mexican Revolution (roughly 1910 to 1920), Claudio Lomnitz writes. The other totems Lomnitz lists are the Virgin of Guadalupe (representing hope) and the image of Benito Juárez (representing reason). Mexican identity derived from the implications in these images. It is the Mexican boast that the gringo denies death, or has a horror of it, or in Europe sees death as tragic or romantic. "But during Mexico's twentieth century," writes Lomnitz, "a gay familiarity with death became a cornerstone of national identity." He continues, "Mexico's nationalization of death has a more nihilistic and lighthearted component. It is a modern refurbishment of a medieval theme."

Disputations on death are a national pastime in Mexico, especially by intellectuals like Lomnitz, or Carlos Fuentes in *This I Believe,* or Octavio Paz when he writes, "The Mexican chases after death, mocks it, courts it, hugs it, and sleeps with it. He thinks of it as his favorite plaything and his most lasting love."

But the skeptical Mexican literary critic and novelist Guillermo Sheridan (quoted in Kathryn A. Sloan's *Death in the City*) sees the obsession with death as a sham, a custom cooked up by self-interested impresarios—"anthropologists, film directors, and artists such as Frida Kahlo"—to which tourists, loving a party, gave a big boost. All these Mexican speculations seem true to me—death as a party, a plaything, a protest, a somber ritual. These notions animated Oaxaca in those first days of November, along with the paradox that manifestations of the death cult—ranging from the comic to the macabre—created a sense of vitality.

Memento mori—remember you must die—is the subtext of Mexican life, and no wonder. Consider the shocking statistics of Mexico's homicides—in 2017, around thirty thousand, the greatest number of annual murders in modern Mexican history. This was exceeded by the murders in 2018, when I was winding up my Mexico trip. No one shrugged at these statistics: the wise ones kept their heads down, they whispered advice, they stayed indoors at night, they locked their doors; the vulnerable ones headed for the border, and safety; the others—the vast majority—continued to live and work as before. The medieval theme was "death comes to all and makes a mockery of us all." And in the street theater and cemetery crapulosities—*borracheras*—of those Days of the Dead, the Mexicans return the compliment: they dress as skeletons, they parade in skull masks, they make gifts of sugar skulls, they engage in macabre dances, they mock death.

But it was not a Mexican intellectual who summed up for me the ambiguities in the Mexican relationship to death. It was Muriel Spark, in her novel *Memento Mori:* "If I had my life over again I should form the habit of nightly composing myself to thoughts of death. I would practice, as it were, the remembrance of death. There is no other practice which so intensifies life. Death, when it approaches, ought not to take one by surprise. It should be part of the full expectancy of life. Without an ever-present sense of death life is insipid."

Was it this death awareness that so vitalized me in Mexico? I was at that point more than halfway through my road trip, and in a lifetime of travel had never felt more fully alive, more eager to wake each morning and see what the day would bring—even when what it might bring was a nighttime vigil in a cemetery and an array of skulls. Mexico was for me a world of struggle, of incident, of questioning, of people under threat and prevailing over their humble circumstances, which was a lesson to me, of venerating the past and being true, being determined to live. I kept thinking, with pleasure, I'm still here!

The image I carried away was that of the solemn old woman crouched by a tombstone at the old cemetery at Xoxocotlán, looking severe in her grief and staring defiantly at me, the intruder.

## San Agustín Yatareni

NOW THAT MY lessons in Mexican were over, having conquered the subjunctive mood, I had free time to range more widely. I visited ruins, beautiful ruins. I revisited Monte Albán. It had been a sophisticated city on a hill, and on its high plateau its stepped, symmetrical pyramids were still a marvel. Building had begun in 500 BC, at a time when Britain was a land of quarrelsome Iron Age tribes painting their bellies blue and huddled in hill forts; around the time of the Greek Parthenon (432 BC) and the Roman Forum, but greater than these, nobler in design, and combining the aesthetic of temples and residences with the power of a citadel.

Monte Albán's stark main plaza was a complex of pyramids, a ball court, stone platforms, and, dug into the hillside, a sequence of underground tombs, the oldest true city in the Americas and one of the oldest in the world. I went to Mitla, where the ruins were fragmentary and overtopped by a gloomy church. A few miles from Mitla, a surprise, the more impressive site of Yagul, a palace with stone villas and a fort built around the same time as Monte Albán, on a terrace cut into a high hill, lesser known than Monte Albán or Mitla, but in its day the center of a community of six thousand people. And now, no one, not even many visitors. The day I drove there, I was the only gawker.

So much for ruins. In search of human architecture I asked an American friend from Huayapam—Linda Hanna, who ran a small posada—if she knew of a village where people had left for the United States, or had returned, having been disenchanted or deported.

"I know just the place."

This was San Agustín Yatareni, a small settlement on a country road outside Oaxaca, just where the road tilts upward, beginning the climb to Huayapam. San Agustín was a quiet, concentrated place, baking in noon heat, few people stirring—the low bulge of the thick-walled church of San Agustín, a modest plaza, small houses fronting on narrow lanes, no sidewalks. The village had a certain touristic charm, attested to by the scattering of taquerias, but was an unpromising place for a villager looking for work; and on its fringes were poor houses, tethered donkeys, and agitated goats. But in spite of its size and somnolence, it proved to be exemplary.

Around 1980 a local man named Adolfo Agustín Santiago departed from San Agustín and headed north to the border. José López Portillo was Mexico's president, his administration well known for corruption and nepotism. He presided over an oil boom, but that was no help to the people in Oaxaca, and oil booms are notorious for creating criminality and greed. (Look at Nigeria, Venezuela, and Angola, oil rich and crooked.) Mexico soon entered a period of economic crisis. There was no work in San Agustín and very little in nearby Oaxaca. The state was the second poorest in Mexico—which it still is, three-quarters of its people living then, as now, in what economists term "extreme poverty."

Somehow, young Adolfo managed to get to New York City, and then to Poughkeepsie, where there were still some factories—Western Publishing, a Fiat factory, some textiles, and IBM had three Hudson Valley plants. In nearby Hyde Park, the Culinary Institute of America was growing. But Poughkeepsie was in decline, becoming cheaper to live in and with opportunities for anyone familiar with tough times, such as a Oaxacan like Adolfo. Western Publishing closed, IBM furloughed thousands of workers, the Culinary Institute still thrived, but Main Street was boarded up. In most respects Poughkeepsie was blue collar and poor, a failing city that continued to fade for decades, and it was so unsafe that many Mexicans kept to seasonal work, returning home in the winter—by common consent, so I heard again and again, crossing the border was a simple matter, until September 2001.

The largest number of Mexicans in Poughkeepsie, by far, were from Oaxaca. Among familiar countrymen, Adolfo stayed. More young men, and women too, followed from San Agustín. The 1990 census recorded 228 Mexicans in Poughkeepsie; now there are thousands, and it is said by people in Poughkeepsie that they have helped revitalize the city. They are employed in the factories that remain there and in the surrounding plants in the Hudson Valley. They have opened shops and restaurants on Main Street. They work in the trades as plumbers and electricians. They have their own radio station and traditional dance troupe, Grupo Folklórico de Poughkeepsie. And they have introduced their own holidays and festivals—the Guelaguetza festival, a traditional Oaxacan event, now attracts thousands of participants and onlookers. Also known as Los Lunes de Cerro, Mondays on the Hill, it is celebrated at the end of July, with costumes and dancing, in Oaxaca and in adjacent villages as well as in Poughkeepsie.

This I learned in conversations with people in San Agustín Yatareni. At any given time, a quarter of the village's population is in Poughkeepsie. The lines of communication are helpful to potential migrants.

I met Antonio Caldera in San Agustín. He looked careworn and resigned, but was eager to talk about his migrant days. In 1989, when he was nineteen, he was in college in Oaxaca, studying mechanical engineering. "But I was bored. I wanted something else, maybe to become a lawyer."

He dropped out of college and applied to study law. But the teachers rebuffed him, saying that they would admit him only if he gave them some money. All he could afford was the tuition. With the idea of earning money, he took a bus to Mexico City, and finding no opportunities there, took another bus to Monterrey. By now he had met five other young men from San Agustín Yatareni, and, using a coyote, they were guided to Tijuana. They holed up in a hotel for several days, and when the signal came—"two knocks on the hotel room door one night"—they slipped out and began to walk east.

"Walk normal," the coyote said, fearing that if they hurried, the police would notice.

Once out of town, they marched. They walked fifty miles, three days to Tecate, and over the border there, where the coyote's contact was waiting with a van at a prearranged spot—this was before cell phones and text messages.

"He drove us to Los Angeles," Antonio said. "Then we flew to New York, and we took a bus to Poughkeepsie. After that, everything was fine."

He worked in a Chinese restaurant and lived in a house with eleven other people, all of them from San Agustín Yatareni. This was still 1989. His monthly expenses were $300, and he usually managed to send $800 a month home to his mother, who kept a farm.

"What about papers?" I asked.

"I had a Social Security card," he said. "The Chinese people gave it to me. They had a business, making Social Security cards. They were from China—they knew about these things."

After ten years, his widowed mother was ailing, and he returned to look after her—glad he was able to help her. He said that almost three-quarters of San Agustín Yatareni was in Poughkeepsie, about half of them with documents. He missed Poughkeepsie and said that he doubted that, given the cartels' control of the border, he would ever be able to return.

I stopped by a small but popular bar and burger joint called Ilegales, which was tucked under a grove of trees at the edge of San Agustín Yatareni, on the Huayapam Road. On the wall was a black-and-white poster showing Donald Trump's face in profile, and in large letters, DON-ALD, TU ERES UN PENDEJO—Donald, You Are a Dickhead. Calling the bar Ilegales was a joke, since the owner of the place, José Miguel Martínez, had been an undocumented migrant for some years in the United States.

A small smiling man in his mid-thirties, in a baseball hat and a T-shirt lettered ILEGALES, fluent in colloquial English, José Miguel looked and talked like any inner-city migrant in the US. We chatted across a table in his bar, though from time to time he jumped up to give an order or explain something to a server. Business was excellent—the place was full, and it was friendly, music playing, laughter coming from the tables, many gringos eating, which meant the word had spread to the tourists in Oaxaca that the burgers were tasty, the beer was cold, and José Miguel's new venture, Ilegal Mezcal, was worth trying.

It had all started so differently. José Miguel was fifteen years old, living in San Agustín Yatareni and doing odd jobs. He was restless, so when his cousin Luis, who was twenty-one, said "Let's go," they set off together, Luis funding the trip.

This was around 1998, in the last years of simpler border crossings, smaller fees to coyotes, and fewer police, but all crossings involved several days of long walks. The two cousins flew to Tijuana, met the coyote, and were driven into the desert, where they began walking for some hours until they came to a river. The river might have been the seasonal arroyo just west of Mexicali, called El Oasis, which forms the edge of the Laguna Salada, a wide river in the summer rainy season, and in a border no-man's-land. This was just south of the Jacumba Wilderness Area, the mountains of piled rock I'd marveled at for their rugged oddness when passing through, near Ocotillo.

"The coyote gave me an inner tube," José Miguel said. "I crossed the river that way, and we were met at the other side and driven to Calexico." By then he had traveled eighty-eight miles from Tijuana. "From there we were taken to Phoenix, and I flew to Philadelphia, where I had some friends. I worked in an Italian restaurant, as a busboy and later as a server. I was earning four dollars an hour, but even so, I managed to save money and send it home."

After three years José Miguel went back and built a house in San Agustín Yatareni. He also fell in love with a local girl. But he missed Philadelphia, and steady work. "I sort of regretted going back." He returned to the States to work, to save some more, but stayed in touch with the girl. When he went back to San Agustín Yatareni to get married, and perhaps move on, he found that the border crossing was much more difficult. Anyway, he was a local guy, and San Agustín was his true home. So he stayed and built Ilegales, and to the bar and burger joint he added a brand of mezcal, also called Ilegales.

He had lived lightly in Philadelphia, undocumented the whole time. He never applied for a green card, nor did he ever have a driver's license or a Social Security card. He did not own a car or drive one. He usually traveled by bus, or by bicycle.

"What do I miss? Food and friends. The diversity of culture," José Miguel said. "And if you work hard, the money's good. This isn't true in Mexico. You can work hard here and still earn very little. What I don't like about Mexico is the paperwork—and especially the poverty. In the States you have poor people, but generally they're the ones who don't want to work. Here we have poor people, but poor because they have no opportunities. It's sad."

Then he looked up. A waitress had a question, someone else was calling out to him, the place was full, a clamor in the kitchen, the clang of tin pots. "Excuse me."

## San Andrés Huayapam

I DROVE UP the road and into the foothills to Huayapam, a simple drive, my car bouncing on the speed bumps, the *topes* and corrugations. A walk to Huayapam was a hearty tradition in the last century for the gringo expatriates living in Oaxaca, a Sunday outing, verging somewhat on slumming, to see a village of exotic Zapotecs in traditional dress and buy a hand-woven shawl or a rug or a newly fired piece of pottery. From the busy town to the quiet country, a mild hike. In *Mornings in Mexico*, D. H. Lawrence recounts his walk to Huayapam—a name he must have misheard and misspelled as "Walk to Huayapa."

A contrarian by nature, Lawrence begins by explaining his reluctance to go and finally how he relents, walking with Frieda and their *mozo* (flunky), Rosalino, and stopping on the way. Not a long walk, but he makes a business of it. Lawrence was one of those highly absorbent few upon whom nothing is wasted. A week in Sardinia gave him the four-hundred-page travel book *Sea and Sardinia*. Less than three months in Oaxaca and he emerged with a full-length novel, a number of short stories, a dozen essays, and some translations. Inflating his one-day walk to Huayapam, he ventures to sum up peasant life in rural Mexico. The essay is a frenzied account of the junket, Frieda nagging, Lawrence ranting, the Oaxacan Rosalino following along, patient and helpful, lugging their gear, playing the role of the comical native sidekick, Sancho Panza to Lawrence's Quixote.

"Humanity enjoying itself is on the whole a dreary spectacle, and holidays are more disheartening than drudgery." Cranky, yes, but this downbeat beginning to the Huayapam piece is not a facetious pose. Tiny, misanthropic Lawrence ("Humanity is a tree of lies!") was a skeptical spectator by nature, not an active participant, and the interruptions of Sundays and holidays kept him—as they keep most serious writers—from his desk and the novel he was invariably writing, *The Plumed Serpent,* on this particular December day in 1924. But he took the walk to Huayapam all the same, and brought his skepticism with him. It must be added that another factor that limited Lawrence's robust appreciation of a ten-mile walk on a hot day at a high altitude was his poor health. He was a physical wreck at the best of times, and in Oaxaca he was diagnosed with malaria, as well as being chronically consumptive, spitting blood some days. Not long after the walk to Huayapam he had his first and nearly fatal tubercular hemorrhage, and died of the disease five years later. But he roused himself for the walk.

Apart from the church, which Lawrence anatomizes in detail, everything about Huayapam itself has changed in the century since he sauntered up the road. Much of the way is urbanized now, or residential. Where Lawrence saw farms, there are now houses. It is the condition of poorly zoned and improvisational Mexico, sprawling into the fields and pastures, huts and shacks accumulating to violate and blight the pastoral. The road is paved, and Oaxaca has spread into the nearer hills.

But that is the foreground. And there would be no point in mentioning Lawrence's piece at all if there was no more than foreground in it. But it is the framing of the walk, the amphitheater of the landscape, and his precision in describing it that gives it beauty and presence. What matters is the sense of place in *Mornings in Mexico,* some of it gone forever, other aspects eternal. It is true of Mexico in general, it is the appeal of the back roads, it is another reason for a road trip, it is the enduring value of Oaxaca.

Away from Huayapam, the background—the dramatic, unbuilt-upon steepness of the sierra—is unaltered from Lawrence's observation of a century ago. "On the left, quite near, bank the stiffly pleated mountains, all the foot-hills, that press savannah-coloured into the savannah of the valley," he writes. "The mountains are clothed smokily with pine, *ocote*, and, like a woman in a gauze *rebozo*, they rear in a rich blue fume that is almost cornflower-blue in the clefts. It is their characteristic, that they are darkest-blue at the top. Like some splendid lizard with a wavering royal-blue crest down the ridge of his back, and pale belly, and soft pinky-fawn claws, on the plain."

A little purple, perhaps, but he makes his point. The physicality of the landscape is matched by the physique of the people he sees, like the bare-breasted laundress slapping at clothes in a river. "She has a beautiful full back, of a deep orange color, and her wet hair is divided and piled." Similarly the naked men bathing: "What beautiful, suave, rich skins these people have; a sort of richness of the flesh." The immediacy and physicality of the essay, Lawrence celebrating the human body, outweighs its fussing and the triviality in the dialogue of the bargaining for fruit or something to eat. In the end, in spite of all the talk and the misunderstandings, he does not get to know anyone or to listen to anyone's story. Huayapam is all surface—brilliant surface ("stiffly pleated mountains," "suave, rich skins"), but with no inner life.

This superficial observation of human architecture has color—flesh like the contours of landscape—but fails to give the essay any staying power. As for the architecture of the pueblo itself, Lawrence makes a timeless observation when he considers the church of San Andrés, like many another remote and isolated church in rural Mexico, how "your heart gives a clutch, feeling the pathos, the isolated tininess of human effort."

What was baffling to Lawrence, and what is unchanged—baffling to many visitors today—is the indigenous language: Huayapam is still a place of Zapotec speakers. And also, that in the absence of political parties, there is a village council that meets regularly to decide the issues of the day, how they affect the town, basing these decisions on traditional Usos y Costumbres—to the frustration of local expatriates and gringos, who wonder whether they have a future here, and if their land tenure is secure, and does anyone like them.

To Lawrence the people in Huayapam are unknowable and obstinate, shrieking "*No hay!*"—Don't have it!—to whatever he requests, or gabbling obscurely in Zapotec. "It is a choice between killing her and hurrying away," he writes of an unhelpful woman. As for the water, "We must get above the village to be able to drink the water without developing typhoid."

That timid squawk of the hemorrhoidal tourist sounded here reflects the tone Lawrence sometimes reveled in, and it was a squawk I wished to avoid. Though Lawrence habitually fought with Frieda, who was habitually unfaithful to him ("You sniffling bitch!") and who casually yelled abuse at locals, he clearly enjoyed his time in Oaxaca—the serenity of the place, the easy friendships with the people, the traditional courtesies, the quality of light: "Then comes Sunday morning, with the peculiar looseness of its sunshine." All these Oaxaca characteristics so helpful to someone who wants to sit quietly and write something.

Many Oaxaqueños, in the city and in villages nearby, had a vivid experience of the United States. I met two in Huayapam who had ventured across the border, the first on a balmy afternoon, under a tree in a garden at the edge of the village.

"I was nineteen when I left for the border," Pedro García Sandoval said. He was thirty-four, yet work and uncertainty had given him the look of an anxious old man. He was employed in Huayapam as a plumber, but his business was slow. He'd been born in the mountains to the west of Oaxaca, in Putla, a district that was partly in Oaxaca and partly in Guerrero. The village was poor. He saw no future there. His older brother was in San Francisco—he'd gone a few years before—and this brother told him how to go about crossing the border.

Recruiters and coyotes visited such poor villages all the time, like door-to-door salesmen, encouraging suitable youths to make the crossing, and collecting down payments, the remainder to be paid on the other side, when the migrant had a job. Pedro paid $1,500 in Putla and took a bus to Mexico City, and one more to Nogales. There he was met by another coyote, with a vehicle, who brought him the fifteen or so miles to Altar, for the crossing at Sasabe. I knew from my time in Nogales that this was one of the easier and popular crossings—just desert, no fence, in the past lightly patrolled, especially on the day Pedro crossed, with a small group that had been assembled by the coyote.

"It was September 2001," Pedro said, shaking his head. "I was crossing the border when the towers fell down. I didn't see any Border Patrol. I walked through the desert to Tucson"—sixty miles, with the coyote and the group of half a dozen young men. "The coyote made a call, and we went to a house in Tucson. We stayed for a few days, then to Los Angeles in a bus, to another house. Finally I took a Greyhound bus to San Francisco, to Bernal Heights, to meet my brother."

"Quite a trip for a young fellow," I said. There was work in Bernal Heights, he said; there were many Mexicans and other Latinos. It was near bus lines and the shipyard. And there were plenty of construction jobs all over the city that was rising on the dot-com boom.

"I was like a grasshopper when I was a little kid," Pedro said. "My brother was in construction. I joined him, I paid the remainder of my money to the coyotes, and I settled down. After a while I helped a plumber, who was also from Oaxaca. Watching him, I became a specialist in plumbing. I stayed in Bernal Heights, met a woman from Oaxaca there, Verónica, and married her. We had two kids, now nine and seven. We were really happy in San Francisco."

"Why did you come back?"

"My father," he said. "He was very sick. This was a year ago. My brother stayed but I came back, and soon after he died. And so here I am, doing plumbing."

He was resigned to living here. There was work in Huayapam, but the pay was far less than in San Francisco, and seventeen years in the States had changed him. Mexico was bureaucratic, the schools were poor, and in many respects he was overqualified for the sort of plumbing he was asked to do. He could not contemplate a return to Bernal Heights, or anywhere in the US—he had a family now, and commitments, and with the price of crossing the border—and the uncertainties—another crossing was out of the question.

"Nevertheless," he said, "here I am." And he smiled sadly. "Home."

I met Ángel Barragán under a tree on a side street in Huayapam. Like Pedro, he was in his mid-thirties, and some of his story was the same—the desert crossing at Altar to Sasabe, for example. But in his case he was in a large group, 102 men and women, and because of the size of the group it was cheaper—an $800 down payment, then more after he arrived and began earning. His younger brother was with him. This was 2006.

"What made you decide to go?"

"To make money," Ángel said, and smiled as though at my simplicity of mind, too dim to grasp this obvious point. "There is no money here."

"You crossed with a lot of people," I said. "That must have been hard."

"It was five days and nights from the border to Tucson," he said, remembering and looking grim. "We had brought one day of food, so we went four days without food. A coyote raped one of the women—well, she couldn't pay the money, so she offered her body."

He considered this and became silent.

"We ate a lot of cactus," he said, using the word *nopales*. The pads of the *nopal*, prickly pear, can be eaten raw or cooked, with a taste—people say—like green beans.

"And you all survived?"

The idea of a hundred people plodding across the desert was hard to imagine—a stream of them, filing on a path through the hot gravel and spiny cactus and mesquite—but none of them were apprehended by the Border Patrol, so Ángel said.

"No one in our group died," Ángel said. "But along the way we saw dead bodies, just lying on the ground. Dead from thirst. Not buried."

"Did you see snakes?"

"During the day, yes, many," he said. "There are always snakes in the desert."

The deal was this: the group assembled by the coyote, or a syndicate, was headed to work on a farm in Huron, California, to harvest lettuce. All of them, like indentured servants. Huron, in Fresno County, with a population of about six thousand at the time of Ángel Barragán's residence, was the city with the highest proportion of Latino or Hispanic people in the United States—98 percent—most of them migrants, working in the fields, a great proportion undocumented.

"Harvesting lettuce, we got about $400 a week. It cost us around $180 a week for room and food and expenses," he said. "It was very hot, sometimes over a hundred degrees. It was no better later, in Santa Rosa, picking grapes—we got about $1,100 every two weeks."

"How much did you send back home?"

"Nothing. After paying rent and food, I had so little left over. See, I was still paying off the coyote."

"What was the name of the vineyard in Santa Rosa?"

"The company was called Star Wines," he said. "I could pick one hundred and fifty boxes of grapes a day. I was in a group of eight guys, most of them from Puebla and Oaxaca. If we picked more grapes than normal, we got extra money. We often picked twelve tons a day."

I questioned this: eight tons was sixteen thousand pounds of grapes. But he insisted the figure was accurate.

"The company would drive us three hours away in a truck to the vineyards," he said. It is two hundred–odd miles from Fresno to Santa Rosa, so this sounded right, but checking later, I could not find a vineyard called Star Wines; maybe I had misunderstood him. "Because of chemicals on the vines we had to wear special suits"—hazmat suits—"and boots. So it was very hot. But the pay was good. I could send some money home. I could earn in a week in the US what would take me a month and a half here. But still it wasn't enough." He reflected on this. "Finally after eight months, when I paid the coyote in full, I came back here. There was no point staying if I couldn't earn extra money."

"How did you come back?"

"In my friend's pickup truck," he said, and brightened, remembering a detail. "As we were crossing the desert we saw the Border Patrol in a helicopter."

"So you're staying here?"

"I'd like to go back—for the money. Some other people have gone to the States from Huayapam. But they've been gone so long I don't think they're coming back. For the past six years I've been trying to build a house here. I have children in school—and you know it costs money for children to be educated in Mexico." He had a son, Román, who was sixteen, and two daughters, Diana, twelve, and Michelle, eleven.

He itemized the amounts: 10,000 pesos for books, uniforms, paper, and pens for the three children—that was $550—and extra for sports equipment. Tuition was 15,000 pesos for each child for a school year. The Mexican government helped a little with a stipend: every two months, 2,000 pesos to keep the kids in school, under a plan called the Program of Opportunity. It was a struggle, and Ángel Barragán's pay in his job as a handyman in Huayapam was just enough to support the family, but there was nothing left over, and he wondered whether he would ever finish building his house.

## *Lost Migrants: Caminos Oaxaca:*
## *Acompañamiento a Migrantes*

WHAT SHOCKED AND stayed with me in Ángel Barragán's story was his saying that "along the way we saw dead bodies, just lying on the ground. Dead from thirst. Not buried." In my inquiries in Oaxaca I found an organization that tracked lost migrants, Caminos Oaxaca: Acompañamiento a Migrantes, so I paid them a visit. The office was less an office than a roomy suburban villa, in a pleasant neighborhood of two-story houses on a quiet street. This was in the Colonia Yalalag, in the community of Santa Lucia del Camino, bordering San Agustín, where I had been a few days earlier. It was three miles from the central part of Oaxaca, the house heavily gated and fenced, like most of the houses near it—like most of the larger residences everywhere in Mexico, land of fortified dwellings. But once inside, having introduced myself, I was struck by the tidiness and hum of activity, young women padding back and forth, shuffling papers, past a wide bright mural of a yellow landscape, of flowers, butterflies, and migrants — migrants as butterflies, butterflies as migrants, the yellow mariposa a symbol of migration.

"We started this organization four years ago," the director, Nancy García, told me in the kitchen of the house, which doubled as a reception area, a coffee machine nearby. Señorita García was a small and earnest woman in her mid-thirties, fast-talking, friendly, on a mission to locate migrants who'd become lost, or who'd disappeared during their crossing.

"I worked for eight years in Oaxaca for an organization that helps Central Americans," she said, "and I realized there was a greater need for Mexicans, so I founded this organization. Our focus is on Oaxacans, especially ones who have disappeared on the way north."

"How do you find out their names?"

"Families come to us and say that a member of their family had gone — that they've lost communication with them. Or the family member says, 'I'll call when I get across,' and they're never heard from again, either on the border or afterward. The people come and say, 'Can you help us find our family member?' So we help them."

I asked the obvious question: "What might have happened to them?"

"So many things! They might have been abducted by the cartels. They might have died crossing. Or they might have been detained, and it can be months or years without a word."

I mentioned that in places on the border, such as the Comedor in Nogales of the Kino Border Initiative, where migrants were sheltered, I'd come across migrants with falsified papers, fake IDs, counterfeit Social Security cards.

"Yes," Nancy said. "They're harder to find. We usually call around and try to locate friends. We use the internet. We use that Nogales place — a good place, the Kino Initiative. The US immigration service doesn't help us at all. Here's an example: before Trump, the pages on the ICE website were bilingual. Now not."

"How many people have disappeared?"

"We have records of about one hundred and twenty people missing from around here, more or less," she said. "We're helping to find eighty of them. The other forty disappeared completely—their families have given up. They're tired, or resigned to the loss."

"Maybe," I said, hesitating, trying for a tactful tone, "maybe some people don't want to be found."

"Yes," she said, and again, "Yes."

We chatted about her hometown of San Antonio, which was a distance from Oaxaca city and mainly agricultural, and how people there had to have three or four jobs in order to get by—odd jobs, making food to sell, driving taxis, cleaning houses. The usual salary was 150 to 250 pesos a day, or $7 to $13. A person hustling on their own would not make more than 600 pesos a week, or $30, which was not enough to live on.

"Has NAFTA made a difference?"

"Not a positive one," she said. "It has made the rich people richer and the poor people poorer. People who leave here are untrained, so they set off across the border to work in the fields in the US, not in the factories."

"And some don't make it."

"Yes. And the ones who've disappeared crossing, most likely they've died. At least it seems so in my experience. The ones who've disappeared in Mexico, most of them have died. In the US they are probably in prison or maybe living under another name. It's our job to find out what happened to them."

I told her what Ángel Barragán had said to me, about seeing corpses scattered unburied in the desert.

"We look for them as best we can," Nancy said. "In general, we don't know how people die. But here's an example. There were some people from a town called San Miguel Lachiguiri." San Miguel is in the Isthmus of Tehuantepec, small (pop. 560, mainly Mixtecs and Zapotecs), coffee-growing, poor, surviving on remittances from migrants. "Six guys from there, migrants, they got to a hotel in Tamaulipas near the border. Two of the six decided to go out and get some food. While they were out, an armed gang came to the hotel—and it was a *levantón*, the group of four lifted, kidnapped. The gang might have been tipped off by someone at the hotel. The two who'd avoided it by going out for food went back home to San Miguel and told of the kidnapping."

"What happened?"

"That's the thing. The four were never heard from again."

"Killed?"

"Not necessarily. They might have been used as forced labor. They might have been made to take drugs across the border. But we found no one, nothing. Gone."

"I've heard of migrants used as forced labor on farms."

"One guy who disappeared returned to his town after twenty years. He escaped—*por un pelo*—by a hair. He'd been doing agri work. He said, 'I wished they'd killed me. I've lost my whole life.' Twenty years! When he got home to Teotitlán"—Teotitlán del Valle, another Zapotec town—"he was so traumatized and angry I couldn't get anything from him."

"This farm, was it in Mexico?"

"He had no idea. Probably in Mexico, but he was captive. All he knew was that it was a farm," she said. "He was poor. He had nothing, like most of the people we work with—people from small towns, families who have no tools to find them, no computers, no access."

"And the ones who don't want to be found?"

"We've found migrants who have another life—a new life, a new family. And the wife here who had us look says, 'At least he could have given me a divorce!'"

"What about the ones in jail?"

"Terrible stories sometimes," she said. "Some guys were drunk in a town in California—fieldworkers. They were arrested on a charge of public nuisance and had to serve two years. Because they were migrants. We found them just as they were about to complete their sentence. And this is the strange part. Because of that, people thought I got them out of jail. After that, we were flooded with requests to get their relatives out of jail!"

All the hassle, all the hard work, all the danger, I said to her. And yet people still risked the frontier.

"The main reason for crossing is economic," Nancy said. "There's also a cultural reason. 'My grandfather went,' 'My father went,' 'My cousin went.' 'And now it's time for me to go.'"

I suggested that it was, in that sense, almost a rite of passage.

"In some cases," she said, "a village or a community here develops its own tradition, of people going to Mexico City, or Guadalajara, or the border, or a specific city in the States, like LA or Phoenix."

This put me in mind of the San Agustín tradition of going to Poughkeepsie.

"And there's this," she said. "Some of the people who come back don't tell the whole story. They say, 'I got new clothes . . . I got money.' They don't talk about how they were almost killed. Or that they were eating out of trash cans. They don't talk about the dark side. So you have this elevated status in the town when you come back. People look up to you. This is especially true of the young ones—they come back and boast. The older ones tend to say how hard it was."

"The men of judgment," I said, using the expression for the old.

"Yes, and it's really tough," she said. "My undocumented friends in the States, I ask them about their life. They say, 'I start work at six a.m. I work until midnight—two shifts. With my first shift I pay my rent, with my second shift I pay for my food.' And they have to repay the loan taken out by the family for them to go, and for a year or so they have to pay off the coyote who got them there."

"Sorry to keep asking, but what's the point?"

"To have a little house, or a shop, or something—anything—here."

"Is it so hard here that people risk their lives to cross the border?"

"I'll tell you how hard, from personal experience," Nancy said, and for the first time in our talk she clutched her hands and seemed exasperated. "I have a little house. My bathroom was outside. My dream was to have a bathroom inside the house. I had to save for three years to get this. So, imagine what life is like in a small village, how unattainable such things are. This is why people try so hard to get to the States. Here they are living on the edge. They go. Sometimes they disappear—die or get lost. We try to find them."

## *Toledo, El Maestro*

THERE WAS ONE man I wished to see in Oaxaca before I left. I had begun to understand, from what he'd done and the ways in which he was praised, that this man, Francisco Toledo, was the embodiment of Oaxaca's vortex of energy. The paradox was that apart from the ubiquity of his work and his achievements, the man himself was invisible. But he was talked about as though he was always present, wraith-like, perhaps listening, the effect of his work always in view.

An artist, an activist, an organizer, and a motivator, Toledo was known as El Maestro. That was an appropriate description: the master, also teacher and authority figure. I saw him as the heart and soul of Oaxaca, and a kind of hero. His work, and the results of his campaigns and his philanthropy, could be seen everywhere, but the man himself was elusive. He hid from journalists, he hated to be photographed, he seldom gave interviews. He no longer attended his own openings, but instead sent his wife and daughter to preside over them while he stayed home, unwilling to speak—a great example of how writers and artists should respond—letting his work speak for him, with greater eloquence.

He was that maddening public figure, a person so determined to avoid being noticed and to maintain his privacy that he becomes the object of exaggerated scrutiny, his privacy constantly under threat. It is the attention seeker and the publicity hound who is consigned to obscurity—or ignored or dismissed. The recluse, the shunner of fame, the "I just want to be alone" escapee—B. Traven was one, so was J. D. Salinger—seems perversely to invite intrusion. Say "Absolutely no interviews," and people beat a path to your door.

Fascinated by his work and his activism, I was provoked to become one of those intruders. Incurable nosiness is the true traveler's essential but least likable trait. I put in a request to see Toledo; I knew someone in Oaxaca who knew his daughter. Toledo had traveled widely in his early life, but he was rooted here in Oaxaca and had lived in the city for decades. He was a critic, a satirist, a portrayer of government abuses and assaults by foreign companies on Mexican life and culture. With protests and demonstrations he defied developers and gringo junk food franchises. Lately he had taken on Monsanto and its use of genetically modified crops, disastrous for traditional farmers in Mexico. A repeated description of the man was "Mexico's greatest living artist."

His daughter Sara said she would help arrange the meeting. She was tall—taller than me—half Danish, helpful, and prepared me for the visit, explaining that her father had not been well. She said that it was in my favor that her father knew that eighteen of my books, in both Spanish and English, were on the shelves of IAGO, the Instituto de Artes Gráficas de Oaxaca, a graphic arts museum and library housed in a colonial building across from the city's famed Santo Domingo church.

IAGO was one of a number of cultural institutions that Toledo had founded. A contemporary art museum, MACO, was another, along with a photographic archive (Toledo was also a distinguished photographer), a rare-book library, a shop that produced handmade paper, and an environmental and cultural protection nonprofit organization. The institutes and exhibitions and libraries were free. Toledo believed that anyone who wished should be allowed to enter the precincts of these places at no charge. As a country boy himself, he hoped that people from small villages, often intimidated by museums and the forbidding entrances of public institutions, would visit, so that local people could look at art produced locally.

I asked Sara if it was true (as I had heard) that upon hearing news that a McDonald's might open in the Zócalo, her indignant father had threatened to strip naked and demonstrate.

"Maybe the threat worked," Sara said. "He didn't take his clothes off, but he would have done so if necessary. In the end, he walked up and down giving away *tamalitas* as a protest. After a year, he won."

Toledo had had help in defying McDonald's. One *compañero* was the Oaxaca artist Guillermo Olguín. A tall, handsome man in his late forties, Olguín had invited me to his walled compound where, under the trees, as chickens pecked at our feet, we drank mezcal and talked—he owned a thriving mezcal business. Olguín was widely traveled. He'd lived in Japan, India, the US, and Cuba, and longed to go to Madagascar. His moody, complex paintings—many of them collages of old photos worked over in black ink or brushstrokes, among withered illegible documents—reflected his travels, his obsessive collecting in foreign bazaars. The paintings seemed like palimpsests, layered memories of journeys in time and space.

"I grew up using the library Toledo founded," Olguín told me. "He's a giant. And he was successful because of his talent, not his connections."

"Tell me about the McDonald's protest."

"Toledo called me and said that they were going to build this thing in the Zócalo," Olguín said. "And would I help? Of course, yes—civil society has a voice. We bought banana leaves for the *tamalitas*. I did the posters. We were the soldiers, you can say, to represent the people. Others joined in. We set up tables, people gathered, we gave out the *tamalitas*—no, Toledo didn't strip naked, as he'd threatened, ha! But it was a happening, and it did the trick."

I mentioned to Olguín that one of my reasons for wishing to see Toledo was that he was just a year older than me. As the years have passed, I have nurtured a special feeling for anyone close to my age. It means that we grew up in the same world, in the austere aftermath of World War II, that we knew the same terrors and tyrants and heroes, as well as the same cultural touchstones, certain fashions, banned books, forbidden words, items of slang, the music of the fifties—rock 'n' roll and jazz. We were in our early twenties in the tumble and conflict of the sixties: the civil rights movement, Vietnam, women's lib, a new way of looking at ourselves and the world, the hope we felt seeing oppressive institutions shaken up; we shared a bellicose mood, too, thanks to guerrilla wars and decolonization in Africa. We had lived through an era when authority was challenged by people like us, from the margins of society, like Toledo's, whose origins were obscure and inauspicious.

Francisco Benjamín López Toledo, the son of a leatherworker—shoemaker and tanner—had been born in a small village near Juchitán de Zaragoza, in the Isthmus of Tehuantepec, nearer to Guatemala than to Mexico City—and being Zapotec, nearer culturally to the ancient pieties of the hinterland, too. While still a child Toledo moved with his family to Minatitlán, near Veracruz, where his father set himself up as a shopkeeper.

Toledo was a dreamy child, much influenced by the myths and legends of a rural upbringing, elements that later emerged in his art. When his parents recognized his talent for drawing they sent him to Mexico City to study graphic art techniques at the Instituto Nacional de Bellas Artes. He was just seventeen, but even so he was singled out for his brilliance, and held his first solo exhibitions two years later, in Mexico City and Fort Worth, Texas. Restless and now solvent, ambitious to know more, but still young—barely twenty—he went to Paris, to continue painting, sculpting, and printmaking.

All these biographical details are freely available in books, catalogs, articles, and online, including the approving words of the French novelist and art critic André Pieyre de Mandiargues, who became acquainted with Toledo's work in Paris: "I know of no other modern artist who is so naturally penetrated with a sacred conception of the universe and a sacred sense of life, who has approached myth and magic with such seriousness and simplicity and who is so purely inspired by ritual and fable."

Nostalgic less for the big world of Mexico than for his remote ancestral world of the Zapotecs, Toledo abandoned Europe and returned home in 1965, first to Juchitán, determined to promote and protect the arts and crafts in his native state of Oaxaca (he designed tapestries with the craftsmen of Teotitlán del Valle), and then moving to Oaxaca city, where he helped create a cultural awakening, with his indignation and his art.

"He works all the time," Sara told me. "He's still painting. He's multitasking. He makes fences of iron—well, they look like fences. They're sculptures. He works with all sorts of materials—felt, carpets, tiles, ceramics, glass, laser cutouts. He makes toys. He makes felt hats for little kids."

"And *tamalitas.*"

"That, too. He's pro-Oaxaca," she said, and laughed softly. "They were going to put up a big statue of Don Quixote somewhere in the city. Another protest. 'If you do this, I will take my clothes off.' After that, no statue!"

Monsanto, more villainous than junk food or a kitschy statue, was the target of another protest. The company had bought 1.7 million acres in Sinaloa in order to produce yellow corn, a genetically modified variety

Monsanto termed "nano corn." Mexico knew a little bit about corn grow-ing, having domesticated corn eight thousand years ago. But Monsanto's importation of its Frankenstein corn was seen as subversive, and that ge-netically modified corn plantings would contaminate ancient native variet-ies. As bad as that, the toxins designed to protect the GMO grain against pests would indiscriminately destroy insects useful to pollination and the natural order.

"Monsanto held some trials," Sara said. "Their corn pollinated the local corn, and it died. They're not allowed to introduce seeds here. The govern-ment banned them after the protests."

Her father, she said, still had strong links with his birthplace in Juchitán. The earthquake that had destroyed the parts of Mexico City where I had been teaching also laid waste to much of the city of Juchitán. Many people were made homeless.

"We formed a group called Amigos de IAGO and set up forty-five soup kitchens in and around Juchitán and in other parts of the Isthmus," Sara said. "We were feeding five thousand people a day for four months, until people got back on their feet."

And she explained that the soup kitchens were not an entirely out-side effort—a charity, doing everything—but rather a cooperative system, mostly operated by the Juchitán people themselves.

"Having something to do was therapeutic for them," Sara said. "It took their mind off the earthquake."

I said that I intended to drive there in a few weeks.

"I can give you some names," she said. "It's a little dangerous now, with so much destruction. People are still desperate."

Not long after this chat with her, she gave me the word: I could meet Toledo at the arts center, where a show of his work was being mounted.

I arrived early enough to have a brisk walk-through of the show and was dazzled by the variety of works—iron sculptures flat against the wall like trellises of metal filigree, lurid posters with denunciations in large let-ters—one of these showed Benito Juárez sleeping on eight or ten ears of corn, and written above him, *Despierta Benito!* (Wake up, Benito!) and *Y di no al maíz transgénico!* (And reject genetically modified maize!). There were hand puppets, hats, lithographs of mottoes, dolls in Zapotec dresses, a felt corn cob labeled *Monsanto* with a skull on it, and serene ink drawings — a large one completely covered with a shoal of beautifully rendered darting shrimp, flashing to one edge of the paper.

"Hello." I looked up from the drawing and saw Toledo walking toward me.

The first thing, the most obvious aspect of the man, was his head — a large head, accentuated by wild hair, much too big for his slender body. He had a slight torso, thin arms, skinny legs, looking doll-like and improbable. He was wide-eyed, unsmiling, and intense, but courtly, austerely polite in the manner of old-fashioned Mexicans. He was dark, Zapotec to his fingertips, and his untucked white cotton shirt made him seem darker. I also felt at once, seeing his crooked smile and the way he bounced when he walked, that he had too much heart and humor to make himself unapproachable. Some people are so generous they have a justifiable fear of the clutches of strangers.

"This is lovely," I said of the drawing of the darting shrimp.

"*Camarones,*" he said, and tapped the glass of the case it lay in, shimmering with life and movement. "I like the way they swim together. You see the pattern?" And as though this explained everything, he added, "Juchitán is near the sea."

With a movement of his hand, he signaled to his daughter that he wanted coffee.

He became animated, smiling, as we walked around the exhibition. At the *Despierta Benito!* poster he said, "This is against the government."

A lithograph under glass was a copy of a seventeenth-century Spanish manuscript listing a Zapotec vocabulary, for the use of missionaries and officials. Another was also based on an old document, but one with images of slavery — men and women, their legs and hands in shackles and chains, titled *De la Esclavitud* (*Of Slavery*).

"This is me," he said of a mass of feathers, titled *Autoretrato en Plumas,* which, with concentration, I discerned was Toledo's face picked out in gray pin feathers, glued to a board, a startling likeness. He laughed as I examined it.

And more: a woodcut of two rhinos copulating, a cracked mirror ("the sister of Snow White"), a spider web in steel wires, a portrait of Albrecht Dürer, his hair and beard rendered with actual hair.

"Dürer was fascinated by hair," Toledo said.

And a large work of many faces, individual portraits of the forty-three students who had been abducted and killed at Ayotzinapa, the faces printed in melancholy tints, like icons.

"Sad," Toledo said. "A tragedy." He steered me out of the exhibit to a small table where two cups of coffee had been placed, along with a pile of books. "Sit, please. You can sign them? For our library."

I signed the books and thanked him for meeting me at short notice. I told him he was the only person in Oaxaca I wished to meet, and when I said this was not simple *adulación*, he dismissed it with a wave of his hand.

"My English is no good."

"It's perfect."

"I'm old, I forget," he said. "I'm going to stop painting sometime."

"Please don't say you're old," I said in Spanish, "because I'm the same age. We are men of judgment."

"Maybe. I like to think so," he said in English.

"I'm interested that you went to Paris when you were very young," I said.

"I was twenty," he said. "But in Paris I was alone, and lonely. I worked, I did painting and prints. Tamayo was kind to me. I felt less lonely with him."

The renowned Mexican painter Rufino Tamayo had gone to Paris in 1949 — fled, perhaps, because he found himself out of sympathy with the passionately political muralists — Rivera, Orozco, and others — and skeptical of revolutionary solutions. Wishing to go his own way, Tamayo took up residence in New York City in 1926 and after the war worked in Paris. He encouraged Toledo to paint in his studio, and though Tamayo was forty years older than Toledo, they had much in common, both Oaxacans of Zapotec ethnicity, both resisting classification, making art in prints, in painting, in sculpture. In the end, Tamayo returned to Oaxaca, like Toledo.

"I came back to be among my own people and my family," Toledo told me. "I wanted to speak Zapoteco again, in Juchitán."

"So you were happy then?"

"No. I couldn't work there," he said. "It was the noise, too much activity. I liked the place. I was home. I could speak Zapoteco—my grandfather and father and others spoke it. I don't speak it well—I understand it. But I wanted to paint, so I left."

"Did you miss Paris?"

He cocked his considerable head. He said, "In Paris I fell in love with a woman. She was Vietnamese. I had an idea. I planned to go to Vietnam with her—this was 1964, when it was very bad there."

"What was your idea in going to Vietnam in wartime?"

"Just to see it," he said simply. "I thought I could teach drawing in classes to American soldiers. And I could meet the girl's parents, but . . ." He shrugged. "The girl's parents would not support my application for a visa. So in the end I left Paris. I went to New York City, but I was lonely there, too."

I mentioned my feeling of meeting someone my own age, how we had both lived through the events of the sixties—Vietnam, demonstrations, political and social upheaval. And he would have experienced at close hand the massacre of students in 1968 in Mexico City.

"You're my age, but you're strong," he said. He clapped me on the shoulder. "Driving your car in Mexico!"

"But I'm sure you drive."

"My wife drives, not me." He tapped his chest regretfully. "My heart. I don't travel. There is danger on roads. There is danger on planes. I don't like airports."

"No one likes airports," I said.

"I don't like the colors in airports. I don't like the colors of the insides of planes. I don't like the smells."

All these seemed to me sensible objections to air travel.

"What happened to the Vietnamese woman?"

"Funny thing. She married a GI and went to live in California," he said. "Now she's a widow, and old, but I still talk to her. She comes to Oaxaca—I see her here, we are friends." He became restless, adjusting his posture on the chair, holding the coffee cup but not drinking. He said, "Have you seen what is happening in Mexico?"

"I've traveled a little bit—driving around. I drove from the border, stopping in towns and talking to people. I stayed awhile in Mexico City. I'm trying to make sense of Mexico."

"Are you having success?"

"Yes. I have Mexican friends. I'm happy!"

"Good for you, amigo!"

We talked about Mexico City. He told me of his studies there, and the artists he'd met. I asked him what he thought of Frida Kahlo, because as a budding artist he would have known her work when she was at the center of attention, as an artist, as a public figure, iconic, adored or disputed over—she died in 1954.

"I started out hating her," he said. "Then later I began to see that she represented something. And outsiders were interested in her. Her life was so complex and painful. So she is something," he said, and in an echo I was to hear about Mexican novelists, sculptors, poets, playwrights, and musicians, wanting an outsider to understand the wealth of Mexican creativity, he added, "But there are so many others!"

To change the subject, and suggest a place I'd been, I clicked on my phone and showed him a photograph I'd taken of a tiny peasant woman in a remote mountain village in the Mixteca.

Toledo peered at the photo and frowned. "She's poor," he said. "Nothing will happen to her. No one cares about her, or people like her. No one cares about the poor, or about their lives. The government doesn't care."

"But these are the people I've been trying to write about, the ones I want to talk to—about their hopes."

"Mexico is in a bad time now," he said. "It's not just the US and Trump. It's other things. Drugs and gangs, and the immigration from Central America." He gestured, spreading his thin arms, his delicate fingers. "Oaxaca is in the middle of it all."

"But you're working. That's the important thing. Tamayo worked until he was ninety."

"He was strong. I'm not," he said. "My studio is here, I'm still painting. I make things from felt, from metal, from paper and cloth. I look at the paintings I've done and I'm not that satisfied. I've done so many! I want to move on and do other things. I'll show you."

He led me back to the exhibition, past the metal sculpture, the felt hats, the light box of transparencies of a human body, pull toys, and laser cuts of insects, including a large black scorpion. He opened a chest in which booklets were piled. I took them to be children's books, but he explained that they were stories he had illustrated.

"I'm a publisher, too," he said. "I published these—I want to publish more."

I picked up a few and leafed through them, impressed by the care with which they had been printed: lovely designs, beautiful typefaces, vivid illustrations—of fabulous animals, jungle foliage, witch-like faces with intimidating noses.

"Maybe you can write a story for me," he said. "I'll make a picture. I'll publish it."

"I'll write one as soon as I have an idea."

"Good, good," he said, and we shook hands, but he did not let go of my hand. He tugged me to the case where, on my arrival, I had seen the large ink drawing of the mass of moving shrimp. He lifted the lid of the case.

"The *camarones*," he said. "I saw you looking at it. Take it—my gift."

He signed it for me, and hugged me, and in a whirl—his bouncing gait, his wild hair—he was gone.

Some time after that, my friend Juan Villoro, strolling in Oaxaca, happened to see Toledo hurrying to his library. Juan said hello and mentioned my visit.

"He's a good gringo," Toledo said, which delighted me. You can't have higher praise than that in Mexico. But Juan had more to report.

He had texted his girlfriend in Mexico City: "I just saw Toledo."

"*Pide un deseo!*" she texted back immediately—Make a wish! Because any encounter with this powerful man was lucky, magical, an occasion to celebrate.

## San Jerónimo Tlacochahuaya

DONE WITH MY lessons in Mexican and my mezcal sessions with the hospitable Guillermo Olguín ("Look for me when you come back," he said), and uplifted by having seen Francisco Toledo, I moved out of Oaxaca city and drove to San Jerónimo Tlacochahuaya, a large but compact and coherent village, like an island in the sea of big fields of agave, garlic, and maize, about fifteen miles to the south. I rented a room in a small posada, Ex-Hacienda Guadalupe. The hacienda was an ancient-looking place set on a hillside, owned and run by Michael Sledge and his partner, Raúl Cabra. Sledge was one of the writing students I'd taught in Mexico City, though "writing student" gives a misleading impression. He was about fifty, widely read, with a scientific background. He had published two excellent books, to good reviews: a novel based on the life and love of Elizabeth Bishop, *The More I Owe You*, and a memoir, *Mother and Son*, about his coming out as a gay man. His work in progress, *Seclusia*, most of which I had read and admired, was a fictional version of the Mexican residence of the English aristocrat Edward James. This extravagant and surrealistic estate of follies and gazebos James built in a valley in the rain forest of San Luis Potosí. James claimed to be the illegitimate son of King Edward VII, was very wealthy, a patron of the arts, a part-time art collector (surrealistic masterpieces), and a full-time eccentric. "But I don't want to build a house," Edward says in Sledge's book. "I want to build a ruin."

Sledge was a patient man, amazingly so, a good-tempered gringo who had lived in Mexico, mainly in Oaxaca, for twelve years, fluent in Spanish, knowledgeable about Mexican customs and literature, well connected, and wise. It was Sledge's lot as a long-term expatriate to have to endure the obnoxious observations of breathless know-it-alls who, on a hectic visit, flying in to Oaxaca for a few days, wrote simplistic pieces about its people and its food, multiplying mistakes and mishearings.

In extolling Oaxaca in the travel pages of a newspaper or magazine, the visiting writer on a weekend junket nearly always romanticized the experience and idealized the state, ignoring the fact that it is one of the poorest areas in the country, and that the city's traffic is maddening and often at a standstill because of political protest blockades or the sheer volume of cars. They bought charmless, machine-made bags, believing them to be hand sewn, and reported that the covered 20th of November Market, near the Zócalo, where they bought the bags, was a traditional *tianguis* rather than a prettified shopping area cooked up specifically for tourists. Gushing over colonial-era churches, these travel writers seldom pointed out that they were built by the forced labor—or slave labor—of the indigenous people, and in praising the church at the ancient ruins in Mitla failed to mention the salient point, that Mitla was a Zapotec religious site that was destroyed so that its stones could be reused to create San Pablo Villa de Mitla church, to displace the old gods and to demonstrate the domination of the colonizing power.

As Sledge told me, with barely suppressed fury, "These writers show a total lack of curiosity or understanding beyond the most superficial perception of the place and people."

I was one of those know-it-alls, but Sledge was helpful in correcting my blunders, and he became an ally in my quest to penetrate the hinterland. Raúl, too, an artist, designer, and entrepreneur, knew the villages of artisans—weavers, sandal makers, plaiters of baskets, ceramicists, and painters.

The Templo de San Jerónimo, designed by Dominicans, built by Zapotecs in the late sixteenth century, was said by Oaxaca guides to be the best example in the whole valley of the high style of interior decoration—baroque on the outside, painted ceilings and archways inside, *retablos* of miracles, every altarpiece and wall and pillar painted, and even the eighteenth-century organ in the loft had cherubic faces daubed on it. The American photographer Paul Strand had come to the village of San Jerónimo Tlacochahuaya in the early 1930s, to take pictures of the church for his iconic portfolio of gravure prints, *Photographs of Mexico* (1940).

But the village was tiny and poor, like hundreds of others in Oaxaca state: a small waffle of streets, a plaza that looked like an afterthought, a number of abandoned houses, a hole-in-the-wall grocery store. The singular church was visible from every street. The whole place was surrounded by plowed fields, the plows pulled by horses or mules, steered by a plowman smacking their flanks with a stick. San Jerónimo was near the road to Mitla, not far from the high terraced ruins of Yagul, and if you took a right on the main road and stayed on it, you'd pass through the Isthmus and Chiapas; if you persevered, you'd end up in Patagonia, since this was the Pan American Highway. In spite of the grand name, the highway was a modest-looking two-lane, Mexico Route 190 at this point, potholed and bumpy for many miles south.

Ex-Hacienda Guadalupe was a thick-walled one-story building of granite blocks that had been restored by Sledge and Raúl. Its footprint was a large hollow square, and its rooms were ranged around the enormous—big as a tennis court—central paved patio, with white plastered walls and a fountain. The whole place was cool and well lit, its shady spots draped with sleeping rescue dogs: perfect for reading and writing. I was happy there. I was undisturbed in my work. I was Don Pablo.

The hacienda was five miles from Tlacolula and its vast, celebrated market, busiest on Sundays and noted for its hawkers, mainly indigenous Zapotecs and Mixtecs, their handicrafts, their fruit and vegetables, their flowers. The pleasure in visiting markets in distant countries is mainly self-indulgent and voyeuristic, but apart from listing the items for sale or describing the faces of the stallholders, not much to report. One market is pretty much like another in its color and profusion, except for what's on offer: dead dogs hung on hooks in the markets in China to be made into stew, sharks in the Philippines, used (American-donated) clothes in Zambia, pickled snakes in Vietnam, endangered species elsewhere. In Juchitán, a month after visiting Tlacolula, I saw buckets of sea turtle eggs for sale, forbidden of course, but tasty: "*Pero muy sabroso, señor.*"

In his "Market Day" essay, D. H. Lawrence mentions the variety of the produce and the crafts, and of the contending Zapotec and Mixtec voices, and then shrewdly observes of markets in general, "To buy and to sell, but above all to commingle." That is the mood of most markets, men boasting, women chatting companionably, boys being boys and flirting, girls being shy, children engaged in improbably difficult jobs: small girls scrubbing pots, small boys hauling heavy sacks—the daunting sight, frequent in Mexico, of child labor.

The streets surrounding Tlacolula Market are closed on Sundays so that the market can sprawl beyond the arcades and the big building itself, allowing stalls to line the streets. The interior is sectioned off, sausages here, chocolate there, aisles of shoes and T-shirts, pink underwear and religious items, and videocassettes. The making of mezcal is a tradition in the town: lots of stalls selling the potent liquor, hawkers tempting passersby with shots. Stacks of flattened salted fish, and at the meat section one odd piece of meat, a small red carcass with an inedible gray bristly tail attached to it, a javelina or skunk pig, perhaps for peccary posole. The beauty of market stalls: piles of heirloom tomatoes, the twenty varieties of sun-dried peppers, clay pots of Oaxacan *mole* sauce.

The faces of the stallholders—old women sitting amid their homegrown fruit and vegetables, baskets of prickly pears, pieces of embroidery—were classic Zapotec, the faces you see on the carved walls of Monte Albán and in high relief on slabs, the same noses and square jaws and in some cases the same headgear of folded cloth. Heavy and hawk-nosed, the women wore full skirts and blouses picked out in stitched flowers, nearly all of them with a headscarf wrapped in the fashion of their particular pueblo, in a twisted kerchief, a swag of thick cloth, or a flattened turban, each one a species of identification and pride. Those in the know could tell where they lived from the style and weave of the cloth.

Tlacolula is incidentally a tourist attraction—big baffled gringos shouldering their way through the narrow aisles of carved skulls and track suits ("Look, Kevin, the old and the new")—but as a traditional *tianguis* that has existed for centuries the market is not organized to please them. How could it be? The dining area serves fatty meat wrapped in greasy bread, fried grasshoppers, and gourds of pulque, and the burned, blistered, wheel-like *tlayudas* do not in the least resemble the smaller dainty ones offered in the cafés of Oaxaca city.

These enterprising market men and women are among the poorest in

Mexico, the ones who hanker to go to the US because they are hard-up, and who hanker to come home, because a market like this exists nowhere else. Like most traditional markets, this one is a meeting place of like-minded people, about selling goods, of course, but also about commingling, seeing friends, and in a state with one of the lowest literacy rates, swapping the news of the day.

In one annex with a high ceiling and the smack of recently tanned leather—pinching the nose, stinging the eyes—the sandal sellers sat among their piles of aromatic footwear. D. H. Lawrence makes a point of talking at length about malodorous sandals, having heard that an essential ingredient in the tanning of Mexican leather is human excrement, a traditional practice still used in parts of the country.

"Meet my sister-in-law," Sledge said at a sandal stall in Tlacolula. This was Sarahi García, who was married to his stepbrother, Richard. One of their businesses—a cottage industry, really—was the making of huaraches, leather flip-flops, and other, more substantial sandals, the very sort that Lawrence haggled over on his visit to the market. ("How much do you give?" "Nothing, because they smell.")

We talked awhile. I said I was interested in meeting people who had been to the States.

"We have many in our village," Sarahi said. "You wouldn't believe how many have crossed the border."

"Why is that?"

"Come to San Dionisio. You can ask them."

## San Dionisio Ocotepec: The Crossing

LIKE MOST OF the people in San Dionisio, Sarahi García's first language was Zapotec. Sarahi did not speak Spanish until she began school, and still spoke Zapotec at home and in the village. It was a specific dialect, which linguists termed Tlacolula Valley Zapotec. When I later met her father, Don Germán, the patriarch of the large García family, I saw in his steady, assessing gaze and skeptical smile a confident man, proud of his lineage, loyal to his culture, and somewhat satirical. Because of her marriage to a gringo, he called Sarahi "La Malinche."

Most people who heard her father say this laughed uncomfortably and averted their eyes. As I had learned in Mexico City, La Malinche, an indigenous Nahua woman also known as Doña Marina, was the young lover, interpreter, and go-between for the conquistador Hernán Cortés. She was also the mother of his first son, Martín. La Malinche was seen by some as a brilliant tactician, and by others as a traitor for sleeping with the enemy. There are still conflicting opinions in Mexico about this singular woman.

Teasing, especially the public sort, as well as the joshing in a joking relationship, always contains an element of hostility. Sarahi bore her father's teasing for her marriage to Richard with forbearance and dignity. She was very beautiful, with delicate features and a kind of hauteur in the way she carried herself, always striding, always wrapped in a colorful scarf. But her father's needling also demonstrated how in Mexico nothing is forgotten, how the past exists in the present. People sometimes mentioned that when a bad habit was criticized—for example, littering, which is one of Mexico's most visible roadside blights—the excuse for it often began, "Well, you see, the Spanish, when they colonized us, did the same thing." Thus, the five-hundred-year-old figure of La Malinche persists in the minds of most Mexicans and is still in dispute—as a paragon of indigenous womanhood, as a temptress, as a traitor.

Sarahi's village, the small hamlet of San Dionisio, was scattered on the slopes of a low hill. Steep and curving streets followed the contours of the slopes, defying the usual Spanish-imposed pattern of right angles. The nearer hills are cultivated—it's an agricultural village. One of the crops is agave, for mezcal production, which is popular and profitable here (the main highway is called La Ruta Mezcal). Another San Dionisio crop is marijuana, bought by visiting narcos, processed, and transshipped north. A mainstay of the village is the steady flow of remittances from San Dionisians who are working in the United States. Sandal making was an option, too, but apart from that and fieldwork, there wasn't much else. Many young men from San Dionisio waited at the roadside at Matatlán—on the main thoroughfare twenty miles away—hoping to be picked up to spend the day as casual laborers, for which they'd earn about $3.

As I was parking my car near Sarahi's house—one-story, but occupying most of a block—an old man approached and said hello and "welcome" in the formal manner of a campesino seeing a stranger in town. We talked for a little while and exchanged names. He was Pedro.

"Have you ever been to the States?"

"I was in the States for seven years, *señor!* I loved it. California—pretty."

"Any problems with the police?"

"No problems at all."

"What were you doing there?"

"*La cosecha,*" he said. The harvest. "Working in the fields."

"You loved the United States but you came back here."

"Yes, because I was sick. And now I'm old. I'm seventy!"

"I'm older than that."

"Not true!"

Another man who returned from the States to his home in San Dionisio was Fortino Ruiz, a sandal maker. He was fifty-one now, but when he was thirty-five he decided to try to cross the border.

"What made you want to cross?" I asked.

"For money—that's all," he said. "People go with an idea in mind. To get money to build a house, or to save money to start a business here. They come back because their family is here. And their future."

In Fortino's case he did not stay long, a few months in Los Angeles, washing dishes. But he hurt his back, was unemployed, and decided to return to San Dionisio.

"But how I got there," he said, brightening. "That was an adventure. But a long story."

"I'm a writer," I said. "I like long stories."

"Okay. I went with four guys from here in 2001," he said, settling into his chair in the yard next to the sandal tannery. "We flew to Tijuana, to find a way to cross. We went from one coyote to another to find the best price and the most security. The coyote we chose charged us one thousand dollars per person, because the route was easier. A harder route would have been cheaper.

"We went to a hotel to make a plan—no money had changed hands. Some guys showed up in a truck. We had never seen them before. We were dropped at a taxi stand in Mexicali. Some other guys met us. They said we were headed for a place called Punta del Cerro, and they took us to a store. One said, 'Buy food and water for two days.'

"By then there were ten of us. We got into three cabs. It was night as we drove off. Rabbits were jumping across the road. It was exciting, it was like a movie!

"About forty minutes later the cabs stopped and we got out. We began walking. We walked until about three in the morning, not on a path, though we could see a sort of way. We ate and we rested, then we set off again. At about four-thirty we found a fence—barbed wire. We squeezed through it. It was the border, of course, but not a serious fence.

"At that point the coyote said, 'No fire. No smoking. No talking. Keep walking.'

"We walked until ten in the morning, and rested, then set off again. Around four or five o'clock that day we came to the desert, and it was very hot. We had backpacks, the water we carried by hand.

"The sun went down. We kept walking, and walked until about one in the morning. It was very cold, and we were tired. We rested awhile, then walked until dawn. Sand got into my shoes, I got blisters, I was limping.

"There were two women with us. They were twenty-two or twenty-three. One of them was lagging behind. I carried her water bottle, another guy carried her backpack. They said they couldn't make it. They began to cry.

"We helped them and struggled on. By this time we had very little water or food left. We asked the coyote, 'How far?'

"He said, 'Our ride is beyond that mountain.' I could see the mountain. The coyote said, 'But it's farther than it appears.'

"He was smoking marijuana. So were the other coyotes, to keep going.

"We arrived at a cave and rested. Now it was about two in the afternoon.

This was the second day—two days of walking. After an hour we began walking again, but I was limping. I'd had two pairs of socks, but they were in shreds and my feet were sore.

"The coyote said, 'We have to climb this mountain.'

"We climbed and climbed. When we got to the top and looked down, we could see big roads and cars and houses. The United States!

"The coyote said, 'This isn't it. We have to go down.'

"Meanwhile, one of the guys had broken his foot while climbing. He said, 'Please give me some water.'

"The coyote said, 'If you can manage to make it down there, you'll save yourself. They'll help you. But it will be the people who'll arrest you.'

"We left him. We didn't know what happened to him. We continued down the mountain and saw tire tracks in the sand.

"The coyote said, 'Let's go. But be careful. Use my footprints. That way, they won't know how many there are of us.' And he told the last man in the group to grab a branch and erase the footprints.

"The Border Patrol spotted us—we saw their lights. Yet there were trees and bushes around us. The coyote said, 'Let's watch and wait.' It was then about two or three in the morning. We heard voices all around us.

"Then we heard, 'Don't move or we'll shoot'—in Spanish. And, 'If anyone is hurt, we can help you.' And they shone a bright light.

"The coyote said, 'You're on your own now. I'm out of here.'

"Everyone except the five of us from San Dionisio ran away. The Border Patrol found us. They captured us and took us to a processing center and gave us food. They treated us with respect. We slept there, and they took us in a bus to Tijuana.

"They said, 'Go home. Don't come back.'

"We discussed this among ourselves. We didn't want to go back to San Dionisio. We decided to try again. We ate something and went to find another coyote. We had money—we hadn't paid the first one!

"The new coyote took us back in a van—there were eight of us now. We were left at a bridge, but in a more mountainous area. This time the coyotes carried the water and doled it out to us. They said it would be a shorter route. We walked and walked—my feet were bleeding. We lost all sense of direction. We asked, 'Where are we?'

"The coyote said, 'We're already in the United States.'

"We walked a day and a night, the same as before. Walk six hours, then rest.

"We came to a little house. There were fifteen people inside, waiting for a ride to Los Angeles. It was near a highway. We stayed there all day and night—no food, no water, no talking. And no bathroom.

"One man found a can that had been left behind. It was empty, but he used a small stick to get the last residue of beans, which he ate. The rest of us were desperate and hungry.

"A truck came to pick us up. Twelve or thirteen went in the first truck—fighting to get in. The second truck came six hours later. The back was open, we pushed in. The driver stopped and bought some beer, and after that he began driving erratically.

"We heard sirens. The Highway Patrol stopped us. They opened the door with their guns drawn. They arrested us and brought us to a station. There, they said, 'Where are you guys going?'

"We were still in their van. One of us who spoke English said, 'We're going to such and such a town to work'—I can't remember the name of the town.

"We heard the Highway Patrol talking outside. Talking and talking. They opened the door of the van and said, 'Okay, get out of here.' They didn't want to deal with us. Too much trouble!

"Someone said, 'Hey, this is Phoenix!'

"We walked all morning. We were dirty and ragged, but we were in the United States. One guy had a Social Security card. We used it to have some money wired to us, and went to a hotel to rest, eat some food, and change our clothes.

"We were told we couldn't take a bus to Los Angeles, because it went through a checkpoint, so we got bus tickets to Las Vegas. The bus was stopped, but we kept our heads down, and eventually went by bus to Los Angeles.

"In the end, we didn't pay anything to the coyotes! In Los Angeles we got in touch with our relatives and friends, and we were picked up. I lived with them near Santa Monica Boulevard."

He fell silent. I asked, "What then?"

"Washing dishes for a few weeks," he said. "Then at another place that served breakfast. I hurt my back. I couldn't work. I wasn't earning anything. I came home. I'm making sandals now."

He had a detailed memory for the handful of days he'd spent trying to cross the border, his adventure. His year in Los Angeles he summarized in a few sentences, as an experience of little consequence.

## Mezcalero

SOMEONE — IT might have been Sarahi — mentioned that at the edge of one of the far hills of San Dionisio there was a *palenque*, a mezcal distillery (called a *vinata* elsewhere in Mexico). This distillery produced high-quality mezcal that was much in demand. It was a family business that had been productive for generations — and by the way, the present mezcalero had been to the United States, another border jumper.

I drove there on a steep unpaved road that led to a notch between two hills and what looked like an encampment — sheds, outhouses, stacks of wood, a tethered horse, smoke rising from a great pyramid of earth and wood, packed solid. Six or seven men toiled with shovels or carried thick chunks of firewood. The impression I had from a distance, approaching it from the road, was of campers, fossicking among their lean-tos and shelters, smacking the smoldering pyramid with shovels and stabbing it with pitchforks.

Up close, the scene resolved itself into something more industrious and coherent, which I often found to be the case in Mexico: what looked like disorder from afar was something harmonious when I peered at it without prejudice.

"*Hola,* welcome — welcome!" It was an unshaven man in a filthy shirt and torn sandals, his baseball hat on sideways, but with a beatific smile and a courtly manner.

This was Crispin García (San Dionisio was mainly Garcías, some of them related), the owner, the *jefe,* the director of operations, and the *patrón.* It would be a great mistake to judge him by his grubby work clothes, because he was not only a highly respected mezcalero, but a wealthy man, his product much sought after. And it turned out he was also an immensely friendly man. He had not known I was going to show up, and yet, in the Mexican way, he made me welcome, introduced me to his crew of mezcalistas, asked me what I wanted to know, and explained the whole operation.

"The oven," he said — *horno* — of the smoking, eight-foot mound of earth and wood. "Or as we say in Zapoteco, a *gorn.*"

The other men and boys laughed, and I realized they were not conversing in Spanish but in Zapoteco. I remarked on this.

"Yes, we speak it all the time," Crispin said. "Our secret language!"

They laughed at this, too, but it was true: the slushy susurrus of Zapotec voices in rural Oaxaca — and in the nearby towns — is incomprehensible to an outsider, not only to a gringo but to Mexicans from other states. Clinging to their language, the language of Monte Albán, with its uniqueness in expressing aspects of that ancient culture, they have made themselves unassailable and remote. Retaining their language was one of the side benefits of being ignored, overlooked, or despised — early writers seldom refer to Zapotecs or Mixtecs or Tzotzils as Mexicans. For Greene or Huxley or Lawrence, it's "Indians" — "the cave man face," "the reptilian gaze." The growing of agave and making of mezcal is one of their traditions, along with their own Day of the Dead, or the Guelaguetza festival, the weaving, the pottery, the fabulous oral literature. So much for "Indians."

"Inside the oven are a lot of agave hearts — *piños,*" Crispin said. "Look, show him what we do." A man held an agave plant and hacked off the thick leaves, making it look like a large, cartoonish pineapple. "We're cooking the *piños.* We'll cook them slowly for the next four days — there are hot rocks inside this oven. After that—"

He led me to a circular cement platform, very smooth and stained the terra-cotta of cooked agave juice. A post in the middle was attached to a log and a large circular stone, a leather harness tangled on the surface.

"This is the mill"—the *molino*—"the millstone"—the *tahona*. "A horse pulls it round and round. It grinds the cooked agave hearts into shreds we call *bagasso*. Over there it's put into those vats"—*tinas*.

Some of the sunken vats were filled with the dark, stringy agave shreds, and from the sour odor it was easy to tell it was stewing in dark broth, swelling and fermenting.

"We mash it, we turn it over," Crispin said, taking me to a big cement sink with an array of copper pipes. "Then we put the liquid in this sink and distill it. Slow is best. A drop at a time! Then into the barrels."

Big blue plastic drums, nine of them, were lined up in one of the sheds. Each one held 200 liters and was sold for 12,000 pesos—$670—which was the reason that Crispin was a wealthy man.

"Now we take some *doa'nhis*."

"*Doa'nhis?*"

"Mezcal." He laughed. "Zapotec word."

He poked a thick bamboo pipe into a barrel and, sucking it, filled the pipe, which he decanted into two halved coconut shells, filling each one with mezcal—colorless, slightly viscous, pricked with bubbles, slopping in the shell. He handed me the bigger shell.

"To you! To friendship!"

"To us!"

And we drank, the first sip a knife blade of liquid slipping down my throat and stinging my eyes, the second sip soothing the laceration of the first sip. The third sip induced a feeling of well-being, warming my face. The second cup percolated to my extremities, a relaxation of fingers and toes, a mollifying of the mind and spirit.

"*Quiero emborracharme*," I said with a gasp. I want to get drunk.

"Forty-five percent alcohol," he said. "Here's how you tell the quality of mezcal." He jiggled the coconut shell. "Bubbles—see the bubbles?"*Burbujas.* "This is good. In Zapoteco the word for bubbles is *cordon*."

"Do you make tequila, too?"

"No. I don't like tequila. It's made from agave but a different process."

He laughed, saying, "They add alcohol," as though accusing the tequila makers of cheating.

"My grandfather and father were mezcaleros," he said. "But it was hard for them. They didn't have a car. They used burros and horses to get the agave from the mountains."

I loved Crispin's gap-toothed grin. We toasted again. He said, "Americans are nice people!"

"You've been to the States?"

"Six years in Los Angeles," he said. "North Hollywood."

"What sort of work?"

"Restaurants. Three years in a Chinese one."

"What was its name?" I said, to tease him.

"Chin-Chin!" he said, and wheezed with laughter. "Then a Japanese one. Cleaning tables, also preparing food."

"How did you cross the border?"

"Coyote—three hundred dollars the first time. That was 1994." He was fifty-seven now, so he had been thirty-three on that trip, and he'd traveled with some other young men from San Dionisio. "Second time I paid a thousand. I crossed near Mexicali, ten hours walking to the freeway."

"Any problems with the police in LA?"

"None! They left me alone. I loved it there. My intention was to save money, then come back here and help my family."

All this time we'd been surrounded by the crew, watching us drink, shouting at each other in Zapoteco, bringing more mezcal in the bamboo pipe from the barrel.

Gesturing to one of the young men, Crispin said, "This is my son, Rodrigo. He's been across!"

Rodrigo was thirty-five, heavyset, with a rueful expression. He said in English, "I paid three thousand to cross the first time. I crossed at Tecate. Five thousand the second time. A lot of money. I had to work two years to pay it off, so I didn't save much. But I liked it there."

"What do you miss about the States?"

"I miss the work. I miss the pretty towns, so quiet," he said sadly.

Crispin knew enough English to understand what his son was saying.

He said in Spanish, "Our family is here. We're happy. I had a lot of work in the States but I never made much money. I'll never cross the border again. Look, I have my mezcal business. And I'm home. Less pressure. I want to make the best mezcal."

He was swaying slightly, balancing a coconut shell of mezcal on his fingertips, still smiling.

"How do you make the best mezcal?"

"You have to cut the agave exactly," he said, with a slicing gesture of his free hand. "The exact cooking. The exact fermenting of the *bagasso*."

He flung his arm around me. He began to speak in Zapoteco, with great force, in a heartfelt way.

"*Eet yelasu nara!*" he said, smiling, but blinking mezcal tears.

"What is he saying?" I asked Rodrigo.

"'Don't forget me.' In Zapoteco."

No, nor would I forget the sunlight slanting through the puffs of smoke from the earthen pile of the oven, or the thatched roofs of the mill and the sheds, the tang of fermenting agave gunk, the horse cropping grass in the valley below, the eager faces of the Zapotec crew, their work-toughened fingers when they shook my hand, or my delirium, part mezcal, part pure traveler's bliss.

## Día Siguiente: Feast Under the Trees

A RECENT DEATH in the García family in San Dionisio meant two weeks of mourning—Mexican mourning, a process of easing the spirit of the dead person into the next world. In this case, the deceased woman was the beloved matriarch, Gabina García, who had died at the age of seventy-one. She had led a full life, having married at the age of fifteen and given birth to seven children, one of them Sarahi's mother.

I was invited to an afternoon meal at the sprawling García compound—a feast, really: about a hundred people were eating in the backyard, under the low boughs of the trees. This was El Día Siguiente—the Following Day—also referred to as a *recalentado,* the word for reheating, the ceremonial warming up of food the day after the burial, for additional guests.

Women and small girls served tripe and liver stew out of a tureen, tortillas wrapped in cloth napkins, chicken hacked apart on platters, pots of vegetables. And mezcal. We sat at long tables, some men conferring on benches, an impromptu kitchen at the back of the garden—a pot of maize being stirred for tomorrow's tortillas amid a drone of voices, the subdued garrulity of the feasting and grieving friends and relations.

"It takes thirteen days for a soul to get to heaven," a woman serving me said, meaning the journey to the afterlife. "We take thirteen tortillas and put them on the house altar after a death. Every day we divide one tortilla into small pieces, and we share it. And we are also sharing it with the departed one."

As I ate at the table with Germán García—sixty-one, the patriarch—I was asked the usual questions: where was I from, what was I work, how did I like Mexico, did I have a wife and children, and what was I doing in this small village?

With the talk about the reverence of ritual mourning in mind, I said, among other things, that I liked Mexican politeness, the small courtesies I'd seen, many of them extended to me in country areas.

This drew a snort of disapproval from an old woman. "No," she said. "In the past we greeted each other four times a day—four greetings. We kissed hands."

"Like this," Sarahi García said, and demonstrated how a person would extend both hands, turned down, offering them to be kissed.

"Yes," the old woman said. "But these days the young people just say 'Hi!'"

"Barbarous Mexico," Germán said. He sat back in his chair, tipped up the broad brim of his hat, and folding his arms importantly, he looked aristocratic in his confidence. "It's a book, *México Bárbaro*, written by a gringo, John Kenneth Turner. You know the book?"

I had to say I did not know the book. I had never heard of John Kenneth Turner. But later I was easily able to find out about this crusading journalist (1879–1948), a precocious socialist (a reader of Marx at the age of sixteen) and a frequent visitor to Mexico at crucial periods, during the Porfirio Díaz years and again at the time of Pancho Villa's Punitive Expedition (1916–17)—humiliating for Mexico as another gringo intrusion, though Villa eluded capture. On his last trip, in 1921, Turner interviewed a powerful Zapatista general. Turner became a hero in Mexico, and the atrocities detailed in his book were so important in rousing revolutionary fervor that the artist Siqueiros included a portrait of Turner among the faces in the vast mob in his mural *The Revolution Against the Porfirian Dictatorship*, on the walls of Chapultepec Castle in Mexico City.

"This gringo Turner was here in Oaxaca just before the revolution," Germán said, stroking his mustache. "He was also in Chiapas and Sonora. He wrote about the indigenous Yaquis in Sonora, how they tried to prevent outsiders from exploiting the copper mines. This was around the turn of the century. So what did the Díaz government do? They exterminated some Yaquis and sent other Yaquis to Yucatán, forcing them to work on the henequen [sisal] plantations. And he describes how the Yaqui women were made to marry Chinese laborers."

"You're a reader," I said.

"Of course. Mainly history."

I was impressed by his passion, by his description of the book I'd never heard of, written by an American a century ago. And this book had appeared around the same time—1910, the turbulent years of Porfirio Díaz—as Charles Macomb Flandrau's *Viva Mexico!*

Had Germán read Flandrau?

"Of course," he said. "And Enrique Krauze and many others."

"Flandrau talked about the courtliness of Mexican manners," I said, thinking of how he had written: "I have heard a half-naked laborer bent double under a sack of coffee-berries murmur, 'With your permission,' as he passed in front of a bricklayer who was repairing a wall."

Germán nodded and with a tactical silence gathered the attention of the table before he said pointedly, "But that was long ago!"

Sitting under a tree at a ritual of mourning and feasting, and being informed of Turner and an era I knew little about (Flandrau's book is genial, with a reference to what he calls "Diazpotism"; Turner's is a bitter polemic), I was humbled. Germán was an indigenous Zapotec. What he remembered most vividly about the book was the persecution of another indigenous group, the Yaquis of Sonora, the attempt by the Mexican government to exterminate some and enslave others. When at last I found the book, I discovered it to be an exhaustive account of the abuses of the Díaz period, of oppression and forced labor in Yucatán, of the connivance of the immigrant Chinese, of massacre in Juchitán, and Turner's terrifying eyewitness description of the sadistic flogging of a Yaqui.

In one of his crueler orders, quoted by Turner, Díaz issued a proclamation: "No more Yaquis are to be deported except in the case of offenses being committed by Yaquis. For every offense hereafter committed by any Yaqui, 500 Yaquis are to be rounded up and deported to Yucatan."

"The Yaquis are Indians," the fair-minded Turner writes later. "They are not white, yet when one converses with them in a language mutually understood one is struck with the likenesses of the mental processes of White and Brown. I was early convinced that the Yaqui and I were more alike in mind than in color. I became convinced, too, that the family attachments of the Yaqui mean quite as much to the Yaqui as the family attachments of the American mean to the American. Conjugal fidelity is the cardinal virtue of the Yaqui home and it seems to be so not because of any tribal superstition of past times or because of any teachings of priests, but because of a constitutional tenderness sweetened more and more with the passing of the years."

Meanwhile, at the funeral feast, women were stirring the big pot of maize kernels, slapping tortillas on a griddle, and passing from table to table with a local delicacy, *pan de cazuela*, bread dipped in chocolate, which we ate with one hand, a glass of mezcal or soda pop in the other.

Germán began speaking about the injustices of the current government, and a young man sat down heavily next to me. In a frantic voice he told me his name was Rojelio, that he was thirty-seven, that he had lived in Fresno for years, and joined a gang, and took drugs.

"It's weird to be back here," he said, his voice rising to a screech. "Nothing works. No water. No electricity. No connection to the outside world. Kids go to school without food. There's no information here. I needed to reconnect with this town, but I can't connect."

He stopped making sense, he was paranoid and accusatory, but his moments of lucidity threw me. Across the table, Germán nibbled the *pan de cazuela*, dabs of chocolate on his mustache, while the small girls, winking and offering more food, tiptoed among the tables.

When I looked past the guests eating and drinking, at the apparent clutter in the compound, I perceived something unexpected.

## Harmony in Disorder

IT WAS A clarifying vision, a Mexican epiphany. The funeral feast the day after the burial was held in the walled back garden of the dead woman's house. But the house was much more than that, a compound occupying a whole corner block in the village, three dwellings, including a sizable shop.

This illustrated something it had taken me a while to understand about Mexican life. At ten long tables, and at half a dozen wooden benches, sat a hundred or more people, old and young, dressed informally in the rustic way, all eating together—the tripe and liver stew, weak broth, plates of fatty meat and gristle hacked off the bone, tortillas, mezcal, and soda. For dessert, *pan de cazuela* dipped in a reddish mixture of cocoa-flavored water.

The steady hum of this meal was surrounded by chaotic rustling: ducks and ducklings underfoot, two dogs, seven querulous chickens pecking near a rusted motor scooter that served as a small table, the spreading branches of the trees for shade, a six-foot-high heap of withered corn cobs, two children riding tricycles bumping into the tables, the yard littered with torn plastic and shreds of paper, and at head height, two slumping lines, one hung with laundry, the other with cow tendons stiffening in the heat—or perhaps pale plasticine jerky. Scattered beneath the rope lines: broken toys, unrecognizable; dismembered dolls, heads and torsos; the collapsed tubular frame of a bike; a cast-off car tire; and an old black engine block half buried in the soil. A junkyard, really, but a purposeful one, and a wakeful dog—when he yawned he seemed to grin satirically, showing his teeth.

Three women stood near huge metal pots, one of the pots four feet in diameter, so big the three women could almost have fit inside, the other pots nearly as big, boiling the maize kernels ("for tomorrow's tortillas"), other women serving food, pouring mezcal, bringing baskets of fruit, cuddling babies, cooking, and in a corner near a hand pump and a basin, three women scrubbing soot-crusted pans. In the roofed, open-sided shed—the ramada—a woman at a table hacked at a slab of meat.

But as I studied the scene, the small children bumping on tricycles or playfully offering food seemed soft and luminous, like dream children.

It was not chaotic; it was a serene tableau, each person engaged and animated in a task—eating, drinking, cooking, cleaning, serving, playing, reminiscing, explaining. It seemed like the interior mechanism of an enormous clock—a Mexican clock, all spare parts, its workings tapping the time, gulping the seconds, clicking on the minutes, a model of symmetry and efficiency: each thing mattered, each person was essential. Even the dog mattered, as the proverb had it: Where there is veneration, even a dog's tooth emits light. It was something I needed to know.

My epiphany was this: a mass of unrelated and jumbled elements deliquescing to a vision, disarray resolving to order, chaos crystallizing to harmony. What had looked like a mess was a rational pattern, the Mexican world making sense to me. It was all ritual, preordained and obeyed; it calmed me and helped me on my way.

## Self-Portrait of a Patriarch

MEETING THE OLDER indigenous man, the patriarch at the funeral feast in a small village in the mountains, who read widely and was articulate, self-aware, and analytical, I wanted to know more. This is his story:

My name is Germán García Martínez. I'm sixty-one years old and grew up in the town of San Dionisio Ocotepec. My parents on my mother's side were farmers, and on my father's side bakers. My father believed in education for women and hard work for men. For that reason, I didn't finish primary school. When I married, I worked a long time with my father, but he didn't allow me to advance. He treated me like a stranger, he didn't pay me a salary, and he always said, "Why do you complain if you have food and a roof over your head?"

My wife and I decided to be independent of him, because one day my eldest daughter got sick and I asked my father for money for the doctor and he said no. My wife started to sell *pepitas* [pumpkin seeds] at church, and I worked for other people until we had saved enough to buy a car. With the car, I began to give rides to people to Tlacolula or Oaxaca. In that time there was no taxi or bus. And I began to transport produce for people who took them to sell in the market. This was how I met people from Yalalag who bought plants and leaves for curing leather. I spoke with them and began to sell them the plants, then I bought a mill and began to grind the plants [*a moler las plantas*], because I could get a better price for them.

My wife and I began to buy huaraches from them and sell them at the market, and it went so well that my father stopped talking to me to the point of disinheriting me, only because I wanted a better life for my children. My mother forced him to give me a plot of land where I built my house, and from that moment he told me that was the only thing I would get from him. So I made my own home.

My wife and I wanted to produce our own huaraches. The first step was to learn how to cure leather. One of the men who bought our plants agreed to teach me, but without taking pay or food or lodging. For a number of years he taught me, and I then began curing our own leather. I realized that he had only taught me the basics, and so we wasted a lot of material. In the end, my wife and I succeeded in curing the leather, and we began to learn how to make huaraches, until finally they came out well. We started to sell, and eventually we had seventy clients. This ended when there was the devaluation of the peso, and the people of our town elected me municipal president. At that time, my mother also died.

The business my wife and I had built began to fail. The people who worked with us started to leave for the United States, and I wasn't able to cure the leather because my responsibilities as municipal president took up all my time. My mother had died and my father loved neither me nor my family because I had been able to advance in life, and he hadn't.

In my office as president, I wanted to organize the community, include women in the town assemblies, revive community service, and build a water treatment plant long before even the city of Oaxaca did so. We separated organic from inorganic trash, paved roads, dug water and drainage systems, provided computers for the schools, and created an association of seven indigenous communities. For three years in this post, I received no salary, because the town is run by what is called Uses and Customs [as noted earlier, Usos y Costumbres — customary law, or self-governance], which I call Abuses and Customs [Abusos y Costumbres]. But I also feel a lot of pride and satisfaction for what I accomplished as president. I paid a heavy price, leaving my business and taking on so much in that post.

I returned to my workshop, now in ruins. I was depressed, and to my mind I thought the solution was to go to the United States. But my wife disagreed; she fought to move forward with the business, and she convinced me not to leave the country, and to keep working here.

My father, on the other hand, was happy I had failed. Those were ten very difficult years, and I am grateful to my wife and children, who were always there pushing and fighting for us to succeed. Now everything is different, from having no food to always having food on the table, and now I can even go out to eat or take a break to rest.

Afterward, the village elected me to be the president of communal lands [another unpaid position, to direct the use of communal properties and the group of townspeople who are authorized to use this land]. In that job I discovered my love of nature and the importance of caring for the environment and using it responsibly. It seemed my ideas pleased some people in our town but annoyed others, so I became frustrated and even angry, but I also knew that if I didn't do it, then no one would.

Today I am a man with strong principles. I don't like corruption. I work for the greater good. I like to read. Some of the books I've read are *Poder y Delirio* [*Power and Passion* by Enrique Krauze], *La Rebelión de los Colgados* [*The Rebellion of the Hanged* by B. Traven], and Turner's *México Bárbaro*. I like to help people. I want to protect our lands and protect and restore the environment.

I believe that education is the key to personal and community development. I work to minimize irresponsible consumerism, and for the youth of my town to be able to compete against globalization, so they can have a better future. I believe that collective action can create transformative changes in my community, and that the young can become fountains of inspiration for communities around the world.


In his own words, Don Germán provided me with a portrait of himself as a whole man, recounting his struggles and achievements. It was a reminder that in its essence, travel is less about landscapes than about people—not power brokers but pedestrians, in the long march of Everyman. Once again, in Mexico, as with my students, my chance encounters with campesinos, with Francisco Toledo and Guillermo Olguín and so many others, I felt lucky in the people I met.

## In the Mixteca Alta: Santa María Ixcatlán

THE CRUNCHY, POPULAR straw hats stacked in the market at Tehuacán, in southeastern Puebla state, and in market stalls farther afield—all of them handmade, of strips of dried palm fronds—were woven in one remote community in the mountains of northern Oaxaca. The bleak village lay like chalky residue in a cup-like valley at the end of a road so bad the place was hardly visited, except for the days of its annual fiesta. On those days, pilgrims came in their thousands to venerate a peculiar relic, the carving of a bruised and tortured Christ, which worked miracles and (so it was said) sometimes dripped real blood.

This poor village was Santa María Ixcatlán, so poor that real money seldom changed hands there. If a villager wished to buy vegetables at the market, or an item at the small shop, or had a bag of maize kernels to grind for tortilla flour at the local *molino,* such a person would probably barter a freshly made straw hat, woven early that morning, and that was the equivalent of money—5 pesos, or 25 cents. Few people had money in Santa María Ixcatlán, but all had palm fiber for hats, because the palms grew wild on the rocky slopes of the steep valleys, and the fronds were free for the picking.

Yet the village was culturally rich, and well known in other respects. The place was famous in the Mixteca not only for its hats of woven palm, but also for durable and finely plaited baskets. The local church was celebrated too, for the carved image in a glass case behind the altar, the lacerated Christ—from the Stations of the Cross, the Lord of the Three Falls—the relic that attracted pilgrims. Add to this, a little distance from the village, in a hollow by a stream, a *palenque* of the most traditional kind making mezcal, employing the simplest tools—wooden pitchforks and leather vats—the fermentation taking place in the stitched hides of cows, filled with liquor and looking (the tight hairy bellies bulging) like fat, dismembered animals hung upside down. Finally, Santa María Ixcatlán was the only community in Mexico of Ixcateco-speaking people, and the language was in danger of dying out: though most in the village of about five hundred people knew some words, only three could chat fluently in Ixcateco, and those folks were in their eighties. The population had grown slightly from the three hundred inhabitants recorded in 1579, when the first Spanish missionaries arrived.

I heard of this unusual village from Raúl Cabra, Michael Sledge's partner. Raúl was a designer and entrepreneur, and he was one of Santa María Ixcatlán's largest employers, of local men and women plaiting baskets—some ornamental, others with a practical purpose (for laundry or desk accessories), to be used in luxury hotels.

"But you'll never find the place," Sledge said.

"I have a map."

"Probably not on a map," he said. "But there's another issue, a more tricky one." He made a face, stroked his beard, and smiled. "There's a story they tell about some strangers in the Mixteca. They show up in a village unannounced and begin asking all sorts of questions. This is before they are properly introduced. They're either from the government or some religious sect. The villagers answer the questions—they're sort of intimidated. But they see the strangers as a threat, and the questions as intrusive. So, after the strangers have passed through the village, all the people gather . . ."

"Stop, stop," I said.

"Don't you want to know how it ends?"

"No more details, please."

"You don't like it?"

"I love the story, 'Strangers with Questions,'" I said. "It's just that I don't want to know too much."

"I still think we should go together. The road is terrible. The village is in the middle of nowhere. You don't know anyone there. But I have some contacts—the basket makers. And my truck has more clearance than your car. I'm telling you, that road is horrendous."

It was a good idea that we set off early, going north, past Oaxaca city and Etla, heading to the toll road, because at the first tollbooth a policeman said, "Blockade up ahead. You can't go through. You'll have to take the side roads," and he pointed into the swirling mist, mountain ridges clawed by erosion, the summits visible as bluish crags.

"The scenic route," Sledge said, turning into a narrow road that led upward, past plowed fields, and curved above the valley. Traveling along one ridge — steepness on both sides — he said, "This was probably the road the Spanish took to get to Oaxaca."

"I know this road," I said. "This was the detour I took when I drove to Oaxaca the first time, in a thunderstorm. Another blockade. This is the Camino Real."

The road continued, winding around the upper slopes, giving onto great vistas, the sierra miles away, the nearer mountains eroded, in the red clay zone of Oaxaca. In the most unlikely and precipitous places, small lopsided huts were propped up on slopes, while cows and horses, tipped sideways to compensate for the angle, browsed in the sparse grass, a slanted landscape of leaning creatures and buildings.

Though I had come south on much of this road on my way to Oaxaca, the rain and dark clouds had obscured the distances then and filled the valleys with mist. I had not realized how deep the valleys were, how high I'd been traveling, but the sun and scattered clouds today revealed the true altitude and the danger — the hairpin bends that were unfenced and unforgiving, the crashed cars tumbled and tipped over at the edges of some of these curves, were proof of that.

Sixty miles of sharp bends and potholes, and then the descent to Nochixtlán, the epicenter of teachers' protests, burned-out buses on the main street, the slogan JUSTICE AND RIGHTS FOR ALL PEOPLE still daubed in red paint on the overpasses, and on the buses more slogans accusing the Mexican president of being an assassin. A Mexican town that has been vandalized by protesters and the opposing forces of police and army — the blackened buses, the burned-out trucks, the scorched and melted street surface wrinkled like lava — is Mexico at its most dystopian, like a vision of a failed future, a world gone wrong, a place to flee.

From the slopes of red clay to the slopes of white clay, we turned east on the side road and came to the village of San Juan Bautista Coixtlahuaca, a vast abandoned sixteenth-century convent looming at its center. At the edge of the village we turned onto a stony road that led northeast across the bald hills—bald because, in the absence of trees, the topsoil had been scoured away by the wind.

A woman in black was walking unsteadily, tottering on the lumpy road ahead of us. We slowed.

"Do you want a ride?"

"Yes, please."

She was elderly, black-shawled, her face pinkish from the raw wind. She climbed into the back seat—it was a crew cab—and she sighed in gratitude. Her face was stiff with shyness and cold.

"Where are you going?" I asked.

"Río Blanco."

"How far is it?"

"One hour, walking."

"What about Santa María Ixcatlán?"

"Very far. I don't go there."

She was well wrapped up, a warm shawl, thick jacket, and long skirt; but her shoes were misshapen, one sole coming adrift. She had a dark, wrinkled face, deep furrows, and the determined set to her jaw made her look unflappable. She was a Mixtec, she said, and yes, she spoke the language all the time.

As for her reason for what I took to be a ten-mile round trip to San Juan Bautista, it was, she said, a *recado:* "I am on an errand."

Most of the landscape was ghost white, blowing dust, infertile, nothing growing, only wind-whipped hollows and those odd scooped shapes you see in some smooth sand dunes.

"And they wonder why people want to leave places like this," Sledge said. "Nothing grows here."

But on other hills some pines had been planted, as a gesture to reforestation, obviously to hold the soil. They were planted in rows, some tenaciously rooted, others dead, brown and brittle and stark, having shed their needles.

"They planted those five years ago," the old woman said.

"What do you grow here?"

"Maize," she said. "Beans. Wheat. Maguey."

"What do you eat?"

"We eat meat—little goats. Red *mole*. Black *mole*. Beans." She frowned and thought a moment. She might have been abashed at the simplicity of the menu. She said, "Pulque bread."

It was perhaps her way of reminding us that they observed festivals in Río Blanco, offering the traditional treat of *pan de pulque*, made with the fermented sap of the maguey plant.

But our truck jounced so badly it was hard to hold a conversation with all the banging, the road more like a dry rocky riverbed than a thoroughfare for wheeled vehicles. Near a sudden creek, I saw geometric plots of land, in large rectangles, marked by low walls of football-sized stones.

"Wheat fields," the old woman said.

She said she rarely went to Oaxaca—it was much too expensive. The first leg was a car or a truck to San Juan Bautista. Then a bus to Nochixtlán. Then another bus. Total, 600 pesos, or $29—prohibitive.

We came to a little bridge, some stone huts beyond it.

"Río Blanco," the woman said, and thanked us and got out.

More miles, of gravel and stones, of dry bouldery fields where nothing grew. The village of Río Poblano, some miles farther on, was a cluster of huts, a small chapel, a fifty-foot section of paved road, then the rocky road again. After a few hours, we descended into more sheltered hollows. What looked like twisted black claws scattered in the white dust were agave plants—not the cultivated agave but the wild variety of maguey they called *criollo*. And descending farther, now with a better view of the wide, greeny-brown valley, I could see the palm trees, fan palms, ten or fifteen feet high, many of them stripped of their fronds. These two plants—the agave and the palm—provided raw material for the artisans in the village, the agave for mezcal, the palms for baskets.

Every community in this part of Mexico is approached through an archway, with its name and lettered word of welcome. We passed under SANTA MARÍA IXCATLÁN and BIENVENIDO, and, still on a high section of road, I could see the whole place: at the base of a rocky hillside, one long street of low, pale, flat-faced cement or adobe huts fronting the curb, at the far end a white church, on a rise to the left a municipal building. No trees visible in the village, no cars on the roads, no people—apparently a ghost town.

On a side road, halfway down the narrow main street, there was a house propped over a ravine. The rooms were stark and cold, cement block walls, with that sour stink of damp concrete, a hard bed, a dirty floor, a bare bulb hanging from a cord—like a jail cell, but a bargain at $5 a night.

"We are busy during the fiesta," the owner, Juana, said. "Now it's very quiet. But you will see some people celebrating the beginning of Lent at night these days. They are the townspeople. Some play music."

And she explained that the name of the town, Ixcatlán, in the Ixcateco language, meant Land of Wild Cotton; in Mixteco, the name was Xula. The place name is significant. Cotton was grown here and throughout Oaxaca for thousands of years, in the Mayan and Aztec empires, and continued well beyond the Spanish conquest. As Sven Beckert describes in his book *Empire of Cotton,* many Nahuatl settlements had the word "cotton" in their name, such as On the Hill of Cotton and On the Cotton Temple.

I asked about the sacred image in the church, the Lord of the Three Falls.

"There was a statue of Christ in Puebla about two hundred years ago," Juana said. "All the villages wanted it. But when they tried to pick it up, they failed. Then a man from here tried. He lifted it easily and brought it to the church, where it is venerated."

The story was a bit more complicated than this, as I found out later.

"But we have no priest," she said. "That is, none in town. A priest comes now and then. He doesn't live here—he lives in Teotitlán." That was twenty miles away. "He charges us eight hundred pesos [$43] to say Mass."

There was no phone line to the town. The Wi-Fi signal was so weak it was not worth logging on. No bus stopped here. As the woman we'd picked up had said, it took a car and two bus rides to get to Oaxaca city.

"At one time a train stopped at a town over the mountains—this was seventy or eighty years ago. Men waited with burros and brought the passengers and travelers to our town."

The town with the railway halt had an odd name. It was called Tecoma-vaca (something like Eat Your Cow); the railway line from Puebla—it was the freight line to Oaxaca city—was shown on my map.

"Some people leave the town," she said, "because they're poor."

"What sort of work do people do here?"

"They cut wood," she said. "Or do palm weaving. There's not enough water to grow crops. They gather maguey for mezcal."

Sledge suggested that we go to where the palm weavers were at work, in a hut, which was also a workshop. And in the hut next door to it we could get something to eat.

We walked down the empty main street to the hut, where smoke was issuing from a tin chimney. The hut was made of adobe and the limestone they called *bijarra*. This was one room, half of it a kitchen, with wide gaps in the roof to let the smoke out. A wood fire was burning in a bricked corner under a *comal*, a clay basin where tortillas were being heated. A black iron pot held a bubbling stew of tripe and goat meat with carrots, beans, and zucchini, with lumps of fraying fat floating on the surface.

Filiberta was the cook. Her two boys served us, and while she went on slapping tortillas, her husband and boys joined us at the table.

Filiberta's husband, José, said grace. After we began eating, I asked if the boys were at school.

"Only junior high," José said. "There is no high school here. He'd have to live in another town to go to high school. At the age of sixteen they have no further option, so they generally leave."

Listening, the older boy, Ignacio, who was twenty, said softly, "I'd like to leave, but I don't know where to go."

"Have you traveled in Mexico?"

He said, "I was in Tehuacán once."

Filiberta said, "Not more than four people from here have gone to the USA. Three came back. One of them stayed."

"People from this town go to Mexico City," José said. "They send money back. Recently some have gone to Querétaro, to work in a factory."

José himself made money building houses, using traditional materials, mostly adobe. This was not profitable—he earned the equivalent of $12 a day; but with Filiberta's cooking and the palm weaving next door, they produced enough to live on.

"This town is more than one thousand years old," José said. "It was a kingdom."

I asked him a few more questions, about the town and the church and its sacred image, but José replied that he didn't know much, and I realized I had embarrassed him by pressing him for details, as though testing him. He was not wrong in saying the town had existed for a thousand years—as a traditional community it was much older than that, and as an Ixcateco stronghold it was a *cacicazgo*—a fiefdom ruled by a cacique, a noble who was also the owner of the whole place.

So we finished the food without saying much more, and it was like eating a meal in a cold village in Tibet, the same sort of tin-roofed hut and drafty room, clouded and thick with woodsmoke from the open fire, the same rough table and simple dishes, the same piety and patience, the stolidity of the people, their look of everlastingness, unreadable in their silence.

When we were done, Filiberta said, "Come next door. Let's see the weavers. And I have to resume weaving."

## Palm Weavers

TODAY THEY WERE sitting together in a small cold cinderblock room, malodorous from the damp and dusty cement walls, but they often sat together outside the house, crouched in a deep hole in the ground they called a *cueva*, a cave, knees bumping. The dampness in the cave moistened the palm and kept it pliable for weaving, and the cave was a refuge from the hot weather. There were six women weaving in the room, Filiberta, Crecencia, Roberta, Margarita, Yolanda, and Alicia. In their midst, one man, Jesús, who was twenty-three.

"Our husbands also do weaving," Crecencia said when I asked. "Men and women do it."

"We learned when we were five years old," Roberta said. She was an older woman and might have been doing this for sixty years.

"Our parents taught us," Crecencia said.

Each was at work on a different sort of basket, intent on slipping the strands of palm fiber through the weave, and they faced me, answering my questions, weaving without looking down, tugging the strand of fiber as someone sewing draws a thread to close a seam. They were making boxes of various sizes, some very small and tight, others large and rectangular and shallow, with lids that fit snugly over them.

"For shirts, when the laundry is returned to the room at the hotel," Alicia said of the box she was making. She was young, recently married, and was glad for the work. It took her a week to make a box with a lid, and for this she was paid 1,500 pesos, about $75, a good wage by local standards, and paid in real money.

Besides the boxes, some of them were making mats—*petates*—big and small, and others fashioning cylindrical containers. They wove all the time, not only here and in the cave but in their spare time at home, listening to music, or sitting at meetings, or in the stands at basketball games. Basketball was popular in the village; there were hoops and a court near the Palacio Municipal, where the village president had an office.

"In the 1700s people here were already weaving like this," Filiberta said.

In fact, long before that. A research student from Texas, Michael Hironymous, reported that the palm weaving in the village had been practiced since pre-Hispanic times, and that a survey carried out in 1579 under King Philip II, the Relaciones Geográficas, specifically mentioned palm weaving here as "the sole economic activity of the community"—more than four centuries of processing palm fronds, stripping and drying them, and making baskets, everyone in the village involved, including small children.

The weavers in the cinderblock room were filling an order for a thousand pieces of different shapes, designed by Raúl Cabra, for a luxury hotel in Cabo San Lucas, in Baja. It was the largest order they'd ever had, and the best paid.

"Has anyone here thought of going to the United States?" I asked.

"There is no tradition for anyone here to go to the United States," Crecencia said.

"We don't know anyone in the United States," Roberta said.

"My husband is in Mexico City," Alicia said. "He said he's going to come and get me. Then I'll live there."

"Maybe he'll send some burros to help you move," Margarita said, teasing the younger woman.

The others laughed and continued weaving, their fingers darting, pushing at palm fiber, tugging it, smoothing the weaving, darting again.

Two of the women had been to Mexico City. Crecencia had been as far as Puebla, but preferred life here—a harder life, but the family was here, and they all did weaving together. Santa María Ixcatlán was by far a better place.

I asked about weaving hats.

"You can make five hats a day. That's twenty-five pesos"—25 cents a hat. "We swap hats for food. All stores take hats in trade."

The village seemed so destitute and isolated, at the end of a bad road. The nearest river was twelve hours away, round-trip, on foot, which was the usual way of going. I asked them to tell me what they liked best about living here.

"History," Filiberta said. "Nature, too. The mountains. The birds."

"We are social here, families get together," Crecencia said. "We eat together—red *mole,* goat meat, cow meat. Even when we are in the cave we are social, and we compete to see who can make a hat or a basket the fastest."

They laughed at this, and recalled the deftest weavers, and teased Jesús, the single male weaver, for lagging. Seeing him wince under the teasing, I asked whether there were any tensions in the village.

"Sometimes," Margarita said. "There can be tensions between goat herders and weavers, because the goats eat the small palms that grow wild. And we complain when some people cut the palms in a bad way, ruining the fronds. But we really don't have any serious tensions."

"Land disputes," Filiberta said.

Yes, they all agreed, land disputes caused problems.

"Customs and traditions, they are strong here," Yolanda said—her first utterance, though she had been watching closely, weaving without looking down.

"But we get along. We have fiestas here," Crecencia said. "Tomorrow there is one—you will see it. Carnaval."

I had not realized: tomorrow was Shrove Tuesday, the next day Ash Wednesday, Miércoles de Ceniza, the first day of Lent.

"There will be music and a procession and masks," Crecencia said. "*Una calenda. Mascaritas.*"

## Carnaval in Santa María Ixcatlán

IT WAS A silent village of closed doors and windows curtained with cardboard, of empty streets where the only movement was a limping dog or a chicken pecking at ants. The main street was narrow and paved, but I never saw a car on it, or any vehicle except a cart pulled by a burro. On the side streets there were a few small shops, open-fronted, piled with canned goods, bottled beer, candy bars, toothpaste, and dried beans in fat sacks, yet the only person I saw in a shop was a man sitting sideways on a stool, his eyes glassy, holding a tumbler of mezcal, too drunk to hold a conversation.

But on this cold night, just after dark, the music started—overblown trumpets and guitars and drums in the distance, blatting brass and plinking strings and the rattle of snare drums. The band ducked from one back street to another (not streets, really, but alleys), and when I finally found the musicians, they were standing beneath the dim streetlamps, to play under available light. But there were so few lamps in the village, the band did not travel far.

They played in front of the shops, too, "Ghost Riders in the Sky" at one, provoking the shop owner to distribute wrapped candy, which they tore open with their teeth, while still playing.

Townsfolk in masks gathered around them, strutting and hopping—the *calenda* the weavers had promised, a procession of celebrants, a hundred of them masked or playing music, about two hundred people watching and following, more than half the village in the poorly lit streets. The masks were grotesque, but they were not the oddest aspect of it. What struck me as unusual was that none of the people were taller than about five feet, so the impression I had was of a village of dwarves, both adults and children, some of them masked, others watching in silence.

The smallest of them I took to be children, though they could have been any age, and they wore monkey masks. One trudging boy in a hairy, toothy dog mask, swinging his arms and nodding, came at me, then veered off. Bearded men, witches and goblins, some made up as clowns, their faces gleaming with paint, girls in dresses wearing wolf masks, strolling in pairs, and all this time the trumpets blaring, the drums determining the pace of the procession.

The women were not women; they were *mascaritas,* men dressed as women, in wigs and gowns, big-breasted, their chests stuffed, their masks depicting coquettes. And when one in a blond wig saw me making notes (*Child in dog mask freaking me out . . .*), I found myself embraced by strong unyielding arms, my face butted by the crimson everted lips on a mask of a woman's face. My height, or perhaps it was my scribbling in an open note-book, made me conspicuous, so I became the object of the amative *mascaritas.* I was not startled; men dressed as women are common in Mexican processions. But I was fascinated by the small size of everyone in the street.

The spectators, watching and following, were Ixcatecos, most of them impassive, a few laughing at the antics of the masked shufflers and the twanging and blatting of the bandsmen, all of them wrapped in blankets or shawls, the women holding babies. The procession moved from street to street, up and down the alleys, to the three shops in the village, until the sound died away and the place became silent once more, severe and Lenten.

I went back to the chilly guesthouse, found a hard chair in the disorder of the kitchen, sat under a fluorescent bulb at a table littered with sticky jars, and ate a burned quesadilla. Then wearily I groped to my cement cell and lay on a slumping mattress with filthy sheets, under a damp mildewed blanket, my head on a stained pillow, and slept like a baby.

## *El Señor de las Tres Caídas*

I WAS WOKEN in the dark of my cold and dirty cubicle by singing somewhere in town, unmistakably lilting and liturgical—a call to prayer, as it turned out. Sledge was already up, waiting by the front door. It was five-thirty on a dark morning on the Ixcatec plateau.

"The church opens at six," he said. "But it closes an hour later."

I yawned and said, "My room is awful."

"That's the best room in the place."

"How so?"

"You have the one with the bathroom."

That small, dank, stone closet, with the wet floor and the dripping pipe and the stinking hopper.

We walked to the church of Santa María in semidarkness. Hurrying, I became slightly breathless, affected by the village's altitude, which was over six thousand feet. The streets were empty, not even a mule cart. A goat was browsing by the roadside.

"This village makes me think of *Pedro Páramo,*" Sledge said.

"I really wonder about that book," I said.

At the top of a little hill at the end of the road stood the white church, a high wall around it, a tree in the churchyard, one of the few trees hereabouts. A little plaque at the gate was lettered *Nunga,* the Ixcateco word for church. Offices, stores, even the local jail, *Ndachika,* and the municipal public toilets—*Dii* for Men, *C'a* for Women—had such plaques near the entrance, giving the name in Ixcateco, or Xwja (*Sh-wa*), its proper name. But the language was on the verge of extinction.

As we approached the church, which was dedicated to the Virgin Mary, the front door swung open, a custodian dragging it with two hands. Another custodian stood near the door, toggling light switches. It was early enough that the interior was still being illuminated, and after a few minutes was brightly lit, the altars blazing, several chapels devoted to various virgins, another to Saint Michael. The church was newly painted; the light intensified the tang of fresh paint. Except for one man, kneeling in a rear pew, praying, the church was empty.

While Sledge examined the paintings, I sat in the front pew, trying to get a look at the object of veneration, the figure of the fallen Christ. It was lodged in a rectangular niche behind the altar, obscured by the tabernacle and a row of flickering electric candles.

The custodian who had opened the door was watching me.

I went to him and whispered, "I would like to go closer. May I?"

"Yes — this way," he said, and gestured to a passageway that circled behind the altar.

As reverently as I could, because I was being severely observed by the custodians I took to be vergers, I shuffled along the tiles and up the stairs to the raised platform where the figure was displayed behind glass. It took me a little while to understand the attitude of the figure, its posture was so odd, a four-foot-long prone carving in a red brocade robe. My first impression was a mass of twisted cloth and the glint of gold objects. Numerous gold rings, chain bracelets, gilded filigree brooches, and medals had been pinned to the robe and to the tapestry behind the fallen Christ: not trinkets but votive offerings.

Christ lay on his stomach, half raised from the fulcrum of his hip joint, his body contorted, one bloody elbow a pivot, his agonized face twisted and uplifted, his eyes staring upward to the heavens. The eyes were the key feature, tormented, seeking help and strength, Christ arrested in a moment of crisis: the ninth station, the Lord of the Three Falls, under the weight of the cross, just before he is kicked by the Roman soldiers and rises again to continue to his crucifixion. The figure seemed to dramatize both suffering and hope. The gold tokens pinned to the robe I took to be offerings donated by pilgrims who had either received help or were seeking it.

The window was so small, the bloodstained figure filling it, and in such a tight space, that it could only be seen in close-up, by squeezing along the narrow passage and up the stairs and pressing your face against the glass to contemplate the tableau of torture.

Sledge had followed me, looking reflective, and like me fearful of not seeming properly pious.

The custodian-vergers stood near the altar as we descended, as though to gauge the extent of our piety.

"*Muy impresionante,*" Sledge said.

"*Muchos milagros?*" I asked.

"Yes, many miracles," one of the men said.

"For the pilgrims," the other man said. "Not so much for the town."

"What sort of miracles?"

"Wishes granted. Health restored. Ailments cured."

And as the hour for viewing had almost expired, the custodians led us to the doorway of the church.

I had more questions: How long had the figure been in the church? Had it—as local people said—been found in a field? Could anyone verify that although many struggled, no one could lift it from where it lay abandoned until a man from Santa María had picked it up? Was the rumor true that it bled from some of its wounds and soaked its robe, and that occasionally the wounds healed?

"It came many years ago" was one answer. It was true that only a man from Santa María Ixcatlán could lift it. Yes, now and then the statue bled, and yes, when cracks were detected, the cracks healed. And the beard needed to be trimmed from time to time, because it was still growing.

It was not a statue, not a carving; El Señor de las Tres Caídas was a living thing, able to bleed, heal, weep, and grow hair. And this was why it commanded the utmost veneration, because it was alive. A living Christ lay on the altar of the church of the Virgin Mary in this remote village.

The most complete account of its origin was given by the American scholar Michael Hironymous in his 2007 dissertation, based on earlier research and his own interviews. The Texas scholar had lived in the village for extended periods in the late 1990s and quizzed the older locals. The statue had been found by a peasant in a field near Tilapa, in southern Puebla state, sometime in the 1840s. The peasant first believed it to be a wounded man, but seeing that it was a Christ figure, he tried to pick it up. In spite of his efforts he could not budge it. A priest was summoned, people from surrounding villages came to wonder at it, and perhaps to move it. Many tried. No one could shift it. The priest anointed it and blessed it.

Then four men from distant Santa María Ixcatlán showed up and easily lifted it, seeming to prove that it belonged to them.

Carrying the figure along the banks of the Río Salado on their way home, they passed the corpses of some men who had been hanged. The proximity of the Christ figure miraculously brought the men back from the dead. The men carrying the figure fell three times on their way to the village—the places where they fell still marked by crosses. A further miracle of El Señor occurred nearer the village: "As he approached Ixcatlán, it is said that all the trees bowed and shed their leaves to carpet the path in his honor."

For about 175 years, on the fourth Friday of Lent, the village had held a weeklong fiesta in honor of El Señor, with Masses and band concerts. This was when the pilgrims arrived, from distant places ("even from the United States"), some of them journeying on foot to mortify themselves. Pilgrims participated in the fiesta, paying for Masses or flowers, some of them carrying wooden crosses up and down the main street. The figure of El Señor was removed from its niche in that week and carried in a litter from street to street, with fireworks at night.

Though the church was dedicated to the Virgin Mary, it was El Señor who was the guiding presence in the village, and the fiesta was a chance for Santa María Ixcatlán to generate income, renting rooms to pilgrims and selling them food—the sort of food I ate in the village, baby goat stew, tripe soup, beans, eggs, salsa, avocados, tortillas, coffee, and mezcal.

But whenever the villagers spoke of the pilgrims, they did so with visible restraint and a grudging tone, letting drop the fact that the village could not really accommodate so many visitors at once; that in that week the pilgrims were everywhere, camped in fields, picnicking in the plaza, and sprawled at the roadsides; that when they finally went away, having said their prayers and worshiped El Señor, they left litter all over the place. This last detail was vividly recalled, more than the business of food selling, or the stalls of drinks, or the Masses, or the fireworks. It was the annoyance of having to clean up after the pilgrims departed.

"*Basura*"—and a deep sigh—"*en todos lados.*"

Trash—everywhere.

## Artisanal Mezcal

THE *PALENQUE* OF Alvarado Álvarez lay in a deep valley east of the village, on a steep gravel road. On the way I saw a small girl carrying a hat and a basket of maize. Sledge, driving his pickup truck, was going slowly on the bad road, so it was easy to stop and say hello. Now I saw that it was not a small girl but an old withered woman in a shawl, no more than four and a half feet tall. Smiling, she seemed friendly, eager to know where I was from and pleased when I complimented her on her newly made hat.

"I am going to the miller's to grind this maize into flour," she said. "I will pay with this hat."

We continued on our way to the lip of the valley, in sight of the granite walls of Loma de los Muertos, the Hillock of the Dead, where I could see terraces, and meadows at the base of the valley. We walked down a long path to a terrace, to a mezcal operation that would have been easily recognized by a Mixteco living long ago, when mezcal was made the same way: by smashing the agave in a tub with a four-foot pestle (*marso*) and fermenting the *bagasso* in sacks sewn of uncured cowhide.

"This is the tradition here," Alvarado said. "Not vats of wood or stone sinks." The cowhide was slippery and so heavy with liquid, the swollen belly stretched and strained the lashed frame of its rack. "The other thing—when it ferments, it cures the skin. And you can taste the difference."

Alvarado employed eight workers for the pounding of the agave *piños* and the distillation in clay pitchers (*jarras*) and pots (*monteras*), the funnel made of an agave spike. It was all done by hand using simple tools—machetes, pestle, pitchforks, animal skins.

"An old method," I said.

"Two hundred years old," he said. "I inherited this from my great-grandfather."

I tasted some of the product. It was 46 percent alcohol, Alvarado said.

"See, it's sweeter, not so aggressive as the usual kind."

He made ten thousand liters a year, selling it directly to bars in Oaxaca for 250 pesos a liter, about $13.50. This was good money. A family of five in the village lived on an average of 700 pesos a month, about $37, which was, as I learned later, much less than a family of the same size in rural Kenya. The average monthly income for Mexico was ten times that, but this rural area was at the periphery of the economy, the poorest people in the country.

Slightly dazed after sampling the mezcal, we left the *palenque* and, Sledge still driving, made our way through the village. We went past the church and the small plaza, under the archway and up the slopes of agave and palms, to the windy plateau, surrounded by mountains: to the east El Mirador, to the north Gandudo, to the southeast Peña de Gavilán and Montón de Piedras, rugged descriptions of stone ridges and ravines.

The landscape seemed, on this return trip, even starker than before, slopes and fields of smooth, wind-scoured limestone, no soil at all except in the occasional acres that had been desperately planted with pine trees. The villages of Río Poblano and Río Blanco looked poorer than Santa María Ixcatlán, and now and then we saw people plodding along the road. Four of them we picked up. They climbed into the bed of the truck, because the back seat of the crew cab was filled with finished woven baskets that we had agreed to take to Oaxaca.

"This road doesn't get easier," Sledge said, driving slowly, dodging potholes.

We talked about what we had seen, the palm weavers, the pre-Lenten procession, the El Señor figure, the *palenque*. "We asked a lot of questions." And he reminded me of the story he'd heard of the strangers who had come to just such a remote village and asked too many questions.

When we got to the paved road, and then the village of San Juan Bautista Coixtlahuaca, we parked, and the riders climbed out to thank us, and made a ritual gesture of offering to pay for the ride.

"Thank you, no money is necessary," I said. "But can you answer some questions instead?"

One of them, an older woman, was Epifania Gutiérrez, about forty, perhaps younger.

"I live and work in Río Poblano," she said. "I am a housewife, and I also work at home. I have six children. My work is making hats. I get seventy pesos for twelve hats. It takes eight days to make that many hats, but of course I don't work all day at it."

This came to just under $4 for eight days' work.

"A person here buys them from me. Then I walk back to Río Poblano."

Epifania's oldest daughter, Angelina, was seventeen. She was accompanying her mother on this cloudy day on the plateau.

"What do you do, Angelina?"

"I help my mother."

The younger of the two men was José Luis Figueroa. He had three children.

"I am a campesino," he said, when I asked his work. "I have cows. When I have a need for money, I sell a cow." A small cow could bring 450 pesos, about $25.

The older man was probably in his sixties. He wore a battered hat. He said he had six children, but they were married. He was a grandfather.

"What do you do?" I asked.

"I am a campesino."

"How do you live?"

"I keep little goats"—*chivitas.*

"Do you eat them or sell them?"

"We eat them. We also sell them."

He earned the same for a goat as José Luis Figueroa did for a small cow.

"I sell maybe six a year."

"What is the name of this pueblo, señor?" I knew the name, but I thought I would ask, for a particular reason.

"It is San Juan Bautista Coixtlahuaca," he said. "See, the old convent."

The broken church was vast and hollowed out and unvisited, monumental in this tiny place, one large belfry, the entryway enclosing doors that were thirty feet high, with an inner courtyard and cloisters, similar in scale to the church in Yanhuitlán, which I'd visited on my way south and was not far from here.

"What is the meaning of 'Coixtlahuaca'?"

*"El llano de los serpientes."*
The plain of snakes.

## Mexicans on Mexico

I WONDERED, AS a writer and reader, but also as a traveler, do you learn anything of value about Mexican life by reading Mexican novels? Why spend all this time on back roads when you could stay home with your feet up, traveling in fiction, and discover Mexico that way?

In Santa María Ixcatlán, Sledge had said, "This village makes me think of *Pedro Páramo*."

When Mexican writers are asked to name an important Mexican novel of the past sixty years or so, they usually suggest *Pedro Páramo* (1955) by Juan Rulfo, rather than, say, any of the thirty-six works of fiction by Carlos Fuentes, or the ten of Jorge Ibargüengoitia, or the sixteen of Martín Luis Guzmán. In other words, none of the big urban novels, but a small rural one of a far-off ghost town. *Pedro Páramo* is a story of futility, deception, decay, and death, which is not so surprising, since these are the enduring themes in Mexican writing, and it seemed to me that both in tradition and popular culture Mexicans were half in love with death, always playing with a human skull as though it was a doll—and it often is, a gaily painted grinning head, or a skeleton costumed as a doll, or a skull of smooth sculpted sugar, made for the fiesta.

"The Mexican . . . is familiar with death, jokes about it, caresses it, sleeps with it, celebrates it; it is one of his favorite toys and his most steadfast love," Octavio Paz writes in *The Labyrinth of Solitude*, with his customary hyperbole. Paz is the most acute of Mexican writers on Mexican life: any observation you might make about Mexico—life or society, identity or belief—has probably been said with greater eloquence in Paz's *Labyrinth* or his poems. He goes on, "True, there is perhaps as much fear in his attitude as that of others, but at least death is not hidden away: he looks at it face to face, with impatience, disdain or irony. 'If they are going to kill me tomorrow, let them kill me right away.'" And: "Our contempt for death is not at odds with the cult we have made of it. Death is present in our fiestas, our games, our loves and our thoughts. To die and kill are ideas that rarely leave us . . . Death revenges us against life, strips it of all its vanities and pretensions and converts it into what it really is: a few neat bones and a dreadful grimace."

He might have added, Is it any wonder that Mexicans are so fatalistic about the drug gangs and beheadings?

Paz says "death," not "dying." Dying is another matter altogether, something to be avoided because it implies pain — an anguished, agonizing process, sometimes lengthy, not a sudden bitter end, but an often prolonged terminal condition. Yet death as a certainty and a promise is the eternal Mexican specter at the feast. Paz is Mexican in his commitment to pessimism: "The reason death cannot frighten us is that 'life has cured us of fear.'"

*Pedro Páramo,* the novel of death, of ghosts, of apparitions, is set in Comala, a remote village in a barren landscape, which is a sort of *inframundo,* the underworld that parts of Mexico sometimes seem. As a traveler in rural towns and villages, I was fascinated by a novel with this setting. I ended up reading it half a dozen times, with growing bewilderment and diminishing pleasure. But the novel is regarded as a Mexican classic, and has been extravagantly praised by Jorge Luis Borges. Gabriel García Márquez said that reading it inspired him to conceive the form of *One Hundred Years of Solitude,* emboldening him in his excursions in juxtaposed realism and fantasy in his fictional Colombian town of Macondo.

*Pedro Páramo* was Rulfo's only novel — novella, really, at just over a hundred pages — and in my opinion a slight one, an elusive narrative of heavy hints, with an elliptical charm, suggesting (as poetry does) events or feelings rather than stating them. In other words, the reader is always somewhat at sea, and has to work to understand the chorus of voices and the time shifts. Obeying his mother's deathbed request, young Juan Preciado journeys to haunted Comala to search for his father, Pedro Páramo, and in doing so encounters ghosts of the past and remnants of his father's history.

It is a novel of fragments, and a landscape sketchily described, of abrupt unexplained transitions, of dreams, and dialogue as whispers. Rulfo had planned to call it *Los Murmullos* (*The Murmurs*).

When Juan dies midway through the novel, the narration is taken up by Dorotea, a beggar, who is — by the way — dead, but has witnessed the town in its better days and known Pedro, his love Susana, and the many other townspeople, a great number — priest, postman, local prophet, cook, and so forth. A literary puzzle of multiple narrators, it is static and mutely defiant like most puzzles, with a circular narration, revolving slowly rather than moving forward. Its handling of time — fluid, the sort literary critics call Faulknerian — and its blurred meanings infuse the narrative with an opacity some scholars believe to confer a mythical quality. The novel is squarely in the tradition of fictional obliquity, of the (God help us) "difficult" novel in need of explanation — you don't read it for pleasure, you study it for a term paper. It's the kind of baffling book that is assigned to a special category, to invite discussion, the book overexamined by postmodernist explicators (hardly a surprise that Susan Sontag, queening pedantically over its obscurity, wrote the introduction to a later edition of *Pedro Páramo*). The novel challenges the reader to find a meaning in it — quite a job, since Rulfo is so little help, assigning all his allusions the same value.

As well as being claimed a masterpiece by Borges and García Márquez, Paz and Fuentes, the much younger Mexican novelist Carmen Boullosa has also praised it. She knew Juan Rulfo as a friend and mentor, but though she is enthusiastic, her praise is off-putting: "The novel is about the Novel: the wonders of storytelling, the power of the literary word that spins so fast it never lets the reader catch it." But I find Boullosa's own novels, in particular *Antes* (*Before*), which is also about a complex search, more satisfying and readable, and just as important.

When I said I had my doubts about *Pedro Páramo*, I was also thinking of a whole shimmering shelf of novels, self-consciously of a bygone literary movement, in this case fantasies and evasions. Like most self-conscious, programmatic literary movements, they obey a fanciful formula, ultimately a pointless parlor trick. This is not to disparage Borges, who is regarded as the father of it all, but only to say that reading Borges's fiction, you're lost on the forking paths of an inimitable and wordy underworld, and not the hard-up hinterland, and the hard-up hinterland is all I have come to care about, not just in Latin America, where magical realism was first defined in the mid-twentieth century (by the Cuban Alejo Carpentier, who called it *lo real maravilloso*), but across the poverty-stricken world.

Magical realism, once gushed over, now seeming somewhat dated and pretentious, was perhaps a third-world reaction to the horrific and hard to bear in daily life, a willful turning away from reality, a flight into banal bedazzlement, as Salman Rushdie, who has made his reputation producing it, described, in *Imaginary Homelands:* "'El realismo magical,' magic realism, at least as practiced by Márquez, is a development out of Surrealism that expresses a genuinely 'Third World' consciousness. It deals with what Naipaul has called 'half-made' societies, in which the impossibly old struggles against the appallingly new, in which public corruptions and private anguishes are somehow more garish and extreme than they ever get in the so-called 'North,' where centuries of wealth and power have formed thick layers over the surface of what's really going on."

I doubt this. Rather than expressing a third-world consciousness (and Naipaul is at pains to be scrupulous, plainspoken, and disenchanted in writing about "half-made" societies), I see it as at worst a third-world writer's affectation and at best a third-world writer's indirection, like a magician's trick of distraction, a fiction that has arisen out of embarrassment, a literary reaction to shameful circumstances or origins. To this point, Naipaul has also said, "More and more today, writers' myths are about the writers themselves." Subjected to scrutiny, abused children make up such whoppers to disguise the reality that they come from unhappy homes. The poor pray for miracles, consoling themselves with fantasy and fables, and in Mexico sometimes enact them in rituals, as though to bring them to life. This combination of sympathy, yearning, and belief abounds in the communities of rural Mexico and permeates them with a consciousness of the supernatural.

This oral tradition of the supernatural has been appropriated by others for fiction. But the term "magical realism" is an academic justification — that is, a pompous way of avoiding the term "fantasy." It is a literature of denial, a literature of hokum, a form of extravagant literary nostalgia for an earlier, animistic era, a culture of masks, sacrifices, apparitions, and fairy tales. It is my friend Salman Rushdie and other literary refugees shrinking from the horrors of India to sit in New York or London and serve up flapdoodle and farce and comic tales of bedazzlement about a prettified peasantry, while half a billion Indians living in poverty on the subcontinent struggle to find their next meal. I admit the wisdom and vitality of García Márquez's novels and short stories, and the power of his imagination, his avoidance of whimsy, his great comic gift. He is the best of this bunch, writing about the hard-up hinterland, yet even his work seems a brilliant confection, fable and allegory not being to my taste. "It's like farting 'Annie Laurie' through a keyhole," Gulley Jimson says. "It may be clever but is it worth the trouble?" I have spent my reading and writing life, and my traveling, trying to see things as they are—not magical at all, but desperate and woeful, illuminated by flashes of hope.

But here is the protestation of a Mexican magical realist, the middle-aged, middle-class editor and modern novelist Ignacio Solares: "I believe in every possible manifestation of spiritual strangeness. I believe in all possible escapes. The only thing I cannot endure is reality, whatever it may be. I believe that the writer is defined by the constant necessity of creating a world, to depart from this world. Literature is more concerned with misery than with happiness. Writing is directly related to frustration. It is a reflection of personal desperation. The writer is profoundly disgusted with his reality." And in an interview in a Mexican magazine, *Revista Zócalo*, Solares said, "It so happens that the one thing unbearable to me is the 'real reality'" ("*Lo que pasa es que para mí lo único insoportable es la 'realidad real'*").

Consider this: Solares is from Ciudad Juárez, border city of narco mayhem, of executions, lynchings, disemboweling, cartel exploitation, and beheadings—the guts spilled and the blood puddled on the main roads, the bodies hung from lampposts or stuffed into trunks, and the heads arranged like tainted cantaloupes on the hoods of parked cars, to suggest to passersby the realities of rough justice.

What rational Mexican—or anyone else—wouldn't find that "*insoportable*"? Yet it is the fiction writer's duty, through the prism of the imagination, to cast a cold eye, and to depict life as it is, life as it should be. In spite of his stated aversion to reality, Solares doesn't seem to scare easily. Provoked by his experience of six members of his family being alcoholics, and three uncles suffering from delirium tremens, he published a powerful account of drinking to oblivion, including interviews with alcoholics, called *Delirium Tremens: Stories of Suffering and Transcendence.* He has, as well, written historical novels, short stories, and plays.

Like most prominent Mexican writers, Solares lives in Mexico City. But you can become lost in the crosscurrents and cliques of literary Mexico — the fantasists, magical realists, dirty realists, poets, novelists of narco lit, and the various literary movements, such as the Boom (Fuentes and others), the Crack Manifesto, and the Wave (La Onda), which produced the younger generation who call themselves the McOndo, and lastly the naturalistic novelists.

One of the many paradoxes of modern Mexican literature is its cosmopolitan influences, especially from Spain and the US. Another paradox is that the movement of writers is toward Mexico City and the wider world, rather than to the hinterland. The regional novelist or short story writer — Mexican versions of the rusticated Chekhov, the Wessex-dwelling Thomas Hardy, the gentleman farmer William Faulkner — hardly exists in Mexico. Mexico is without a Cormac McCarthy scribbling in seclusion, or a sequestered Thomas Pynchon — though Pynchon himself wrote some of his novel *V* while living in Mexico, perhaps in Mazatlán, a town pointedly mentioned in *The Crying of Lot 49.*

Carlos Fuentes suggested a reason for the attraction of Mexico City, and the absence of regionalism, in his introduction to *Yankee Invasion,* Solares's novel — a realistic one — about the humiliating siege, capture, and occupation of Mexico City by the US Army in 1847 and 1848.

"Mexico has had a highly centralized cultural and political history," Fuentes wrote. "Since the reign of the Aztecs (to 1521) and the colonial (1521–1810) and independent (1810 to the present) periods, Mexico City has been the crown and magnet of Mexican life. A nation isolated within itself by a geography of volcanoes, mountain ranges, deserts and jungles, Mexico has always found a semblance of unity in the capital city . . . The majority of Mexico's writers, whatever their regional origin, end up in Mexico City: government, art, education, politics, are all centered in what was previously known as '*la region más transparente*' where the air is clear."

"An incomplete country," Fuentes said in *This I Believe* (*En Esto Creo*)—another way of saying an underdeveloped country, or in newer, politer usage, an emerging economy. "Mexico is the portrait of a creation that never rests because its work is still unfinished." He goes on, "The search for a national identity—the nation-narrative—has left us perplexed for centuries."

This is not surprising, since regionalism is so underrepresented—rejected by being prettified or consigned to the shelf of old-fashioned narratives, along with Agustín Yáñez, *On the Edge of the Storm* (*Al Filo del Agua*), set in Jalisco, or Rosario Castellanos's (as yet untranslated) *Balún Canán*, set in her native Chiapas. Both those writers lived in Mexico City, and Castellanos ended up in Israel. Apart from the Zapatistas—to their credit, in their self-governed, self-regulated state—anyone with education or ambition or a dream of ease or modernity, anyone yearning for transformation or to achieve escape velocity, ups and leaves for Mexico City.

It is perhaps a reflex of wishful thinking that impels the Mexican novelist to create the fiction of the small village as a place where amazing things happen. One example is Jorge Ibargüengoitia's *The Dead Girls*, a narrative of mysterious murders and disappearances set in a village in Guanajuato (a state that recorded sixty-two murders in the first ten days of 2018). Another is the high-octane hullaballoo and time travel (magical realism again) of Elena Garro's small-town saga, *Recollections of Things to Come* (*Los Recuerdos del Porvenir*). But these are brilliant exceptions, for in most Mexican writing there is little nostalgia for the village, only a hatred and fear of its severity and suffocating provincialism.

A village is where you're reminded you are poor, where you starve and die; it is a place to flee. ("Take me with you—take me away from here," an old woman said to me later in my trip in a village in the Isthmus. "I don't care where you come from. I want to go there.") These days a village is seen as insecure, the haunt of thieves and cartels and drug traffickers. Although relieved by the occasional fiesta, the village is the epitome of Mexican isolation, because of "a geography of volcanoes, mountain ranges, deserts and jungles." In Octavio Paz's bewitching metaphor, this geography encloses a labyrinth of solitude.

Yet it seemed to me, after spending some time there as a volunteer teacher, that Mexico City was much more of a labyrinth, a place from which—in spite of the stimulation of its street life and jollifications, its gourmet food and its hundred museums—I longed to escape, to see the villages, in order to know Mexico better. A pair of novellas, published under the title *Lost in the City,* by Ignacio Solares, are a good example of the Mexico City nightmare and give a taste of the Mexican tendency toward the surreal and the impressionistic, a book like a bad dream.

We are never quite sure why Cristina, in Solares's novella "Tree of Desire," decides to leave home. She is ten years old. Her father is violent, but his violence is unexplained. She tells herself, with the squinting vagueness of a child, "Someday one has to leave." And so she does, taking her four-year-old brother, Joaquín, with her. What follows is a plotless ordeal, as the two children confront one brute after another—and this includes a priest who drives them out of a church. They meet a humpbacked beggar, Angustias, who befriends them and takes them into her shack, where they meet her abusive partner, Jesús, and they soon realize they are captives. They are beaten, Joaquín is tied up, Cristina is forced to steal, and the children living in squalor witness Angustias and Jesús in drunken fornication a few feet away, a scene of sexual horror that Cristina, with an air of detachment, finds mildly amusing. It is only when Jesús stabs Angustias to death that Cristina is provoked to flee on a train. In a final irony, she comes face-to-face with her hideous father at the railway station, and is left to an uncertain fate.

In the accompanying novella, "Serafín," the eponymous child Serafín, who is about eleven, decides to go in search of his father, who has abruptly left the village for Mexico City—the search for a missing father another link with *Pedro Páramo.* Their village, Aguichapan, is probably in Guanajuato (a nearby town, Tierra Blanca, is mentioned); it is poor, backward, forgotten, hopeless—reasons the father gives for leaving, though he has a local girl, "Cipriano's daughter," in tow, to debauch. Like Cristina, Serafín encounters in his search the hostility of strangers, the ugliness, indifference, and violence of the city, and he becomes lost in dreams and in ambivalent memories of Aguichapan. He is at last picked up by a terrifying old man, who turns out to be Jesús, the murderer from the previous novella, who brings Serafín to his slum shack, where he describes the stabbing of his lover. Serafín escapes, meets people who have known his father, and after many conflicts tracks him down, the father bringing the story to an end by saying blandly of the reunion, "What are you doing here?"

What ought to make these stories nightmarish is that the main characters are small children—strangers and afraid, in a world they never made—resourceful but impressionable and vulnerable, indeed innocent victims. Though presented as horror stories, and though the terrors and monsters of the city are portrayed in every particular, the settings themselves, the villages (or slum, in the case of Cristina), are hastily depicted. What saves the stories from being terrifying is that they are unconvincing.

Ixtepec, the small, remote town in Elena Garro's *Recollections of Things to Come* (1963), is a stop on a railway line, but otherwise remote and existing in oblivion. Like other Mexican towns in fiction, it represents failure, neglect, isolation, and decay—the Faulkner attributes, crushed by history. Though *Pedro Páramo* was published in 1955, Garro's work is credited as the first Mexican novel to anticipate magical realism. Incidentally, Garro was married for twenty-two years to Octavio Paz, and the breakup of their marriage was so acrimonious that one of her publishers reported, "Garro herself said that everything she did was driven by hatred for Octavio Paz: she had breakfast hating Octavio Paz, she had lunch hating Octavio Paz, and she wrote hating Octavio Paz."

The paradox of the title is reflected in the book, a typical sentence of which is "He struggled with various memories, and the memories of what had happened were the only thing that was unreal to him." The first half of the book concerns the sudden appearance of a man in the small town, who is whispered about as "the stranger" and finally discovered to be Felipe Hurtado. He is a disrupter of Ixtepec because "he came for her"—the woman being the young, beautiful Julia Andrade, "the love object." Julia is the mistress of General Rosas, a commanding presence in the town, a jealous and arrogant bully and the embodiment of Mexican machismo.

The love story is suspenseful, but the novel, emphatic in its distortions of reality, plays tricks with time in the same way as the townspeople do. One of the servants, Felix, stops the clock every night in the grand house so that the family can exist outside time: "After dinner, when Felix stopped the clock, he let his unlived memory run freely. The calendar also imprisoned him in anecdotic time and deprived him of the other time that lived within him."

General Rosas suspects that he is about to be subjected to being cuckolded, the worst of Mexican masculine indignities. In a memorable scene, abasing himself, he appeals to his lover: "Julia, is there a part of your body that no one has kissed?" When she says she is pure, "her lie grazed the nape of his neck." Julia and Felipe's escape from the town ends the first part of the novel.

Set during the Cristero Rebellion of the late 1920s, the novel shifts, in part two, to a narrative set in a specific historical period, but with fantastic flourishes. The family of Joaquín and Matilde Meléndez, the occupants of the Hotel Jardín, and the patrons of Luchi's brothel are as central to the town as they are central to the novel. But the town is isolated in wilderness. The religious persecution in the second half is violent — stabbings, beatings, humiliation, and hangings, with a massacre at the end. An Indian is whipped to death, and the Indians living on its margins are hated by the landowners for their perceived primitivism. "If only we could exterminate all the Indians! They are the disgrace of Mexico!" and "Indians all look alike — that's why they're dangerous." Written with passion and a particularity in observation that gives it life, the book leaves the impression at last of the inhumanity of the dominant characters and a brutishness that arises from the town's isolation; the notion that a Mexican village or small town is always a dead end.

Laura Esquivel's *Like Water for Chocolate* is essentially a romantic novel, written with chatty familiarity, blending the occurrences of everyday life — and many recipes — with casual fantasy. The food, the gourmandizing, the specific ingredients in the novel, give it life. What other novel dares to elaborate the making of a dish like *champandongo*, a sort of layered Latin lasagna. Yet I often have the feeling Esquivel is winking at the reader as she writes, an occasional cuteness that overwhelms her related novel, *Swift as Desire*. Here, a belated revelation of the clairvoyant Júbilo turns out to be a shaggy dog story. Still, Esquivel has a heightened intensity of observation that seems to me a gift of Mexican women writers, perhaps because as women and nurturers they are forced so often to wait, studying their condition, being patient, existing in suspense. But that patience provokes in them an active inner life and intense emotion; it is a patience that men lack, demanding that you see, rather than persuading you, as Esquivel does, with detail:

"She stopped grinding, straightened up, and proudly lifted her chest so Pedro could see it better. His scrutiny changed their relationship forever. After that penetrating look that saw through clothes, nothing would ever be the same. Tita saw through her own flesh how fire transformed the elements, how a lump of corn flour is changed into a tortilla, how a soul that hasn't been warmed by the fire of love is lifeless, like a useless ball of corn flour. In a few moments' time, Pedro had transformed Tita's breasts from chaste to experienced flesh, without even touching them."

Or: "Instead of eating, she would stare at her hands for hours on end. She would regard them like a baby, marveling that they belonged to her. She could move them however she pleased, yet she didn't know what to do with them, other than knitting. She had never taken time to stop and think about these things."

I had struggled with Carlos Fuentes. He is regarded in the United States as the best-known and perhaps greatest Mexican writer; he lived and taught in the US and made many famous friends—writers and celebrities. A determined partygoer, with homes in London and Paris, as well as an atelier in Mexico City, Fuentes had an undeniable cosmopolitan panache: he was, after all, Mexico's ambassador to France for a time, and he had the savoir faire to carry out his diplomatic duties. (Not many writers become diplomats, though Washington Irving was our chargé d'affaires in London, and Nathaniel Hawthorne was made American consul in Liverpool as a reward for writing a sycophantic book about President Franklin Pierce.) Fuentes was prolific in many different genres, but seemed to me flawed. His border fictions in *The Crystal Frontier* are fanciful and unrealized, and his novel *Diana,* based on his humiliating affair with the actress Jean Seberg, is mawkish and confused, and revealed him as a ludicrous lover, spurned by a psychotic gringa who was two-timing him (so he says) with a Black Panther.

*The Death of Artemio Cruz,* said to be his masterpiece, seemed to me a dense and overwritten Mexican version of *Citizen Kane* (but without any of the film's bitter humor), a corporate monster fantasizing on his death-bed, often in the future tense, about his enemies. I attempted *Terra Nostra,* which seemed even worse and, I decided, unreadable. It seemed I was not wrong. Fuentes publicly boasted of this eight-hundred-page novel: "I never think about the reader. Not at all. *Terra Nostra* is not made for readers ... When I wrote it I was absolutely certain that nobody would read it, and in fact I wrote it with that in mind ... I gave myself the luxury of writing a book without readers."

His novella about enduring love, *Aura,* is one of his contributions to Mexican magical realism, though it is in part a pastiche of Henry James's *The Aspern Papers.* Fuentes's essays and pithier observations on Mexican life rang true to me, but I often felt that perhaps the problem was my confusion, not Fuentes's bombast and opacity, until I read an essay in the *New Republic* about the man and his work by the Mexican historian, biographer, and literary critic Enrique Krauze.

In this essay, Krauze declares his responsibility by quoting Albert Camus: "To see nuances and understand, not to dogmatize and confuse." But then he flicks open his *navaja*—the lethal Mexican fighting knife—and leaps for the jugular. He calls Fuentes a fraud, a poseur, a "Guerrilla Dandy" ("For the Guerrilla Dandy, there is no frontier between reality and fiction"), someone suffering an identity crisis, out of touch with Mexican life, and overeager to win readers in America with his falsifications. "His work simplifies the country; his view is frivolous, unrealistic, and, all too often, false." False and unpersuasive, because he spends so little time in Mexico and hobnobs with the A-listers in European and American big cities.

"In 1950 Mexico City was in the process of taking on the physiognomy of other modern capitals where Fuentes had been," Krauze writes. "He did not see the need, therefore, to go deeper into the countryside, where the reality of Mexico was more profound. His exploration of the city, although superficial, was incessant and orgiastic. Like a bedazzled and perplexed tourist, he lived the city of leisure, the nocturnal city, the show-biz city."

To me, Fuentes's obsession with grandiosity seems harmless, naïve, and somewhat lovable. In "Spoils," a story in *The Crystal Frontier*, the main character, Dionisio, a chef studying in the US, conjectures, "How many Mexicans spoke decent English? Dionisio knew of only two, Jorge Castañeda and Carlos Fuentes." Another story is dedicated to Castañeda.

I wrote a long, jeering review in the *New York Times* of his *Diana*—the Jean Seberg fiasco of unrequited ardor—when it came out in 1995, and decided it was merely childish. I began in this way: "Sexual postures can look so funny and vulnerable that the very notion of the distinguished author of this inch-from-the-truth novel, Carlos Fuentes . . . engaged in buccal coition with an American actress in a hotel in Mexico City is irresistible to the point where it is almost possible to overlook the book's excesses and delusions. That *Diana: The Goddess Who Hunts Alone* also seems a seedy form of self-parody is one of the crueler wounds the author inflicts on himself, but this is a risk you run when you embark on autobiographical fiction. Another issue is the question of tone: are you boasting or complaining? Yet another is pomposity: 'I began to be haunted by the idea that Diana was a work of art that had to be destroyed to be possessed.' (Trust a philanderer to have a fancy prose style.)" And so on for another nine hundred words, to "an entirely humorless and strangely sclerotic novel."

But Fuentes's refusal to go deeper into "the countryside, where the reality of Mexico was more profound" (as Krauze wrote) was one of the objections I had to so much of Mexican fiction. Fuentes saw himself as the Mexican Balzac, yet "he never came to know the country that would be the central theme of his work. He thought he could resolve the deafness of his origins by turning it inside out: history, society, the life of the city, would be assimilated to the raging tumult of its voices. Balzac's characters still survive in the literary and popular memory of Europe. Nobody in Mexico remembers the characters of Fuentes." Resembling one of his villains, Fuentes is "a macho, a stud, an Artemio Cruz who treats words like whores." Krauze concludes, "Carlos Fuentes . . . has created only one extraordinary character: Carlos Fuentes."

That crack seems intended as abuse, but the more you know about Fuentes, the more tempting the idea that Fuentes's life was vast and rich, his circle of friends luminous and accomplished, and his family life fractured and tragic—his youthful adored son and daughter apparent suicides, six years apart. Asked about them, Fuentes's reply was stoical: "*Ellos me acompañan cuando escribo*" (They accompany me when I write). A full biography of Fuentes has not been written, but it would be, as Krauze unconsciously suggests, an extraordinary account of a man in the throes of the last infirmity of a noble mind.

Fuentes, who seems to have loved the limelight and charming his interviewers, inspired this besotted observation from a *New York Times* reporter in 1982: "Mr. Fuentes flashes a matinee idol smile. He has dark good looks and the easy grace of one descended from a solid line of bankers, merchants, and landed gentry. The son of a diplomat, he grew up in Washington . . . He is an aristocrat in style, a revolutionary in thought."

Providing ammo to his enemies, Fuentes confided in this interview (meant to promote his play *Orchids in the Moonlight*, which was being produced in Cambridge, Massachusetts), "My work is probably becoming less and less Mexican . . . I've lived outside my country for a long time. Maybe I've paid my nationalistic dues by now."

Krauze and others seized on such pomposities. His attack was merciless, and his urban sniping was cruel—good fun for the spectator, painful for Fuentes. But since Octavio Paz was the owner of Krauze's magazine, *Vuelta*, it is perhaps understandable that Krauze was twisting the knife to please his patron, Fuentes's rival. Once a Mexican intellectual has done violence to another Mexican intellectual, nothing remains of the carnage to anatomize. They are like cartel assassins in this respect.

Fuentes was faulted for spending so little time in Mexico, for teaching in American universities, for living and writing in Paris. But this travel and foreign residence is a characteristic of many other Mexican writers. The links with Spain are age-old. A great number of the male writers besides Fuentes and Paz have been diplomats, the foreign service a form of liberation for Mexican intellectuals. Paz in Paris was a friend of Samuel Beckett, Fuentes in Paris was a friend of Malraux and Mitterrand, and in New York of William Styron. But the younger writers are the true cosmopolitans, taking advantage of the way the world has contracted, beginning as exchange students, backpackers, and tourists, chasing experience. It seemed remarkable to me how widely and well Mexican writers travel. All but one of the writers in the *taller* I conducted in Mexico City had been to the US, and most of them had been to Europe.

As I had noticed in my *taller*, what impressed me in Guadalupe Nettel's *Natural Histories* was the wide experience expressed in the stories, of love and marriage (generally disastrous) and of travel (beautifully observed). And I was struck by how cosmopolitan Guadalupe and many of the others were, since Mexico City was connected to the world—perhaps more to the big world than to the hard-up hinterland.

Mexican writers are infatuated with Mexico City, but you can't blame them: it is like a separate country where every *chilango*'s back is turned to the countryside. So it seemed that my students and my friends were dealing with the new realities, and were often looking at their big city or beyond Mexico. But this also meant that the Mexico I was seeing was underrepresented in Mexican fiction, so I put the books aside, got into my car, and drove down the road again.

## *The* Inframundo

IN SANTA MARÍA Ixcatlán, and earlier in San Dionisio Ocotepec—where I had spent time with the mourners at their feast and with the mezcalero Crispin—I'd felt I'd driven slowly down a back road into a village so small and unregarded it was like being in the underworld, the *inframundo* of

Mexican traditional belief. Of course that is fanciful: the villages were on the map, they were productive in their way, with cottage industries like weaving or sandal making, and all of them celebrated the holidays, venerated the dead, were lavish with their weddings and funerals, and engaged in masquerades.

But it is easy in Mexico to leave the main road, take a side road, turn into a narrow track, and wind up in the past, and the past often seems like an underworld. What troubles the poor villager in Mexico (and in Africa and elsewhere) is what troubled the villagers of the distant past: the difficulty of finding firewood for cooking, or grazing land for the goats, or transport to the market, or the scarcity of water, or the maddening entanglement of debt. Of course, most people know the burden of debt, but what makes the indebted Mexican villager exceptional are the tiny amounts involved in what is a matter of life and death.

I drove to the village of Santa Cruz Papalutla, not far from San Jerónimo, and in a sequence of narrowing roads found myself in another underworld. Here the activity was bamboo weaving—bamboo grew wild in canebrakes; it was harvested, dried, and split, then made into baskets. Santa Cruz was also the past, a village of horses and carts, a man pushing a mule-drawn plow into the dry ground, opening a furrow, breaking clods of earth in a field he'd soon plant with garlic, the other income-producing activity in the village. And boys in some horse-drawn carts rode them, flicking whips, standing like charioteers.

In a family compound on a back lane, watched over by three elderly women, I asked to see Magdalena, to whom I'd had a formal introduction. A young woman who introduced herself as Mónica said, "She is my mother. She will be back soon."

We talked awhile near the weaving table—strands and strips of cane, partly finished baskets, and the clutter of drying bamboo. One of Mónica's three small children kicked a ball against a rain barrel. The old women, in the shady corner of the open yard, only appeared to be sitting in judgment; in fact, they were fascinated by the gringo who had just blundered into the compound and tripped against the sleeping dog.

"My husband was in the US for seven years," Mónica said. "He was feeling insecure there, and at the same time his father was sick. So five years ago he came back."

"Does he miss the work?"

"A bit. Most people come back from the States and find the work here in the fields too arduous and poorly paid."

I thought of the man I had just seen in the field struggling along a furrow with his old-fashioned plow blade, smacking his mule with a long switch.

"They usually want to go back to the States," Mónica said.

"Have you been there?"

"To the border, Nuevo Laredo," she said. "I worked six months with a family, looking after two children. I came back because I was separated from my family. And the pay was not much. I earned 1,500 pesos [$83] a month in Nuevo Laredo. Here, for the same work, I would get 1,000 [$55]."

Mónica excused herself to go and calm her small son, who was kicking a ball and perhaps upsetting the three old women.

Soon Magdalena arrived—she'd been to the market—and, thinking I'd come to buy a basket, she showed me some in various sizes and described how she'd designed them. She had three children, the eldest thirty-six, the youngest twenty-six. Mónica was thirty-two, and Magdalena herself was fifty-two, so she'd had her first child at the age of sixteen—not so unusual in the underworld of Mexico.

The baskets were beautifully made, the sunlight dazzling the simple objects in the compound, but I sensed a melancholy in Magdalena, the slow solemn way she handled the baskets, her head tipped to the side, her sad eyes, a grimness at her mouth, the way she sighed when she got up to look for another basket, a heaviness in demeanor.

She was deeply in debt, though it took a while for me to get to that delicate subject.

"I'd like to go to Texas," she said. "I have a friend in Laredo. I'd find work there easily. I get along with everyone. They call me Aunt. I'd cook for a family. They'd pay me 3,500 pesos [$195] a month." She fell silent. "My main reason is the economy here."

"How long would you stay there?"

"No more than eight months, because I have responsibilities here." She glanced at the three old women—her mother, her aunts, perhaps. "But I want to do it with an official permit. I don't want to cross illegally."

"How do you get a permit?"

"I went to the government office here. They help migrants with temporary work permits." She went slack and heavy and sad again. "You see, I had to borrow 70,000 pesos because of my husband's illness. It was kidney stones. He had so many they had to operate."

"That's a lot of money," I said. It was almost $4,000.

"I'm broke now. I owe money. And there's the interest on the loan," she said. "While I wait for the permit, I am making baskets and weaving."

"How did you learn to weave?" I asked, wishing to lighten the conversation.

"My parents taught me how to weave cane," she said, and became sorrowful again. "No one is interested anymore. My children don't do it. Look at this basket." It was about a foot in diameter, with a handle, a small wastebasket, perhaps. "This takes two days to make, sometimes two and a half. I sell it for 220 pesos. That's 100 pesos a day"—$5.50. "So I supplement my income by cooking for people in town. But there's a lot of competition for cooks."

"How do you repay the loan?"

"Monthly. I pay 2,200 every month for the loan. Sixty is the principal and the rest is interest."

It was a bank loan, at a high rate of interest. It seemed to me impossible that Magdalena would ever clear the debt, since so much was needed for the interest.

"What happens if you don't have the money?"

"If you don't pay, they send lawyers. They take things from you."

"What sorts of things?"

"They take your refrigerator. They take appliances. They make a public spectacle. It is terrible. I would lose status. No one would trust me again."

While we talked, another old woman joined the three in the shady corner, and two other women—younger, whom I took to be Magdalena's other daughters—came from inside the house, the six of them watching

Magdalena and me. They had the anxious air of dependents, people need-ing to be looked after; and of course somewhere in the house was Magda-lena's husband, convalescing from his surgery.

In a low voice Magdalena said, "I can't tell my family I want to go."

"This is a beautiful basket," I said, picking up the small one with the handle. "How much?"

"Whatever you wish to give."

I gave her $40, which was four times what she'd said it was worth earlier. She crushed the money in her hand, enclosing it in her fist, and looked burdened.

As I left, slipping through the bamboo gateway, I saw a man in a blue helmet parking a motorcycle, lifting it onto its kickstand. He then took out a notebook and tapped one page with a pen. I said hello, and he gave me a cheery reply. Keeping his helmet on, he seemed somewhat unreadable and rather forbidding. Then I saw the logo on his shirt: *Banca Azteca.* The debt collector.

## San Baltazar Guelavila

IN THE SMALL Zapotec-speaking town of San Baltazar Guelavila, I asked Felipe, a local man, the meaning of "Guelavila."

"It means Night of Hell, sir," Felipe said.

"And this river?"

"It is the River of Red Ants, sir."

"That hill is impressive."

"It is the Hill of the Nine Points, sir," Felipe said, indicating the separate small peaks of the ridge with a dabbing finger. "Our soul goes there when we die."

"The maize in the market is colorful."

"Our maize has four colors," he said with pride. "Red, white, purple, and blue. It is from ancient times."

"That big snake painted on the side of the house," I said, "it's unusual."

We were in the center of town, near the plaza and the market. The town itself was off the main road south of Oaxaca, at the end of a potholed track three miles into the mountains. A mural painted on the flat, forty-foot-high end-side of an adobe building near us depicted the blue archway entrance of the town, a man plowing a field, a woman making tortillas, and another man digging a chopped agave plant to cook in an oven for mezcal. But the largest image in the mural was a sensuous snake, coiled around one upright of the blue archway. The snake's singular feature was a rose blossom attached to — apparently growing from — the top of its greenish head.

"The snake is a symbol of our town," Felipe said. "We believe that local people hunted this snake with the rose on its head day and night, because capturing it would bring us good luck."

"Wouldn't it be dangerous to capture a snake that size?" It was thick, with a darting tongue, and in the mural about thirty feet long.

"No danger, sir. Because no one ever caught the snake, and as a result they never had good luck."

Felipe was a cotton weaver who made scarves and caps, his looms located in a two-story building at the edge of San Baltazar. Making adobe and distilling mezcal were the town's other industries. Felipe had been to the States. He gave me the most succinct version of a border crossing.

"I crossed the border. Everyone was kind. My bosses were good to me. The thing I missed most was eating with my family. It's very lonely in the United States. So I came home."

All this time, whenever I arrived in a town like this, I was under the influence of my memories of the people I'd met — many Oaxacans — on the border. Many of the men in San Baltazar had been to the States, including a certain man who Felipe, clearing his throat with an awkward cough, warned me had a superior attitude as a result of having spent a lot of time over the border. That sometimes happened. A person went across, spent years in the States, then returned *presumido* (stuck-up).

I asked Felipe whether he could round up some returnees from the States and meet me under a tree near the weaving operation, the building with the looms. It was a lovely morning in San Baltazar, finches flitting in the boughs of the big shade tree. We sat on folding chairs, the men, young and old, sitting or standing, and the dog of one of the older men lay snoring at his feet. The sun streaming through the boughs gave them shadow-carved faces.

From his tone, I was sure the first man to speak was the stuck-up one. He was not conceited, but he was the loudest, the most reckless, and in a society where modesty was valued and boasting frowned upon, he might have seemed intimidating. But he was funny in the way of a person wishing to take charge, so humor took the sting out of his bluster.

"My name is Nilo," he said. "Like the river."

A big man in a dirty red T-shirt, he reclined on the thick upraised roots of the tree, wagging a sandal on one foot, and rather than facing me, he shouted his answers to the fifteen others gathered there.

"It's an adventure!" he shouted. "You leave your family—you don't know whether you'll live or die!"

This dramatic opening seized the attention of the others, and hearing the shout in his sleep, the dog twitched one of his ears.

"Where did you cross?" I asked.

"Tecate—I walked across," he said. "It was easy then. I was with twenty-six people, four from this town, the rest from Mexico City. I paid 450 pesos, which is nothing, really"—about $25 that morning. "Now they charge 15,000"—$830. "But you can always get someone to pay, and then you pay them back. Listen, if you work hard, you can pay it all off in a year."

Nilo's confidence and his casual way with sums of money impressed the younger men. And they must have noticed, as I did, that Nilo was the grubbiest man in the group, with squashed sandals and dusty trousers, now and then lifting his T-shirt to wipe the sweat from his face, exposing his rounded belly.

"Doing what sort of work?" I asked.

"Construction. I was in roofing."

"How do you get hired?"

"Not a problem!" he yelled, enlightening me. "The guys doing the hiring are from here! Oaxacans. My brother's in Utah—he's been there twenty-seven years. I was in the States for fifteen." He nodded with authority. "I would have stayed, but my mother was getting old."

As though to puncture Nilo's bluster and give it a sense of reality, Felipe said, "It's dangerous. All sorts of bad things can happen if you go with a stranger to the border. They might kidnap you and force you to get money from your family. You say, 'I can't pay.' So they make you take drugs across."

Nilo shrugged and made a face, as if to convey the thought, Hey, bad things happen everywhere.

"My brother," Felipe went on, "the coyote dropped him at a house near the border. The people at the house robbed my brother of everything he had. It was obvious they were in cahoots with the coyote."

"The *polleros* come here all the time," the old man with the dog said, using the variant word for coyote. "They look for people who want to cross. I went with one — it was '93. I flew to Tijuana and tried to cross in a car. I was sent back that time, but the second time I made it. I was there a year and a half, working in construction and doing other things. I never made much money, so I came home."

I said, "Given the fact that there are dangers, and it costs money to go across, is it worth it?"

"Yes," Felipe said. "If all you've got is a roof and nothing else, you go there. I was twenty-three when I went. I didn't even have a roof. And there's more work now than before. I went across, worked in construction and tree trimming, then got a job in a Chinese restaurant — doing dishes, then I was an assistant chef."

"Why did you come back?"

"I couldn't save enough money," Felipe said. "Even after eight years I was still struggling."

Nilo tugged at his grubby shirt and howled in contradiction, saying, "If you know how to save, you can save 8,000 in six months." I took this to mean pesos, about $440.

"At the Chinese restaurant I was making $150 every two weeks," Felipe said, and raising his voice, added, "I got into debt. I ate Chinese food for a year and a half. I never want to eat Chinese food ever again."

I asked him the name of the restaurant.

"Chow Mein House," he said. "In Azusa."

Azusa is just off the 210 Freeway of Pasadena, on the way to Rancho Cucamonga, though Felipe lived in a house with other migrants in Covina, and took the bus to Citrus Avenue and Chow Mein House.

"How about you?" I asked a young man who'd been listening in silence. He said his name was Isaac. "Have you been to the States?"

"No. But I'd like to see another place. To see how they live there. To know it."

Another man piped up, "I'd like to leave here and find markets for my work."

"What is your work?"

"Weaving," he said, and explained, "Making rebozos and ponchos and shawls."

"You should go. It's amazing," Nilo said, talking over the man. "It's like being a goat in a green valley! You see it and you want to eat it all! You drink and eat and spend money!"

The old man with the dog said, "The work is hard. The pay is low. And sometimes there's no work."

"You can't say there's no work!" Nilo said. "There's always this"—and he began gesturing—"you go into a department store, pick up some things, rip off the security tags, steal the things, and sell them on the street." Encouraged by the men's laughter, he went on, "Or go to a grocery store, fill your shirt with shrimp"—he lifted his shirt and bunched it with his fists, the imaginary shrimp, to make his point—"and you walk out and sell the shrimp."

I said, "By the way, that's against the law. You can go to jail."

"He's joking," one of the men said, in case I got the wrong idea about Nilo.

"Here in San Baltazar I was a rebellious young man," Nilo said. "My father was gone. I broke windows. My mother was useless. Mothers can be weak! I was always drunk and getting into trouble. I needed my father."

"Where was your father?"

"In California! He went when I was nine," Nilo said. "It was the most beautiful time of my life."

"I had no free time," Felipe said, protesting. "I worked. I was tired. I slept. Then I worked again."

I asked, "Did you see anything in California that you wanted to bring back here?"

"A community well," he said. "We need more water here."

Two women and two young girls walked from behind a one-story adobe building, the women carrying pitchers on their shoulders, the girls carrying clay bowls, a sudden biblical glimpse—attending women in long skirts, bearing drinks.

"*Tejate,*" Isaac said. "It tastes good."

The liquid poured into the bowls was gray, with a grainy texture and a scum of bubbles on the surface, and it tasted sweetish, a thick soup of—so they explained—maize, *flor de cacao,* peanuts, coconut, and roasted mamey seeds, or *pixtle* in Zapotec. Because of the extensive grinding, kneading, roasting, and toasting of ingredients, this pre-Hispanic concoction is called one of the most labor-intensive drinks on earth.

"Important people used to drink this," Felipe said, and by important people, he was harking back six hundred years, because (in the long memory of Mexico) he meant Zapotec royalty, for whom *tejate* was reserved.

"Drink, Don Pablo! You are welcome here!"

Except for Nilo, the rest of the men were weavers, spending all day at a loom. Nilo explained that he had diabetes and was no longer strong. "Because of my diabetes they wanted to cut my leg off!" But he had refused, and stubbornly, defiantly still walked, though he had no work.

Felipe guided me into the nearby building and upstairs to the weaving room, where there were seven head-high wooden looms, some of the weavers sitting, thrusting the shuttles at right angles through the tight threads, pulling the beams down, working the treadles, and in all that effort—the rattle of skeletal frames and the stamping of treadles—lengthening the cloth by one thread.

(Recalling that, it seems a fit image for what I am doing now, fussing with my fingers and hesitating, then tightening the line and starting again, minutes passing, this memory of weaving enlarged by one sentence.)

Some of the men who had been seated under the tree, talking to me, took their places on benches at looms and resumed weaving. With the clacking and chattering of the wooden machinery in this upstairs workshop, it was hard to hold a conversation, yet I noticed that the men were speaking in a language that was not Spanish.

I beckoned Isaac to a balcony and said, "Are you speaking Zapotec?"

"Yes," he said. "We speak Zapotec among ourselves."

A man listening said, "It's like having a secret language! You can talk about someone who doesn't speak it and say anything you want while in their presence."

The town of San Baltazar was completely bilingual, the school taught in both Spanish and Zapotec. But Isaac's son Alejandro, who was fourteen and said he was a student, was not in school that day, though school was in session. Alejandro was sitting at a loom, weaving lengths of black cloth.

"How's business?" I asked Isaac.

"Demand is unstable," he said.

"Yet we keep working," Felipe said. "We work twelve hours a day. It's hard. It's like working in the States."


## The Story of the Brujo

SAN BALTAZAR GUELAVILA was not especially known for its weaving, its adobe, or its mezcal, but it was celebrated for Las Salinas, its hot spring, which bubbled in a deep ravine to the southwest, the valley of the Cerro Oscura—the Hidden Hill. I ought to see it, the weavers said.

"Is it far?"

"A little far."

That implied very far, and it proved to be the case—it was miles below the town, on a rocky track, circling both sides of a ravine, and would take an hour and a half to get to the valley bottom. This was in the heat of the day, and it meant they'd have to take off work to get there. But none of the men had a car, and there was no regular transport into the valley, so they seized on the opportunity of my having a vehicle and said that I must not miss this wonder of nature. The truth was they wanted a ride, an outing, a lark, to see it again themselves and paddle their bare feet and wiggle their toes in the mineral water.

On the way there, the car sliding and tipping on the loose rocks of the road, they told me a story of a witch, each of the men chipping in with a detail or a bit of dialogue.

"There was a *brujo* here," someone said—a sorcerer. "He was so powerful he could eat a whole cow in one sitting." This was amazing, but it also meant that people's cows were disappearing. "So they decided to kill the *brujo.*"

"His name was Tomás Olivera. He lived in this area, near San Baltazar."

"They looked all over for him—in the hills, in the valleys, even in the town. But no one could find him to kill him, and of course to save their cows that were still disappearing, the *brujo* devouring them."

"At last someone saw him high in a cactus, holding on. They surrounded him, with rifles."

"Tomás Olivera said, 'Please don't shoot me in my body. I have enough holes in my flesh. Shoot me in a hole I already have.'"

"Because he was high up in the cactus, they decided to shoot him in his *culo*—a chosen hole."

"So they raised their rifles and pulled the triggers, but the guns would not go off. The guns were bewitched! And the next thing they heard was the voice of Tomás Olivera."

"He said, 'I am over here!'"

"They ran to that spot, but he wasn't there. He was throwing his voice. They were unable to find him, although they kept hearing him: 'I am here' and 'I am over here.'"

"At last, as they were still trying to find him, he disappeared into a bottle and was gone forever."

. . .

Magical realism in the remote village? No, just something fanciful, a cock-and-bull story, like the local legend of the elusive snake with the rose on its head—a tall tale to help pass the time on the slow descent into the deep valley.

The hot spring was a pool in a declivity of rock, yellowed with a large, smooth, crystalline scab of hardened minerals from the water. The excitement of the men was like the sudden urgency of children on an outing, dancing along the log bridge that spanned the narrow river, also called Las Salinas, jumping from flat stone to flat stone on the little ledge, and taking their sandals off and wading in the river through the opening between the limestone walls to see the cataract splashing down the cliff face.

At the end of the day, back at the big house near the weaving compound, one of the men said, "Now, we eat." And he explained that this was the house of the patriarch, Alejandro Martínez.

I was led through a bamboo fence, a nearby horse tethered to a tree, and onto a veranda where a long table had been set with plates and glasses.

Ten of us at the table, all men, Don Alejandro sitting at the far end, and through the door to the house I could see another long table, eight or ten women seated with children, and older women preparing the platters of food. Young women brought the platters out to us, slices of sinewy meat, beans, tortillas, avocados, tomatoes, salsa, shredded cabbage, and glasses of goat milk—a pale, viscous liquid they called *agua de avena.*

While we ate, and talked about the hot spring, and the thrill of crossing the border, and the snake with the rose on its head, Don Alejandro went inside to sit with the women and children, and I counted twenty-four adults altogether eating, some of them family, some weavers, and the one gringo. It was an event, it was a party, and it was also an affirmation of family and community; and I understood Felipe—who was at the table—who had said to me how everyone in the States had been kind to him, but "the thing I missed most was eating with my family."

## PART FOUR

# The Road to
# Nueva Maravilla

## To the Isthmus: Juchitán

THE APPARENT STRAIGHTNESS and regularity of the road south from San Baltazar Guelavila to the Isthmus of Tehuantepec is misleading, because in less than an hour it narrows and lifts, veering at a sharp angle — a ribbon of ledge cut into the rock face of the sierra. I had vertigo and a fearsome illusion of slippage on many of the curves where, at the edge, the sheer drop was half a mile into a canyon, and what seemed like villages or people or goats at the bottom were nothing more than a twinkling mirage.

And the distance to Juchitán — about 175 miles, which isn't much — is misleading, too, because they are vertical miles, rising and falling. And because of the rumors of bandits — highwaymen, carjackers, con men — and the fact of roadblocks, this is not a busy road: some scary trucks, the odd bus, not many passenger vehicles. It is hard to document banditry in Mexico, because the police often turn a blind eye — or the police may also be bandits. John Gibler's reporting on the killings of the forty-three students in Guerrero state (which is next door) established that many police departments were corrupt, and some members of the force were cartel operatives or narcotraffickers. When the police are crooked, the innocent are victims. As the Federale said smilingly to me, "You know what we can do to you?"

The roadblocks on this highway had a history. They were occasionally teachers' roadblocks, but more often they were Triqui roadblocks.

The Triqui people are an indigenous group of about twenty thousand fluent speakers who live in and around San Juan Copala, a small town in the municipality of Santiago Juxtlahuaca, in the mountains to the west of Oaxaca state. San Juan is about eighty miles from Oaxaca city as the crow flies and many more miles by the winding roads. The tenacious Triqui decided that they had had enough of being cheated, sidelined, and ignored by the federal government and the Oaxacan state government. In 2006, inspired by the 1994 uprising of the Zapatistas in Chiapas, the Triqui distanced themselves from the Mexican state and declared the Autonomous Municipality of San Juan Copala.

Popular resistance in Mexico is nearly always met with deadly force: demonstrations often end in brutality, now and then with the murder of demonstrators, and occasionally in massacres. Not long after the Triqui declaration of autonomy, the federal government formed a paramilitary group to suppress the dissenters, and it gave the fierce group a picturesque name, the Union for the Social Well-Being of the Triqui Region, its acronym the almost jocular UBISORT.

"Social well-being" became a Mexican euphemism for oppression or targeted assassination. Twenty protesters were killed by police or paramilitaries in 2006, a year during which the state was frequently challenged by demonstrations. In 2008 two Triqui women were murdered by UBISORT. And a year later the Mexican government tried to starve out the Triqui by blockading San Juan Copala, shutting off water and electricity and preventing the delivery of food. This led to demonstrations in Oaxaca's Zócalo, which, in the course of the police action to shut the protesters down, became a pitched battle, with many wounded.

When in 2010 an aid caravan attempted to help the besieged town of San Juan Copala, it was ambushed by UBISORT, the irresistible Union for the Social Well-Being of the Triqui Region. Two people in the caravan were murdered, twelve went missing, and scores were wounded. The murder victims (shot in the head) were a Mexican woman who directed a human rights group and an observer from Finland; a journalist was pursued and shot in the foot, and two Triqui women were kidnapped. The Triqui people were prevented from entering or leaving the town. This resulted in more protests, more attacks, more roadblocks, and the rise of another resistance group, called MULT (the Unification Movement for the Triqui Struggle). Eight years later, the Triqui trying to return to their land were foiled by the government—foiled in a Mexican way, the government agreeing formally to resettlement but preventing it from happening. This "Yes, then again, no" maddened the Triqui and inflamed their defiance.

San Juan Copala lies in a remote mountain fastness. So in order to gain headlines, protests have to be held in the most prominent places — the city center of Oaxaca or on a major road. In June 2017 a large, well-organized series of protests occurred all over Oaxaca state, as sixteen blockades shut down the main highways. Route 190 is a central artery where any disorder is bound to be a headline. The most recent ones had been about eight months before I arrived here, but since the issue of Triqui autonomy had been left unresolved, there was always the possibility of more roadblocks and more mayhem.

I was driving down a road that had been a site of barricades and paramilitary opposition, a thoroughfare of delay and confrontation. I was also driving to meet the Zapatistas. Juan Villoro had asked me, on behalf of Comandante Marcos, supreme leader of the Zapatistas, whether I would be interested in attending a Zapatista event, announced as a "Conversatorio" of the EZLN, the Zapatista Army of National Liberation.

I had the pamphlets and discussion papers in my bag, with a personal invitation from the Comandante himself. This would be catnip for the paramilitaries if I were stopped and searched.

The road south glittered in the sun, and there was little traffic, the motorists scared away by rumors of Triqui defiance. There were only big trucks for me to contend with — empty roads on the switchbacks and zigzags through the barren ranges in the shadow of Cerro El Labrador.

But as with all travel in Mexico, which I thought of as life on the plain of snakes, you can take nothing for granted. The amiable policeman might be a thief, and around the bend of the serene-looking road there might be a roadblock manned by carjackers or furious protesters. Not long after I arrived in Chiapas, a group of round-the-world cyclists was deliberately rammed by a car; two of the cyclists were killed and all of them robbed. To the natural anxieties of road travel (breakdowns, flat tires, dead ends) I added a heightened awareness of looming shadows. Mexicans speak of this all the time, especially to the gringo on the road. No one is more cautious or more prompt with warnings than the Mexican away from the security of his pueblo.

Weaving through the canyons, I came to the small town of San Pedro Totolapan and stopped for a cup of coffee in a roadside café. It was empty except for four whispering men at a table, who fell silent as I passed and—unusual in Oaxaca—with no exchange of greetings. I made a point of not lingering, and drinking my coffee outside, felt the melancholy of the isolated town, its sunlit desolation, an improvised place for travelers on the road, stopping for gas or a *garnache*—street snack—such as a taco or a tamale or, here in Oaxaca, a *tlayuda*.

The river below, deep in the canyon I saw on my map, was the Rio Grande—very wide but mostly dry, not much more than a trickle of water in the middle. I came to more opportunistic villages, offering food and tire repair, Las Margaritas and El Camarón, and at the latter place the road began to descend and straighten, so that I could see an expanse of flat plain ahead, dust brown and dotted with cactus and trees withered in the heat of the Isthmus.

That plain gave onto tropical lushness, the sea-level foliage of palms and cane fields and mango orchards. Seeing signs to the main town of the region, Tehuantepec, I thought: I made it—as though I'd squeezed through the gauntlet of the mountain passes and was here among other cars, on my way to Juchitán.

Juchitán was a detour, one of those places that look convenient on the map, but on arrival a place of pure horror.


## *Terremoto*

I ENTERED MY room in the Hotel Xcaanda (the word means "dream" in Zapotec), the only hotel left standing in the city of Juchitán de Zaragoza, and I put down my bag. In that moment of releasing it, the room shook as though thumped by a giant fist, and jogged my body. A sickly threat of upchuck stirred in my throat, and a wiggle under my foot soles loosened my legs, the floor of the room briefly fluid, as if I was up to my ankles in liquid, sinking and flowing sideways. A moment later the floor was solid again, firm under my tremulous body.

"An aftershock," Francisco Ramos told me later.

Francisco was a photographer, a friend of Toledo's daughter Sara, who put us in touch. He meant of the earthquake—or rather, quakes: this was six months after two deadly quakes shook the city.

I asked, "Do you get many aftershocks?"

"Thousands. We get them every day. It will happen again today, more shakes. You'll see."

I had seen the results of the Puebla quake that damaged the buildings in Mexico City in the month before I began teaching there, the cracked facades and exposed rooms where walls had fallen, the piles of rubble in the streets—the damage had been particularly severe in the neighborhood of my classroom. The same earthquake that had disrupted parts of Mexico City had destroyed much of Juchitán, toppling most of its buildings. Less than two weeks later another one rocked the city, and houses that had been cracked but had withstood the first one tumbled to the ground when the second hit. And so the city was wrecked.

They were the worst earthquakes in Mexico in a hundred years, the first one on September 7, 2017, registering 8.2 ("Great" on the Richter scale, causing "Major Damage"), and for a full minute the movement was so violent that people said they were unable to stand, and fell, or were banged into walls, terrified by the earth rolling under them. And there was the noise—screams mingled with the dry rumble of thudding blocks of concrete. Most of the thirty-one arches gave way in the Palacio Municipal in Juchitán's central plaza. The bell tower of the city's main church, the Parroquia de San Vicente Ferrer, crashed to the ground, and a whole thick wall of the church collapsed, flattening a car. Houses cracked and fell, suddenly dropping in their heaviness, becoming a heap of irregular masonry under a dust cloud.

A minute later, thousands were made homeless and many died. And as the residents began to dig out their belongings and bury their dead, the second earthquake, on September 19, shook them again, with a force of 6.1

("Strong" on the Richter scale, characterized by "Violent Shaking"), flinging more houses to the ground, killing again, until the death toll reached over 100 — it climbed to 380 dead in the country at large. A third of the homes in Juchitán were uninhabitable — thousands of structures in a city of 100,000 people. And there were aftershocks, often two or three a day, some of them severe enough to knock pots off shelves or dislodge tiles from a roof.

Months later, the commonest sounds in the streets of the city were the scrape of shoveling and the rhythmic crack of pickaxes against fallen cement. People were scooping their ruined houses into the street — in front of every plot where there had once been a house, there was a heap of shattered brick and stone.

"No international money is coming in now," Francisco Ramos said. "But people are slowly rebuilding."

The early stages of rebuilding involved digging out debris, clearing the broken brickwork, and creating a pile of rubble to be hauled away; only then could a house be raised. It was all pick and shovel work. And because the roads were filled with these rubble piles, they were impassable. Local transport in Juchitán was mostly three-wheelers — moto-taxis, scooters refitted for passengers; but even these small, nimble vehicles couldn't squeeze through the bottlenecks. After a hundred yards the driver would say, "I'll drop you here. You'll have to walk the rest of the way."

In many respects, because of the extent of the destruction, Juchitán looked as though the earthquake had just hit. No houses had been rebuilt — at best, they'd been braced with timbers against the possibility of another tremor, and many people were living under canvas or plastic shelters, open-sided, their sleeping mats and stoves visible, children picking their way through the broken rock. The whole city was in a state of disrepair, a sensational disorder so irrational and shocking it had the dangerous look of great ugliness — a face of violence.

The damage was not only to the structures in the city — old solid buildings smashed to bits, thick walls lying in chunks, historic structures propped up by logs. The social fabric had also been torn to shreds. Something seismic had affected the mood of the people, in the way the aftermath of a natural disaster creates mayhem, offers opportunities to the lawless, or feeds a sense of anarchy.

"I need to warn you about a few things," Francisco said. "This city is not safe."

"Tell me."

"Don't walk in town alone."

"Why—is it bad?"

"People are robbed all the time."

"Often?"

"Every day," he said. *Cada día.* And repeated it. "Every day."

What added to the sense of insecurity, the vulnerability of the Juchitecos, was the outdoor life that people had begun to live since the earthquake: spending the day in the open air, under trees, on folding chairs in the street; sleeping under canvas awnings; cooking over wood fires; washing in buckets or plastic basins. People were exposed, easy targets in all their pathetic helplessness.

Yet in the daylight hours, the men, and many women, toiled at their ruins, disposing of the fragments of their houses, heaping them in the street. The whole town was unfinished, dusty, noisy, cluttered with temporary fences and improvised shelters.

"And these moto-taxis," Francisco said of the scooters. "Don't take them at night. Take a car." Seeing that I was looking for an explanation, he said, "If someone sees you in a moto-taxi, they'll reach in and grab you and take your things."

It was late afternoon. We walked around the side streets, busy with diggers, shovelers, and laborers slamming pickaxes against chunks of debris, and men steering wheelbarrows piled with broken bricks. Women and children washed clothes in buckets, the younger girls holding the family infants. The worst of the quake had struck the center of town, or at least that was how it looked—it was the area with the oldest buildings, the biggest ones, now broken apart. The covered market had been moved to an open space. The church was heavily cracked, and the remaining steeple had shifted sideways and was held up with thick scaffolding. Because the church was too dangerous to enter, services were held nearby in an open-sided makeshift ramada, canvas stretched over poles.

On the corner of a crossroads in the Cheguigo neighborhood, an old man stood before a new whitewashed two-room house. He was Cándido Carrasco, and said he was an artist. He showed me his paintings — Zapotec legends of birds and deer, romantic scenes of women in diaphanous gowns on the battlements of castles. But he was a local hero as a painter of banners, which are worn by captains in the Juchitán fiesta called the Watering of the Fruits. Known locally as Don Cándido, he had won prizes for his artwork and was celebrated for his banners.

"What happened, Don Cándido?"

"My house fell on me," he said. "I was trapped for five hours. My neighbors rescued me. But now, see, my new house."

The market sprawled — not a specific location in the center, but penetrating the side streets, tumbling through the town. A balding man in a yellow dress — men wearing women's clothes, it seemed, were common in Juchitán — twitched his skirt and offered me mangoes piled high at a stall. Elsewhere an egg seller called my attention to tin washbasins filled with pinkish eggs, golf-ball-sized, some of them smooth, others sun-dried and shrunken, hundreds of them to a basin.

"Turtle eggs," Francisco said, and explained that they were gathered from turtle nests on the coast, a mile away.

"Isn't collecting turtle eggs illegal?"

"Nothing is illegal here," Francisco said with a crooked smile.

Olive ridley turtles laid these eggs every year in the dunes just above the tidemark on the coasts of Oaxaca and Chiapas; hawksbill turtles did the same. One glance at the basins of turtle eggs in the Juchitán market was a vivid explanation of the reason these two species were on the verge of extinction.

The market sold iguanas, too. They were also endangered, and so popular, the six or seven women who had iguana stalls sold all the carcasses first thing in the morning. They were a Zapotec delicacy, specific to Juchitán; the market women caught them in the fields and rivers, sometimes using hunting dogs. They caught and sold another endangered creature, the bird they called the *alcaraván*—the Eurasian stone curlew—excellent when roasted and served with salsa (so people said).

"They sell armadillos, too," Francisco said. "But they're strange. If you don't kill them right away, no sooner have you put them on the ground than they're like El Chapo. They dig a tunnel and they're gone."

Tureens held spiced and cooked goat heads, staring with sightless eyes, defying you to eat them. And fried cow's blood, the blood poured into a *comal* and sizzled, then served up as a side dish called simply *sangre*, blood. Stalls with sports clothes, stalls with ducks and chickens, stalls displaying the arts of the Isthmus, including the elaborate embroidery called *caveira*, flowers picked out on blouses and skirts, touches of pictorial color amid the gray devastation. And some of the market women were dressed in the Zapotec style, with lacy petticoats and huipils—tunics brilliantly set off by embroidered flowers or birds.

Tucked beneath one of the reinforced arches of the Palacio Municipal, a man was selling ice cream. Farther along a man was plunking a guitar, watched by a small group of people, and in another archway at the end of the palace—city hall, actually—a bedsheet had been hung up and a movie was being shown.

It was a flickering black-and-white film—a comedy, it seemed, judging by the laughter of the people squatting on the cobblestones of the plaza or sitting on folding chairs. I took a seat.

"An old movie," Francisco said. "That man was very popular."

The man was singing, flirting with a doe-eyed beauty in a frilly blouse.

"Pedro Infante," Francisco said.

"You've seen this movie before?"

"Everyone in Mexico knows this movie. It is *Nosotros, los Pobres*."

*We, the Poor* dated from 1948, which made it seventy years old, but Pedro Infante, who died in 1957, had enduring fame in Mexico—one of his nicknames was El Inmortal. Given the travails of its hero, Pepe el Toro, a carpenter with a ramshackle shop in a Mexican slum—his spell in jail, having been wrongly arrested, his devotion to his dying mother and his small daughter—this was a perfect movie for Juchitán. In this scene of devastation, a city so broken by the earthquake that everyone lived in the streets, and ate and slept under trees, for entertainment the Juchitecos sat in folding chairs in the ruins and watched a splotchy black-and-white movie about people who were worse off than they were, and laughed through their tears.

Some of the women watching the movie wore heavy makeup and tight skirts — legs crossed, kicking their high heels — their upswept hairdos gleaming with oil, their big fingers laced together on their thick thighs. Those old-fashioned Mexican beauties, like the mango seller in the yellow dress in the market, were not women. They were *muxes* — "mooshes" — for which Juchitán is famed, men who dressed as women but were physically male. As Francisco remarked to me of the *muxes* watching the movie, they had probably just ended a shift at a beauty parlor, where *muxes* were often manicurists, or had closed their stall at the market, because many of the market women were *muxes*, or they were prostitutes — because many *muxes* ply their trade on back streets; when night falls, they linger in the shadows of the shattered arcades.

The *muxes* regard themselves as a third sex and say they are unique to the Isthmus. Unlike Spanish, the Zapotec language is accommodating — in Zapotec, as in English, there are no grammatical genders. You wouldn't know from the Zapotec word *ijueze* (friend) whether the friend was male or female. The presence of the *muxes* among the homeless and bombed-out Juchitecos, the cruising street thieves, the guitar player, the children hawking candy, and the exhausted construction workers — all this enhanced the doomsday atmosphere, the sense that the End Time was upon us and everyone was living in the street, in a world turned upside down, watching movies amid the ruins.

A distraction in the main plaza was the noise of birds, thousands of black birds that looked to me like grackles, flights of them alighting on tree boughs and making a shrill racket. They were great-tailed grackles, as I was to find out, filling the plaza with their shrieks and adding to the mood of chaos.

"Do people have a fear of being inside?" I asked.

The streets were thronged with people standing and sitting, mixing cement, patching walls, and selling nuts and fruit. Yet the windows and doorways that were still intact had no lights in them. And with the tangles of wires hanging loose in the street for the temporary lights, and the lanes blocked by rubble, it looked like a war zone, but a heavily populated one.

"Yes, they are afraid in their houses."

Earlier in the day, Francisco and I had eaten fish and shrimp in a restaurant of long trestle tables enclosed in a high-ceilinged, steamy tent—the fish from the seaside town of Salina Cruz on the Gulf of Tehuantepec. And I wondered, as you wonder over fish in Mexico: Am I being poisoned?

Dinner was served next to an open-air improvised kitchen-diner, in a backyard where lightbulbs were strung overhead—a vacant lot between two broken buildings. The kitchen, in a corner, threw up greasy smoke, the diners sat in plastic chairs, a ladder was propped against one of the cracked walls, and a motorcycle was parked near the stack of tortillas. What looked at first like festive bunting was laundry drying on a line, sheets and pajamas and the pink pennants of ladies' bloomers.

Families dined sedately, talking in low voices, a table of a dozen people smilingly celebrating a birthday (presents formally presented and ritually unwrapped, the guest of honor an older woman in a blue dress), all of them eating and drinking. And this being a Mexican restaurant of a sort, children chased each other, teasing in singsong, and small babies bawled in their mothers' arms.

I thought, as I had in San Dionisio, how this jumbled and malodorous backyard of people and junk and laundry, when studied objectively for a long moment, represented a kind of order, everything in place for a purpose, and—chewing the torpedo of my *tlacoyo de frijol* and nibbling at spicy shrimp—more than mere order: it was an example of pure harmony.

I went back to the Hotel Xcaanda and was sick as a dog.

## The Squitters

IT IS A truism that Mexican travel usually involves a spell of gut sickness, known in Mexican slang as *chorro*, a splash. Because the ailment is almost inevitable, shared by most travelers, it is unremarkable—hardly worth a mention, and a bore when it is introduced in a conversation or as a paragraph in a book. Many travelers can top my squitters story, two days and two nights of paralytic misery in Juchitán, made all the more miserable by the humid heat, 97 degrees in the shade most days, and the unbreathable night air thickened with the shrill, triphammer racket of grackles, the sour tang of smoke from the smoldering ruins of buildings, the cooking fires, the dust thrown up by skidding scooters, and the stink of pulverized adobe of the wrecked town. I thought I might be critically dehydrated and need an IV drip, not just my home remedies of salted water and sports drinks and no food. I had bowel-shattering cramps and light-headedness, with the obsessive mental cataloging: was it the slippery shrimp, or the sinister stew, or the bulging tacos, or maybe the *tlacoyo* eaten in the stinking backyard? Possibly the sip of tainted water when I brushed my teeth. It doesn't matter. You wait for the dizziness to pass, the paralysis to ease, the cramps to abate, the appetite to return, drinking Epix and Jumex sports drinks to rehydrate, praying it's not dysentery, and dreading another aftershock of the quake and the threat of upchuck. And one day you wake, as I did, and you're restored and ready to hit the road again.

The only justification for my mentioning it now is to say that while I was laid up with the squitters in Juchitán, I remembered Francisco Toledo's request in Oaxaca—"Maybe you can write a story for me. I'll make a picture. I'll publish it"—and to kill time, I wrote the story.

## *The Palenque*

THE TWO TRUDGING men had arrived just before dawn, so I was told. Traveling among the cold, huddled villages of the Mixteca Alta in rural Oaxaca, I took the story to be true. But I also felt it was intended as a cautionary tale, a warning to me, since I was—like the strangers in it—also a stranger, with many questions.

The drifting morning mist under the low sky was whipped with blown grit (the story continued). The men moved through the valley past the wind-scoured hillside and the bouldery slopes, where the *quijote* claws of agave clumps were upright and stark in the thin topsoil: the small uncultivated agave, the wild kind known as *criollo*.

The first of the morning sun, a blur, then a stripe of light puddling pinky purple in the mist, lit the two men from behind, putting their faces in shadow. So the goatherd, who saw them plodding along the road and scattering his animals, found their darkened faces unreadable. Their clothes were unfamiliar—identical—like uniforms, a suggestion of officialdom.

Seeing the goatherd stumbling across the loose stones of the field, following his animals, one of the men called out, "Wait—don't go. We want to talk to you."

The voice was friendly, yet when the goatherd turned and the men were facing the sunrise, their apparent friendliness did not persuade him, because now their faces were illuminated by the weak rays of the dawn, the muted violet giving them the yellow eyes and sallow skin and bluish lips of corpses—especially ghoulish on that hillside of dark agave claws, the boulders like tombstones.

"We're strangers here."

That was so obvious to the goatherd it seemed like a feeble way of tricking him. Anyway, as strangers there was nothing they could offer him in the way of reassurance; strangers came here only to carry something away, never to improve the village. And it was known that strangers were confident intruders who lingered just long enough to seize what they were looking for—baskets, woven hats, mezcal from the *palenque*—then move on.

But the road was bad, sixty stony miles, because in places it also served as a seasonal arroyo, snaking up the valleys and along the hills, a thoroughfare of rubble that prevented any cars from traveling on it. Only drivers in the biggest trucks dared it, the flatbeds that brought barrels of oil and carried away drums of mezcal.

Now the two men were close, their faces still eerily lit. They were dressed warmly, in thick woolen jackets and black trousers, but what the goatherd noticed was that their heavy boots were shiny—disconcertingly so, for how was it that the men could appear at the end of a long stony road and not have dusty boots? It was as though they had dropped from the sky.

Aware of the suddenness of the strangers and their fine clothes, the goatherd kept his distance. But like all goatherds he carried a wooden staff that he used to guide his animals, tapping their flanks or pounding the stones with it, to direct them to where some grass still grew on the eroded slopes. And the staff served as a weapon, a cudgel he'd used on a maddened dog once, clubbing him senseless as the dog gnawed at his sandal, leaving slobber on his toes.

"We just want to ask a few questions."

That and something else alarmed the goatherd: they were each wearing a little badge on the lapel of their woolen coats. The idea that they were officials, that they had status of some kind, was as worrying as their being strangers.

"We won't hurt you."

Anyone who said that had a violent intention—otherwise, why would they deny it?

Raising his staff chest-high to defend himself, the goatherd backed away.

One of the men unfolded a large sheet of paper. Its whiteness, its paradoxical purity in this field of dark stones and blown dust and agave claws, seemed like something malign.

Flourishing a blue pen, the first man said, "What's your name, and where is your house?"

This was too much for the goatherd. He turned aside, and with long strides he made his way across the slope, not showing fear but moving with determination through the agave plants. The goats followed, as though sensing he was leading them to a place of better grazing.

The two strangers watched him go, pondering his departure with bewildered frustration. And when he'd dropped from view in the steepness of the hill, the men turned and picked their way back to the road, heading for the village in the valley below. They could see the whole of it, the one long street interrupted in the middle by a square of plaza, and a white church with two spires at the end, at the edge of town.

The narrow rough road became a wider paved street at a brick and stucco archway, the formal entrance to the village, a saint's name and the

Mixtec name of the place after it inscribed in green-flecked gold on the crossbar of the arch. Unlike other village archways, the place name was not followed by the word "Welcome."

From the archway onward the road was straight and smooth, dividing the village in half, all the houses fronting the street, outbuildings—kitchens—just behind them, woodsmoke rising from them at this hour, paddocks and wash houses and latrines, and small backyard corrals where burros were tethered, tugging on their ropes.

The entire village of single-story houses lay on this one street, from the archway to the plaza and onward, to the far end, the church. No people were visible, though the woodsmoke indicated that cooking was under way. A dog trotted sideways, its head down, the only movement on the street, pausing to worry a thing half hidden in shadow—a rag, a cat—then ducking into an alleyway.

One of the strangers began writing on the bright page on his clipboard as the other knocked at the door of the first house. No one answered, but when he knocked again the wooden door opened just wide enough to reveal a face.

The face was squarish and heavy, with a wide forehead, beaky nose, broad mouth, and jutting chin, similar to the ones on the bas-reliefs of the ancient ruins near here, a face from a temple wall, but flesh, dark cheeks and coarse black hair—a woman in the crack of the door with a long braid lying against her back.

She peered with narrowed eyes, saying nothing.

"Good day," the first stranger said. "May we ask you some questions?"

At this, the woman's gaze became intense and rueful, a fastening onto the questioner's face, as though regretting she had noted his features.

"We are from the health department," the other stranger explained. "We're carrying out a medical survey."

As he spoke, he wrote on his pad, seeming to note the number of the house stenciled on the door. The first stranger said, "May I ask your name?"

The woman said, "Atalia," and pushed the door, and when it was shut came the bump of wood clapping behind it, a sound like an exclamation mark, barring the door.

At the next house, a slit in the middle of the door flicked open, a dark eye against it.

The first stranger repeated his question, the eye blinked, and the muffled reply sounded like "Juana."

"How many people live here?"

"Many" was the muffled reply. "All of them are men—my husband, my strong boys. Dogs, too."

But after this assertion there was silence, not the macho growl from the interior the strangers expected. And before any of the strangers could speak, the tiny opening in the door squeezed shut, like the closing of an eye.

Crossing the road to the houses on the other side, the strangers noticed a man standing a distance away, at the level of the plaza. They seemed to recognize him as the goatherd, who had somehow entered the village and overtaken them. He held his staff across his body as if for protection, his head tilted up in an attitude of triumph.

The first stranger smiled at the boasting goatherd and, now on the other side of the road, knocked again.

This time the door was opened—slowly, but wide enough for the man standing in the doorway to be wholly revealed. He was middle-aged and mustached, the same smooth ancient face, the hue of an old plank of wood, the broad mouth and heavy jaw giving him a look of stubbornness.

Yet he answered the questions, offered his name and that of his wife, the ages of his children—three of them—and gave his profession as mezcalero.

All this time he was glancing across the road at the houses the strangers had just left.

"Your children," the first stranger asked, "are they at home?"

The man shook his head and his features softened. His stubborn expression was smoothed, as he slowly smiled and threw the door open.

"Come inside! Have a cup!"

The strangers hesitated, but encouraged by the man's shouts, they stepped past him into the small room, dimly lit and smelling of dampness and woodsmoke. Meanwhile, the man had uncorked a slender bottle and was pouring the clear liquid into two china cups.

"Teacups," one of the strangers said.

"Better than tea, my friends."

And when they had downed the liquid, and gasped with pleasure, he poured two more, and was wagging the bottle at them, against their protests, as they slipped out the front door, thanking him.

The small boy at the next house—an agave gatherer, he said, though he could hardly have been more than eight or ten—answered for his parents. They were at the *palenque,* he said.

"Doing what?"

He said they were preparing the *piñas,* chopping the *quijotes* from the agave he had harvested. He said their names, but was unable to spell them.

Then he bowed his head and whispered, seeming to pray, "You must go now."

Smiling at him, their lips still damp, their eyes glassy from the mezcal, they started across the road again and winked at each other, the self-mockery of drudges going about their rounds—yet they were brisk, approaching another front door.

At that moment, a loud, familiar metallic note was sounded that penetrated their bodies and rang in their ears, the spirited shriek of a trumpet and the rattle of a snare drum, followed by the blatting of a trombone. They turned to see four men following them—the fourth was strumming a guitar, drowned out by the louder instruments. They were dressed in ragged coats, and two wore hats woven of palm strips, and their boot heels were worn flat. But the music was glorious, the drumming and trumpeting brightening the air and filling the road with life.

The strangers had to raise their voices to compete with the loud music, and they could not help but smile when, one after another, the villagers came to where they stood holding a bottle of mezcal and two glasses, urging the men to have a drink. Although the demeanor of the campesinos was friendly, their replies were terse, but they divulged enough for the strangers to fill in the blanks of the questionnaire.

"Is this about taxes?" one woman asked.

"It is to help you," the second stranger said.

"How did you find us?" another woman asked, pouring mezcal.

"It wasn't easy. Your road is very poor."

"It is poor for a reason," the woman said, and clutched her apron, which was stained as though with tobacco juice. Seeing them glance at her apron, she said, "It is from the *palenque*."

By the time the strangers reached the plaza, a bricked square edged with dry bushes, the musicians had mounted the roofed platform in the middle where they played, their music echoing from nearby houses. The strangers sat on a hard bench, scribbling for a while, nodding to the beat of the music, summarizing what they had been told. Women passed them, some carrying wood in their arms, others leading burros burdened with wood, a bundle on each side. The goatherd was nowhere to be seen.

"God bless you!" a woman cried.

Dizzy from mezcal, the strangers sighed in relief at the greeting, glad to be half done, the church at the end of the road much closer—close enough to see that it was a ruin, the sort of hollowed-out, roofless building they'd seen elsewhere, an old convent, open to the elements, just walls and broken buttresses and symmetrical stonework, arched openings where there had been windows and doors, and no worshipers—a broken church, a wall around it, melancholy in its vastness and abandonment.

"Who sent you?" a man at the next house asked, and then, just as quickly, chuckled, saying, "Never mind. It doesn't matter."

"I'm happy to tell you," the first stranger said, and peering closer, added, "I see your family's at home," and looked past the man to a woman seated at a table. She kept her face in profile, not looking at them. Something about her was so familiar, the stranger said, "Atalia?"

The woman laughed in a chattering, teasing way, and the strangers waved. To them, these small, dark villagers looked alike, so it might not have been the woman from up the road, that first house.

"Welcome," the man in the doorway said. "How can I help you?"

"To tell you the truth," the second stranger said, raising his voice against the music, "this isn't easy. All we need are some simple answers."

The man spoke with urgency. "You've come this far—the church is just up the road. You're almost there."

And the strangers looked toward the church, where some villagers had begun to gather at the perimeter wall, and their presence seemed to vitalize the ruin, their veneration—if that's what it was—giving it a purpose.

The man in the doorway said, "They are mezcaleros. We are all mezcaleros."

"At the church?"

"Not a church anymore. For years it has been our *palenque*. Instead of praying we make mezcal," the man said. "You've seen the agave growing in the hills around here. It is the wild kind. It makes the best mezcal. And not only that—we know how to cook the *piñas* at just the right temperature. They will be heating the rocks soon." He smiled and said, "What do you want to know?"

He gave his name as Felipe, and the names of his children, and he scoffed when the strangers asked if it was a problem that there was no school in the village.

"We don't need a school. We have a *palenque*. There we worship and we work. There's always work for people who are willing," the man said.

"How many more houses?" the first stranger said to his partner.

But it was the man, Felipe, who answered. "Not many. Maybe twelve. You will find the people cooperative—they'll answer your questions." He seemed eager for them to stay, to complete their work. "And then—just there—the church, and you'll be finished."

"It's not easy, coming to a village like this and asking questions."

"It's not easy to answer such questions."

"I guess not," the first stranger said, glancing down at his clipboard, adding, "Felipe."

But the man frowned, seeming bewildered by the name.

The remaining houses, as the man had promised, were more forthcoming, the people candid and cooperative, offering names and ages, satisfying the strangers. And when the two men reached the churchyard and saw some villagers, they said, "We're done. We deserve another drink!"

"In here," a man said. It was the goatherd, speaking in a confident voice, beckoning them into the gateway in the perimeter wall of the ruined church, to the churchyard.

There, in a large circular pit, a fire roared so hot a white eye blazed at its center. Nearby was the familiar apparatus of a *palenque:* the cement platform of a mill, a grinder upon it—an enormous stone mill wheel; the pit of agave shredded into reddish fibers; the vats of sweetish fermenting pulp; sinks and suspended copper pipes set up for distillation; and empty barrels to be filled.

Somehow the villagers had found their way here, slipping behind the main street, perhaps, like the goatherd. Many of them the strangers recognized, a hundred or more in all.

But it was the fire that attracted the two men in this high valley of drifting mist. They went to the edge of the pit to warm their hands, and called again for a drink.

"This is for you," a man said, in a voice they knew as Felipe's, and he raised his hand.

Just then the first blow was struck, a sudden thump like the bar clapping behind the door to secure it, and more blows, landing with such force the men were briefly blinded. They were merely stunned, but numb and helpless, tottering, until they were manhandled into the pit, where they howled.

Logs were flung over them, pinning them to the flames. Then the agave *piñas* were piled upon them, and covered with soil, to be baked.

## Amurabi and the Muxes

THE THREE JUCHITECO women staring into the mirrors of their compacts, as though at an adored friend, touching up their makeup in the lobby of the Hotel Xcaanda, were *muxes*. One conjecture, since the term referred to a trans woman, was that *muxe* (sometimes *muxhe*) was an early colonial corruption of the Spanish word for woman, *mujer*. There were *muxes* in the market selling fruit, and *muxes* cruising the back streets, looking for customers or sex partners. *Muxes* strolled hand in hand—beautifully dressed in sequined gowns and high heels—through the littered streets. Beefy *muxes* in tight frocks walked with soberly dressed families. A chain-smoking TV crew from Japan sat in the hotel waiting for written permission from the municipal president's office to interview *muxes* for a Japanese freak show. Their fixer, Elvis Guerra, a local poet and *muxe* go-between, held my hand, his fingers damp in the heat, and said sweetly, "I can tell you so many amazing things."

I wanted to know everything.

Francisco said, "There's a man here who likes your books. He is an expert on *muxes.*"

The man was Amurabi Mendez, a genial fellow of about forty-five, and we found him in his workplace a few streets from the main plaza. He owned a shop named Kiddo, retailing children's clothing—T-shirts, shorts, sneakers, backpacks, all the merchandise brightly colored and seeming to match Amurabi's sunny disposition. He was slightly built and slim, boyish in a cheerful, winning way. But any hint of the epicene was misleading; he had studied engineering, ran this business, and was a serious writer. He was, as I learned later, widely traveled, and his English was excellent.

"Sorry to hear you were sick," he said.

"Everyone gets sick. *Chorro.*"

"That's true," he said, laughing at the rude word. "I read *The Mosquito Coast* when I was an engineering student in Mexico City. I loved it. I'm so happy to see the author in our poor town of Juchitán."

I asked him about his own writing.

"I've written a lot about the earthquake," he said. "I was here and lived through it."

"Must have been terrifying," I said.

"Yes, but so many good things happened—inspiring things," he said, to my banal remark. "One day after the quake there were people selling in the market. The houses were destroyed, chaos everywhere, but life was going on, people were active. Here it was, just twenty-four hours after the disaster, and some people were clearing their houses, trying to rebuild. Other people were selling flowers, fruit, meat, and at the stalls women were cooking, making *garnaches.* It was great. It was inspiring to see how determined they were to survive."

In the caste-conscious Mexican mind, Amurabi was a mestizo, that ethnic group of shifting definitions, his mother indigenous Zapotec, his father identifying as Mexican—but of course they were both of them Mexican, his father a little more Latinate. His mother was born and raised in San Carlos Yautepec, about eighty miles from Oaxaca city, up the Royal Road I had just traveled, but the pueblo was a distance off that road, and isolated, a few thousand people, most of them Zapotec, clinging to a mountainside.

"My father was macho," Amurabi said. "He called my mother names. 'Indian.' 'Ignorant.' 'Primitive.' He would demand, 'Don't speak your language!'"

"Poor woman," I said. "But what effect did that have on you?"

"My mother was so ashamed, she didn't want us to speak the language," he said. "So when I was in Mexico City as a student, I didn't want anyone to know I was Zapotec. That shame became mine."

"Do you feel that way now?"

"No, not at all. I came back here—I'm proud!"

All this time we were standing at the front of his shop, in the midst of blue backpacks and multicolored T-shirts and rows of girls' summer dresses.

"Ask Amurabi about the *muxes*," Francisco Ramos said. "He's the expert."

"Let's meet later," Amurabi said. "I know a place."

The place was Bar Jardín, a sports bar on an easy-to-remember back street, Cinco de Mayo, with TV screens showing soccer matches, tables of yelling fans, and a loud band. Yet such a noisy place seemed to stimulate energetic talk and encourage confidences, or at least frankness, because the speaker was competing with a defiant cacophony and who cared what was said? We drank beer and shouted back and forth.

"The first thing to know," Amurabi said, "is that a *muxe* is totally woman. A gay man attracted to a *muxe*—it's somehow not right. The *muxe* wants to think, 'I'm his girl—whatever he wants!'"

"Because he's my guy!" I said. "A macho guy!"

"Yes," Amurabi said. "He hit me and it felt like a kiss!"

"That's shocking."

"It's a song," Amurabi said, and riffed a little: "Yeah, yeah. 'He hit me, and I knew he loved me.' Oh, yeah."

"So *muxes* are not gay."

"Not at all. I'm gay. I know!" he said. "There's a huge difference between being *muxe* and gay. Gays have a tough time in Mexican life. They call us *mayate*. What is *mayate*—dung beetle? It's also slang for a black person. In Latin America generally, gays are mocked. At the World Cup last year there were chants: '*Ehhh puto!*' and '*El que no salta es un chileno maricón*'—'He who doesn't jump is a Chilean faggot.' It's awful homophobic stuff." But he laughed and drank and then said, "Francisco says you met Elvis Guerra."

"Yes, the other day at the hotel. He was lining up some *muxes* for a Japanese TV show."

"He's a poet. He has also tried to change the whole perspective and get people to understand. There's a new generation of *muxes* now."

"For example?"

"They can be tops—these days, lots of *muxes* want to be tops," Amurabi said, using the sexual terminology (common in S & M code) for the dominant partner. "They don't see themselves as having to be bottoms. Older *muxes* are totally bottoms. And in the past, *muxes* wouldn't fall in love with each other, but now it happens. The old idea was that they were transvestites and wouldn't fall in love. That's old thinking."

I wondered how a *muxe* emerged in a family. It is well known that Zapotec society is essentially matriarchal, that women dominate the economy—it is obvious in the market—and it is said that Zapotec women not only run the household but are the decision makers in family affairs. I asked Amurabi whether it was the mother in the family who singled out the possible *muxe* from her brood.

"Yes, the family notices certain behavior when they're young," he said. "And things go from there. But it's not easy. *Muxes* find it hard to get jobs sometimes. They become hairdressers, they do women's nails. Clothing designers. Embroidery. Dancers. They might become prostitutes to earn a living, especially the young and beautiful ones." He glanced at his watch.

"Right now"—it was ten at night—"many *muxes* are busy being prostitutes. They're cruising," and he waved his hand beyond the shouting soccer fans and the TV screens in the direction of the back streets.

"I saw some in the market."

"Not young ones."

"Maybe not."

"But for most *muxes* their destiny is the streets, because the school is closed to them. The university—it's not open to them. In school, the teacher says, 'You are Francisco.' 'No, I am Rosa.' 'No, you are Francisco!' And they get so sad."

*Their destiny is the streets*—I admired its concision. "You were saying it's not much better being gay here in Mexico?"

He laughed. He said, "This very bar—I walked in here with some of my gay friends a little while ago. We were talking, blah, blah, blah. And we heard 'They're *putos.*' And *jotos.* And *mampo.* And *mayate.*"

"I know *puto* is 'queer.' What are those others?"

"Faggot," he said. "*Mampo* is mainly a Juchitán word. There's so many others. *Hueco*—that's Guatemala, too. *Culero* means 'lazy' but also means 'queer,' like *maricón*. We are always laughed at."

That was putting it mildly. One of the clearest denunciations of homophobia in Mexico was made by the masked Zapatista Subcomandante Marcos in conversation with Gabriel García Márquez in 2001, when Marcos appeared in Mexico City from his jungle stronghold. García Márquez had said that Marcos did not appear to be a traditional Latin American leftist.

Marcos said that such leftists ignored two important social groups, the indigenous people and the minorities. "Even if we took off our ski masks we would not be as marginalized as gays, lesbians, and transsexuals," Marcos explained. "These sectors of society have not only been ignored by the traditional Left in Latin America during previous decades—an ignorance that still persists today—but the theoretical model of Marxist-Leninism has been to leave them out or consider them as part of the problem to be eliminated. The homosexual, for example, is suspected as a traitor, as a malignant force for the movement and for the socialist state. And the Indian is a backward element that impedes the forces of production."

Amurabi, gay and indigenous, was not just laughed at but was regarded as a problem. He said the homophobia arose from the ambiguity that lay behind much of Mexican machismo, and he explained it with a joke.

"Paul, you know the saying: What's the difference between a gay Mexican and a straight Mexican?"

"Tell me."

"Six beers."

He said he was proudest of all of the *muxe* gala, called La Vela—the Vigil—a grand event held every November in Juchitán, often attended by ten thousand people, a thousand of them *muxes,* all dressed in finery—music, dancing, feasting, hooking up.

"Juchitecas have no inhibitions," one of Mexico's most illustrious writers, the poet, essayist, and journalist Andrés Henestrosa (1906–2008), had written. Henestrosa was born in a Zapotec-speaking family in the small town of San Francisco Ixhuatán, east of Juchitán. He studied in Juchitán and spent his life promoting Zapotec language and culture. A friend and collaborator of Francisco Toledo, he was as expressive in speaking about his culture as Toledo has been in painting it. Henestrosa had added, "There is nothing they can't say nor anything they can't do. The Juchiteca has no shame; in Zapotec there are no bad words."

"Because of the earthquake, La Vela wasn't held last year," Amurabi said, "but we're going to have it this year. This is something special. It's just here in the Isthmus—*muxes* only happen here."

The main church in Juchitán is the Parroquia de San Vicente Ferrer. One of the traditions here is that God gave Saint Ferrer a bag of *muxes* to scatter throughout Mexico. But when the saint arrived in Juchitán, the bag fell apart and all the *muxes* ended up in this one place.

"It's why we are totally in love with this town. We're proud of it. It's our heritage. I think there were *muxes* here a thousand years ago." Amurabi thought a moment. "This pride—it got us through the traumatic earthquake."

## Ixtepec and the Shelter

JUCHITÁN IS A stop on the railway line from Guatemala. Exactly forty years before, I had ridden this train from Veracruz, ending up in the border town of Tapachula, on my months-long overland trip to Patagonia. Hanging out the window then, I noted the names of nearby towns in my book, Tonalá and Pijijiapan. Now the railway is in decline; it is merely a freight train rumbling up from the Guatemalan frontier, nicknamed the Beast, carrying migrants as much as three thousand miles in separate journeys on the roofs of its boxcars, an ordeal that has been vividly chronicled by Oscar Martínez in his grim account of the migrant route and the brutal varieties of human trafficking, *The Beast: Riding the Rails and Dodging Narcos on the Migrant Trail.* He boarded "the Beast, the snake, the machine, the monster" in Ixtepec—indeed, he claims in his book that he rode this train eight times with only minor mishaps. Many riders do not survive a single trip.

Migrants topple from the speeding boxcars and are crushed by the fall, or lose their arms or legs under the steel wheels. And throughout the route they are preyed upon by rapists and thieves. "Assailants hop on the train whenever it stops, to hide among the migrants," Martínez writes. "Sometimes the conductor, in previously made agreement with the assailants, slows the train down enough so that they can jump right on." These are the petty thieves and opportunists who live near the tracks in outlying areas, but the kidnappings of women on the Beast, a frequent occurrence that ends with the women forced into prostitution or slave labor in narco camps, "are orchestrated by highly organized gangs."

The so-called Caravan of 2018—a wave of migrants, including many women and children, fleeing violence in Central America—that arrived at the US border (at which point the mothers were parted from their children and each locked up separately) originated fifty miles southeast of here, in Arriaga. In the period I was in the Isthmus, thousands of migrants headed north from Central America, and many of them stopped in the nearby town of Ixtepec—because they were exhausted and hungry, and Juchitán was too starved and broken to accommodate them. And also because in Ixtepec there was a migrant shelter, somewhat like the Kino Initiative in Nogales. Oscar Martínez mentions this place in his book as "Father Alejandro Solalinde's shelter."

This part of the Isthmus is hot and flat and unenchanted. Through the steamy savanna of foul-looking canals, of thick grass and ragged palms, the road was potholed and the heat oppressive—over a hundred degrees the day I drove from Juchitán. I went by a series of back roads, and discovered that Juchitán, in comparison to other places, seemed spared the worst of the quake. Hidden in the tall grass was the small pottery-making town of Asunción Ixtaltepec. There, not much had been left standing: the Palacio Municipal and the church of the Virgin of the Asunción were so cracked they looked unfixable. The surrounding peanut and bean fields—the mainstay of the economy—were parched and neglected, and Río los Perros—Dogs River—was an oxbow of stagnation.

The road was so hemmed in by the dense grass that the town of Ixtepec did not appear until I was almost upon it. It was a depot town, the railway cut the place in half, and it too had suffered earthquake damage. But the cinderblock huts were so small and low to the ground, many of them seemed whole. Another hidden town, of poor houses on broken streets, bars on the shop windows spoke of thievishness, and at piles of garbage on street corners pariah dogs were tearing at wastepaper and scraps.

This place of obvious misery was heaven for a bewildered migrant.

The migrant shelter, an *albergue* (hostel), was a walled compound secured by a heavy gate, on a back lane in a poor barrio called La Soledad, in itself a pitiful name meaning "loneliness" or "solitude." The barrio was obviously an area where other migrants were living, mainly men and mostly desperate-looking, holed up in shacks and crouched under plastic sheeting. An encampment of migrants lay across the lane from the shelter, where the formal name was painted in large letters on the outer wall, ALBERGUE DE MIGRANTES, and under a picture of wandering figures, HERMANOS EN EL CAMINO, Brothers on the Road. And inscribed over it the biblical text from Matthew 25:35: "*Tuve hambre y me dieron de comer...*" "For I was hungry and you gave me something to eat, I was thirsty and you gave me something to drink, I was a stranger and you invited me in."

A radical priest originally from Texcoco, Padre Alejandro Solalinde, founded the shelter in 2007, when he recognized that this area, pinched geographically and economically, was the focus of criminal activity against migrants. (And although Father Solalinde has received many awards, he has also received many death threats, so he has from time to time needed to hide to save himself.) The shelter's mission statement says, "Due to Ixtepec's strategic and geopolitical importance in the Isthmus of Tehuantepec, it has been chosen by many gangs as the center of operations. It is the most desirable location for extracting enormous amounts of money from migrants, by any means possible." Among the extortionists, the statement continues, are "Municipal, State and Federal Police."

The website offers what it calls "Volunteering Opportunities": "At the shelter Hermanos en el Camino, we are all volunteers! This is your opportunity to support our migrant brothers and have a life-changing experience."

And once I convinced the gatekeeper that I was a harmless gringo, merely seeking information, almost the first person I met was an American volunteer, Junet (Junie) Bedayn, from Grass Valley, California, a thin, sweet-faced eighteen-year-old in an ankle-length flower-patterned dress and sandals, her hair covered with a kerchief.

"*Hola, bienvenido,*" she said, and realizing I was a fellow American, she slipped into English, laughing a little, and explained how she had gotten there. Hoping to do something productive between high school graduation in Grass Valley and her first semester at Columbia University, she had found the Hermanos en el Camino website and the description of the ways volunteers could help. So instead of waiting on tables at a bistro in Grass Valley, or teaching kids to swim at a camp, or staring at a screen posting images on Instagram, she applied to the *albergue* and explained her qualifications: an honor student, fluent in Spanish, sympathetic to the plight of migrants, and committed to spending two or three months volunteering at the shelter.

"You're eighteen!" I said, remembering that when I was eighteen I was a lifeguard at a public swimming pool in Boston. When I was not covertly reading in my tall lifeguard chair (it was my *On the Road* and *Generation of Vipers* summer), I was horsing around with the other lifeguards and locker room attendants, who called me Paulie.

But Junie Bedayn at that age got herself to the Isthmus of Tehuantepec alone, and defying the popular view that migrants were pests, she was volunteering to work among them and to learn by doing.

"The tough part was convincing my mother and my aunt that I'd be all right," she said. Not long before she applied, her father had passed away, so I could easily understand her mother's anxiety. But Junie had prevailed. She had traveled by bus from Oaxaca, and had fallen seriously ill soon after arriving ("I forgot that you're not supposed to drink the water"). There were some nuns on the staff, but only two other volunteers. Junie was now essential to the running of the shelter. And this whole outside section of shelter was occupied by young men — lean, grubby, hungry-looking, and idle, many of them having a siesta on straw mats and others eyeing this pretty but practical girl. But being brisk, Junie was unfazed.

"That's the dormitory," she said, of a four-story building at the far side of the compound. She pointed to a wide crack in the wall. "That's earthquake damage. So a lot of the migrants don't want to sleep inside — they think it will fall down. They sleep over here," and she indicated a large concrete slab, where many of them were supine.

There were eighty men in the shelter, which was a small number. The usual number of migrants was two hundred, and they had housed as many as four hundred at a time, all from Guatemala, Honduras, or El Salvador. I tried to imagine four hundred homeless, penniless, hungry men lingering here for a week at a time, looking for ways to travel farther north. Many of them would be injured or sick, or traumatized by the journey from Central America and the train trip from Arriaga. I mentioned this.

"We have two doctors and two nurses in the shelter," Junie said. "As you can imagine, they're pretty busy."

"Did the Caravan stop here?"

"They passed by — what? — I guess a few weeks ago," she said. "We fed all of them."

In a low voice, nodding toward the men lying on the mats, I said, "What do these guys do all day?"

"They listen to music, they play games. Some of them do paintings — see those paintings hung up there?"

Rectangles of paper daubed with rustic scenes, of white-shirted farmers in rows of green crops, of stiffened cows and goats, and other paintings of groups of dancers, gaily dressed in red, some of them masked. Farms and fiestas.

"Actually, most of them do some sort of work," Junie said. "They're picked up at six-thirty in the morning and they do construction in town. There's a lot for them to do, what with the earthquake damage. They get three hundred pesos a day, and they come back in the afternoon."

"What's their goal?"

"Most everyone is headed north," she said. "Some of them are waiting for Mexican residency."

"And they're all men?" I said.

"No. We have twelve women and four children at the moment," she said, and started across the compound to a smaller, fenced-in building that bordered a playground.

As we approached the chain-link fence, a woman of about thirty in casual clothes — slacks and a blue blouse — saw us and said hello. This was Ana Luz Minerva, who was here volunteering and also collecting material for her doctoral dissertation. She was Spanish speaking and candid.

"I'm studying children traveling alone from Central America," she said.

"Are there many?"

"Oh, yes. Some as young as eight, going solo."

"I don't get it. Why so young?"

"Because the gangs in Salvador and Honduras are recruiting children as assassins, and it's harder and harder for the gangs to find them, so the children are getting younger — the assassins, I mean. The children I'm concerned with are trying to escape."

"How do they recruit them?" The word was *reclutamiento.*

"The gangs take them and threaten to kill their mothers," Ana Luz said.

"That seems pretty persuasive."

"And sometimes they do it."

"There's no one to stop them?"

"In some of the towns there's vigilante justice—'cleaning up the streets,' they call it, killing the gang members, because the police do nothing."

As we were speaking under a tree, adjacent to the women's shelter, a young woman passed by, saying hello.

"She's here with her two children," Ana Luz said. "Often families travel together. The other day we had a woman of twenty-six traveling alone, with four children."

"Sometimes women are raped," Junie said. "One who came here was raped by fourteen men."

"She told you that?" I said. "What did she say?"

"She was kind of resigned to it. She said, 'It had to happen, for me to get farther on.'"

Ana Luz said, "For a while the Zetas were kidnapping migrants and forcing them to hand over their telephone numbers, to collect ransom from their families. That's less of a problem now. Drugs are the main problem."

"What sort of drugs?"

"Marijuana, crack, meth," Junie said calmly, her innocent, late-teenage face clouded with a flicker of concern. "But users are always kicked out of here. You'll see them across the street, in that squatter camp."

Both Ana Luz and Junie said they had to get back to work—on this sweltering day, at this underfunded shelter on a littered back lane buzzing with blowflies, in a remote town in the Isthmus.

I said, "I admire you both a lot for what you're doing. And Junie, your mother should be very proud."

"She worries about me," Junie said. We were walking back through the compound, and the office where a nun—a supervisor—was peering at a computer screen, and twenty men were slouched on their mats, watching us pass by. "But I worry about these people."

Outside, in the lane of the barrio, I saw the squatter camp—the druggies, the rejects from the shelter, the tough guys, the tortured-looking youths, about thirty of them. Four of them stood on the roof of the hut, calling out to me, asking for money. They stayed behind a barrier they had made—as aliens in Ixtepec, they had created a fortified camp out of junk wood, plastic sheeting, and wire. The stranded souls stared, sullenly complaining, isolated in their grim encampment. They were lost and vulnerable. I couldn't blame them for resenting the ease with which I walked to my parked car, preparing to slip away.

But then an odd thing happened that distracted and silenced them. About fifty feet up the road, a *muxe* walked out of a hut and through a gateway in a fence of scrap wood. Broad-shouldered and heavyset, apparently a man in a party dress, she came toward me, her plastic sandals scuffing the gravel in the dusty lane. Approaching me, she passed by the crowd of migrant men from Honduras and Guatemala and El Salvador, where *muxes* were unknown but machismo predominated. On this hot afternoon, the *muxe*—middle-aged, with long black hair, wearing a tight black sparkly dress—ambled past gracefully, almost haughtily, in no particular hurry, while the fascinated migrants stared, gaping in their rags.

## *To San Cristóbal*

ON AN IMPULSE, soon after the visit in Ciudad Ixtepec, I drove back to the main road and headed east to San Cristóbal de las Casas, past the lagoons of Juchitán, and the hot fields of torn and flopped-over grass, for my rendezvous with the Zapatistas. It seemed that ever since the border at Reynosa, 1,400 miles away, I had been traveling on a royal road through a plain of snakes.

Mexico is rich in many tourist-friendly respects—the traditional hospitality, the varieties of food, the elaborate fiestas, the gusto of the language, the consolations of family and faith. These attractive attributes are well known to the vacationer, and are the pride and boast of the Mexican. But there is more, and some of it is not pretty, and all of it is complicated.

Set against these conventional satisfactions was the melancholy fact that life in Mexico is dangerous for nearly everyone—the fat cats in Mexico City, frantic about their safety, had armed guards; the poor in their huts and shacks defended themselves with upright shards of glass cemented to the tops of their garden walls, or failing that, heavily barred windows. Living behind fortifications, a high wall or a fence, was a visible pattern of Mexican life. La Vida Mexicana was a vision of battlements. The very rich behind their ramparts made themselves bulletproof, the middle classes were walled in, and even the poorest lived in enclosed compounds, irrationally comforted by wobbly bamboo fences and fierce guard dogs, as I saw in the villages of the Mixteca Alta.

And though I found Mexicans to be instinctively welcoming, there was a murmur of hesitation behind every first encounter. In a suspicious shadow of their nature — the haunted substratum of darkness in their history, a marker in their DNA of survival and self-preservation — Mexicans had also to regard every stranger as a potential threat. The way forward in any relationship was based on trust, but trust was not taken for granted. It was something you had to earn. *Ganar el respeto* — to win respect — was a Mexican imperative; more profound was *ganar la confianza*, to win trust. You might be an informal friend, a casual *amigo*, but before you were respected and trusted, every nuance of your interactions was evaluated: your mood, your generosity, your openness, your reliability, even your posture, the way you stood or sat. Only then would a Mexican say, *Se ganó mi confianza* — He won my trust. Then you were a *compadre*.

This was why I felt Mexican friendship to be unusually surprising and generous, the chosen friend grateful and relieved, the friendship at times more subtle, durable, and deeper than love. *Abrazos* is the salutation on most friends' messages: hugs. *Querido*, the frequent greeting: dear. *Compa*, an intimate way of saying *compañero*.

I have always extolled the virtues of traveling alone, seeking the solitary path, staying anonymous and meditative in the Zen of the open road — and I still think that silence, exile, and cunning (James Joyce's words of defense) are useful strategies to any wanderer, especially one who wishes to write.

But Mexico is full of contradictions for the visitor. You can sit in Cancún nursing a mojito and toying with a taco in utter bliss, needing nothing but a little money and the smile of a waiter sprinting to your table: millions do that. But the gringo on a back road in his own car is another matter, and much resembles the Mexican in his or her lack of protection, and fatal vulnerabilities. Reflecting in Juchitán, I had to admit that I could never have gotten this far in the country, or penetrated it so intimately, without the help of Mexican friends.

Because in Mexico Mundo, life on the plain of snakes was so uncertain, every venture out of the security of the home could become dramatic and precarious. One of the more bizarre cruelties of the country, found in both its political and criminal cultures — and of course the two often overlap — were sudden disappearances. As I found out from the humanitarian organization Caminos Oaxaca: Acompañamiento a Migrantes, hundreds of migrants disappeared en route to the border; the feistier journalists disappeared; the forty-three students from Ayotzinapa disappeared; virtually every day people went missing in Mexico, kidnapped, abducted, lifted, deleted, never to be heard from again.

On the days I was on the road in the Isthmus pondering this, two large demonstrations were held, in Mexico City and in Guadalajara, using the disappearance of three film-school students in Jalisco to call attention to what they called "an epidemic," the disappearance of many others. Their slogan was "We Are Not Three — We Are Many." Very many, based on official statistics from Mexico's Secretariat of the Interior: the whereabouts of 15,516 people aged between thirteen and twenty-nine years remain unknown. The number of those younger than eighteen is more than 7,000. The Washington Office on Latin America, an advocacy group that promotes human rights in the Americas, released a statement in 2017 saying that over 32,000 people have disappeared in Mexico in the last decade. Mexicans told me that however tragic it was to confront the visible certainties of a murder, it was much harder for a family to deal with the agonizing bafflement of a vanishing.

Most Mexicans I met said urgently to me, "Be careful," and many went into great detail: places to avoid, how to store my car for the night so it wouldn't be vandalized or stolen, where to walk, how to observe the protocols of village life: "Always talk to the municipal president, introduce yourself, before you ask a single question of anyone." (And as I write this, I think: Does any American think to take a Mexican visitor to the US aside and offer such cautions?) Mexicans had ample reasons to be cynical politically. And they often warned me of the police, though I'd now had enough experiences with them to be wary, not only of the well-armed Federales in dark glasses, but also the shambling, potbellied local cops with their hats tipped sideways, glassy-eyed with greed at a roadblock and peering into my car, stroking their mustache and calculating the amount they could reasonably demand to release me.

Mexican police: whenever I saw a black-and-white squad car parked by the side of a road I was traveling—and this was a frequent sight—I drove past in a state of apprehension, and was unspeakably happy when I looked in my rear-view mirror and saw that it had not pulled out to pursue me.

The natural protections that Americans take for granted are almost unknown in Mexico. Most Mexicans lived without security, and in general for good reasons; political leadership was uninspiring. I thought of the Mexican woman tourist I had casually met at Monte Albán, who shook her head sadly and said, "Unfortunately we live in Colima"—a small state on the Pacific Coast, the drug route—"and when we travel by car we always have to go in a convoy, because the roads are not secure."

When the poor stoical peasant man in San Juan Bautista Coixtlahuaca told me that the meaning of the Mixtec word was "the plain of snakes," I had a perfect image for the contradictions of Mexican life: its glory, as the plumed serpent, Quetzalcoatl, the supreme, dragon-like deity, the god of wind and fire and creation, worshiped by the Aztecs; and the snake as the dangerous lurker.

"The most important pre-Hispanic deity was Quetzalcoatl," my writer friend Diego Olavarría told me later. "Many places in Mexico have the serpent in their names: Coatzacoalcos, Coatepec. And 'Cancún,' in Maya, means Nest of Serpents." And he elaborated: "Although our foundational myth, and our coat of arms, suggests that snakes are forces of evil that must be devoured by the virtuous eagles, the truth is more complicated than that. The eagles soar in the sky alone, but we Mexicans share the land with snakes."

It seemed to me that insecurity was a dominant theme in Mexican history, which is why people prayed for salvation and for miracles: to the Virgin of Guadalupe, to Saint Jude Thaddeus (San Judas Tadeo), to Santísima

Muerte—Holy Death; to Jesús Malverde the narco saint; and to other spirit saviors. And it was why, from time to time, when a real savior appeared dramatically from nowhere to rescue the country, that person was elevated. It was the history of Emiliano Zapata, of Pancho Villa, of Lázaro Cárdenas—revolutionaries and reformers, but more than that, protectors of their people.

Because, in general, Mexicans lived unprotected. Knowing their vulnerabilities, they had long ago ceased to yearn for anyone to care. The lesson I had learned in Mexico was that, more than almost any other person I had met in my life of travel, the Mexican was diligent in his or her self-sufficiency. This strategy to survive drove them from their villages and slums to cross the border—sometimes to share in the ideals of American life, but perhaps more often to toil as field hands or fruit pickers and to clean hotel rooms, grateful for the work.

The most recent incarnation of savior revolutionaries, and the most tested, were the Zapatistas. From my first glimpse in the news in 1994 of the masked figure of Subcomandante Marcos leaving the Lacandón jungle and appearing in San Cristóbal de las Casas on horseback, under the banner of the Ejército Zapatista Liberación Nacional, the Zapatista Army of National Liberation, I had wanted to meet him and to know more. Like many revolutionaries, he was regarded by some as a pest, by others as a charismatic leader, to still others as the savior and protector that poor and indigenous Mexicans needed. And it was odd: no one knew Subcomandante Marcos's real name, no one knew where he lived in the jungle, and no one had ever seen his face.

I was headed to his territory, to the "Conversatorio" in San Cristóbal, organized by his people, where he might or might not appear.

Bowling in my car through the savanna on the straight flat road: this too was a royal road, of the lowland Isthmus of Tehuantepec, sea level and steamy, a hot wind blowing from the northeast. The wind was so strong it rocked the chassis and pushed at the big trucks ahead of me, making them unsteady and hard to pass, as they seemed like buttocky hippos on wheels, ostentatiously sashaying on the road. But this wind, called the Tehuano, was useful, too—I passed numerous wind farms, miles of turbines like giant fans, their rotors whirring, pumping juice into the national grid.

The Camino Real gained radically in altitude, from the coast to more than a mile high. After sixty or eighty miles of buffeting wind and blown-down grass, the road climbed out of Oaxaca state into Chiapas, at Arriaga—the migrant railhead. Still climbing, the road rose to almost 1,700 feet at Tuxtla Gutiérrez. This industrial and commercial city of half a million, enclosed in a high valley, was well known to air passengers, because in order to get to any of the towns beyond it in Chiapas—and that included San Cristóbal, and tourists going to Cancún or Mérida—one of the main hubs was Tuxtla's international airport, named for one of its local heroes. This hero was Ángel Albino Corzo, who, after a life of sacrifice and idealism, headed to his hometown of Chiapa, about nine miles from Tuxtla, for a well-deserved retirement from the fray, and was murdered.

My interest in Tuxtla was related to the Zapatistas. After their emergence in San Cristóbal in 1994 and the confrontation with police and federal troops, the Mexican government proposed a solution in a peacemaking pact, the San Andrés Accords of that year. But it turned out to be a ruse, and when the government reneged on it a few years later, more than ten thousand protesters mobbed the streets of Tuxtla to press for action—for reforms and elections. A Tuxtla politician and activist, Rubicel Ruíz Gamboa, was a supporter of the Zapatistas, a champion of indigenous rights, and a man eager to promote land reform, as well as the leader of the Independent Peasant Union. In 1998, as he was headed to his home in Tuxtla, a car drove up next to his and two men riddled his car with bullets, killing him. Mexicans, like Americans, have a habit of assassinating their benefactors—in 1919, Emiliano Zapata was murdered.

The murder of Ruíz was thought to be a tactic to sabotage any renewal of the peace talks between the Zapatistas and the government. The San Andrés Accords remain in a legal limbo, unimplemented by the government and jeered at by the Zapatistas, another example of the Mexican government strategy of inaction, the political theory of doing nothing, on the assumption that humans have a habit of forgetting—a perverse assumption, since Mexico seemed to me a nation torn by total recall.

It was obvious from the graffiti on the walls and the rock faces from Tuxtla to San Cristóbal that no one had forgotten the abuses of the government or the revolutionary fervor of the Zapatistas, soon to celebrate their quarter century of dominance in Chiapas, and still masked.

A dramatic feature at the eastern edge of Tuxtla is a great cloven gorge, Sumidero Canyon, over the Grijalva River, near where Corzo was murdered and not far from where Rubicel Ruíz Gamboa was gunned down, and like many another place with a history of mayhem, deceptively beautiful. Birds twittered in the trees on this lovely day, hawks revolved in the sky, bushy trees and wooded slopes blanketed the sierra—no villages, and hardly a house on the *autopista* that circumvented the old royal road of the friars winding through the mountains. Less than an hour from Tuxtla, I was at the lip of a deep valley, looking down at a tight cluster of houses on the valley floor, and soon after was driving on the cobbled, one-car-width streets of San Cristóbal de las Casas.

After the 90-degree weather of the coast, it was a relief to experience the misty heights and blobby, rain-fattened clouds of San Cristóbal—at night in the 40s, a city that experienced freezing temperatures in the winter, and sometimes snow. The city Graham Greene had found intolerable and primitive ("I want to get out of this bloody country") was now bustling and chic, with curio shops and boutiques, or so it seemed.

## Oventic: *Resistir Es Existir* *(To Resist Is to Exist)*

AT FIRST GLANCE, San Cristóbal de las Casas seems a city of tourists, seeking the restaurants, the ecclesiastical architecture, the enormous, maze-like market, and the handicrafts (knitted shawls, jewelry of local amber, needlework, lacquerware, leatherwork), or headed by bus to the ruins of Palenque. Some represent Zapaturismo—drawn to the city that saw the emergence of the Zapatistas, and looking for appropriate caps and T-shirts. Look closer and it becomes clear that the tourists are flaneurs—*paseantes,* a local might say—and that it is a city populated mainly by Mexicans, of the many Mayan language groups, in this region the Tzotzil and the Tzetzal, murmuring in their own idiom. Look closer still, on foot in the outskirts, gasping from the altitude, and you see that its people are badly housed, with few social services, mostly poor, mostly indigenous.

These are the sturdy but faceless folk in the Long March of Everyman, the descendants of indigenous people of the pre-conquest. In Aztec, Zapotec, and Nahuatl society they were the laborers and peasants. They were remote from the rulers, the *tlatoani,* the secret societies of the Eagle and Jaguar warriors, the elegant nobility, the various categories of priests and priestesses—all of whom were privileged.

They were the *maceualli,* in Nahua society, indigenous commoners whose farms supplied the elite with maize, beans, squash, tomatoes, potatoes, sarsaparilla, and the pods they called *chocolatl.* They raised turkeys and harvested the buds of cacti, and medicinal herbs, and the sunflower, native to Mexico, and because it resembled a defensive weapon, known to the Aztecs as *chimalxochitl,* the shield flower.

The farmer, unprivileged and poor, was for centuries overlooked by historians. An early exception was Jacques Soustelle, the great pre-Columbian scholar and anthropologist who, at the beginning of *Daily Life of the Aztecs on the Eve of the Spanish Conquest,* wrote how it was necessary to speak of him, "because after the disaster of 1521"—the conquest—"and the total collapse of all authority, all concepts, the whole frame of society and all religion, he alone survived, and he alone still lives."

That was written in 1955. It remains true today. "Yes, we speak it [Zapotec] all the time. Our secret language!" the mezcalero Crispin García told me in San Dionisio, laughing, hinting at secret lives and secret histories. And I heard the same from Zapotecs in San Baltazar Guelavila and elsewhere. There are one million indigenous people in Chiapas, one third of the population, most of them Mayan related, twelve language groups, conversing in the same words as they have for a thousand years, many of them for whom Spanish is a second language, and some who do not speak Spanish at all. A third of Indian children never see a schoolroom, health facilities are scarce, and the per capita income in Chiapas is the same as in Kenya.

*Con la paciencia muda de hormiga,* "With the silent patience of the ant"—in Samuel Beckett's translation of Alfonso Reyes's poem "Yerbas del Tarahumara"—the so-called Indians have experienced fits of rebellion from the days of the Spanish conquest, but have always been sidelined or beaten into submission. The city of San Cristóbal de las Casas memorializes the name of the man who denounced the slavery and oppression of Indians, the sixteenth-century Spanish friar (and bishop of Chiapas) Bartolomé de las Casas. B. Traven's six jungle novels, especially *The Rebellion of the Hanged* and *The General from the Jungle,* are a dramatization, in the years of the Mexican Revolution, of unrest, debt slavery, and forced labor in Chiapas, where in the 1920s Traven spent many months living among the lumberjacks and peasants, and the indigenous people, whom he championed (and somewhat romanticized) in his work. His novel *The White Rose* describes the eternal Mexican struggle between the Indian, who has a spiritual feeling for the land, and greedy corporate interests (in this case American) that exploit the land to get rich and become overlords. When Traven died in 1969, his widow scattered his ashes from a plane over the Lacandón jungle, and it seems as though the Zapatista movement rose from the ashes of the elusive revolutionary writer.

On my drive from Juchitán into this mountain town I had reflected on the notion of how most Mexicans are unprotected in their lives and in their work, and are at pains to create strategies to avert the dangers they face. In this regard, no one is more vulnerable or exploited than the Mexican Indian. And the recognition of this vulnerability is at the heart of the Zapatista movement, which had its origin in the demand for dignity and justice for the indigenous people of Chiapas. I have also mentioned how important it is for the understanding and the safety of a solitary traveler in Mexico, especially a gringo alone in his car, to have Mexican friends. After my teaching stint in Mexico City, and earning the students' respect, I had twenty-four good friends, with whom I was now in regular touch. Their characteristic greeting was "How can we help you, Don Pablo?"

My friend the writer Juan Villoro had wangled an invitation for me to attend the secret Conversatorio, sponsored by the Zapatistas. I had agreed to meet Juan at a certain *parador* on one of those narrow San Cristóbal streets.

Months before, in Colonia Roma, over a dinner of hog jaw, Juan had deflected my questions about his life and work, and had told me about his father, Luis, a philosopher. This exile from Spain, with a scholarly interest in the nuances of Mayan languages, had traveled widely in Chiapas and been a close observer of the indigenous people there. In 1950 he published his seminal book on the evolving consciousness of indigenous people, *The Major Moments of Indigenism in Mexico.*

Now, in San Cristóbal, Juan became a bit more candid. In the last years of Luis Villoro's teaching at the Autonomous Metropolitan University (UAM), one of his twenty-something colleagues, a professor in the School of Arts and Sciences, was a highly intelligent sociologist, born in 1957 in Tampico, Tamaulipas. As a youth he'd been educated by Jesuits at the Instituto Cultural Tampico. His name was Rafael Sebastián Guillén Vicente. The campus at Xochimilco was famously radical, at the forefront in protests. Of the hundreds of victims of the Tlatelolco massacre in 1968, many had been UAM students. A student at the time, Ilan Stavans (later the author of *The Hispanic Condition* and many other books), five years younger than Guillén, described this firebrand as "bright and articulate," with a "sharp intellect and infectious verbosity."

This young professor, Rafael Guillén, was the man who entered the Lacandón jungle in 1984 and emerged ten years later in a ski mask, on horseback, with the nom de guerre of Subcomandante Marcos, leader of the Zapatistas, the head of an army of thousands, declaring his rebellion from the balconies of municipal buildings and, to seize the attention of the Mexican republic, occupying seven cities. The largest of the occupied cities was San Cristóbal.

"My father was a friend and adviser to the Zapatistas," Juan said. "He was close to Marcos and shared many of his ideas. I've sort of taken on this responsibility, which is why I'm here."

"What did the Zapatistas think of your father?"

"They admired him, they read his books," Juan said. "And he was passionate about their rebellion. Imagine, he asked to be buried at one of the important Zapatista villages, Oventic. He's buried under a special tree there — I can't think of the name of this tree in English, but it's a rare one. We call it *zotzte.*"

"Where is Oventic — in the jungle?"

"No. At the edge of a valley in the mountains, a beautiful place. But one of those forbidden Zapatista *caracoles.*"

I smiled because I'd seen the word on menus: *caracol* means "snail." You might find one minced in your tasty ceviche. I asked Juan to clarify.

He said, "It's the Zapatista name for a village or settlement. A nice name, I think. They identify with the resolute, slow-moving snail."

"How far away is Oventic?"

"A couple of hours' drive. The road is good."

"I have a car."

"*Querido* Pablo, the traveler!" he said. "The tricky part is that strangers — non-Zapatistas — are not welcome." He thought a moment. "But I can say you're visiting the grave of my father, paying respects. That will mean something to them. I'll call the *comandante* there who's in charge, Compañero David. I know him. We'll take a chance."

"Tell me about the Conversatorio."

It would be a clandestine EZLN meeting, held over some days, he explained, open to approved delegates and Zapatista sympathizers, with the theme "Miradas, Escuchas, Palabras: Prohibido Pensar?" (Glances, Listeners, Words: Forbidden Thought?) The place chosen for the meeting was a Zapatista college, CIDECI-UniTierra, a fenced-in location in a small, battered, ironically named colonia, Nueva Maravilla (New Miracle), at the northern edge of San Cristóbal. CIDECI stood for Centro Indígena de Capacitación Integral, the Indigenous Center for Integral Learning. It was effectively a university with a curriculum of alternative education, its courses ranging from practical farming to political theory — a place built and financed by the Zapatistas, where young graduates from the high schools in the *caracoles* went to study. There were about thirty *caracoles* — autonomous municipalities — located all over Chiapas.

"I'm looking forward to the Zapatista event."

"Good. I put you down as a speaker."

This threw me a little. I said, "What subject?"

"Whatever you want to talk about."

"Will Marcos be there?"

"Lately he's taken another nom de guerre, Galeano. And no one ever knows his movements," Juan said. "But there'll be some other Mexican writers, and you and I will be there!"

That was another feature of Mexican life, a result of scarcity and the need to seize the day: spontaneity and improvisation. From a jaunt to San Cristóbal to attend a Zapatista conference, where I assumed I would be in the audience, I now found I was a speaker.

And more spontaneity: the next day, Juan received permission from his *comandante* contact for me to visit the *caracol* of Oventic.

On the way to Oventic I stopped at the town of Chamula, famous for its weird church observances, where the interior of the basilica of San Juan Bautista was ablaze with flames. Worshipers crouched on the floor arranging candles, fifty or a hundred in symmetrical patterns, then lighting them and, in the candlelight, drinking Coca-Cola and ritually burping—eructation believed to be salutary—and splashing libations of Coke on the church floor, which was covered with sand.

There were no pews, there were no priests, there was no Mass or formal service. It was a gathering of *curanderos*—medicine men—and those wishing to be cured. Other solemn groups were chanting, passing hens' eggs around the faces and bodies of prayerful pilgrims in a *limpia*—a purification—or holding a squawking chicken near a kneeling devotee, and a moment later the chicken's neck was wrung, and the softened, drooping carcass placed near the candles.

As I watched, a man approached me holding a bottle and a glass. He said, "Mezcal," and poured me a slug and offered it. I drank it, blinked away the dazzle in my eyes, thanked him, and kept looking.

It was a fusion of pre-Hispanic traditions and Christian dogma, the result an observance involving a mass of candles, throttled chickens, and soda pop. (But sheep are sacred, never harmed or eaten: the town of Chamula is full of grazing sheep.) Added to these rituals was a chance for retribution, because if the chosen saint did not grant the supplicant's wish, the deity could be punished, just as the Zapotecs and Mayans punished their gods and saints, lashing their images with whips. In this church, the statues of saints, which had been ceremonially draped, with an uttered prayer, could be stripped of their robe if the prayer was not answered.

A far cry from this fantastication of beliefs, and a sensible remedy, was in the mountains. Past the villages of Shanate and Callejón, the big town of San Andrés Larráinzar and the smaller one of Talanquita, was the Zapatista *caracol* of Oventic, behind a forbidding steel gate, heavily padlocked and chained shut. Its back turned to the material world, it was a stronghold of rationality and rebellion, where the casual visitor met large unwelcoming signs, printed with variations of Go Away and No Trespassing in red and black block letters.

These were the cool forested highlands of Chiapas, of small farms where woodcutters were clearing the slopes for planting, and stacking the logs to be split for firewood or building material. The deep valleys were terraced for gardens and looked dark and fertile, irrigated by streams that were fed by the bridal veils of splashing waterfalls. The land was plowed and hoed by hand, the woodcutters wielding axes; this physical labor gave the workers the look of ownership. ("*La tierra es de quien la trabaja con sus manos,*" Emiliano Zapata had once said: The land belongs to those who work it with their hands.) It was like rural Mexico from another era. The lush hills and rugged mountains beyond looked like nothing I'd seen up to now in Mexico, but resembled the landscape I remembered from long ago in Guatemala, which was not far away.

Oventic, the community, was a cluster of paved streets of woodframe buildings painted with murals—the face of Zapata visible on one, a woman in a mask, doe-eyed but defiant, on another. And a sign near the gate: PARA TODOS TODO, NADA PARA NOSOTROS. For All, Plenty—For Us, Nothing.

The road I'd arrived on had been empty, no tourists, no travelers, no strangers; it was a back road that, had I stayed on it for three more hours, would have brought me to the town of Teapa, in Tabasco, which was nowhere. The roads in Oventic that I could see behind the gate were empty of vehicles, and when I called out, no human appeared to respond. Hearing my voice, a dog stirred, twitching his tail where he lay in the shade of a veranda. Among the No Trespassing signs was another, more forbidding one: ESTÁ USTED EN TERRITORIO ZAPATISTA EN REBELDÍA — AQUÍ MANDA EL PUEBLO Y EL GOBIERNO OBEDECE, You Are in Zapatista Territory in Rebellion — Here the People Rule and the Government Must Obey, with the acronym MARZ, representing Municipio Autónomo Rebelde Zapatista — Zapatista Rebel Autonomous Municipality.

"*Hola!*" I called out again, and waited.

After some minutes two Zapatista men in black masks stepped from the veranda of a distant building and trudged slowly toward me. Facing me from behind the iron gate, but without a greeting, the one holding a clipboard said, "Who are you?"

Seeking his eyes in the slits of the mask, I told him my name and added, "I am here to visit the tomb of Luis Villoro and to say hello."

He passed me the clipboard through the bars and said, "Write your name."

When I had written it, the two men conferred for a moment, then trudged away, back to the distant building.

I waited at the gate in bright sunlight, a soft breeze freshening and lifting the leaves on the thick boughs of nearby trees. I could see into the valley and beyond, to another mountain range, bluish under a clear blue sky. Apart from the faint birdsong and the flutter of leaves, there was no sound. I was not conspicuous, standing at the locked gate, because there was no one to observe me.

It was a historic place, a *caracol* given the sonorous name Resistencia y Rebeldía por la Humanidad. In 1996, two years after the Zapatistas emerged from the jungle, an event was held here, the First Intercontinental Encounter for Humanity and Against Neoliberalism. Thousands attended, from more than forty countries.

"Behind us are you," Marcos said at the time. "Behind our face masks is the face of all women excluded. Of all the indigenous people forgotten.

Of all homosexuals persecuted. Of young people belittled. Of all migrants beaten. Of all people imprisoned for their thought or word. Of all workers humiliated. Of all who died in oblivion. Of all the simple and ordinary men and women who don't count, who are not seen, who are not named, who have no tomorrow." And he ended with, "Today thousands of little worlds in the continents practice a principle here, in the mountains of southeastern Mexico: the principle of building a new and good world, one world in which many worlds fit."

Now, after ten minutes, the men were trudging back. They went to the side and opened a smaller gate, with a step like a stile, and I passed into the self-contained and secret settlement of Oventic. Saying nothing, the two men walked slowly toward a building, gaily painted with birds and rainbows and Mexican dancers on the outside, stark and shabby inside—the anteroom of an office.

One of my masked men knocked softly on a door, and when it opened a crack I saw the averted face of a man inside. I could not understand the whispers, speaking Tzotzil probably, and then the door shut. After more minutes, a man emerged from the room—possibly the same man, but he wore a bandanna around the lower portion of his face, like a desperado in an old cowboy movie.

"You want to see the tomb?" the masked man said, a mild voice that did not match the forbidding mask.

"Thank you, yes."

He led me outside to a narrow path that descended to a grove of trees, and as we walked, two women began following. They too were masked—the black knitted ski masks favored by Zapatistas. They kept their arms folded.

"No pictures of people," the man in the bandanna said.

"What about these lovely painted houses?"

"Yes, you can take pictures of those."

The side of the house with the pair of staring long-lashed eyes enclosed in a mask. The upright ear of corn, a masked head at its tip, and the banner SOMOS RAÍZ, We Are the Root, an allusion to the fact that the indigenous people here, and elsewhere in Mexico, believe an ear of corn to be essential to their creation myth. On another white exterior wall, an outline map of

Africa enclosing a poem beginning, "Le rêve d'un monde / Immense et en eau profonde, / Où les mensonges immondes / Qu'on diffuse sur les ondes," and the initials JKK. A poetic snippet, sounding like the work of a novice creative writing student: "The dream of a wide world and in deep water where unclean lies are scattered on the waves." Much later I discovered that JKK stood for Joseph Kokou Koffigoh, a Togolese politician who had served as prime minister of Togo for three years in the 1990s. Driven from power, he believed himself to possess a lyric gift, and perhaps he had been present here, twenty years before, at the First Intercontinental Encounter for Humanity and Against Neoliberalism.

Another mural, *Vivan las Luchas de los Kurdos y los Zapatistas,* asserted solidarity with the Kurds, mustached Middle Easterners in kaffiyehs dancing around a fire with Zapatista women.

Another: rugged mountains with women's eyes peering from just beneath their summits, and the message, *Somos la Tierra Creciendo la Autonomía,* We Are the Land, Growing Autonomy.

A huge black slogan on the side of a big building was lettered *Oventic Sakamchen Territorio Libre,* flanked by masked figures. Near it was a portrait of Che Guevara and a series of upraised fists beside a fluttering dove of peace.

And more: women masked with bandannas, Zapatistas with rifles, Zapata himself looking benign under the brim of his vast sombrero, and another iconic one of his face with fierce eyes, brandishing a rifle, and still another, a whole door, his sombrero off, bandoliers of bullets crisscrossing his chest. The entire town was painted in bright primary colors: snails, rainbows, lovely children — some of the murals depicting men dancing across a wall, with the circus quality of Fernand Léger or the fanciful weightlessness, toy-like shapes, and floating figures of Marc Chagall, especially so in their aquatic colors.

It seemed that Oventic also had administrative offices for other *caracoles* in the vicinity, and these offices' exteriors were brilliantly painted. Apart from the portraits of Zapata, every face was masked, even the woman painted on the front wall of the Women's Office, the Oficina de Mujeres por la Dignidad: she was holding a flower in an upraised hand, steadying a rifle in the other, and had a child slung on her back—the child was masked. On one vivid wall a large brown snail was shown wearing a ski mask. It was a village not of faces, but of woolly balaclavas.

Beautiful paintings. They were not the indignant narrative murals of Rivera or Siqueiros, but decorative and cheery, the rifles like toys, the animals in them joyous, many of them bordered with flowers.

The masked man took me to the grave, under a tree, enclosed by an iron fence—I suppose to keep the goats or cows away.

"A special tree," I said, because that's what Juan had told me.

"It is a *zotzte*," the masked man said.

"What is its name in the Mexican idiom?" I asked.

"I only know its Tzotzil name. I don't know any other name."

With star-shaped reddish leaves and spreading boughs, it was an American sweetgum, prolific in the Deep South, so I discovered later.

On the concrete marker of the tomb were these words: *Compañero y Filósofo Don Luis Villoro Toranzo, 1922–2014 — Tu ejemplo siempre vivirá!*

I wrote this in my notebook, watched by the slender masked man and the two masked women, their arms still folded in postures of impatience.

"May I see more of Oventic?"

"If you wish," the masked man said.

Gesturing tentatively, I began to say, "Does it extend—"

Interrupting, he said, "It is everything that you can see," and his more expansive gesture took in the whole valley, the foothills beyond, and the mountain range in the distance. Then he became exasperated and said, "Go with her," indicating the stouter of the two women, and gave her an order.

As she led the way, I began to ask a question. I wanted to know how many people lived here.

"I don't speak Spanish," she said in mumbled Spanish.

We walked in silence from building to building, from mural to mural, downhill to where larger buildings loomed, the wider walls allowing for more ambitious murals. Even the grocery stores were painted, one with snails, another (*Tienda la Resistencia*) with Zapatista guerrillas. We passed an auditorium, a broad, one-story, flat-roofed structure as big as a high school gym. The entire floor was covered with rows of simple benches, hundreds of them. It was just a room, but cavernous, and the benches indicated that it might accommodate the whole community of Oventic. The many hard benches inspired in me two opposing thoughts: the prospect of a people's democracy, like a New England town meeting, and the dreary one of people having to sit for hours listening to speeches about political theory. Perhaps the room represented a mixture of both.

Farther down the hill I saw a terrace with a basketball court and what were obviously school buildings, because at the grassy periphery of the schoolyard, boys and girls, none of them masked, sat in groups or sprawled, chatting among themselves. It was a rest period for the hundred or so students, all of them neatly dressed, smiling when they saw me, but subdued in their greetings. They displayed none of the gusto, the shrieks and teasing, I'd seen among village schoolchildren elsewhere in Mexico. This reserve made them seem more watchful, and the intensity of gaze suggested intelligence.

I said hello. They said hello back. But none were prepared to hold a conversation with the gringo. It seemed obnoxious for me to intrude on them during their recess, and the aura that enclosed their whispers and their repose was peaceful: no music, no loud talk, no contention, a great calm, so odd yet so welcome in a schoolyard.

In contrast to their formality and restraint, a slogan on the wall of the school exhorted, RESISTIR ES EXISTIR. To Resist Is to Exist.

Surrounding the school, the village proper lay on side streets and lanes, small woodframe cottages and modest houses, most of them with vegetable gardens adjoining them. Deeper in the valley the communal gardens were well tended and fruitful. Another building housed a health clinic.

The masked woman trudged ahead, silently leading me, stopping when I stopped, moving on when I resumed walking.

I had never been in a place like this, a community that was a kind of sanctuary, wood-plank buildings elaborately painted, quiet except for birdsong. I saw no machines, no motorized vehicles, nothing new. The simplicity impressed me. The absence of modernity made it seem gentle and earnest—a community built by hand, carpentered houses, colorfully painted walls, and no sign (as in the other Mexico) of American products or American influence, an utter indifference to El Norte.

I was free to go anywhere in Oventic—the gardens, the chicken farm, the basketball court, and I could even buy a hand-knitted Zapatista mask in one of the shops. But it was impossible for me to engage anyone in conversation.

After my circuit of the place, I started up the hill. Passing another exuberantly painted building, I saw two men sitting on the porch, and recognized from their shirts that they were the men who had admitted me ("Sign your name"). But they were no longer masked. I stopped to say hello.

"No masks," I said.

They shrugged. Though it was a place painted in bright colors and slogans, those colors and slogans had to suffice for explanations. For the visitor, an un-Mexican atmosphere, almost of a cloister: no idle talk, no chitchat, with the subdued and serene mood of an ashram.

"But you were wearing them before."

This observation was met with silence. So I said, "Why?"

"For security," one of the men said.

I thanked him and walked away, grateful to be here, to have a glimpse into an important Zapatista *caracol.* It was a self-governing community of resistance, and to my question, "How can Mexican people protect themselves from criminals and crooked police and wicked government?," the answer was: In a Zapatista stronghold like Oventic, and there were thirty-seven more just like it all over Chiapas.

## Zapatistas

THE REBELLION, NOW thirty-five years old, had begun modestly, as dialogue, talk, and preparation in jungle villages, the cataloging of grievances. Then came the training of soldiers, the organization of communities, searching for common ground and unity—years of this in the depths of obscure settlements in the cloud forests and mists of the Lacandón jungle.

It was not Che Guevara marching with his men into Katanga, rousing the reluctant Baluba, and within weeks opening fire on Congolese troops and white mercenaries—and failing miserably. In Chiapas, the instigator was a scholar with a knack for writing parables, part of a delegation, who conducted seminars on the tactics of rebellion, and this went on peaceably for a decade.

"For ten years we prepared for the first few minutes of the year 1994," Subcomandante Marcos, the scholar-rebel, wrote in his introduction to *The Fire and the Word*, a detailed history of the Zapatista movement by Gloria Muñoz Ramírez, published in 2008. And Marcos had met receptive people: years before the Zapatistas entered the jungle, the peasants of Chiapas had openly objected to their being despised by the government and exploited by mining and logging interests. "When the Zapatista Army first came to our villages, around 1984, 1985, we had already taken part in peaceful struggles," Comandante Abraham says in Ramírez's book. "The people were already protesting against the government."

"The movements which work revolutions in the world are born out of the dreams and visions in a peasant's heart on a hillside," Joyce writes in *Ulysses*. "For them the earth is not an exploitable ground but the living mother."

The first Zapatistas to penetrate the Lacandón jungle with rebellious intentions, in late 1983, were six indigenous men and women from Chiapas, who camped under trees and in mountain meadows, keeping apart from traditional villages, naming their little band the Zapatista Army of National Liberation, the EZLN. Other like-minded Mexicans joined them a year later, including Rafael Guillén, who on rusticating himself changed his identity, adopting the nom de guerre Subcomandante Marcos. "Sub" because he saw himself as taking orders from the indigenous *comandantes* who'd preceded him.

These men and woman circulated among the villages, befriending the campesinos, educating and arming the farmers and woodcutters, who taught them the Tzotzil language and familiarized them with their beliefs. One central Tzotzil tenet affirmed harmony with the natural world, asserting that trees and bushes have souls, and every human has two souls.

One soul is in the body and the other resides elsewhere, in an animal — a possum, a monkey, a jaguar, a bat ("Tzotzil" comes from the Mayan word for bat) — the power animal and protective creature, a spirit companion. In the peaceable kingdom of Lacandona, Tzotzils could not harm an animal without harming themselves.

By degrees the Zapatistas won converts, and an army began to form. Ten years passed, and then the drama of confrontation began. Led by Marcos, the Zapatista army marched on San Cristóbal, electrifying the country and precipitating violence — the killing by the Mexican army of Zapatista soldiers, and later the massacre of civilians, mainly women and children, at a place called Acteal. In 2001, provoked by the intransigence of the Mexican government over a peace agreement, Marcos led his masked army north, two thousand miles by a roundabout route through the major cities of Mexico, and finally to the Zócalo in Mexico City, where, cheered by a crowd of hundreds of thousands, he raised his fist in the air and gave a rousing speech.

"We are here to shout for and to demand democracy, liberty, and justice," he declaimed. "The government thinks that today marks the end of an earthquake. They think that we are just a photograph, an anecdote, a spectacle. Those in high places know it but do not want to say it. After today, the people who are the color of the earth will never again be forgotten."

What those well-wishers in the Zócalo did not know was that this triumphant arrival had taken seventeen years of preparation. Only after three years, enduring the rigors of the rainy jungle, the insects, the mud and discomfort, were the Zapatistas invited to enter an indigenous village — a vivid example of how long it takes to *ganar la confianza*. It was not until 1989 that an army was raised, a core group of 1,300 soldiers, men and women. When the Mexican government began privatizing traditionally communal plots of agricultural land (known as *ejidos*), the indigenous people, landless and hungry, began to appeal to the Zapatista movement for relief. In 1993 the number of EZLN soldiers numbered about 3,000, and the high command of the EZLN approved a military offensive, deciding to come into the open.

The day the Zapatistas declared themselves was a significant one, January 1, 1994, the day the North American Free Trade Agreement went into effect. NAFTA was regarded by the Zapatistas (and many others) as exploitative, and disastrous for small farmers all over Mexico. On the morning of his appearance in San Cristóbal, Marcos said to some tourists, "We apologize for the inconveniences, but this is a revolution." He later clarified, saying it was a rebellion, not a revolution. "We are one people," he said, and repeated, "We are the color of the earth."

The armed uprising shocked Mexico, the more so because seven towns were occupied, including San Cristóbal and Ocosingo, and hundreds of ranches. Marcos climbed to the balcony of the municipal presidential building in San Cristóbal and read the First Declaration of the Lacandón Jungle.

"We are a product of 500 years of struggle," he said. "First against slavery, then during the War of Independence against Spain led by insurgents, then to avoid being absorbed by North American imperialism, then to promulgate our constitution and expel the French empire from our soil, and later the dictatorship of Porfirio Díaz denied us the just application of the Reform laws and the people rebelled and leaders like Villa and Zapata emerged, poor men just like us. We have been denied the most elemental preparation so they can use us as cannon fodder and pillage the wealth of our country. They don't care that we have nothing, absolutely nothing, not even a roof over our heads, no land, no work, no health care, no food nor education. Nor are we able to freely and democratically elect our political representatives, nor is there independence from foreigners, nor is there peace, nor justice for ourselves and our children. But today, we say, 'Ya basta!'—enough is enough!"

He was masked. Some people asked who he was. He said, "I am only a mestizo—a man of the people who struggles so that these terrible inequalities will no longer be suffered in our country. I am a combatant."

All of Marcos's listeners were attentive, many of them sympathetic, and even ones who were skeptical of his ability to change Mexico significantly were impressed by the inclusiveness of his message. One of my well-educated, middle-class students from the *taller*, Valerie Miranda, told me,

"I am not a big fan of Zapatistas, but I always admired the way Marcos unified Mexicans under one identity—mestizo. *'No hay ya el "ustedes" y el "nosotros," porque todos somos ya el color que somos de la tierra. El color de la tierra!'* [There's no more "you" or "us," because all of us are now the color we are, the color of the earth.] The land, the earth, is such a huge deal here. There's something beautiful in making it part of us."

The Mexican government's response to such idealistic sentiments was to send planes to Chiapas and drop bombs on indigenous communities. They killed 145 people. In the next few days there were pitched battles in the towns of Ocosingo and Altamiranos, thousands shooting, many casualties on each side. On January 12, 1994, a ceasefire was proposed, and by the end of the year the Zapatistas announced that they had created thirty-eight autonomous indigenous municipalities in Chiapas. In *The Zapatista Reader* (edited by Tom Hayden), Jorge Mancillas—a writer, activist, and neurobiologist—quotes a Zapatista soldier's response to being asked where the movement had arisen from: "We came from the depths of oblivion. From an abyss so deep, our voices could not be heard. So dark, we could not be seen. We emerged from the deepest depths of oblivion."

The Zapatista success, a result of shrewd organization, thoughtful planning, and rebel passion, alarmed the American investors in NAFTA to such an extent that, a year after Marcos declared his rebellion, Chase Manhattan Bank issued a memo on January 13, 1995, calling for the Mexican government "to eliminate the Zapatistas to demonstrate their effective control of the national territory and of security policy." The Mexican government responded to this memo by invading Zapatista territory and pushing twenty thousand peasants off their land.

When, thereafter, tens of thousands of Mexican troops occupied Chiapas, the Zapatistas proposed peace talks and met in a town near Oventic to thrash out the details. This effort culminated in the San Andrés Accords on indigenous rights and culture, "outlining a program for land reform, indigenous autonomy and cultural rights."

As a delaying tactic, the Mexican government niggled over the accords, disputing parts of it related to issues of justice and democracy, and they ultimately succeeded in getting what they wanted—an impasse. Historically, the Mexican government and the drug cartels have often resorted to mass killing to solve complex problems—the massacre option. And so, in December 1997, paramilitaries linked to the governing PRI party descended on the Chiapas town of Acteal (about twelve miles north of San Cristóbal), surprising some people praying at a shrine. This was a community group calling themselves Las Abejas, the Bees, who supported the aims of the Zapatistas.

The intruders attacked, slaughtering 45 of them with machetes and bullets, all indigenous campesinos, 21 women, 15 children, and 9 men. Hundreds were wounded in six hours of sniper fire. Soon after, about 150 foreign observers who were gathering information on the massacre were expelled from Mexico. More murders in the ensuing years culminated in the two-week, 2,000-mile Zapatista march to Mexico City, where 250,000 people cheered Marcos in supporting the peace accords.

One of the observers in Mexico City was José Saramago, the Nobel Prize–winning Portuguese novelist. He wrote, "The Zapatistas covered their faces to make themselves visible and now in effect we have finally seen them."

"Here we are. We are the forgotten heart of the country, and we represent the dignity of rebellion," Marcos said from his podium in the Plaza de la Constitutión—the Zócalo, the center of the city, the heart of Mexico.

A few days before his speech, Marcos had given an interview to the French paper *Le Monde*. "This is not Marcos's march nor the EZLN's," he said. "It is the march of the poor, the march of all the Indian peoples. It's intended to show that the days of fear are over." It was an ethnic rebellion, he said. "Of all the people in Mexico, the Indians are the most forgotten."

Marcos became a familiar voice, if not a familiar face. His favorite authors, he said, were Cervantes, Lewis Carroll, García Márquez, Brecht, Borges, García Lorca, and Shakespeare. *Hamlet* and *Macbeth*, he added, were essential studies in power. He was not interested in maintaining control as an army, explaining, "The military man is an absurdity, because he must always rely on a weapon to be able to convince others that his ideas are the ones that should be followed." He went on, "Our movement has no future if it is military. If the EZLN perpetuates itself as a military organization it is bound to fail."

As for his mask: "It's about being anonymous, not because we fear for ourselves but rather so they cannot corrupt us." He also said, "We are the Zapatistas, the smallest of the small, those who cover their faces to be seen, the dead that die to live."

NAFTA, he said, was a tool of the sort of globalization that he characterized as a sinister power grab by international corporations to subvert governments all over the world. "The world's new masters have no need to govern directly. National governments take on the role of running things on their behalf. This is what the new order means—unification of the world into one single market. States are simply enterprises with managers in the guise of governments, and the new regional alliances bear more of a resemblance to shopping malls than to political federations. The unification produced by neoliberalism is economic: in the giant planetary hypermarket it is only commodities that circulate freely, not people."

Corporate interests connive with third-world tyrants to supply goods and services and raw materials. The United States and Europe and China—everywhere: "the globalization of exploitation."

It was what I had seen on the border, the clusters of foreign-owned factories, exploiting their workers in distressed communities to save money and increase profits. In a prescient essay, Marcos wrote in 1997, "As a world system, neoliberalism is a new war for the conquest of territory. The ending of the Third World War—meaning the Cold War—in no sense means that the world has gone beyond the bi-polar and found stability under the domination of a new victor. Because while there was certainly a defeat (of the socialist camp), it is hard to say who won . . . The defeat of the 'evil empire' has opened up new markets, and the struggle over them is leading to a New World War, the Fourth."

As Apple Corporation was expanding in China, and Microsoft in India, and textile and appliance companies were setting up factories in Mexico, South Korea, and Thailand, Marcos was writing, "Vast territories, wealth, and above all, a huge and available workforce lie waiting for the world's new master but, while there is only one position as master available, there are many aspiring candidates."

In his determination to be independent, and no one's case or client, Marcos has also railed against the paternalism of many charities and NGOs. In the "Thirteenth Estela," of the Zapatista Calendar of Resistance, in 2003, he denounced the sort of aid in the form of charity and handouts advocated by celebrities and church groups, and "a more sophisticated handout — the practice of some NGOs and international organizations [that] decide what the communities need . . . without even consulting them." How they "impose not only certain projects but also the times and ways of implementing them. Imagine the exasperation of a community that needs drinking water, and what they get is a library, one that needs a school for children, and gets a course on herbal medicine."

This clear thinking resonated with me. All my adult life, beginning with my teaching in Africa as a Peace Corps volunteer, I have tried to understand how to reconcile the nature of poverty, the role of charity, the intervention of aid organizations, and the maneuverings of governments, especially those in the third world. After repeated visits to Africa over fifty years, I concluded that foreign aid as it is conventionally practiced is essentially a failure, futile in relieving poverty, and often harmful, relieving the ills of a few at the expense of the many. Most charities are diabolically self-interested, proselytizing evangelists, tax-avoidance scammers with schemes to buff up the image of the founder — often someone in disgrace or mired in scandal or obscenely rich. Claiming to be apolitical, such charities allow authoritarian governments and kleptocracies to go on existing, because the charities do the governments' work, and in doing so, prevent oppressed people from understanding how they are being exploited.

The best example I have seen close up is the presence of China in Africa, offering rogue aid to despots in return for valuable commodities. The United States once did this in small and subtle ways; China now does it conspicuously and with impunity. When I took my Africa trips for *Dark Star Safari* and *The Last Train to Zona Verde* I saw how with backhanders or huge loans China bought dictatorships in Zimbabwe, Kenya, Sudan, and Angola, in order to obtain ivory, gold, bauxite, oil, and much else, leaving the countries in deep and sometimes unpayable debt—indeed debt slavery. But the United States still does the same in many countries, taking advantage of a government's indifference to human rights abuses.

This is the reason Apple (dodging taxes, exploiting Chinese workers, pretending to care) is a trillion-dollar company, one of China's best friends. When someone like Bill Gates or Tim Cook makes noises about helping the poor, while conniving with China to use cheap labor and turning a blind eye to China's human rights brutalities (a million Uighurs imprisoned to be brainwashed in Xinjiang, the persecution of gay men and women, the suppression of news, and other abuses), you just want to laugh. In the years Bill Clinton sold the American people on NAFTA, he did not say how it would remove manufacturing from communities in the United States (the many instances I recounted in *Deep South*), nor did he seem to know or care how it would destroy the lives of farmers in Mexico with genetically modified crops, as I heard from Francisco Toledo's organization in Oaxaca.

It took me years to see that charities and NGOs are profitable businesses, many of them subversive ones. The average Peace Corps volunteer gains greatly in experience by living for two years in, say, an African dictatorship, but the result is demoralizing rather than uplifting for the citizens of the host country: in my experience the Peace Corps volunteers' students, instead of becoming teachers themselves, immigrate to Europe or the US. Subcomandante Marcos's term for this seemingly well-intentioned but ultimately self-serving effort is neoliberalism, which in the United States is as rampant among Democrats as Republicans.

Another humane aspect of the Zapatista struggle that has annoyed many other rebel groups is their refusal to engage in the killing of ordinary citizens. Bombings by the Irish Republican Army—cheered and often financed by some Irish Americans—were condemned by the Zapatistas as savage and inhumane, and of course the targeting of civilians is a grave breach of the Geneva Conventions, punishable as a war crime. (I recalled that whenever a bomb went off in a market square in Ulster, killing bystanders, either the IRA or the Ulster Defence Association took credit for it and crowed, or said nothing and let the innocent bleed to death.) And the same goes for the brutalities of ISIS and Al Qaeda.

As for Basque separatists and their bombing campaigns in Spain, Marcos wrote in 2002, "We consider the struggle of the Basque people for sovereignty just and legitimate, but neither this noble cause, nor any other, can justify the sacrifice of civilian lives. Not only does it not lead to any political gain, even if it did, the human cost is unpayable. We condemn military actions that hurt civilians. And we condemn them equally, whether they come from ETA [Basque nationalists] or from the Spanish state, from Al Qaeda or George W. Bush, from Israelis or Palestinians, or anyone who under different names or initials, claiming state, ideological or religious reasons, makes victims of children, women, old people and men who have nothing to do with the matter."

This is the clearest possible statement of the dignity of rebellion and the limits of resistance, a rational way of looking at the world, and a means to go about fixing it: "to build a world in which many worlds fit." In what has been described as the world's first postmodern revolution, Marcos's temperament—and actions—were those of a pacifist. I admired him for valuing the lives of civilians, I identified with him in his passion for writing, I was enlightened by his parables—the rabbit, the fox, Durito the beetle. I was in awe of his stamina in existing in one of the most inhospitable jungles on earth, and I was happy to be invited to the Zapatista event.


## *The Road to Nueva Maravilla*

WITH TIME TO kill in San Cristóbal, I made a tour of the restaurants; I sat in the cafés and drank Chiapas coffee or sipped mezcal; I wandered around the market, where women in the black goat-hair skirts that I'd seen in Chamula, and Indians from nearby valleys, were hawking their harvests of unfamiliar fruit: orange-fleshed mamey, papausa—a small scaly ball with sweet pinkish pulp—huayas, pear-sized guavas, the prickly pear they call *tuna* (but tuna fish is *atún*), the bitter xoconostle, granadilla, and mangoes. The altitude made me trembly and mostly abstemious. I concentrated on *caldos*—soups—bread soup, corn soup, tortilla soup, posole and the thick Chiapas stew, *caldo tlalpeño*.

One of those dinners I shared with Juan Villoro, who said, "You know the presidential election is coming up in July?" (We were speaking in April 2018.) "One of Marcos's proposals is to put up a Zapatista candidate for president. Marcos has the idea of supporting an indigenous woman, Marichuy Patricio."

"Does she have a chance?"

"No, it's a symbolic gesture," Juan said. "But she's a good person and she'd make a great president. You'll meet her."

Marichuy was the name she was known by, but her full name was María de Jesús Patricio Martínez. She was in her fifties, from a Nahua community in Tuxpan, Jalisco. Fluent in Nahuatl, trained as a traditional healer, she had her own clinic. She was prominent as an activist for the cause of indigenous people to the extent that the Zapatistas, who normally distanced themselves from Mexican elections, saying they were a sham, supported Marichuy's candidacy, representing the National Indigenous Congress, in the coming election. To appear on the ballot, she'd need to collect almost 900,000 signatures.

"What about Obrador?" I asked, because Andrés Manuel López Obrador was said to be a man of the people and also the most popular candidate.

"The Zapatistas have objections to him," Juan said. And he listed them: Obrador had a lot of former members of the discredited ruling party, the PRI, on his team. One of them, Esteban Moctezuma, his secretary of education, had been in charge of the persecution of the Zapatistas, and though he'd also participated in secret peace talks with them, he had issued an arrest order for Marcos. Obrador would not change much; the most he'd do is enhance the same economic system, with a few popular corrections. Obrador had no program to address the Indian communities—worse than that, he had approved economic strategies that would destroy large indigenous territories.

So much for Obrador—who later went on to win the election.

As I was debating whether to go zip-lining or on a hike, take a day trip to the ruins at Palenque or a drive to Ocosingo, I got the word from Juan.

"An unmarked white van will be parked at the Zócalo end of Francisco Madero at three o'clock," he said. "The traffic is always bad, and the roads are terrible. It might take an hour to get to the Conversatorio in Nueva Maravilla."

The anonymous van was at the appointed spot. I got in and introduced myself to the others inside: an older woman lawyer, two men — a professor and a philosopher — and a gentle middle-aged Indian woman, who said, "I am Marichuy" — the presidential candidate.

But the van lurching on the bumpy road prevented any further conversation, as we passed through the barrios — La Hormiga (the Ant), Progreso, America Libre — to La Cronistas Street, turned into Los Profesores, and on through narrowing side streets until we reached Calle Jon Chamula, hardly a street, potholed and badly paved to the end. This was the colonia of Nueva Maravilla. The van paused at a gate in a high fence, bearing a sign indicating that this was the Zapatista institute, UniTierra, low yellow buildings with red-tiled roofs and murals.

Subdued but watchful, the attendees circulated among stands selling food or Zapatista emblems. They were all ages, some wearing ski masks or balaclavas, others looking professorial, still more in the casual clothes of college students, who I guessed were undergraduates here.

Marichuy was greeted affectionately by groups of indigenous women in embroidered blouses and full skirts, and they escorted her toward a building that proved to be the auditorium.

Juan called out to me, and I joined him to register.

"*Colectivo?*" the woman at the registration desk asked.

It usually meant a bus or taxi, but here it meant the political group to which I might belong.

"None," I said, and I was assigned a badge, the space for my *colectivo* left blank. Juan and I entered the building, taking seats up front, near the stage, where Marichuy and some other women were already seated. The auditorium was nearly full, with perhaps four hundred murmuring people. Two large murals at the back of the stage were brightly lit, one showing an indigenous woman in a white blouse and apron, kneeling with her hands clasped, the other a dark-skinned man staring across the top of his mask, a red bandanna covering the lower portion of his face.

"This man over there," Juan said of an elderly Mexican man wearing a beret. "That is Pablo González Casanova, a sociologist and radical reformer. He was president of the National University of Mexico in the 1970s. But he was too radical for them. And he's still radical. How old do you think he is?"

"No idea."

"He's ninety-six," Juan whispered. "An *hombre de juicio*. Just like you, *querido amigo*."

Nothing happened for about twenty minutes, during which the talking in the auditorium produced a dull, engine-like howl you hear in most theaters before the curtain rises.

Then, in an instant, there was a squeezing of the air, a hush, then silence.

It was hard to imagine a great hall of chattering people suddenly ceasing—and intensifying the hush was a concentration of everyone's attention on the right-hand side of the stage, where five masked men had mounted the stairs and were taking seats.

Four of the masked men were hardly five feet tall in their boots, gnome-like in thick black jackets, a few with peasants' black wide-brimmed hats jammed on their heads, the others with brimmed or beaked camouflage headgear—bush hats. The fifth man was stout and much taller than the others, also dressed in black. What I took to be an armband was a torn sleeve around his biceps, his red shirt showing through. His brown cloth cap, a red star sewn to the front, was sensationally crushed and faded. Only his eyes showed in his mask, which was not the "ski mask" I had expected, but the sort of hood I associated with executioners in wicked folktales—the beefy masked man holding a cleaver-like ax. But this man held a notebook. Inserted in his mask at the level of his mouth was a briar pipe. His arms were heavy with his black sleeves, his back and shoulders were thick, and he was half turned away, talking with his men, who looked even smaller in their chairs, their arms folded across their chests, listening intently. This big man was Subcomandante Marcos.

It was not the man but the mask that silenced the big hall. "Everything behind the mask is mysterious," Elias Canetti writes in *Crowds and Power.* "When the mask is taken seriously . . . no one must know what lies behind it. A mask expresses much, but hides even more. Above all it *separates.* Charged with a menace, which must not be precisely known — one element of which, indeed, is the fact that it cannot be known — it comes close to the spectator, but remains clearly separated from him. It threatens him with the secret dammed up behind it."

In the dead silence the whole room seemed to be holding its breath. There was no applause, not a murmur. Marcos seated himself and opened and flattened the notebook. There was apprehension, as when a whale surfaces and rises — as in *Moby-Dick,* where Melville speaks of the lovely tail and body of the whale and, "Thou shalt see my back parts, my tail, he seems to say, but my face shall not be seen. But I cannot completely make out his back parts; and hint what he will about his face, I say again he has no face."

"*Compañeros y compañeras,* brothers and sisters," he began, speaking out of his mask. "Welcome to our Conversatorio." And he glanced at Juan Villoro and welcomed him with an unusual legal term, as "*mi hermano bajo protesta*" — my undercover brother.

He spoke easily, not reading but as though in conversation, using an informal chatting shorthand, saying *compas* instead of *compañeros.* But this was so sudden — his bursting on the stage — his physical presence overwhelmed his words. We were not listening at first; we were watching. And this, I realized, was the aura of a charismatic figure with a rich history. The dazzle of one's first encounter — mine, at any rate — was deafening.

"Let me introduce Marichuy," he said, "our sister, our healer from Tuxpan," and as he spoke, praising her, the impassive middle-aged woman in her embroidered blouse sat with her hands folded, staring at us.

Still seated, Marichuy began to speak of her bid to be president of Mexico — her struggle to obtain signatures, how the system worked against her. I was lost in the details of this, but it seemed a certain computer program or a specific phone was necessary in order for someone to register a signature online. I also thought how most of the telephone accounts in Mexico were the property of one man, Carlos Slim, who owned the monopoly Telmex. Marichuy said she had gotten 300,000 signatures.

"Not enough," said Marcos, interrupting, not ranting but speaking reasonably, "and you know why? Because the system is rigged."

His remarks—asides, really—were so offhand I could barely understand them. But his eyes, flashing in the slit of his mask, were expressive, active, readable, like those of a Muslim woman in a yashmak. "She is a healer, a traditional *curandera*," he said at one point. "She healed her mother." These were interjections. "She belongs to the town of Guadalajara—they recognize traditional healing."

To loud applause, Marichuy sat down, and Marcos called out, "Where's Alicia? Alicia, please stand up."

A young woman sitting near me at the front stood, smiling shyly.

"She is a great *compa*. They were going to put her in jail. But she fooled them. She is going to college instead."

As Alicia sat, Marcos resumed, talking about the system that had defeated Marichuy. And perhaps because he was masked, preventing him from showing any facial expressions, his gestures were expressive, his hands and arms chopping and slicing, pointing with his tobacco pipe, his tone cajoling, beseeching, sounding at times like someone bargaining.

"They think we're romantics," he said, reading quotations from political journalists. "Zapatistas—romantics? Not at all. We represent the forgotten people, the heart of the country. Not so, Obrador. And here is an example of the schizophrenia of Mexican political power," he went on, reading. "Here, Obrador says that Marichuy shouldn't be a candidate—that she'd be a bad candidate. And later on, after Obrador is sure she doesn't have enough signatures, when she is no longer a threat to him, he says how she would have been a true candidate of the people. Hypocrisy!"

He spoke at length and fluently about women. "Women make the decisions, women are the backbone of our cause," but, he said, "I don't know what goes on among women behind closed doors. Maybe they get manicures and talk about Hegel's dialectic!"

The laughter in the hall encouraged him further, and he seemed to be enjoying himself, in full flow, a torrent of denunciations and asides. I found it so hard to concentrate I could not take notes.

"Never mind the Right, never mind the conservatives," he was saying. "We know what they're going to say. But the voices of the Left were the strongest against Marichuy's candidacy. We had no idea how many people would resist her — people who should have known better, who should have supported her. She's indigenous and a hard worker and mother, they say. But they refuse to talk about her as a wife" — because her role as a diligent, indigenous mother was regarded by macho Mexicans as a hindrance, but being a strong wife amply qualified her. "Seeing Marichuy as a wife, young women no longer regard the family as an impediment to the struggle. Being a wife in a strong family would make any woman a better president.

"What does she have to do to qualify for president — how do we change? What is enough?" he asked, his voice piercing the hall. "The forty-three students being killed were not enough. The women who have disappeared were not enough. We would need a hundred thousand people dead in the streets to have enough visibility, so that people would finally say, 'Let her run. Let poor little [*pobrecita*] Marichuy run.'"

He spoke of the dynamics between men and women. "Now I'm going to speak badly of women," he said sarcastically, and went on to describe powerful, clear-thinking women whose fate in life is having to deal with egotistical, manipulative men. And with a sort of play-acting, he teased the youths in his movement.

"Young Zapatistas — you know what they like?" He mumbled inaudibly into the microphone. "They like" mumble-mumble. "They really like" mumble-mumble. Finally, with reluctance, "They like — reggaeton. There, you made me say it!"

Annoyed, as any sixty-one-year-old freedom fighter would be, having liberated a Mexican state and then being forced to listen to the musical preferences of this freedom, a squashy combination of Jamaican reggae, Puerto Rican hip-hop, and the songs of Daddy Yankee (Ramón Luis Ayala), self-crowned King of Reggaeton, among them the hit "Despacito."

Marcos stood and called to the back of the auditorium, "Now I'd like to introduce our *compañeras*. Come here!"

For the next ten minutes or more, a hundred women in knitted hood-like masks walked slowly down the narrow side aisle in single file. In contrast to their masks, they wore frilly, lacy blouses and woven wool skirts. All attention was on them, the strange beauty of so many masked women in a silent procession—masks, masks, masks. I thought of what José Donoso had written: "Behind the face of the mask there is never a face. There is always another mask. The masks are you, and the mask below the mask is also you ... All different masks serve a purpose, you use them because they help you to live ... You have to defend yourself."

Glancing back at the stage, crowded with masked women, I saw Marcos raising his arms in an "I give up!" gesture of helplessness and comic exasperation. With that, his men clustered about him and he swiftly vanished by a rear door, leaving his pipe on the table.

## *Compañero Escritor*

MORE CHIAPANECA SOUP, more mezcal, a visit to the cathedral of San Cristóbal, a morning spent making notes for my talk, and then a whisper from Juan Villoro that the white van would be waiting, this time at a different location. Marichuy was at the appointed spot, the writer Cristina Rivera Garza and her husband, and some others. We slid into the van and headed anonymously down the cobbled streets, past the tourists and around the Parque Principal, going north, the barrios growing poorer with each mile.

I talked a bit with Cristina Rivera Garza, a distinguished Mexican American author of many short stories and novels, including *No One Will See Me Cry*, a multilayered historical novel of sleuthing and identity, which I'd read in Mexico City. She told me she was living in Houston, but had taken a similar trip to mine along the border. Having been born in the border town of Matamoros, she confirmed my feeling that there was a *frontera* culture, with the added complexity of members of the same family (such as hers) living on both sides.

"I've driven up and down the border," I said. "I've crossed a lot of borders in my life, but never one like the Mexican border. The little bridges that cross from Texas. The simple stroll from Douglas to Agua Prieta. The doorway in the iron fence in Nogales—that's like Alice going down the rabbit hole."

Cristina agreed, and in the jolting van told me of her experiences on the border. A reliable witness, she had once told an interviewer, "I am interested in borders, borders of all kinds, geopolitical borders and conceptual borders, borders of gender and genre, borders between life and death. I spend most of my time thinking of ways to cross such borders. How come we are allowed, even invited at times, to walk over some of them but are prevented from even approaching others?"

Sentiments I agreed with. Soon the van was headed through the high gate of the UniTierra, to the Conversatorio, and I was summoned by Juan.

"Compañero Manuel wants to talk with you," Juan said, indicating a man sitting on a bench on the veranda of one of the low, tile-roofed buildings.

He was an older man, probably sixty, in the plain dark clothes and combat cap of a Zapatista, but he was not masked. None of the men or women had new uniforms, but they wore old patched clothes with dignity and panache, and this being chilly Chiapas, they were all dressed warmly. Compañero Manuel greeted me with a hug and asked, "Are you ready, *compañero?*"

"I've got a little talk prepared," I said.

"In Spanish or in English?"

"I'm starting off in Spanish as an introduction, then will talk in English."

He called to a slender fellow in a vest. "This is Alejandro. He'll translate for you."

I shook hands with Alejandro and asked, "Will the Comandante be there when I speak?"

"We don't know," Compañero Manuel said, wrinkling his nose. "Maybe. Maybe not. We don't know his movements."

The auditorium was full, as on the previous day, but when the program began, Comandante Marcos was not onstage, nor were any of his entourage. The opening session was devoted to documentaries made recently in Mexico.

The first film was *Tobias*, written and directed by two young Mexican filmmakers, Francisca D'Acosta and Ramiro Pedraza. This portrait of a village boy with ambitions of traveling with his school basketball team to a tournament in Barcelona was about much more than basketball. The team's first challenge is to raise the money to take the trip. This accomplished, Tobias, who has never left his village in the Isthmus, undergoes a cleansing by a *curandero*—the egg ceremony I'd seen in Chamula—and then solicits travel advice from the village elders. Tobias's mother is as key a figure to his fulfilling his ambitions as the mothers in *Hoop Dreams*, a powerful American documentary it somewhat resembled.

In all the preliminary basketball games, the boys are outmatched physically—they're small and skinny village kids playing against taller urban athletes. But they shoot the ball accurately, and they are nimble enough to dribble around the other players. They make it to Barcelona, win one game, lose another, and are soon back in Mexico, grateful to be home, having had a glimpse of the world. A good-hearted film, *Tobias* is an intimate look at village life and beyond, through the eyes of a boy determined to excel in his sport and make his family proud. But it also showed the emphatic isolation of a poor Mexican village, and this seemed to recommend it to the approving Zapatistas.

*Somos Lengua* (*We Are Language*) was a movie about rap music in Mexico, made by forty-year-old Kyzza Terrazas. I found it a shocking film, not just for its language, as brutal in Mexican rap lingo as in American, but in its atmosphere of cruelty, the slums and tenements of Mexican cities, the mean streets of Guadalajara and Torreón and Escobedo, terrifying stories of arrests and brawls, the miseries and infernalities of poverty. The rappers were evangelical in their belief that their music was liberating, that it bestowed self-esteem and pride. "Rap is a way out of this terrible life," one rapper asserts, with the repeated Zapatista message of "the power we get through words . . . to write so that death doesn't have the last word."

It seemed so odd to be watching the Mexican rappers, foulmouthed and defiant, in the mode of American rap and hip-hop. I disliked the cacophonous music, I found the grunted lyrics excruciating, but Terrazas, concentrating on the lives of the rappers, the struggle and the day-to-day, made me care.

When the lights came up, Comandante Marcos was seated onstage, some of his men in chairs behind him, two masked women at the table, and seeing him, the crowd in the auditorium became watchful and fell silent.

At that point the Comandante beckoned to me, calling out, *"Venga, Compañero Escritor!"*

I walked to the edge of the stage, where he met me at the top of the steps and gave me a hug, embracing me with peculiar force, and this shared energy eased me. I had been apprehensive—a stranger in Chiapas, a visible gringo among the Tzotzils and Tzeltales, an old man in street clothes and a Stetson among the masked Zapatistas. The hug calmed me in a way that went beyond helpful reassurance. A hug has been proven to produce a neurochemical called oxytocin, which flashes through your body, warming it and healing it, making the hugged one feel safe. The Comandante did not release me immediately, as I expected. He held me and said, "Welcome."

Perhaps I was projecting, dazzled to be meeting a man I regarded as a hero. In her incomplete but perceptive book *Survivors in Mexico,* published after her death, Rebecca West, reflecting on Trotsky in Coyoacán, writes, "The men who excite adoration, who are what is called natural leaders (which means really that people feel an unnatural readiness to follow them), are usually empty. Human beings need hollow containers in which they can place their fantasies and admire them, just as they need flower vases if they are to decorate their homes with flowers."

Napoleon was one of these, she wrote, a man who exhibited "no outward signs of having any private thoughts or feelings that would give the slightest pleasure to any stranger." But Leon Trotsky was exceptional, not an empty vessel, but "one of the great men within whom there was something resembling the inner vexations suffered by us lesser animals." I felt the Comandante was another exception, not merely because he was a brilliant tactician and advocate for indigenous rights, but because he seemed to me a gifted writer who was able to convey the *gusto* of his inner life and the sinuous dialectics of his thinking. In the progress of the struggle—even masked and secluded in the jungle—in his prolific essays and updates, his parables and denunciations, he had grown from the masked rebel on horseback to a philosopher-leader, uneasy in exciting adoration and always deflecting such attention to the men and women in the Zapatista movement.

I wasn't projecting. I knew him, as I knew other writers, by his work. He was about my height, but bulky under his black jacket, with a strong grip. He introduced me to his *compas,* six of them today, whispering to me each man's name. They were small, all of them heavily masked, their jackets zipped to their chin, hats pulled tight.

Their hands were the hands of manual laborers, farmers, stonemasons, ditch diggers, lumberjacks, and plowmen, hands scaly and hard, stiff fingers, more like tree roots. They were not the hands of commissars or bureaucrats. They held on, gripping my soft writer's hands with their crusty workers' hands. Their strong handshakes made the men seem bigger somehow, their grip conveying power.

These impressions were vivid because I was so self-conscious of being out of my element, quaking a little, nerving myself for what was to come.

When we were seated at a long table on the stage, the Comandante addressed the audience, saying casually, "Thanks for showing us your films. I remember how in the 1980s we went from village to village in the jungle, showing movies with a small camera, and then later we used a TV set and a VHS. Kyzza came to us when he was young, and now here he is, showing us his film. What we'd like is a film about us sometime, and maybe these documentarians can do it." Then he turned to me and said, "And now it is my pleasure to welcome *Compa Paul—Compañero Escritor,* our visitor from the United States."

"*Muchas gracias, Comandante,*" I said, and continued in Spanish. "Brothers, sisters, *compañeros, compañeras*—Zapatista friends—thank you for your friendly welcome. I am speaking in your idiom, but it must be obvious to you that I am a poor speaker. I'm sorry to say that I speak Spanish like a child. On the other hand, I speak English like a normal *gabacho.* I think I write English like a sensible person, but here's the paradox. I dream like a genius!" This was a version of something Nabokov once said about himself, and it seemed to resonate, eliciting a little laughter.

"To you, I am sure I seem like just another gringo. But in fact I am also part indigenous — the proudest part of my secret being. My paternal grandmother was a Menominee, a nation of people who lived in what is now Wisconsin, a people who lived in that region for six thousand years. This knowledge helps me understand your struggle a little better, because the indigenous people of the United States have been massacred and cheated and pushed to the margins ever since the first colonizers arrived on the continent. I share your defiance, and for this I am happy to be among you."

I slid aside the papers on which I'd written this, and resumed in English, stopping after every few sentences for Alejandro to translate.

Many years ago, I said, wishing to discover more about the world, I'd become a teacher in Africa, in a remote school. At that time, many African countries were in revolt, rejecting colonialism and becoming independent. I was just a schoolteacher in the bush, learning the language. At the same time, Che Guevara had arrived to launch an offensive in the Congo against Katanga separatists. The record of his experience he put in his book *Congo Diary,* which he called "the history of a failure."

His insurgency was a failure, I said, because he did not spend much time in the Congo, he had a slender grasp of Swahili, and he did not understand the innate caution that prevailed among people in an African village. Che wrote of how the Cubans felt superior, "like people who had come to give advice." He had found himself not among revolutionaries, but among con- servative-thinking, or at least cautious, subsistence farmers and fishermen. Even the young African combatants who had been trained as guerrillas in Maoist China were reluctant to fight on their arrival in Che's camp. They had been away, they were homesick, and they wanted to go back to their villages, eat their traditional food, and see their families. Che was baffled by their sentimental nostalgia for village life and their lack of revolutionary zeal, as he wrote in his dispirited book, an essential guide to avoiding mistakes in a country not your own.

The Zapatistas had spent ten years in the jungle, I went on, not fighting but making friends, trying to understand the grievances of the indigenous people, and by degrees creating an army of rebels. The Zapatistas' patience, their humanity, and their resolve, I felt, were their most admirable qualities.

I then talked about my Mexico trip, how I'd driven from my home in Massachusetts, how the road I'd set out on had led me here to Nueva Maravilla — we were at two ends of the same road. I'd also traveled the length of the border, looking closely at both sides: the fields on the US side where Mexican migrants worked for low wages, the factories on the Mexican side where Mexicans from the poorer parts of Mexico were employed, also poorly paid. This was the blighting effect of NAFTA, which boasted of raising people's standard of living while at the same time exploiting them.

"I have seen this with my own eyes," I said. "For the quarter million people living in one colonia in Ciudad Juárez, working in the factories and living in the slums, there is only one high school. But for about fifty families in Oventic, there are two schools. Oventic is a great model for educating and enlightening a community, a peaceful place as well as a dynamic one, with a human scale, beautiful and productive and most of all self-sufficient."

I finished by saying how vulnerable Mexicans seemed to me, how unprotected, and how impressed I was by their bravery, and the ways in which they sustained themselves through work and family, without much help from the government.

Slightly numb from giving this little testimonial, I turned to the Comandante and thanked him again for allowing me to share these experiences of traveling through Mexico.

In the informal style that characterized the Conversatorio, he said (Alejandro translating for me), "We appreciate your being here. It is very important for us to think that we are not alone — that we have friends not only in Mexico, but also in other countries. I don't hold your being an American against you. We want friends of all races, from all countries . . ."

Then, more rapidly—faster than I could take notes—he talked about isolation, the seclusion of living deep in the mountains of southeastern Mexico, in the jungle where it usually rained. Because of that isolation, the Zapatistas needed friends from all over. He indicated me, the filmmakers, Juan Villoro, and the philosopher Pablo Casanova, whom he complimented on his great age and his passion.

"*Compa Escritor*," he went on, speaking directly to me but more slowly, "we're glad you're here. But even more, we want you to return. I appreciate what this *compa* said about Oventic—how it is a model, with good schools and a clinic and gardens. That's why it's important that the *compa* returns." And, his voice rising to a slight peroration, "We want to be a movement with no borders!"

This was cheered by the audience. He waited for the noise to subside, playing with his pipe.

"*Compa Escritor*—come back," he said. "Many people travel here with revolutionary intentions, and then what happens? They become courtesans of politics, conservative in their thinking. Come back, *compa*, come back. We want you to keep having a relationship with us. We don't want to be merely an anecdote in your recollection of being here."

He then opened a folder, took out a sheaf of papers, and read a short, episodic story he'd written about the experiences of a rabbit traveling among other animals.

Although Alejandro was ably translating, I was distracted by the Comandante's proscription about not wanting to be merely an anecdote, because it is in the nature of travel to collect and value telling anecdotes. Yet this experience was something else, a clarification of much that I had seen in my traveling life, an elaboration of the challenges of poverty and development, the curse of bad government and predatory corporations, the struggle of people living on the plain of snakes who wish to choose their own destiny.

Being welcomed in this way by the Zapatistas—embraced, accepted, listened to—I felt I had been admitted to a band of brothers and sisters who had resisted all that was negative and destructive in Mexican life. They had built their movement upon everything that was humane and enduring in the traditions of these indigenous people, the world's aristocrats. It was not a back-to-nature movement or a violent upheaval but a reminder of what Mexico needed: an example to the whole country, and the world, of the power of resistance and the assertion of human rights.

As impressed as I was to meet the Comandante (El Sup, as he is sometimes known), I was just as reassured to make the acquaintance of Pablo González Casanova, the sociologist and historian. Juan Villoro had mentioned that Casanova was "too radical" for UNAM, Mexico's national university, and had resigned. I asked Casanova about this, and he went into more detail. He'd been the director of the Center for Interdisciplinary Research in Sciences and Humanities at UNAM. When, in 2000, a detachment of federal police stormed onto the campus to arrest students who were striking, he strenuously objected, condemned the police action, and resigned his post. He had written many books, including one considered a classic, *Democracy in Mexico*, described by a Mexican critic as "a pioneer in the research on democratic processes in Mexico, constituting the first systematic study on the structure of power, based on empirical research and animated by a critical theory."

Casanova was genial, approachable in conversation yet silent, and attentive at the meeting—held in high regard by the Zapatistas for his lifelong defense of indigenous people. He was not by nature a bivouacker in the jungle, yet he made no fuss about traveling from Mexico City to Chiapas to spend days in an obscure location, in a hard chair, listening to speeches and debates and watching films. Seated near him, I could see he was nearly always nodding in appreciation, his face blazing with intelligence, fully engaged, an activist, an optimist, a visionary, and still radical at ninety-six—a great example to me.

Marcos stood and asked Casanova to please join him in standing. The old man smiled and doffed his cap, rose from his chair and stood soldierly straight.

"For your work, your support, and your guidance," Marcos said, "I appoint you to the rank of *comandante* [in the EZLN]."

Hearing this, all the Zapatistas on the stage and in the audience stood and saluted him, their eyes shining in the slits of their black masks, and Casanova saluted back in acknowledgment.

This demonstration of respect and admiration thrilled me, and gave me the gift of hope that I might have twenty more years. I felt this widely read man must have known in his old age the lines of T. S. Eliot in "East Coker" ("Old men ought to be explorers") or the epiphany Czesław Miłosz had described in "Late Ripeness":

Not soon, as late as the approach of my ninetieth year
I felt a door opening in me and I entered
the clarity of early morning.

I had begun my trip to Mexico in a mood of dejection and self-pity, feeling shunned, overlooked, ignored, rejected — easily identifying with migrants and Mexicans, who knew that same feeling of being despised. I'd hoped the trip would be salutary, a cure for my sour mood, and so it proved. I was uplifted, smiling when I set off for home, my hand on my heart, promising to return. In my time in Mexico I'd published pieces in Mexican literary magazines, among them *Letras Libres* and the *Revista de la Universidad de México,* made many friends with Mexican writers, spoken at a number of literary and political events, and found a Mexican publisher, Almadía. One of the greatest thrills in travel is to know the satisfaction of arrival, and to find oneself among friends.

I knew, always, that I would be a worker in the vineyard,
as are all men and women living at the same time,
whether they are aware of it or not.

Or as the Mexican saying (*dicho*) had it: *Arrieros somos y en el camino andamos* — All of us are mule drivers, headed down the road.

## PART FIVE

*The Way Back*

## To the Border: My Last Mordida

I TOOK THE migrant route all the way north, except instead of riding on top of a rattling boxcar of the Beast, or in a clanking bus or a narco van, I was speeding in my own car, leaving San Cristóbal de las Casas. "I'm going to miss San Cristóbal," a man says in Charles Portis's *Gringos.* "This place is cool and pleasant the year round, a fat man's dream."

The *autopista* was closed that day—I was waved back by a policeman—so I took the old winding road on the eastern slopes of the Sierra Madre del Sur, the narrow track that had been cleared by the Dominican friars from Oaxaca in their pursuit of converts, and the conquistadors in search of gold. The Comandante was not indulging in euphemism in speaking of the five hundred years of persecution of the indigenous people of Chiapas.

When the conquistadors came this way as soldiers and tax collectors in 1524, looking for slave labor and gold, they fought to subdue the Tzotzils, who were startled and enraged by this intrusion of strangers. The Tzotzils called themselves Batsil winik'otik, the True People. This was their own land. So they responded by flinging rocks and shooting arrows, and they climbed to ridges like the ones on this road, and "mocked the Spanish, hurling small quantities of gold at them and inviting them to try and take the rest that they had within their walls." But they were no match for Spanish-forged twelve-foot lances and pikes, broadswords and crossbows. In 1526, at the Battle of Tepetchia, many Tzotzils, facing defeat, jumped to their deaths from Sumidero Canyon into the Grijalva River rather than be taken alive and enslaved. The history of Chiapas is a litany of invasion, massacre, punitive missions, and extermination, at last defended and redeemed by the Zapatistas.

The road hugged the high slopes, sometimes obscured in cloud, in sunny places allowing glimpses into lush valleys below, so deep they seemed like abysses. For many years this slow track was the main road to San Cristóbal, and was still known as the Carretera Internacional, because it leads to Guatemala and beyond; but the new, straighter *autopista* superseded it in 2006. The only town on this old winding road was Navenchauc, a community of low square houses, most of them made of rough unpainted cement blocks, lining mongrel-haunted lanes.

From the cold six-thousand-foot heights of the Sierra Madre de Chiapas, the road twisted down four thousand feet through the forest to the heat of Tuxtla Gutiérrez, then dropped two thousand more on a straight road to the hot gusts of wind and dense humidity of the sea-level tropics, crossing from Chiapas into Oaxaca. There, at a roadblock, a policeman in a sweat-stained shirt, clawing the air, directed me off the road. He was an older man, weary-looking and yawning, scowling at my Massachusetts license plate, his manner, in the Mexican policeman way, peevish.

"Is this your car?"

"Yes. I have papers—my Vehicle Importation Permit, my insurance, my license," I said, and began fossicking in the plump folders in my briefcase.

Something in my manner, perhaps my reciting my documentation, my fussing, wearied him further. "You can go," he said.

I bypassed Juchitán this time, circumvented Tehuantepec, and entered the hills, climbing back into the sierra, sun-dried, dust-blown, and arid—the biscuit-brown, baked-looking mountains of upland Oaxaca.

Around midafternoon I stopped to eat in La Reforma, a small town aslant on the mountainside, scattered on both sides of the road, one building signposted RESTAURANTE ROSA. It was a good-sized family house, the parlor furnished with two dining tables. No other diners today.

"Welcome." Three women greeted me, three generations: an old woman at a stove, her daughter busying herself sifting maize flour, the gawky granddaughter sprawled on a wooden chair—her long legs stretched out, her feet on the arm of another chair.

"Where are you going?" the old woman asked.

"The border," I said. "To the United States."

"Take me with you!" she cried out, and gripped my arm.

The others laughed at her, but it was an old woman's impudence, forgivable and comic. Still, she held on to me with bony fingers.

"What will you do there?"

"I can cook. I can clean your house. I can look after you. Take me with you—take me away from here. I don't care where you come from. I want to go there." She let go of my arm to stand aside and put on a pleading face that was also intentionally clownish. "Please come back for me."

Her daughter by now had made me the quesadilla I'd asked for, and brought it on a plate with a cup of black coffee. The granddaughter was laughing softly, wagging her bare brown feet. She was languid and beautiful, with a long, sallow Modigliani face, sharp eyes, and slender fingers.

"How old are you?" I asked, to change the subject.

"Twelve."

Provoked by my question, the old woman's daughter—the girl's mother—approached me and sized me up. "How old are *you*, señor?"

"*Adivina.*" Take a guess.

She studied me, she did not speak, she cocked her head, pursed her lips, and pressed a finger to her cheek, in actressy reflection, liking the suspense she was creating.

"Seventy-six," she said. Tilting her head back, looking haughty, she was triumphant.

"But I'm a *cabrón*," I said, thumping my chest.

They shrieked, because the word had a belittling meaning here, not "dude," as I had meant, but "dickhead."

Later, passing the sign for the side road to San Dionisio, I remembered the mezcalero Crispin García earnestly whispering to me in Zapotec. I spent two days in San Jerónimo Tlacochahuaya. I stayed again at Ex-Hacienda Guadalupe, and knowing that I wouldn't get another good meal for days, I had lunch alone in Oaxaca at the rooftop Casa Oaxaca. A young woman at the next table, in tight jeans, flashed a smile at me, and gathering her long black hair in her pretty hand, tossed it over her shoulder and turned, bending over, so that I could see the embroidered patch on her back pocket: *Eat Pray Fuck.*

The next day, I left San Jerónimo at sunup and drove down the dirt road past the agave and garlic fields onto the main road and beyond Oaxaca city and Etla. There was no blockade today at siege-prone Nochixtlán, where the footbridge still bore the slogan of the last demonstration, JUS-TICE AND RIGHTS FOR ALL PEOPLE, and the rusted, burned-out bus still lay where I had last seen it.

The deep ravines of the Mixteca Alta, farther on, were the most dramatic, the emptiest, I'd seen in Mexico. High peaks rose to the southwest, and deep down, the river looked black from this height, and the valley lay in shadow. At a steep part of the road, I saw a small boy, no more than nine or ten, treading close to the curb, balancing a bundle of slender, eight-foot bamboo poles on his shoulder—no houses or side roads anywhere, the small, solitary figure with his awkward burden.

The first time I'd driven near here, I'd had to detour into the countryside, slewing and skidding on goopy rain-sodden roads in slurries of mud, through a thunderstorm with three hitchhikers. But today I was speeding, going faster when the road flattened nearer Puebla. Next to the highway, always the signs of old Mexico, goatherds shuffling in the tall grass beyond the guardrails, the goats kicking up dust.

Circling the outskirts of San Luis Potosí, I saw police cars on the verge, and my palms grew damp. Making sure I was not followed, I gunned the car into the desert, passing the familiar stands of *palma china* that seemed emblematic of the deserts in northern Mexico.

As I passed the Santa Muerte shrine at Los Lobos, I considered stopping, just to talk again to the priestess. I rejected this as frivolous, yet I still had my Santa Muerte beads and the skeleton image dangling from my rear-view mirror. Was it his glimpse of this weird relic that caused the peevish policeman at the roadblock in the Isthmus to send me on my way?

In the dark back streets of Matehuala, looking for a place to stay, I remembered the friendly motel, Las Palmas, where I'd slept on the way south: behind a strong fence, secure for my car, with clean rooms, and local food.

"You are coming from?" the clerk at the reception desk asked. She was tall, in a tailored suit that was perhaps her uniform, and looked superior and chic, well dressed and poised.

I told her Oaxaca.

"Did you eat grasshoppers?"

"Lots of them. Ants, too. Very tasty."

She pursed her pretty lips. "We have better food here."

*Cabuches* were in season, the buds of the biznaga (or barrel) cactus, like baby Brussels sprouts. I had a plate of them, and the other Matehuala specialty again, *cabrito al horno,* baby goat baked with the skin on, tender and slimy.

The waiter, Hilário, asked me whether I was going north. I said yes.

"Don't go through Reynosa. It's bad there."

"I was planning to go that way."

"No." He was firm. "My home is in Monterrey. I know Reynosa is dangerous right now. Especially this week."

"What about Ciudad Alemán?"

"Better, I think."

Driving through the small settlements in the heat and glare the next day—every building and every road sign, even the shepherds and the women and children carrying bundles, all coated with a fine film of dust—a feeling of melancholy descended on me. I guessed this was because of the self I remembered from being here long before, the dejected man who had no idea where he was going. But I was a different person now, because I knew where I had been. Instead of being purified by suffering—sometimes the consequence of a travel ordeal—I had made friends on the road through the plain of snakes, and that had lifted my spirits.

I had marveled at this desert landscape on my trip south; it still bewitched me with its stark beauty and unexpected wildness. Taking a side route away from Saltillo, I found myself circling the steep, gravelly brown mountains that serve as the dramatic backdrop to Monterrey, so simple and shapely, with sharp peaks and knife-like ridge lines, such an amazing eruption of sierra, yet so close to the flat land of Texas just north.

From this simplicity and rugged beauty I saw the density of Monterrey in its populous valley, the confusion of roads, the sun beating down on the mass of white, flat-topped houses that looked hot and Moroccan. I headed east and then north along the edge of Monterrey, through industrial suburbs and fenced compounds of bleak tenements, east to Cadereyta Jiménez—notorious for gangs—to Cerralvo (a restaurant, a gas pump), following signs to Ciudad Mier.

The road north was flat and straight through the fields of mesquite and tall grass, sparsely inhabited, only a few roadside villages and very few other cars.

Fiddling with the radio in my car, I heard music from a Monterrey station, classical music I had not heard anywhere else in Mexico, and happened upon a lovely piece (violin, cello, piano) I'd heard before, but couldn't name. This sweet soundtrack soothed me and sped me onward, past the tall grass and twisted trees.

Long before, in Ciudad Alemán, on my traverse of the border, a shopkeeper had said to me, "Don't go outside town. Twenty miles away are the *ranchitos*, and the mafia."

I was traveling in the area of the *ranchitos* and the mafia now. It was around here, so the shopkeeper had suggested, the cartels were located. Just here, a year before, a series of Santa Muerte shrines had been found, forming a route through the semidesert and the thickets of low bush, as a way of guiding and protecting the narcos. Looking closely at passing buildings, I saw no people, just broken windows, empty stores, abandoned houses, and collapsed fences, suggesting fear and chaos. General Treviño to Las Auras—a huge villa off the road, and a ranch unambiguously named Ganadores—Winners.

"And that was the Notturno in E-flat Major by Franz Schubert," the woman on the Monterrey radio station said as the music ended.

There were not many big houses—perhaps three in the hundred miles from Monterrey—but each fancy villa seemed to represent drug money.

At a road junction near the town of Mier I stopped to let a truck pass and was surrounded by eight youths pressing their faces against my windows.

"What's up?"

Shaking a tin can at me, one boy said, "We're collecting money for the Queen of the Day."

I put some coins in the can and said, "Where's the queen?"

A girl pushed past the boys and smiled at me. She wore a black, lacy see-through blouse, tight-fighting shorts, and—on this hot back street in Nuevo León—white patent-leather high heels. She placed a hand on each cheek, tilted her head like a stage coquette, and pouted moodily.

"I am the queen," she said. Her fingernails were sparkly against her cheeks.

I asked of the eight of them, "Which of you have been to the US?"

Two of them said they had been across, to the Texas town of Roma, about six miles away. The torment of Ciudad Mier, suffering in its dust and neglect, was that the fabulous kingdom of money was just down the street and over the narrow river.

I was exhilarated as I set off, but a blocked road and a detour sign sent me into a deserted village, where I began to worry—a dirt road, no signs, ruined buildings, like driving into the sort of entrapment I'd been warned about. I kept on, fretting, until I saw a paved road in the distance, and took it. A mile or so farther on, the curio shops, the taqueria where I'd once had a meal, the shop where I'd seen a pear-shaped, orange-haired piñata in the shape of Donald Trump, the plaza where I'd had a shoeshine.

Although Texas was just across the river, no gringos circulated here. I was hungry, so I went back to the taqueria. Then I bought an ice cream. I sat in the plaza and had my shoes shined, savoring the delay.

But when I told the shoeshine man, Héctor, the route I had come, he said, "You're very lucky."

I didn't think much about that remark. Without a hitch I crossed the international bridge to Roma. A boy on a Jet Ski skidded in circles on the Rio Grande below the bridge. I had taken a simple detour from Monterrey, as Hilário had suggested in Matehuala, a safe back road through the eastern suburbs of Monterrey and Cadereyta Jiménez. This sparsely traveled road, Route 54, was flat, straight, pretty, and placid-looking, through low woods and grazing land of the cattle *ranchitos* and a few small towns.

But "You're very lucky" preyed on my mind. And later I researched the recent history of the area and found that Route 54 was strategic for human and drug smuggling, that this whole border state of Nuevo León had become a battlefield on which the Zetas and the Gulf cartel vied for dominance. Kidnappings and mayhem were common; in the manufacturing town of Cadereyta Jiménez (broom factory, oil refinery, workers' tenements) five municipal employees were massacred in 2012, and in the same year, in San Juan, a town just seventy-five miles southwest of Roma, forty-nine bodies were discovered dumped on the federal highway I'd traveled, all of them decapitated and dismembered, all of them young men, and none of them (because of the butchery) easily identifiable. Near the bodies was a *narcomensaje*—a large Z spray-painted on the road, the sign that Los Zetas had been responsible, and a warning to rivals and the authorities.

Yes, I was lucky—incredibly so. Lucky in the people I met, lucky in the friends I made, lucky even in my mishaps, my always emerging unharmed, with a tale to tell. More than fifty years of this, ever the fortunate traveler.

I'd arrived safely in Roma, but I was not done. I needed to apply for a refund on my Vehicle Importation Permit, and renew my visa. So I drove along the Texas side of the border to McAllen and then crossed into Mexico again, to the customs office in a building just inside the Reynosa frontier.

"I can't do any of your visa paperwork today," the clerk said. He wore a baseball cap and was dressed, as many men in Mexican border offices are dressed, no matter how senior, like a farmer or a field hand. "I can give you a refund on your permit, but there's a three-day waiting period for the visa."

"I can't come back in three days. I need it now."

"This is the law."

I pleaded a little, explaining the inconvenience.

"Maybe talk to that man."

He indicated a man in black, but looking agricultural, like the others. I explained my dilemma. He too told me about the specified waiting period.

A stark government sign on the wall behind the man's head cautioned me, in large black letters in two languages, ANY ATTEMPT TO OFFER A

BRIBE OR A TIP TO AN OFFICIAL IS FORBIDDEN, AND PUNISHABLE
BY LAW.

"I realize it's a problem," I said, and explained that I needed it now.

He listened carefully, then beckoned me into his office, nearer the warning sign. He rifled through my papers. I noticed that one of his rings was a toothy skull, silver, with red stones for eyes, nudging and nibbling a hairy knuckle when he flicked that finger. He looked me up and down, seeming to make a mental calculation.

"Yes. I can help you," he said in a whisper. "But it will cost something."

At such a moment the wary traveler thinks: given the severe sign, and the willingness of the man, this must be a trap. I offer the bribe and then I am arrested for the crime of offering a bribe. But this was the plain of snakes.

"*Cuánto cuesta?*" I mouthed.

Fumbling with a ballpoint pen and agitatedly clicking it, seeming with each click to make a mental calculation, he finally gripped it and wrote "180" on a small piece of paper. Just as quickly he crumpled the paper, pinched it small, and pocketed it.

"Pesos?"

He snorted a little, and hoicked: a Mexican negative. I turned away and covertly selected nine $20 bills from my wallet, folded and flattened them, and palmed them to him. He did not thank me. He clucked softly, a satisfying ungumming of his sticky tongue, and made the money disappear. Then he prepared my documents and wished me a good journey.

*This must not be an anecdote,* I remembered, driving across the border, and I was almost tearful, hearing the echo of the Zapotec whisper, "*Eet yelasu nara,*" Don't forget me.